MW01087935

AZ-900: Microsoft Azure Fundamentals

Study Guide with Practice Questions & Labs
Sixth Edition

Document Control

Proposal Name	:	Microsoft Azure Fundamentals
Document Edition	:	Sixth
Document Release Date	:	20th February 2024
Reference	:	AZ-900
IPS Product Code	:	20240102130106

Feedback:
If you have any comments regarding the quality of this book or otherwise alter it to suit your needs better, you can contact us through email at info@ipspecialist.net
Please include the book's title and ISBN in your message.

About IPSpecialist

LTD. IS COMMITTED TO EXCELLENCE AND DEDICATED TO YOUR SUCCESS.

Our philosophy is to treat our customers like family. We want you to succeed and are willing to do everything possible to help you make it happen. We have the proof to back up our claims. We strive to accelerate billions of careers with great courses, accessibility, and affordability. We believe continuous learning and knowledge evolution are the most important things to keep re-skilling and up-skilling the world.

Planning and creating a specific goal is where IPSpecialist helps. We can create a career track that suits your visions and develop the competencies you need to become a professional Network Engineer. We can also assist you with the execution and evaluation of your proficiency level based on the career track you choose, as they are customized to fit your specific goals.

We help you STAND OUT through our detailed IP training content packages.

Course Features:

❖ Self-Paced Learning
   • Learn at your own pace and in your own time
❖ Covers Complete Exam Blueprint
   • Prep for the exam with confidence
❖ Case Study-Based Learning
   • Relate the content to real-life scenarios
❖ Subscriptions that Suit You
   • Get more and pay less with IPS subscriptions
❖ Career Advisory Services
   • Let the industry experts plan your career journey
❖ Virtual Labs to test your skills
   • With IPS vRacks, you can evaluate your exam preparations
❖ Practice Questions
   • Practice questions to measure your preparation standards
❖ On Request Digital Certification
   • On request: digital certification from IPSpecialist LTD.

About the Authors:

This book has been compiled with the help of multiple professional engineers. These engineers specialize in different fields, e.g., Networking, Security, Cloud, Big Data, IoT, etc. Each engineer develops content in their specialized field that is compiled to form a comprehensive certification guide.

About the Technical Reviewers:

Nouman Ahmed Khan

AWS/Azure/GCP-Architect, CCDE, CCIEx5 (R&S, SP, Security, DC, Wireless), CISSP, CISA, CISM, CRISC, ISO27K-LA is a Solution Architect working with a global telecommunication provider. He works with enterprises, mega-projects, and service providers to help them select the best-fit technology solutions. He also works as a consultant to understand customer business processes and helps select an appropriate technology strategy to support business goals. He has more than eighteen years of experience working with global clients. One of his notable experiences was his tenure with a large managed security services provider, where he was responsible for managing the complete MSSP product portfolio. With his extensive knowledge and expertise in various areas of technology, including cloud computing, network infrastructure, security, and risk management, Nouman has become a trusted advisor for his clients.

Abubakar Saeed

Having started from the grassroots level as an engineer and contributed to the Introduction of internet in Pakistan and elsewhere, a professional journey of over twenty-nine years in various organizations, national and international. Experienced in leading businesses with a focus on Innovation and Transformation.

He is also experienced in Managing, Consulting, Designing, and implementing projects. Heading Operations, Solutions Design, and Integration. Emphasizing on adhering to Project timelines and delivering as per customer expectations, advocate for adopting technology to simplify operations and enhance efficiency.

Dr. Fahad Abdali

Dr. Fahad Abdali is a seasoned leader with extensive experience in managing diverse businesses. With an impressive twenty years track record, Dr. Abdali brings a wealth of expertise to the table. Holding a bachelor's degree from the NED University of Engineers & Technology and Ph.D. from the University of Karachi, he has consistently demonstrated a deep commitment to academic excellence and professional growth. Driven by a passion for innovation and a keen understanding of industry dynamics, he has successfully navigated complex challenges, driving growth and fostering organizational success.

Mehwish Jawed

Mehwish Jawed is working as a Senior Research Analyst. She holds a Master's and Bachelors of Engineering degree in Telecommunication Engineering from NED University of Engineering and Technology. She also worked under the supervision of HEC Approved supervisor. She has more than three published papers, including both conference and journal papers. She has a great knowledge of TWDM Passive Optical Network (PON). She also worked as a Project Engineer, Robotic Trainer in a private institute and has research skills in the field of communication networks. She has both technical knowledge and industry-sounding information, which she utilizes effectively when needed. She has expertise in cloud platforms such as AWS, GCP, Oracle, and Microsoft Azure.

Hareem Khan

Hareem Khan is currently working as a Technical Content Developer, having command over networking and security. She has completed training in CCNA and Cybersecurity. She holds a BE in Telecommunications Engineering from the NED University of Engineering and Technology. She has strong knowledge of all the basics of IP and Security Networks and Routing and Switching Protocols. She has worked on various certification courses of Azure, Microsoft, and GCP. She is part of the content development team and has expertise on Azure, Microsoft, Security and GCP labs.

Free Resources:

For Free Resources: Please visit our website and register to access your desired Resources Or contact us at: info@ipspecialist.net

Career Report: This report is a step-by-step guide for a novice who wants to develop his/her career in computer networks. It answers the following queries:

- What are the current scenarios and prospects?
- Is this industry moving toward saturation, or are new opportunities knocking at the door?
- What will the monetary benefits be?
- Why get certified?
- How to plan, and when will I complete the certifications if I start today?
- Is there any career track I can follow to accomplish the specialization level?

Furthermore, this guide provides a comprehensive career path toward being a specialist in networking and highlights the tracks needed to obtain certification.

IPS Personalized Technical Support for Customers: Good customer service means helping customers efficiently and in a friendly manner. It is essential to be able to handle issues for customers and do your best to ensure they are satisfied. Good service is one of the most important things that can set our business apart from others.
Excellent customer service will attract more customers and attain maximum customer retention.

IPS offers personalized TECH support to its customers to provide better value for money. If you have any queries related to technology and labs, you can ask our technical team for assistance via Live Chat or Email.

Our Products

Study Guides
IPSpecialist Study Guides are the ideal guides to developing the hands-on skills necessary to pass the exam. Our workbooks cover the official exam blueprint and explain the technology with real-life case study-based labs. The content covered in each workbook consists of individually focused technology topics presented in an easy-to-follow, goal-oriented, step-by-step approach. Every scenario features detailed breakdowns and thorough verifications to help you completely understand the task and associated technology.

We extensively used mind maps in our workbooks to visually explain the technology. Our workbooks have become a widely used tool to learn and remember information effectively.

Practice Questions
IP Specialists' Practice Questions are dedicatedly designed from a certification exam perspective. The collection of these questions from our Study Guides is prepared to keep the exam blueprint in mind, covering not only important but necessary topics. It is an ideal document to practice and revise your certification.

Exam Cram
Our Exam Cram notes are a concise bundling of condensed notes of the complete exam blueprint. It is an ideal and handy document to help you remember the most important technology concepts related to the certification exam.

Hands-on Labs
IPSpecialist Hands-on Labs are the fastest and easiest way to learn real-world use cases. These labs are carefully designed to prepare you for the certification exams and your next job role. Whether you are starting to learn technology or solving a real-world scenario, our labs will help you learn the core concepts in no time.

IPSpecialist self-paced labs are designed by subject matter experts and provide an opportunity to use products in a variety of pre-designed scenarios and common use cases, giving you hands-on practice in a simulated environment to help you gain confidence. You have the flexibility to choose from topics and products about which you want to learn more.

Companion Guide

Companion Guides are portable desk guides for the IPSpecialist course materials that users (students, professionals, and experts) can access at any time and from any location. Companion Guides are intended to supplement online course material by assisting users in concentrating on key ideas and planning their study time for quizzes and examinations.

Content at a Glance

Course Introduction..26

Chapter 01: Introduction to Azure...31

Chapter 02: Compute..77

Chapter 03: Networking 141

Chapter 04: Storage 173

Chapter 05: Databases 206

Chapter 06: Authentication and Authorization...235

Chapter 07: Azure Core Solutions and Management Tools.......................260

Chapter 08: Security 318

Chapter 09: Privacy, Compliance, and Trust..367

Chapter 10: Pricing 426

Chapter 11: Managing and Deploying Azure Resources............................453

Chapter 12: Support 491

Answers..502

Acronyms 534

References 537

About Our Products 543

Table of Contents

Course Introduction...**26**

Introduction 26

Course Objectives...26

Why AZ-900? 26

Importance of this Certification..26

What you will learn in this course? 27

Who is this course for? 28

Career Growth with this course 28

Prerequisties 29

Recertification 29

Mind Map 30

Chapter 01: Introduction to Azure **31**

Introduction 31

What is Cloud Computing? 31

Benefits of Cloud Computing 31

The Economy of Cloud Computing...32

Consumption-based Model 32

Technical Terms 34

Manageability in the Cloud 35

Types of Cloud Computing 35

Shared Responsibility Model 40

Cloud Computing Deployments Models 41

What is Azure? 44

Azure Marketplace 45

Physical Infrastructure 45

Management Infrastructure...50

Azure Subscriptions 52

Azure Services..54

How to Interact with Azure 67

Creating an Account on Azure 69

Mind Map 72

Practice Questions 72

Chapter 02: Compute **77**

Introduction 77

Azure Virtual Machines 77

    Linux-Based Machine in Azure 77

    Windows-Based Machine in Azure 77

    Features..78

    Examples of when to use VMs..79

    Moving to the Cloud with VMs: 80

    VM Resource 80

Lab 2-01: Create an Azure Resource 81

    Service Introduction...81

    Problem...81

    Solution 81

Azure VMware Solution..86

Scale Sets...86

    Benefits..87

    Use Case 87

Application Hosting Options 87

    App Services..88

What are Azure Containers? 91

    Azure Container Instances 91

    Azure Container Instances (ACI) 91

Azure Kubernetes Service...93

    Kubernetes 93

    Azure Kubernetes Service 93

Azure Functions 98

    Use Case 98

    Features 98

Azure Virtual Desktop 99

    Key Features...99

    How to Reduce Cost Using Azure Virtual Desktop?..................................99

Remote Desktop Protocol (RDP) 100

Connect Windows Azure VM using RDP 100

Enhance Security 101

Multi-session Windows 10 or Windows 11 deployment 101

Lab 2-02: Configuration of Windows Virtual Machine in Azure using RDP 102

Service Introduction 102

Problem 102

Solution 102

Lab 2-03: Azure App Services 128

Service Introduction 128

Problem 128

Solution 128

Mind Map 136

Practice Questions 137

Chapter 03: Networking 141

Introduction 141

Virtual Network 142

Cloud Advantages 143

Load Balancer 145

Technical Terms of Load Balancer 146

Benefits of Load Balancer 147

Introduction to VPN Gateway 147

VPN Gateway 148

High-Availability Scenarios for VPN Gateways 150

Azure ExpressRoute 150

Advanatges of ExpressRoute 151

Connectivity to Microsoft Cloud Services with ExpressRoute 151

ExpressRoute Connectivity Model 152

ExpressRoute Failover 153

Zone-Redundant Gateways 154

Co-location at a Cloud Exchange with ExpressRoute 154

Security Considerations with ExpressRoute 154

Application Gateway 154

    Benefits of Application Gateway 155

Content Delivery Network.. 156

    Benefits of CDN 157

Traffic Manager 158

Azure DNS 158

    Key Benefits of Azure DNS 158

Lab 3-01: Creating a Virtual Network Connection 159

    Service Introduction.. 159

    Problem.. 160

    Solution 160

Mind Map 168

Practice Questions 168

Chapter 04: Storage **173**

Introduction 173

Storage Account 173

Azure Storage Redundancy 174

    Redundancy in a Primary Region... 174

    Redundancy in a Secondary Region 175

Azure Storage 178

    Blob Storage.. 178

    Disk Storage.. 180

    File Storage 181

    Key Benefits of Azure Files 182

    Archive 183

    Queue Storage 183

    Table Storage 183

    Benefits of Azure Storage.. 183

Identify Azure Data Migration Options 184

    Azure Migrate.. 184

    Azure Data Box.. 185

Identify File Movement Options... 186

AzCopy 186

Storage Explorer 186

Azure File Sync 187

Lab 4-01: Creating a Storage Account 187

Service Introduction 187

Problem 187

Solution 187

Lab 4-02: Create a Storage Blob 193

Service Introduction 193

Problem 193

Solution 193

Mind Map 201

Practice Questions 203

Chapter 05: Databases 206

Introduction 206

Databases 206

Cosmos DB 207

Azure SQL 208

Lab 5-01: Create Cosmos DB and SQL Database 209

Service Introduction 209

Problem 209

Solution 209

Azure Database for MySQL 228

Azure Database for Postgre SQL 229

Database Migration Service 229

Azure Big Data and Analytics 231

Mind Map 232

Practice Questions 232

Chapter 06: Authentication and Authorization 235

Introduction 235

Identity Services 235

Authentication 236

Authorization 236

Authentication vs. Authorization.. 236

Access Management 237

Microsoft Entra ID 237

Active Directory.. 237

Describe Microsoft Entra ID 238

Hybrid Cloud Architecture 241

Azure External Identities 241

Lab 6-01: Azure Entra ID 243

Service Introduction... 243

Problem 243

Solution 243

Multi-Factor Authentication 247

How does an MFA Work? 247

Conditional Access 248

Uses of Conditional Access 249

Lab 6-02: Multi-Factor Authentication 249

Service Introduction... 249

Problem 249

Solution 249

Mind Map 256

Practice Questions 257

Chapter 07: Azure Core Solutions and Management Tools 260

Introduction 260

Choosing the Best Azure IoT Service for Your Application 260

Internet of Things... 260

Identify the product options... 260

IoT Services... 261

Azure IoT Edge 264

Working of IoT Edge 265

Analyze the Decision Criteria 266

Use IoT Hub.. 267

Use IoT Central..268

Use Azure Sphere 269

Big Data..269

Azure Data Lake Analytics...270

HDInsight 270

Azure Databricks 270

Big Data Outcomes 270

Lab 7-01: Explore the Azure IoT Hub and Register a Device...271

Service Introduction...271

Problem...271

Solution 271

Choosing the Best AI Service for Your Needs 285

Artificial Intelligence..285

Identify the Product Options 285

Azure AI Service (Formerly Azure Cognitive Services)..286

Azure Machine Learning...286

Azure Machine Learning Studio...287

Azure Bot Service 287

Analyze the Decision Criteria...287

Use Machine Learning for decision support systems 288

Use Cognitive Services for Data Analysis..289

Use Bot Service for Interactive Chat Experiences 290

Choosing the Best Azure Serverless Technology for Your Business Scenario 291

Serverless 291

Identify the Product Options 291

Analyze the Decision Criteria...292

Use Azure Logic Apps 294

Choosing the Best Tools to Help Organizations Build Better Solutions........................295

DevOps..295

Analyze the Decision Criteria...296

Use Azure DevOps to manage the application development lifecycle.............................297

Use GitHub to contribute to open-source software..298

Use Azure DevTest Labs to manage testing environments...299

Choosing the Best Monitoring Service for Visibility, Insight, and Outage Mitigation 299

    Identify your product options 299

    Analyze the Decision Criteria 302

    Use Azure Advisor 302

    Use Azure Monitor 303

    Use Azure Service Health 304

Choosing the Best Tools for Managing and Configuring your Azure Environment 305

    Identify the Product Options 305

    Analyze the decision criteria 306

    Use the Azure Portal to understand and manage your cloud environment visually 307

    Use Azure PowerShell for one-off administrative tasks 308

    Use the Azure CLI for One-Off Administrative Tasks 308

    Use the Azure Mobile App to Manage Azure on the Go 309

    Use ARM Templates to Deploy an Entire Cloud Infrastructure 309

Lab 7-02: Azure AI Service 310

    Service Introduction 310

    Problem 310

    Solution 310

Mind Map 313

Practice Questions 313

Chapter 08: Security **318**

Introduction 318

    Why Security is Important..318

Zero Trust Model..319

    Adjusting to Zero Trust..320

Defense in Depth..320

    Physical 321

    Identity and Access 321

    Perimeter 321

    Network 321

    Compute..322

    Application 322

Data 322

Securing Network Connectivity 322

Azure Firewall 323

Distributed Denial-of-Service Attacks (DDoS) 324

Network Security Groups 325

Application Security Group 326

Microsoft Defender for Cloud 327

Protection wherever you deploy 328

Azure Native Protection 328

Defend your hybrid resources 329

Defend running resources on other clouds 329

Access, Secure, and Defend 329

Sections in Microsoft Defender for Cloud 332

How to use Microsoft Defender for Cloud? 333

Azure Key Vault 333

Features of Key Vault 334

Azure Information Protection 335

Advanced Threat Protection 336

Are Users Unreliable? 336

Features of Advanced Threat Protection 336

Cyber-Attack Kill-Chain 336

Azure Sentinel 337

Azure Dedicated Host 338

Combine Azure Services to Create a Complete Network Security Solution 339

Secure the Perimeter Layer 339

Secure the Network Layer 339

Combine Services 339

Lab 8-01: Azure Key Vault 340

Service Introduction 340

Problem 340

Solution 340

Lab 8-02: Network Access to VM using NSG 348

Service Introduction..348

Problem...348

Solution..348

Mind Map 362

Practice Questions 362

Chapter 09: Privacy, Compliance, and Trust.................................367

Introduction 367

Build a Cloud Governance Strategy on Azure 367

Governance 367

Concept of Resource Groups 367

Tagging...370

Azure Role-Based Access Control 372

RBAC 372

Secure Azure Resources with RBAC 379

Introduction..379

Role-Based Access Control 380

Secure Resources with RBAC..380

Azure Policy..382

Use Policies to Enforce Standards 383

Azure Policy Initiatives 399

Azure Blueprint 400

Cloud Adoption Framework for Azure 400

Azure Advisor for Security Assistance 400

Use Locks to Protect Resources 401

Resource Locks 401

Purpose of Azure Resource Locks 401

Types of Resource Locks 402

Use Locks to Protect Resources...403

Lab 9-01: Azure Resource Locks 405

Service Introduction..405

Problem...405

Solution..405

Subscription Governance Strategy 412

Billing 412

Access Control 412

Subscription Limit 412

Azure Monitor 412

Outcomes 414

Azure Service Health 414

Demo 9-01: Azure Monitor 415

Compliance 417

Industry Compliance 417

Azure Compliance Manager 418

Azure Government Cloud 418

China Region 418

Privacy 419

Trust 419

Service Trust Portal 420

Mind Map 422

Practice Questions 423

Chapter 10: Pricing 426

Introduction 426

Subscriptions 426

Offer Types 427

Management Groups 427

Azure Cost Management 428

Budget Alerts 429

Credit Alerts 429

Department Spending Quota Alerts 429

Budgets 429

Azure Free Account 429

Pricing Factors 430

Resource Size 430

Resource Type 430

Location 430

Bandwidth... 430

Pricing Calculator.. 431

Steps for Using Pricing Calculator 432

Total Cost of Ownership (TCO) Calculator 433

Lab 10-01: Estimate and Compare Workload Costs by using the Pricing Calculator.................... 435

Service Introduction.. 435

Problem.. 435

Solution.. 436

Best Practices for Minimizing Azure Costs 442

Spending Limits.. 442

Quotas.. 442

Tags 442

Reserved Instances 443

Azure Advisor 443

Lab 10-02: Using the Pricing Calculator... 444

Service Introduction.. 444

Problem.. 444

Solution.. 444

Mind Map 449

Practice Questions 450

Chapter 11: Managing and Deploying Azure Resources..453

Introduction 453

Azure Resource Groups.. 453

Azure Resource Manager 453

Purpose of ARM Templates 453

Infrastructure as Code.. 454

Consistent Deployment 454

Automation.. 454

Benefits of Azure Resource Manager 454

Bicep: A Declarative Language for Azure Resource Deployment 455

Structure of ARM Templates... 456

Resource as Code 456

Template Format 457

Working with ARM Templates 462

Deploy to a Resource Group 463

Deployment Modes 463

Deployment Tools 463

Deploy a Resource with Azure CLI.. 463

Benefits of Azure Resource Manager 464

Lab 11-01: Working with ARM Templates 465

Service Introduction.. 465

Problem.. 465

Solution 465

Azure Arc 475

What can Azure Arc do Outside of Azure? 475

Azure App Service 475

Lab 11-02: Create a Website Hosted in Azure 476

Service Introduction.. 476

Problem.. 476

Solution 476

Mind Map 488

Practice Questions 489

Chapter 12: Support **491**

Introduction 491

Plans... 491

Plan Inclusions- Paid Plans... 491

Tickets.. 492

Submitting a Ticket... 493

Channels 494

Knowledge Center 495

Service Level Agreement.. 495

Properties... 495

Service Life Cycle... 496

Gathering Customers Data 496

Stages 496

Demo 12-01: Using Preview Services 496

Mind Map 498

Practice Questions 499

Answers **502**

Chapter 01: Introduction to Azure 502

Chapter 02: Compute 505

Chapter 03: Networking 508

Chapter 04: Storage 511

Chapter 05: Databases 513

Chapter 06: Authentication and Authorization 515

Chapter 07: Azure Core Solutions and Management Tools 518

Chapter 08: Security 522

Chapter 09: Privacy, Compliance, and Trust 524

Chapter 10: Pricing 527

Chapter 11: Managing and Deploying Azure Resources 530

Chapter 12: Support 532

Acronyms **534**

References **537**

About Our Products **543**

Microsoft Certifications

Microsoft Azure Certifications are industry-recognized credentials that validate your technical Cloud skills and expertise while assisting your career growth. These are one of the most valuable IT certifications since Azure has established an overwhelming growth rate in the public cloud market. Even with several tough competitors such as Amazon Web Services, Google Cloud Engine, and Rackspace, Azure will be the dominant public cloud platform today, with an astounding collection of proprietary services that continues to grow.

In this certification, we will discuss cloud concepts where we will learn the core benefits of using Azure, like high availability, scalability, etc. We will talk about the Azure Architecture in which cloud resources are put together to work at best; Azure Compute, where you will learn how to run applications in Azure; Networking, in which the discussion is on how Azure resources communicate with each other; Storage, where you put all of your data and have different ways of storing it. We will also cover databases used for data storage, their efficient retrieval as per demand, and ensuring that the users have the right access to the resources. Also, we will counter some complex scenarios with their solutions. We will have discussions on important topics like Security, which makes Azure the best secure choice for your applications and functions; Privacy, Compliance, and Trust which make sure services ensure privacy; and how you stay compliant with standards. As well as, pricing in Azure to stay ahead on cost.

AZ-900 is the first certification of Microsoft Azure, the foundational certificate in Azure. After this certification, you can prove to the world that you are proficient and have the credibility to reach the highest point of your professional life.

Value of Azure Certifications

Microsoft emphasizes sound conceptual knowledge of its entire platform and hands-on experience with the Azure infrastructure and its many unique and complex components and services.

For Individuals

- Demonstrate your expertise in designing, deploying, and operating highly available, cost-effective, and secured applications on Microsoft Azure.
- Gain recognition and visibility of your proven skills and proficiency with Azure.
- Earn tangible benefits such as access to the Microsoft Certified Community, getting invited to Microsoft Certification Appreciation Receptions and Lounges, obtaining Microsoft Certification Practice Exam Voucher and Digital Badge for certification validation, and Microsoft Certified Logo usage.
- Foster credibility with your employer and peers.

For Employers

- Identify skilled professionals to lead IT initiatives with Cloud technologies.
- To implement your workloads and projects on the Azure platform, reduce risks and costs.
- Increase customer satisfaction.

Types of Certifications

Role-based Certification

- _Fundamental_ - Validates overall understanding of the Azure Cloud.

- *Associate*- Technical role-based certifications. No pre-requisite is required.
- *Expert*- Highest level technical role-based certification.

About Microsoft Certified: <u>Microsoft Azure Fundamentals</u>

Exam Questions	Case study, short answer, repeated answer, MCQs
Number of Questions	40-60
Time to Complete	85 minutes
Exam Fee	99 USD

Candidates for AZ-900 exam should have the foundational knowledge of cloud services and how those services are provided with Microsoft Azure. The exam is intended for candidates who are just beginning to work with cloud-based solutions and services or are new to Azure. The Azure Fundamentals exam is an opportunity to prove knowledge of cloud concepts, Azure services, Azure workloads, security and privacy in Azure, and Azure pricing and support. Candidates should be familiar with general technology concepts, including networking, storage, compute, application support, and application development. Azure Fundamentals can be used to prepare for other Azure role-based or specialty certifications, but it is not a prerequisite for any of them.

This exam measures your ability to accomplish the following technical tasks:

- Describe cloud concepts   25-30%
- Describe Azure architecture and services   35-40%
- Describe Azure management and governance   30-35%

Recommended Knowledge

- Identify the benefits and considerations of using cloud services
- Describe the differences between categories of cloud services
- Describe the differences between types of cloud computing
- Describe the core Azure architectural components
- Describe core resources available in Azure
- Describe core solutions available in Azure
- Describe Azure management tools
- Describe Azure security features
- Describe Azure network security
- Describe core Azure identity services
- Describe Azure governance features
- Describe privacy and compliance resources
- Describe methods for planning and managing costs
- Describe Azure Service Level Agreements (SLAs) and service lifecycles

All the required information is included in this Study Guide.

	Domain	Percentage
Domain 1	Describe cloud concepts	25-30%
Domain 2	Describe Azure architecture and services	35-40%
Domain 3	Describe Azure management and governance	30-35%

Course Introduction

Introduction

AZ-900 is the first certification of Microsoft Azure, the foundational certificate in Azure. After this certification, you can prove to the world that you are proficient and have the credibility to reach the highest point of your professional life. This course validates your basic understanding of cloud services and how Microsoft Azure provides them. It covers the basics of Azure cloud computing, including core Azure services, subscription management, security, privacy, compliance, and trust.

Course Objectives

- **Cloud Concepts:** Understand the fundamentals of cloud computing, including deployment models, service models, and the benefits of cloud services.
- **Azure Services**: Explore core Azure services and products, learning how they contribute to building and managing applications in the cloud.
- **Azure Pricing and Support:** Gain insights into Azure pricing models, Service Level Agreements (SLA), and how to manage costs effectively.
- **Azure Governance and Compliance:** Learn about implementing and managing Azure policies, Role-Based Access Control (RBAC), and monitoring in Azure.
- **Azure Identity, Privacy, and Data Protection:** Dive into Microsoft Entra ID, Multi-Factor Authentication (MFA), and data protection features in Azure.
- **Azure Solutions**: Explore Internet of Things (IoT), Artificial Intelligence (AI), and Big Data and Analytics solutions in Azure.

Why AZ-900?

- It serves as a foundational certification for individuals new to Azure.
- It provides a broad overview of key cloud concepts and Azure services.
- It prepares you for more advanced Azure certifications.

Importance of this Certification

The AZ-900 certification holds significance as it establishes a foundational understanding of cloud computing principles and introduces key Azure services. Recognized by Microsoft, this certification validates individuals' knowledge of fundamental concepts such as cloud concepts, core Azure services, security, compliance, privacy, and pricing. It serves as an entry point for those pursuing a career in cloud computing, providing a valuable credential for job seekers and professionals seeking to broaden their skill set. Additionally, for business and technical decision-makers, the AZ-900 certification offers insights into Azure's capabilities, aiding in informed decision-making about cloud adoption. Overall, the certification is a recognized benchmark that enhances career opportunities and lays the groundwork for pursuing more advanced Azure certifications.

What you will learn in this course?

In the Microsoft Azure Fundamentals (AZ-900) course, you will acquire a foundational understanding of cloud computing and Microsoft Azure services. Here is an overview of what you will learn in this course:

Cloud Concepts

- Understand the basic principles of cloud computing.
- Differentiate between various cloud deployment models, such as public, private, and hybrid clouds.
- Explore service models, including Infrastructure as a Service (IaaS), Platform as a Service (PaaS), and Software as a Service (SaaS).

Azure Services Overview:

- Explore key Azure services and products.
- Understand the core architectural components of Azure.
- Learn how to use Azure solutions and management tools.

Azure Pricing and Support:

- Gain insights into Azure pricing models and factors influencing costs.
- Understand Service Level Agreements (SLA) and the service lifecycle.
- Learn how to manage Azure costs effectively.

Azure Governance and Compliance:

- Implement and manage Azure policies for resource organization and control.
- Understand Role-Based Access Control (RBAC) for managing access to Azure resources.
- Explore monitoring and reporting tools in Azure.

Azure Identity, Privacy, and Data Protection:

- Dive into Microsoft Entra ID (Azure AD) and its role in identity management.
- Explore features like Multi-Factor Authentication (MFA) and Identity Protection.
- Understand data protection features in Azure, including Azure Information Protection.

Azure Solutions:

- Explore key Azure solutions, including Internet of Things (IoT), Artificial Intelligence (AI), and Big Data and Analytics.
- Understand how these solutions can be applied to real-world scenarios.

Azure Management Tools:

- Navigate the Azure Portal and perform tasks using Azure PowerShell and Azure CLI.
- Understand Azure Resource Manager (ARM) templates for infrastructure as code.
- Explore Azure Monitor and Microsoft Defender for Cloud for management and monitoring.

Security, Privacy, Compliance, and Trust:

- Learn about Microsoft Defender for Cloud for threat protection.
- Understand the role of Azure Key Vault in secure key management.
- Explore compliance features in Azure, including GDPR and other standards.

By the end of this course, you will have a solid foundation in cloud computing concepts and a practical understanding of how to use Microsoft Azure services effectively. Additionally, you'll be well-prepared to take the AZ-900 exam, earning a certification that validates your Azure fundamentals knowledge.

Who is this course for?

The Microsoft Azure AZ-900 exam and its associated course, Microsoft Azure Fundamentals, are designed for individuals who are new to Azure and cloud computing and want to build a foundational understanding of Microsoft's cloud services. This course is ideal for:

IT Professionals: Those who are exploring cloud technologies and want to understand the basics of Azure services. This can include individuals in roles such as system administrators, network administrators, and other IT roles.

Developers: Developers who are getting started with cloud development and need to understand how Azure services can be used to build, deploy, and manage applications in the cloud.

Business Decision Makers: Non-technical professionals, such as business analysts or managers, who need to make informed decisions about adopting cloud services and want a foundational understanding of Azure.

Students and Educators: Students pursuing a career in IT or individuals teaching IT-related courses can benefit from this course to ensure they have a solid understanding of fundamental cloud concepts and Azure services.

Anyone Interested in Cloud Computing: Individuals who are curious about cloud computing in general and want to gain knowledge and skills in using Azure services.

Career Growth with this course

The impact of obtaining the Microsoft Azure Fundamentals (AZ-900) certification on salary increment can vary based on several factors, including your current job role, the industry you're in, geographical location, level of experience, and overall demand for cloud-related skills in your region. Here are some general considerations:

Career Advancement: Earning a certification like AZ-900 can contribute to career advancement, making you a more competitive candidate for roles related to cloud computing and Microsoft Azure. With career progression, salary increments are often a natural outcome.

As per Payscale, the annual average compensation of a cloud solutions architect in the United States is approximately $128,000. Starting out in the field, an individual should anticipate making about $85,000; with experience, this can increase to $170,000 or higher in 2024.

Industry Demand: The demand for cloud skills, including those related to Microsoft Azure, is generally high. Organizations are increasingly adopting cloud technologies, and professionals with relevant certifications may be sought after, potentially leading to better compensation.

Negotiation Power: Certifications can enhance your negotiating power during salary discussions. Employers often value certifications as they demonstrate a commitment to professional development and a certain level of expertise.

Market Trends: Keep an eye on market trends and salary surveys specific to your industry and location. Researching average salaries for roles related to Azure or cloud computing in your area can provide insights into potential salary increments.

Job Role Specifics: If your current or desired role involves significant use of Microsoft Azure services, the AZ-900 certification can be particularly beneficial. Specialized roles often come with higher salaries, and certifications can contribute to your suitability for such positions.

Advanced Certifications: While AZ-900 is an entry-level certification, pursuing more advanced Azure certifications (e.g., Azure Administrator, Azure Developer, or Azure Solutions Architect) can further increase your earning potential. Advanced certifications are often associated with more specialized and higher-paying roles.

Prerequisties

There is no prior certification required for this course however, Microsoft recommends some general skills and knowledge that may be beneficial before taking the AZ-900 course:

Familiarity with basic IT concepts: A general understanding of basic IT concepts, such as networking, storage, and computing, can be helpful.

Basic understanding of cloud computing: While not mandatory, having a basic awareness of cloud computing concepts will make it easier to grasp the content covered in the course.

Experience using internet browsers: The course materials and labs may involve using web-based interfaces, so familiarity with internet browsers is beneficial.

Recertification

The specific recertification requirements can vary depending on the certification track and the policies set by Microsoft. Here are some general points regarding recertification:

Certification Validity Period: Many Microsoft certifications, including the Azure certifications, have a validity period (usually two years). After this period, the certification may expire.

Recertification Exams: To maintain certification, individuals may need to pass a recertification exam or take a specific set of exams. Microsoft may update the certification exams to reflect changes in technology and services.

Mind Map

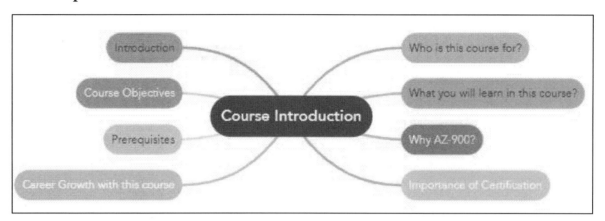

Figure 01: Mind Map

Chapter 01: Introduction to Azure

Introduction

Azure, like Google and Amazon Cloud Platforms, is Microsoft's Cloud Platform. It is typically a platform that allows us to use Microsoft tools. Earlier, we were required to invest tremendous money, energy, physical space, etc., to set up a huge IT infrastructure. Microsoft Azure released us from such circumstances, offering us virtual machines (VM), fast data processing, analytical tools, and monitoring instruments that significantly simplified our work. Azure pricing is also simpler and cheaper. It is commonly referred to as "Pay as You Go," meaning you only pay for the services when you are using them. Microsoft launched Azure's Windows at the beginning of October 2008, but it went live in 2010. Later, in 2014, Microsoft changed the name from "Windows Azure" to "Microsoft Azure. It has become one of the leading cloud services used today and is only growing bigger by the day.

What is Cloud Computing?

Cloud Computing is storing data and accessing computers over the internet. It is the delivery of different computing services like servers, software, analytics, databases, and storage via the internet. Computing resources are delivered on-demand through a cloud service platform with pay-as-you-go pricing. The companies that are providing services are termed "Cloud Providers." There are several cloud providers, with the major ones being Amazon, Google, and Azure.

Benefits of Cloud Computing

We are all aware that cloud computing has greatly changed traditional business thinking for IT resources. There are many benefits of cloud computing. Some of these are:

1. **Cost**

   Cloud computing eliminates the capital cost of buying hardware and software and of building and running in-house data centers – server racks, 24-hour electricity for power and cooling, etc.

2. **Scale Globally**

   Cloud computing services can scale with elasticity. In the cloud, IT resources are provided, with more or less computing power, storage, and bandwidth, as per requirement and from the right place.

3. **Increase Speed and Agility**

   New IT resources are readily available so that resources can be scaled up infinitely according to demand. This leads to a dramatic increase in agility for organizations.

4. **Security**

   The protection of their data is one of the main problems for any organization, regardless of its size and industry. Infringements of data and other cyber-crimes can devastate a company's revenue, customer loyalty, and positioning. Cloud provides many advanced security features to

strengthen the security of the overall company. It also helps in protecting your data, application, and infrastructure.

Reliability

Cloud computing allows data backup, disaster recovery, and business continuity, a business's readiness to maintain critical functions after an emergency or disruption. These events can include security breaches, natural disasters, and power outages as data can be replicated in the network of the cloud supplier on multiple redundant sites.

Predictability in the Cloud

Predictability in the cloud is a cornerstone that empowers businesses to advance with confidence. It revolves around two essential facets: performance predictability and cost predictability, both profoundly influenced by the Microsoft Azure Well-Architected Framework. Constructing a solution aligned with this framework assures a dependable blend of cost and performance.

Performance: Ensuring Consistent Customer Experiences

Anticipating the resources required for a seamless customer experience is at the heart of performance predictability. Cloud concepts such as autoscaling, load balancing, and high availability play pivotal roles in achieving this. In scenarios of increased demand, autoscaling dynamically deploys additional resources to meet requirements, subsequently scaling down during decreased demand. In situations of uneven traffic distribution, load balancing efficiently redistributes the load to less burdened areas, ensuring consistent performance.

Cost: Navigating Cloud Spend with Confidence

Cost predictability centers on forecasting and understanding the expenditure associated with cloud resources. Cloud platforms enable real-time tracking of resource usage, ensuring efficient utilization. Leveraging data analytics, businesses can discern patterns and trends, facilitating strategic resource deployment. Operating in the cloud provides the ability to predict future costs, allowing for proactive adjustments in resource allocation. Tools like Total Cost of Ownership (TCO) or the Pricing Calculator offer estimates, offering insights into potential cloud spending and empowering businesses to make informed decisions.

The Economy of Cloud Computing

The PAY AS YOU GO technique is the economic foundation of cloud computing. Users/Customers should only be required to pay for how they use cloud services. The users will undoubtedly benefit from it. Thus, everyone can benefit greatly economically from the Cloud. The removal of some indirect costs associated with assets like software licenses and support is another benefit. Users can access software applications in the cloud on a subscription basis for free because the cloud provider still owns the rights to the software-providing service.

Consumption-based Model

Two sorts of costs should be considered when contrasting IT infrastructure options. Operations Expenditures (OpEx) and Capital Expenditures (CapEx)

CapEx often involves a one-time, upfront expense to acquire or secure tangible resources. It includes constructing a new building, repaving the parking lot, constructing a data center, or purchasing a corporate vehicle.

OpEx, on the other hand, involves a one-time purchase of goods or services. It can be used to pay for convention center rentals, company car leases, or cloud service contracts.

Due to its consumption-based business model, cloud computing falls under OpEx. You do not pay for the physical infrastructure, electricity, security, or any other costs related to running a data center when you use cloud computing. Rather, you are charged for the IT resources you employ. You do not have to pay for any IT resources for the month if you do not use any.

 **EXAM TIP:**

Capital Expenditure (CapEx) is the expenditure to maintain or acquire fixed assets by spending money. This includes land, equipment, etc.

Operational Expenditure (OpEx) is the cost of a product or a system that is running on a day-to-day basis, like electricity, printer papers, etc.

This consumption-based strategy offers several advantages, such as:

- No up-front expenses
- No need to invest in and maintain the expensive infrastructure that consumers might not fully use
- The capacity to pay for additional resources as needed
- The capability of ceasing to pay for resources that are no longer required

In a conventional data center, you attempt to predict future resource requirements. If you overestimate, you may waste money by spending more on your data center than is necessary. If you underestimate, your data center will quickly hit capacity, and the performance of your apps and services could suffer. It can take a while to fix a data center that is under-provisioned. More hardware might need to be ordered, acquired, and installed. You will also need to add power, cooling, and networking for the additional hardware.

In a cloud-based paradigm, you do not have to stress about accurately estimating your resource requirements. You can add additional virtual machines if you discover that you require more. You remove computers if demand decreases and you no longer require as many virtual machines. Either way, you only pay for the virtual machines you use, not for any "excess capacity" the cloud provider may have.

Compare Cloud Pricing Model

The distribution of computing services via the internet utilizing a pay-as-you-go pricing mechanism is known as cloud computing. Usually, you only pay for the cloud services you really utilize, which benefits you by:

- Manage and plan your operating expenses
- Better manage your infrastructure
- Scale up as your company's demands evolve

In other words, cloud computing is the practice of renting compute and storage from another party's data center. Resources in the cloud can be handled similarly to resources in your local data center. Contrary

to your own data center, you must return cloud resources after utilizing them all. You only pay for what you use.

You rent CPUs and storage for the duration of your need rather than retaining them in your data center. The underlying infrastructure is maintained for you by the cloud provider. With the cloud, you can deliver cutting-edge solutions to your users and rapidly resolve your most difficult business difficulties.

Mostly in Azure, the pricing is hourly, like VMs, App Services, etc. A Virtual Machine (VM) is a compute resource that uses software instead of a physical computer to run programs and deploy apps. There is also consumption-based pricing, which is based on the execution of the function, per second use of the resource, or both. An example of consumption-based pricing is Azure Function.

Technical Terms

To understand Cloud Computing, you need to understand some technical terms.

- **High Availability (HA)** - It is the core of cloud computing. As we know, in traditional server environments, companies own several hardware, and the workload is limited to this hardware capacity. In case of extra load, capacity cannot be increased, whereas, sometimes, this hardware seems extra for the workload. In the cloud, you do not own any hardware, and adding servers is just a click away. With this method, you get high availability for your servers by replacing the failed server instantly with the new one. HA depends on the number of VMs that you set up to cover in case one goes down
- **Fault Tolerance** - For resilience in the cloud, fault tolerance is also an important factor. Fault tolerance gives you zero downtime, meaning that if there is any fault from Azure's side, then it is immediately mitigated by Azure itself
- **Disaster Recovery (DR)** – This is used in case of any catastrophic disaster like a cyber-attack. There is a plan in DR to recover your business from these critical systems or in normal operations if such an event occurs. DR has designated time to recover and a recovery point
- **Scalability** - In cloud computing, scalability means adding or removing resources easily and quickly as per demand. It is important in such a situation where you do not know the actual number of resources that are needed. Auto-scaling is an approach for scalability depending on your requirement by defining the threshold
- **Elasticity** - Elasticity is the capacity to dynamically extend or minimize network resources to respond to autonomous working load adjustments and optimize the use of resources. This can contribute to overall cost savings for services
- **Agility** - Agility is the capability to adapt quickly and efficiently to changes in the business environment. Agility also refers to the ability to develop, test, and deploy business-led software applications quickly. Instead of providing and managing services, Cloud Agility lets businesses concentrate on other issues such as security, monitoring, and analysis

EXAM TIP: For exam preparation, one must be familiar with all the terms like HA, Fault Tolerance, DR, Elasticity, Scalability, and Agility.

Vertical scaling

Vertical scaling, also known as scaling up, is a technical approach in which the capacity of a single server or hardware resource is increased to accommodate higher workloads or enhance performance. This involves upgrading the existing hardware by adding more computational power, memory, storage, or

network bandwidth. For example, increasing the CPU capacity involves upgrading to a more powerful processor or adding additional processors to the existing system. Similarly, expanding memory (RAM), growing storage capacity, and enhancing network bandwidth are common practices in vertical scaling. This approach contrasts with horizontal scaling, where additional resources are added by connecting multiple entities in a distributed manner. The decision to opt for vertical scaling is often based on factors such as the nature of the application, scalability requirements, and the overall system architecture. It is a suitable choice when applications can benefit from a single, robust server to meet increased demands.

Horizontal scaling

Horizontal scaling, also known as scaling out, is a technical strategy focused on expanding a system's capacity by adding more resources horizontally—specifically, by incorporating additional servers into the infrastructure. Unlike vertical scaling, which involves enhancing the capabilities of a single server, horizontal scaling distributes the workload across multiple servers. This approach is characterized by the addition of more servers to the existing architecture, each operating independently and collectively managing the increased demands on the system. Load balancing mechanisms play a crucial role in horizontal scaling, ensuring that incoming tasks or requests are evenly distributed across the servers to prevent performance bottlenecks. Often aligned with distributed architectures, horizontal scaling promotes resilience, fault tolerance, and improved scalability, making it particularly advantageous for applications that can be segmented into independent and parallelizable components. Cloud computing and containerization technologies further facilitate horizontal scaling by enabling organizations to dynamically adjust resources based on demand, supporting flexibility and responsiveness in changing operational requirements. The choice between vertical and horizontal scaling depends on the specific characteristics and needs of the application or system architecture.

Manageability in the Cloud

The alternatives for management are a key advantage of cloud computing. In this section, you will learn about two different types of manageability for cloud computing, both of which have great advantages.

Management of the Cloud

You may manage your cloud resources by managing the cloud. Within the cloud, you can:

- Deploy resources at the appropriate scale automatically as needed
- Remove the need for manual configuration by deploying resources based on a template that has already been configured
- Resources' conditions will be tracked, and failing ones will be replaced automatically
- To be informed about performance in real-time, receive automatic alerts based on preset metrics

Management in the Cloud

How you can manage your cloud environment and resources is referred to as management in the cloud. These are manageable:

- Using web portal
- Using command-line interface
- Using API
- Using PowerShell

Types of Cloud Computing

Cloud computing is a broad word that refers to a set of services that provide organizations with a low-cost way to expand their IT capacity and usefulness.

Businesses can choose where, when, and how they employ cloud computing to ensure an efficient and dependable IT solution based on their individual needs.

Infrastructure as a Service (IaaS), Platform as a Service (PaaS), and Software as a Service (SaaS) are the three basic cloud computing service models. Although there are evident distinctions between the three and what they can offer a business in terms of storage and resource sharing, they can also interact to build a single cloud computing paradigm.

Software as a Service

Cloud providers take over both servers and code. Cloud providers host and maintain the applications and underlying infrastructure for SaaS and handle updates such as software upgrades and security patches. A security patch is a method of updating systems, applications, or software by inserting code to fill in, or "patch," the vulnerability. This helps secure the system against an attack. Users link the app over the internet, usually through their phone, tablet, or PC, using their web browser.

This first service is Software as a Service (SaaS) and is considered the largest and most popular use of cloud computing today. It continues to grow as it replaces traditional on-device software with web-based alternatives. Rapidly moving programs to the cloud, often using a subscription-based model, making the software browser-accessible, eliminating the need to install client software, and, in many cases, making it cross-platform and accessible on the broad set of devices that we use today. Some examples include Gmail, Google Drive, Power BI, Microsoft Office 365, etc.

Platform as a Service

Cloud computing platforms that provide an on-demand environment to build, test, deliver, and manage software applications are called Platform as a Service. PaaS is designed to facilitate the fast development of web or mobile apps for developers without setting or maintaining the underlying server, storage, network, and database infrastructure needed for development.

Platform as a Service (PaaS) is a platform, which runs on a single VM and is designed to support the complete application life cycle, typically for website building, testing, deploying, managing, and updating. This service allows you to avoid the expense and complexity of buying, installing, and managing software licenses. Instead, you manage the applications and services you deploy, and the cloud service provider typically manages everything else. One example of such a service is the Azure App Service platform for hosting web apps and services, and the other is Structured Query Language (SQL) in Azure, which provides an enterprise-grade cloud-based version of SQL Server in the cloud. Enterprise-grade describes products that integrate into an infrastructure with a minimum of complexity and offer transparent proxy support. It includes Google, Microsoft Azure, Amazon Web Service (AWS), etc.

Infrastructure as a Service

An Infrastructure as a Service (IaaS) enables a server in the cloud or Virtual Machine (VM) instance that you would have complete control over. This offering is closer to an on-premises VM. IaaS requires you to manage the virtual machine's operating system and disk and networking attributes. Hardware management is taken care of, and a remote desktop is utilized to manage the VM. IaaS is a great solution where multiple applications running on a single VM are needed to fulfill the needs of third-party software.

> **Note:** It gives you a basic IT infrastructure for Cloud IT, like VMs, Data Storage, Networks, and OS on a pay-as-you-go model.

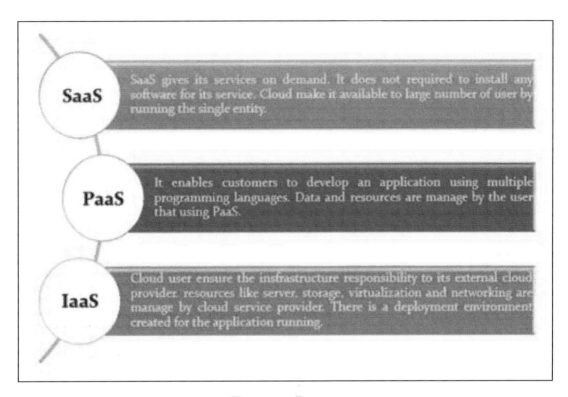

Figure 1-01: Features

Serverless

Overlapping PaaS, serverless computing concentrates on creating application functionality without continually spending time maintaining the required server and infrastructure. The cloud provider is responsible for configuration, capacity planning, and server governance. Cloud capacity planning aims to match demand with available resources. It analyzes what systems are already in place, measuring their performance and predicting demand. Your organization can then provision and allocate cloud resources based on that demand. Cloud governance is a set of practices that help ensure users operate in the cloud in ways that they want, that the operations are efficient, and that the user can monitor and correct operations as needed. The highly scalable and event-based serverless architectures only use resources when a particular task or trigger takes place.

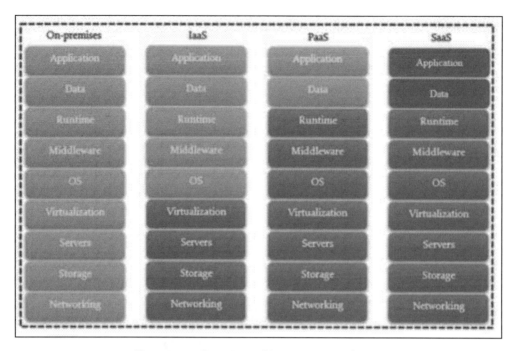

Figure 1-02: Overview of SaaS, PaaS, and IaaS

SaaS: Common Scenarios

Software as a Service (SaaS) allows you to use built-in cloud-based applications over the internet. The most common examples include email, a sophisticated business app like Customer Relationship Management (CRM), Enterprise Resource Planning (ERP), etc. This service allows you to only pay for the app that you use according to the pay-as-you-go model.

Advantages

There are several advantages of SaaS. These include, but are not limited to:

Easy access to cloud-based apps – SaaS provides easy access to cloud-based apps without installing and updating hardware and software. This service gives access to sophisticated applications such as CRM and ERP, making it affordable for businesses and organizations. They do not have to worry about how to manage and deploy applications.

Use free client software – Most clients can run the application directly from their browser without downloading and installing it.

Global access – With this cloud-based service, all data is directly stored in the cloud with some security. Users and clients can access the information and required data from any device connected to the internet.

PaaS: Common Scenarios

PaaS provides a complete deployment environment in the cloud. You can build, deploy, and run from simple to complex applications. You can use and scale services and resources according to the pay-as-you-go model and access them over the secure and reliable internet.

The following are common scenarios that use PaaS:

- **Development Framework** – PaaS provides a framework that enables you to deploy and run from simple to complex cloud-based applications over a secure internet connection. Cloud

features include providing high availability, reliability, scalability, and multi-tenant capabilities used by PaaS to reduce the coding overhead in deploying a framework.

- **Analytics and Business Intelligence** – Some tools provided as a service allow you to examine big data. Organizations and businesses most commonly use the service to improve forecasting, product decision, investment frameworks, project workflows, etc.

Advantages

There are several advantages of PaaS. These include, but are not limited to:

Reduces deployment time – PaaS provides a lot of pre-coded built applications so you can quickly deploy new applications.

Option for multiple platforms – This service offers you an option to deploy services and resources for multiple platforms.

Use of artificialized tools – As PaaS follows the pay-as-you-go approach, most organizations and business intelligence can use sophisticated tools they could not afford to purchase.

Supports geographically distributed teams – With PaaS, you can make a development framework over the internet. Multiple development teams can work together on the same idea from anywhere in the world.

Manages application lifecycle – PaaS cloud service enables you to efficiently manage the application lifecycle, such as building, testing, managing, deploying, etc.

IaaS: Common Scenarios

IaaS enables you to quickly meet the demand by scaling the resources according to need. It avoids having to buy and maintain physical architecture and infrastructure. Each service is offered as a separate component, and you only pay for the service you use.

The following are some common scenarios that use IaaS:

- **Hosting a Website** – You get more control than traditional website hosting when you host a website or run a website over IaaS
- **Web Apps** – IaaS supports the infrastructure of web apps, including storage, web, and application servers. An organization can deploy web apps on IaaS and scale resources to meet the demand.
- **Storage, Backup, and Recovery** – Storage management sometimes becomes very complex. IaaS makes it easy to manage, simplify, backup, and recover.
- **High-Performance Computing** – When working with traffic requiring high-performance computing, you can run these workloads in the cloud while avoiding hardware complexities and only paying for what you use.
- **Big Data Analysis** – IaaS provides the processing power for big data analysis.

Advantages

There are several advantages of IaaS.

Reduced Costs – This service eliminates the up-front cost of hardware and allows you to only pay for the resources and services that you use. This cloud service is often used by businesses looking for new ideas, and it allows you to deploy computing infrastructure quickly.

Better Business Continuity and Disaster Recovery – This service is better for disaster recovery because it allows scaling resources and services to meet the demand. This service is also best suited for business continuity and high availability.

Fast Response – You can deploy apps and deliver them to the user faster with IaaS managing the underlying infrastructure.

Scalable, Reliable, and Flexible – IaaS cloud services provide scalable, reliable, and flexible services that meet the Service Level Agreement (SLA).

EXAM TIP: Cloud computing provides the resources and services to meet demands over the internet. It provides services using three service models.

SaaS: Delivers cloud-based applications.

PaaS: Provides the deployment and development environment for users to use this environment for their cloud-based applications.

IaaS: Allows you to manage and scale resources to meet demands and use resources according to the pay-as-you-go model without any of the underlying hardware infrastructures.

Services	Advantages	Disadvantages
SaaS	Allows comprehensive access Available at any place A unique feature for collaboration work	Restrictions Dictate overall execution due to internet coverage
PaaS	Low cost Developed as publicly and privately Easy for web apps	No control over virtual machines Problem of relocation
IaaS	Automate the installation of hardware Easier for users to install cloud services	Very Expensive

Table 1-01: SaaS, PaaS, and IaaS

Shared Responsibility Model

Although you might be familiar with the shared responsibility concept, you might not know what it entails or how it affects cloud computing.

Start with an ordinary business data center. The business is in charge of the upkeep of the building, security, and, in the event of a disaster, maintenance or replacement of the servers. The equipment and software required to keep the data center operational are all the responsibility of the IT department.

Additionally, they probably must ensure that all systems are patched and running the most recent version.

The shared responsibility model divides these duties between the cloud provider and the customer. The cloud provider is accountable for network connectivity, electricity, cooling, and physical security. It would not make sense for the consumer to be in charge of any of those duties as they are not related to the fact that they are colocated with the data center.

The consumer is also in charge of the data and information kept in the cloud. You would not want your information to be accessible to the cloud provider. Access security is another consumer responsibility, so ensure you only grant access to people who require it.

Then, depending on the circumstance, culpability may vary for some things. The cloud provider will maintain the actual database if you utilize a cloud SQL database. The information that is entered into the database is still under your control. You would be in charge of database patches and updates as well as managing the data and information stored in the database if you deployed a virtual machine and installed a SQL database on it.

You are entirely in charge of an on-premises data center. With cloud computing, these obligations change. The cloud service types—Infrastructure as a Service (IaaS), Platform as a Service (PaaS), and Software as a Service (SaaS)—that are addressed later in this learning path are closely related to the shared responsibility paradigm. IaaS places the greatest amount of responsibility on the user, with the cloud provider being in charge of the fundamentals of connectivity, power, and physical security. SaaS, on the other hand, gives the cloud provider the lion's share of the blame. PaaS, a hybrid of IaaS and SaaS, occupies a middle ground and evenly divides responsibilities between the cloud provider and the customer.

The shared responsibility model outlines who is in charge of what, depending on the kind of cloud service, as seen in the picture below.

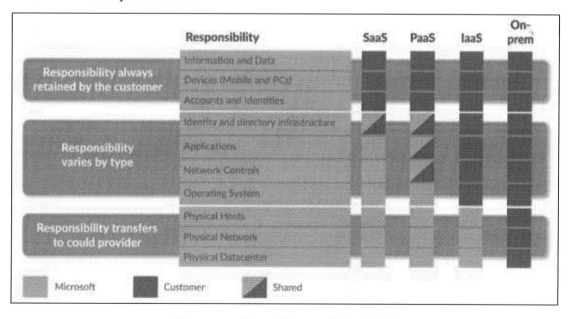

Figure 1-03: Shared Responsibility Model

Cloud Computing Deployments Models

We know that all clouds are not the same, and not every business requirement for cloud computing is the same. Therefore, to meet the requirements, different models, types, and services have been used. Firstly, you must decide how the cloud service is being applied by finding the cloud deployment type or Architecture.

When you shift some of the on-premises applications to the cloud, the next decision you have to make is how to deploy them. There are four ways to deploy and integrate cloud services into your application architecture and infrastructure:

- Public Cloud
- Private Cloud
- Hybrid Cloud
- Community Cloud

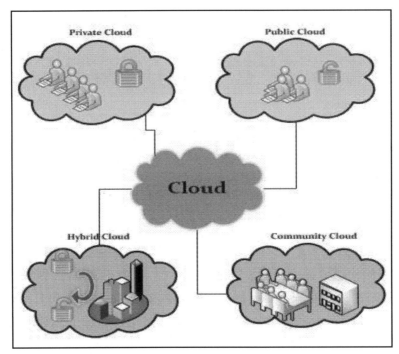

Figure 1-04: Cloud Deployment Models

Public Cloud

The public cloud is the most common approach that is open to all organizations. All resources, such as servers and disks, are owned and managed by the cloud provider in the public cloud. Microsoft Azure is an example. The cloud service provider carries out the maintenance, operation, and monitoring. The physical hardware is shared with other organizations, and your view is virtualized. Your data is secure and isolated. However, the cloud provider decides where it is stored and where your logic runs. The primary advantage of this approach is the lower cost, scalability, and flexibility. You are only required to pay for what you use; you scale on-demand based on your need, and there is no need to purchase and maintain expensive hardware.

Why Public Cloud?

Several applications allow you to use the public cloud:

- **Service Consumption** – Service consumption through an on-demand or subscription model charges you only for the CPU usage, storage, and other resources that you have used or reserved for use in the future
- **No hardware requirement** – With the public cloud, there is no requirement to purchase, maintain, or manage the physical architecture and infrastructure.
- **Automation** – It provides a quick response by using a web portal or scripts
- **Geographical distribution** – With this cloud approach, you can store data in the location nearest to the user without having to maintain data centers
- **Minimize Hardware Monitoring** –With a public cloud, you are free from maintaining hardware, as the service provider is responsible for this.

Private Cloud

The second approach is called a private cloud. This is where computing resources are used exclusively by a business or organization. It can be physically located on-premises or managed by a cloud provider. The maintenance, operation, and monitoring come under the private network owned by that organization. In addition to scalability and reliability, it has very high-level security. Microsoft Azure supports a private cloud through Azure Stack, bringing Azure infrastructure into your data center. A private cloud allows for more security and control. This might be necessary for legal compliance. For example, government agencies or financial institutions may have more stringent data storage requirements that require a private cloud.

Why Private Cloud?

Several applications allow you to use the private cloud:

- **Pre-Existing Environment** – A private cloud allows using an existing operating environment with solution expertise
- **Legacy Application** – Private cloud can be used to handle business-critical legacy applications
- **Data Authority and Security** – The cloud can be used to secure data

Hybrid Cloud

A hybrid cloud allows a user to access both public and private cloud resources within a single access environment. In a hybrid cloud, some of your data and applications run on your private infrastructure, and some run in Azure on the public cloud. This cloud model can be used in various ways, such as a migration approach to gradually transition your app and services out of your private data center into Azure. This allows for better testing and easier migration. This cloud model can also be used for segmenting work. You can connect to the environment together with a secure private network to pass data back and forth. Part of the data is processed in your private local infrastructure, and the rest is processed in the cloud. In this case, the hybrid cloud can be used for cloud bursting. You can upload work to the cloud when your internet data center hits the maximum workload. You can then scale and burst up workloads to leverage Azure and then drop back down to internal resources when the load returns to normal.

Why Hybrid Cloud?

Several applications allow you to use a hybrid cloud:

- **Existing Hardware Investment** – Most businesses prefer to use their existing hardware and operating environment
- **Use for Regulation** – Most regulatory frameworks require their data to exist on-site

- **Easy Migration** – With this cloud, you can shift data from on-premises to the cloud when required

Community Cloud

This model allows the user to access the group of organizations for its services. It can provide a sharing mechanism, but its security is higher than a public cloud and lower than a private cloud.

Why Community Cloud?

Community Cloud is a cloud computing model that serves a specific community or group of organizations, allowing them to collaborate, share resources, and communicate within a secure and customized environment. It provides a shared infrastructure with features tailored to the unique needs and interests of the community members.

Why Multi-Cloud?

Adopting a multi-cloud strategy is driven by the desire to enhance organizational resilience, flexibility, and performance. By distributing workloads across multiple cloud providers, businesses can mitigate the risk of service disruptions associated with a single provider, ensuring continuous operations. This approach also avoids vendor lock-in, allowing organizations to negotiate favorable terms and switch services more easily. Furthermore, a multi-cloud approach enables organizations to optimize performance by leveraging the strengths of different providers for specific workloads. It facilitates compliance with data residency requirements and industry regulations, as organizations can choose providers with the appropriate geographic locations and certifications. Cost optimization is achievable by leveraging pricing variations among providers for specific services. Additionally, a multi-cloud strategy fosters innovation by enabling access to the latest technologies and best-of-breed solutions offered by various providers. Overall, embracing a multi-cloud approach empowers organizations to build a resilient, flexible, and cost-effective IT infrastructure.

What is Azure?

Microsoft Azure is known as Windows Azure, and it is a Public Cloud. In the above discussion, we have already learned about Public Cloud. As for Azure, it is an expanding cloud service that helps companies efficiently tackle their challenges. It is free to build, manage, and deploy applications with your favorite tools and frames in a huge, global network. Azure is considered to offer both IaaS and PaaS. Azure offers over 100 services, from executing existing applications on virtual machines to exploring new tech paradigms like smart bots and mixed reality.

To use Azure, you first need to set up an Azure account directly by going to "Azure.com" or with the help of a representative. You can sign-up to Azure as a Free account with free USD 200 credit and 25+ free services.

Azure, for example, offers AI and machine learning tools that can communicate with your customers through vision, hearing, and speech. It also offers solutions for the storage of massive amounts of data, which are increasing rapidly. Azure services give solutions that, without Cloud resources, are much more expensive.

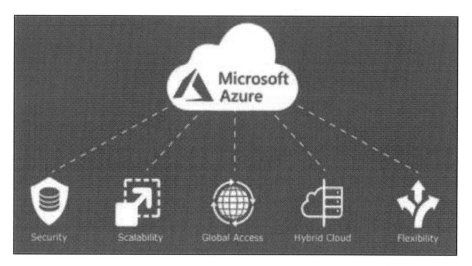

Figure 1-05: Azure Benefits

Azure Marketplace

The Azure marketplace offers technical solutions and services from Microsoft and partners to build and extend Azure products and services. It has all kinds of services and applications like VMs, Templates, apps, Azure-managed services, etc. There is an Azure App Store in your mobile for buying cloud services, where you have a variety of solutions, including base Operating System (OS), database, security, networking, and developer tools. To access all of these, you can either go directly to the marketplace's website, use Azure Command-Line Interface (CLI), or integrate with PowerShell. From the catalog, you can add anything to your subscription. Some services are free, and some are charged. To publish your product in the marketplace, you need to become a partner with Microsoft so that it becomes a distribution channel for your business.

Physical Infrastructure

Data centers are the first component of Azure's physical infrastructure. The data centers are conceptually equivalent to huge corporate data centers. They are buildings with racks of resources and specialized power, cooling, and networking equipment.

Azure has data centers all around the world because it is a worldwide cloud service. These particular data centers, however, are not immediately reachable. To help you achieve resilience and dependability for your business-critical workloads, data centers are organized into Azure Regions or Azure Availability Zones.

You can interactively explore the underlying Azure architecture on the Global Infrastructure webpage.

Azure Data center

Suppose you purchased services in Azure such as SQL database, web hosting virtual machine, or one of the many services offered by Azure. All these services run on a physical infrastructure underneath some services. A physical facility that hosts these services is called a data center. It is used to host a group of network servers, and a typical data center has its power pooling and networking infrastructure.

Geography

Azure divides the world into geographies defined by geopolitical boundaries or country borders. Azure geography is a discrete market typically containing two or more regions that preserve data residency and compliance boundaries.

This division has several benefits.

- Geographies allow customers with specific data residency and compliance needs to keep their data and applications close
- Geographies ensure that data residency, sovereignty, compliance, and resiliency requirements are honored within geographical boundaries
- Geographies are fault-tolerant to withstand complete region failure through their connection to dedicated high-capacity networking infrastructure

Global Footprint

Azure has more global regions than any other cloud provider — which offers the scale required to bring users around the world closer to applications, preserve residency, and provide customers with comprehensive compliance and resilience options. There are 54 regions of Azure that are available around the world, with 140 regions.

Regions

Regions are geographical areas where Azure is present to deploy the Azure resources. It is a set of data centers with a latency-defined perimeter connected via a dedicated regional low-latency network. There are region-specific services, but some core services like storage and VMs are live by default in all regions.

> EXAM TIP: A Dedicated Regional Low Latency network means there is a fiber connection between data centers in the region.

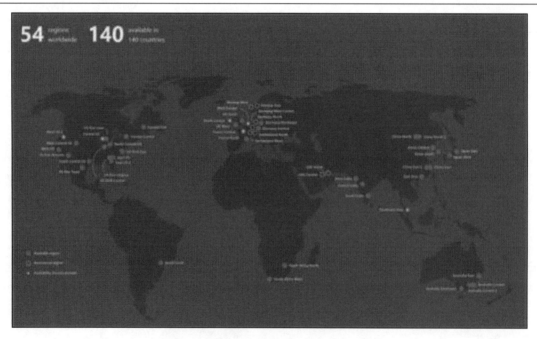

Figure 1-06: Azure Geographical Region

How to Choose a Region?

When choosing a region, you need to think about three things mainly:

- **Location**- To reduce the latency, choose a region closest to the user
- **Features**- All features are not available in all regions, so select a region where your specific feature is available
- **Price**- Service prices in Azure vary from region to region

Why are regions important?

No other cloud service has as many international regions as Azure. With these zones, you have the freedom to deliver applications near your users wherever they may be. Global regions offer greater scalability and redundancy. They maintain data residency for your services as well. Data residency refers to the physical or geographic location of an organization's data or information.

Special Regions

When building out your apps for compliance or legal requirements, you may want to use one of the specialized Azure regions. Here are a few examples:

- **US regions** - These Azure regions offer physically and logically network-isolated instances for U.S. government agencies and partners, including US DoD (Department of Defense) Central, US Gov Virginia, US Gov Iowa, and more. These data centers have additional compliance certifications and are run by screened U.S. employees.
- **China North, China East, and other areas** - Through a special collaboration between Microsoft and 21Vianet, in which Microsoft does not directly administer the data centers, these regions are now accessible.

Note: You locate the location of your resources using regions. You should also be familiar with the terms "geography" and "availability zone".

Azure Region Pair

One or more data centers are used to create availability zones. Within each region, there are at least three zones. An outage significant enough to affect two data centers might occur in the event of a major calamity. Azure builds region pairings because of this.

What is a pair of regions?

Each Azure region is linked with a neighboring region that is at least 300 miles apart and located in the same geographic area (such as the US, Europe, or Asia). This method enables the replication of resources (such as VM storage) across geography, which lowers the possibility of interruptions brought on by occurrences like natural disasters, armed conflict, power outages, or physical network outages that simultaneously affect both locations. Services would automatically failover to the other area in its region pair, for instance, if one region in a pair were to be affected by a natural disaster. Failover is the ability to switch automatically and seamlessly to a reliable backup system.

West US and East US are two examples of region pairs in Azure, as are South East Asia and East Asia.

The relationship between geography, region pairs, regions, and data centers is shown in the diagram below.

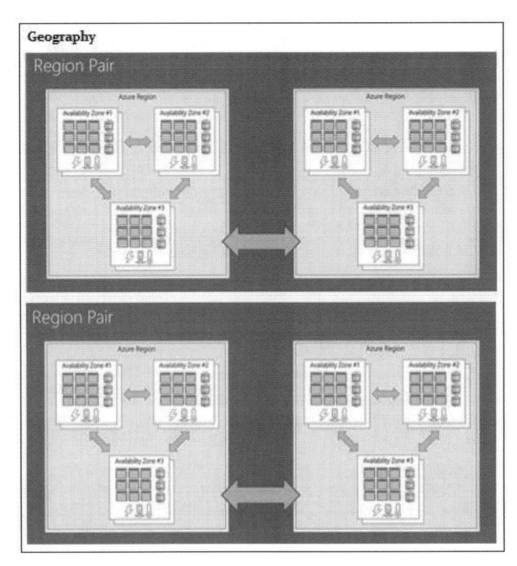

Figure 1-07: Region-Pair Concept

You can use the pair of regions to deliver dependable services and data redundancy because they are directly linked and separated enough to be shielded from local disasters. Some services use region pairs to automatically geo-redundantly store data.

Region pairs also provide the following benefits:

- One region out of each pair is given priority in the event of a significant Azure outage to ensure that at least one gets back online as soon as possible for applications hosted in that region pair.
- To reduce downtime and the chance of an application outage, planned Azure upgrades are applied to paired regions one area at a time.
- Except for Brazil South, data continues to live within the same geographic region as its mate for tax and law enforcement authorities.

Sovereign Regions

Azure has both ordinary regions and sovereign regions. The Azure instances, known as sovereign regions, are separate from the main Azure instance. You might need to use a sovereign region for compliance or legal reasons.

These Azure sovereign regions:

- Instances of Azure that are physically and logically network-isolated for use by US government organizations and partners include US DoD (Department of Defense) Central, US Gov Virginia, US Gov Iowa, and more. These data centers have additional compliance certifications and are run by US employees who have been thoroughly vetted
- Through an innovative collaboration between Microsoft and 21Vianet, whereby Microsoft does not directly run the data centers, several regions—including China East, China North, and others—are made available

Availability Set

An Availability Set is a logical grouping function that can be used to separate VM resources from each other. Azure must ensure that your VMs are operating across several physical servers, device tables, storage units, and network switches within an availability set. If a hardware or software failure occurs, only the VMs will be impacted, and the overall solution will remain operational.

Availability Zone

Availability Zones (AZ) are locations within an Azure region that are physically separate. An availability zone comprises one or more independently operating systems and a network of data centers. Each region has a minimum of three zones.

Availability zones allow clients to run high-availability and low-latency mission-critical applications.

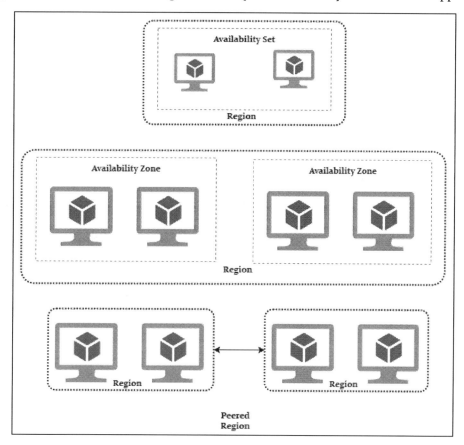

Figure 1-08: Region, AZ, and Paired Region

Management Infrastructure

Azure resources and resource groups, subscriptions, and accounts make up the management infrastructure. Planning your projects and products within Azure will be easier if you understand the hierarchical structure.

Azure Resource Manager (ARM)

Azure Resource Manager gives you the tools needed to organize and secure your resources. It is a fundamental service that is used to install and manage Azure resources. It comes with a management layer that enables you to create, upgrade, and delete Azure subscription tools. After deployment, you use management tools like access control, locks, and tags to keep your resources safe and organized.

Resource

A Resource is a manageable item that is available in Azure, like VM, storage, databases, etc. Each resource can reside only in one resource group.

Resource Groups

Resource Groups are where you deploy your resources. Here, you need to identify which resource group you want to deploy a resource to. It is like a container where all resources of a solution or the resources that you want to manage in a group reside. The resource from the resource group can be added or removed at any time. You can move your resources from one group to another, and the resources of multiple regions can also be in one resource group. With the resource group, you have access control to the resource. The resources in different resource groups can interact with each other.

Logical Groups

Resource groups are used to organize and manage Azure resources. You can add order and organization to your Azure resources by grouping similar usage, type, or location resources. Because materials are often so disorganized, logical grouping is the component that you might be the most interested in.

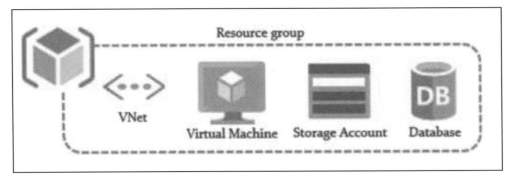

Figure 1-09: Logical Grouping

Lifecycle

When you delete a resource group, it also deletes all of the resources included within it. Organizing resources by life cycle can be advantageous in non-production contexts where you might test an experiment and then discard it. It is simple to remove a collection of resources at once using resource groups.

Authorization

Role-Based Access Control (RBAC) permissions allow you to grant users the specific rights they need to perform their jobs. RBAC permission can also be applied to resource groups. You may simplify administration and limit access to only what is required by applying RBAC rights to a resource group.

IT personnel can manage settings, developers can have read-only access, and administrators can have complete control at all times. You can also prevent resources from being deleted accidentally.

By enabling resource locks, you can block the ability to delete a resource or prevent changes to it by marking it as read-only.

Resource Provider

Resource provider supplies the resources for the resource manager.

A group of REST operations known as an Azure resource provider is what gives an Azure service its capabilities. For example, Microsoft.KeyVault is a resource provider for the Key Vault service. The resource provider defines REST operations for working with vaults, secrets, keys, and certificates.

You can deploy Azure resources to your account based on the definitions provided by the resource provider.

Resource Manager Template

Resource Manager Template is a JavaScript Object Notation (JSON) file that defines the resources deployed in the resource group. It also defines the dependencies between the deployed resources. With this template, resources can be deployed in a consistent and repeatable way.

ARM Benefits

- You have group resource handling like deploying, management, and monitoring
- You get consistency; For example, when you deploy resources, it will happen in the same way every time
- You get the dependency of each resource so that no other dependency will get into the resource
- Access Control is built-in to assign access to the users
- With tagging, it is easier to identify the resource in the future
- For billing, you can use tagging to stay on top

 EXAM TIP: The resource group is not a resource; it helps in the structure of Azure Architecture.

Azure Resource Manager has several features you can use to organize resources, enforce standards, and protect your critical Azure resources from accidental deletion. The resource groups are just like a container for resources deployed on Azure. By placing resources of similar usage, type, or location in the same resource group, you can provide some order and organization to your Azure resources.

Tags

Tags allow you to improve the organization of your resources even further. You can use tags to associate custom details with a resource or resource group, such as the cost center or billing department.

Resource groups and tags are best-suited for helping you organize existing resources or groups.

Azure policies are used to make sure that the new resource uses the same rules. The policies defined by Azure ensure that new resources use the same tags as existing resources.

Azure Subscriptions

You can get authenticated and authorized access to Azure services with an Azure subscription. It also enables you to allocate resources. An Azure subscription is a logical unit of Azure services linked to an Azure account, which is Microsoft Entra ID (formerly Azure AD).

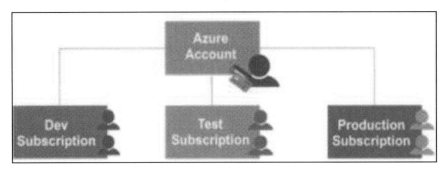

Figure 1-10: Azure Subscriptions

A single subscription or many subscriptions with different charging models and access-management rules can be added to an account. Azure subscriptions can be used to set limits on Azure products, services, and resources. You can utilize one of the two types of subscription boundaries:

Billing Boundary

This subscription type determines how an Azure account is billed for utilizing Azure. For different types of billing requirements, you can create several subscriptions. To help you organize and manage your costs, Azure creates special billing reports and invoices for each subscription.

Access Control Boundary

Azure's access-management policies are applied at the subscription level, and you can build several subscriptions to suit different corporate structures. Within a company, you have several departments to which you can apply different Azure subscription policies. This payment approach enables you to manage and control access to user resources through subscriptions.

Create Additional Azure Subscriptions

You might want to set up several subscriptions for resource or billing management. You could, for example, create several subscriptions to separate the following:

Environments: You can build subscriptions to set up various environments for development and testing, security, or isolating data for compliance while managing your resources. Because resource access restriction happens at the subscription level, this approach is highly beneficial.

Organizational Structures: Subscriptions can be created to reflect various organizational structures. You could, for example, limit a team to lower-cost resources while giving the IT department complete control. With this design, you can manage and regulate access to the resources that users provide within each subscription.

Billing: For billing purposes, you may want to create multiple subscriptions. You want to create subscriptions to control and track costs based on your demands because costs are initially aggregated at the subscription level. For example, you might wish to set up two subscriptions for production workloads and development and testing workloads.

You may also require additional subscriptions as a result of the following:

Subscription Limits: Subscriptions are subject to certain restrictions. For example, the maximum number of Azure ExpressRoute circuits per subscription is '10'. When creating subscriptions on your account, keep those limitations in mind. Additional memberships may be required if you exceed such limits in specific instances.

Customize billing to meet your needs

You can organize your subscriptions into invoice parts if you have many. Each invoice section is a line item on the invoice that shows the monthly charges. For example, your company may require a single invoice yet wish to organize costs by department, team, or project.

Depending on your needs, you can create several invoices within the same billing account. Create additional billing profiles to accomplish this. Each billing profile has its invoice and payment mechanism each month.

An overview of how billing is structured is shown in the diagram below. Your billing may be set up differently if you have previously signed up for Azure or if your company has an Enterprise Agreement.

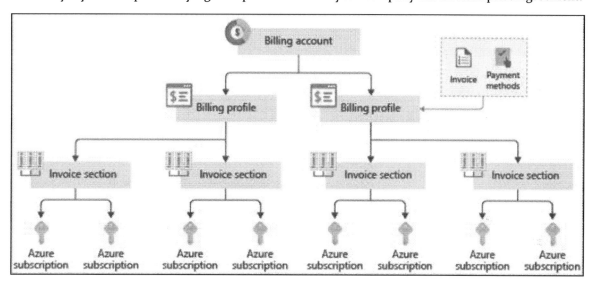

Figure 1-11: Azure Subscription

Azure Management Groups

If your company has a lot of subscriptions, you will need a way to keep track of access, regulations, and compliance for all of them. Over and above subscriptions, Azure management groups provide a level of scope. Subscriptions are organized into containers called management groups, and the management groups are subject to your governance rules. All subscribers within a management group automatically inherit the management group's conditions. Regardless of the sort of subscriptions you have, management groups provide enterprise-level management on a wide scale. The subscriptions of a single management group must all trust the same Azure AD tenant.

Essential Facts about Management Groups

- 10,000 management groups can be supported in a single directory
- A management group tree can support up to six layers of depth; this restriction does not apply to the root or subscription levels

- Each management group and subscription can support only one parent
- Each management team has a large number of children
- Each directory has a single hierarchy that contains all subscriptions and management groups

Management group, subscriptions, and resource group hierarchy

1. Hierarchy with Policies for VM Locations:

To enforce strict governance and ensure specific policies across Azure resources, you can establish a hierarchical structure with management groups. For example, create a management group named "Production" and apply a policy limiting Virtual Machine (VM) locations to the "US West" region within this group. Policies set at the management group level automatically inherit all subscriptions under that management group, ensuring consistent enforcement. This policy, once defined, cannot be altered by individual resources or subscription owners, enhancing overall governance and compliance.

Example Hierarchy:

- ➢ Management Group: Production
- • Subscription 1
- • Subscription 2
- • Resource Group A
   - ➢ VM 1
- • Resource Group B
   - ➢ VM 2

In this setup, the policy limiting VM locations to US West is inherited by all VMs under Subscription 1 and Subscription 2.

2. Centralized User Access Management With Azure RBAC:

Streamlining user access across multiple subscriptions can be achieved by organizing subscriptions under a management group and leveraging Azure Role-Based Access Control (Azure RBAC). Instead of individually scripting RBAC assignments for each subscription, you can assign roles at the management group level. This single assignment cascades down to all sub-management groups, subscriptions, resource groups, and resources underneath, simplifying access control.

Example Hierarchy:

- ➢ Management Group: Access Control
- • Subscription A
- • Subscription B
- • Resource Group X
- • Resource Group Y

By assigning an Azure RBAC role (e.g., Contributor) to the "Access Control" management group, users gain access to all resources within Subscription A and Subscription B, including any future subscriptions or resources added to this hierarchy. This centralized approach enhances security, reduces administrative overhead, and ensures consistent access policies across the Azure environment.

Azure Services

There are several available services and features in Azure. The most commonly used categories are:

- Compute
- Networking
- Storage
- Mobile
- Databases
- Web
- Internet of Things
- Big Data
- Artificial Intelligence
- Security and Identity
- Monitoring and Management

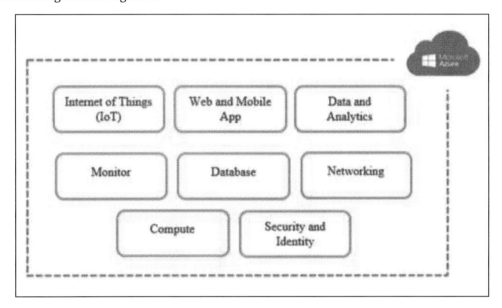

Figure 1-12: Azure Services

Compute

In Azure, there are several options available for application and service hosting. Azure Compute provides you with an infrastructure where you can run your applications.

- **Azure Virtual Machine** - These are Linux and Windows VMs on-demand with your desired configuration hosted in Azure. (Red Hat Enterprise Linux)CentOS, Oracle Linux, RHEL, Debian, OpenSUSE, SUSE LES, and Ubuntu have supported Linux distributions. There are 6 types of VMs with 28 families. There is a set amount of Memory, vCPUs, and Temporary Storage. You can also attach additional data disks to these VMs. Pricing is based on per-minute billing. Reserved VMs are also available for significant discounts; you can get discounts of up to 72% on a pay-as-you-go model
- **App Service** – This PaaS provides a fully managed platform for creating cloud applications for the web and mobile. It hosts web applications, mobile app backends, RESTful APIs, and automated business processes. The programming languages that App Service supports are .NET, .NET Core, Ruby, Java, PHP, Node.js, and Python
- **Azure Function** is a serverless compute that enables you to run code on-demand automatically. Azure Function is an event-driven service for accelerating app development. FaaS executes the

code in response to an event or trigger. Its billing is done when the code is executed; in the idle state, it is not charged. Its supported languages are C#, F#, and JavaScript, and currently, Java is in a preview state. Azure Function is a part of App Services that can run in App Service Plans (from free to isolated plans). In the free account, the first 1 million executions per month are free

- **Azure Batch** is a managed service for batch processing jobs like running large-scale parallel and High-Performance Computing (HPC) applications. It can scale to tens, hundreds, or thousands of virtual machines as per requirement. It supports both Windows and Linux compute nodes. This service is free, and you only need to pay for the resource used in your task

- **Azure Kubernetes Service** – A managed Kubernetes Container Orchestration is used for simplifying the deployment, management, and operations of Kubernetes. It gives you automatic upgrades and patching. Azure Kubernetes Service enables you to manage the cluster of VMs on which the containerized app is running. It also supports other orchestration like DC/OS, Docker, and Unmanaged Kubernetes, but these are not managed. Here, you only need to pay for agent nodes, not for the master node

- **Azure Container Instance** – It is a containerized service that is used to run an application on Azure without provisioning the VMs and servers. You can easily run the container with a single command. It gives you an individual container as a service. Azure Container Instance is the fastest and easiest way to run a container in Azure. It is good for applications that run in an isolated container. The applications are publicly addressable, and you can design the container spec. The billing is based per second.

- **Service Fabric** – It is a distributed network framework that is capable of operating in various environments, Azure, and on-site. It creates Windows and Linux micro-services and orchestrates containers. Multiple Azure and Microsoft services like Skype, CosmosDB, Cortana, etc use Service Fabric. It supports both stateful and stateless microservices. Its supported community is .NET, but it also supports other languages and containers

- **Cloud Services** – It is a managed service for cloud applications. Cloud Services is a PaaS offered by Azure. It is similar to App Services but with the difference that you can remote it into VMs. It creates highly available, flexible cloud applications and APIs to concentrate on software rather than hardware. It has two types of services: Web Roles which are websites and web apps, and Worker Roles which are for asynchronous processing

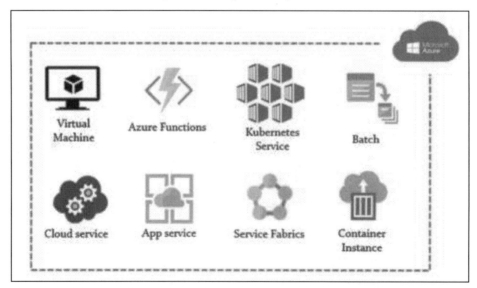

Figure 1-13: Azure Compute

Networking

The key function of Azure networking is the relation between compute resources and access to applications. In Azure, a network interface includes several options in global Microsoft Azure data centers that link the outside world to services and apps. There are various networking services in Azure that can be used individually or together. Azure networking provides you with the most secure environment for your data as compared to any other Cloud Platform.

- **Virtual Networks** – They allow your Azure resources to communicate with each other over the internet or on-premises network in a secure way. Also known as VNET is an isolated network where you host your VMs, VM Scale Sets, and App Service environments. Virtual Networks are composed of subnets with user-defined routes where you define the route to send the traffic and the destination from where it comes in. With Virtual Network, you can add Security Groups and outbound internet access to the resources. In Virtual Network, you have the capability of VNET Peering, where you connect two VNETs. VNET peering can be done within the same region or across the region for global coverage. However, across-region VNET peering is currently only supported in a few regions. A Service Endpoint feature also enables you to access the services within your VNET by creating a private connection to that resource rather than using the internet. This endpoint feature is only available in Storage accounts and databases

- **Azure Load Balancer** – It balances the incoming and outgoing traffic to and from the application resources and service endpoints. Azure Load Balancer gives basic load balancing features to your VMs and operates at layer 4 (Transport layer of the OSI model). It has a public or internal load balancer. A public load balancer is internet-facing, while an internal load balancer is used within the VNET. Azure Load Balancer provides regional load balancing by routing traffic over availability zones and into your VNets. It provides internal load balancing by routing traffic across and from your local resources within VNET. It has HTTP or TCP-based probes for health checks and availability. It also uses hash-based load balancing to balance the load inside the VMs that are behind your load balancer

- **Application Gateway** – It is a cloud load balancing device to handle web app traffic. It is Layer 7 load balancing that uses HTTP-based round-robin. It optimizes application service delivery while increasing security for applications with a web application firewall. It also offers some other features like SSL Offloading (SSL offloading is the process of removing the SSL based encryption from incoming traffic that a web server receives to relieve it from decryption of data), and stickiness for some cookies-based session affinity at the backend to maintain the state for the user between the connection of the user with a single VM. It also provides support for client-connected applications by Web Socket. Application has internal and external load balancing, similar to the public and internal load balancer, but they are at a higher level

- **VPN Gateway** – This sends encrypted traffic across the public internet between an Azure virtual network and an on-site location. Azure Virtual Networks are accessed through high-performance VPN Gateways in a secure way over the internet. VPN Gateway supports both Site-to-Site VPN and Point-to-Site VPN. You have one VPN gateway per VNET; then, you can have multiple connections per VPN Gateway. In that, you can perform Static or Dynamic Routing

- **Azure Domain Name System (DNS)** – This hosts DNS domains with the same credentials as Microsoft Azure infrastructure to provide name resolution, a fast DNS response, and high domain availability. In Azure DNS, you cannot purchase the Domain name. For DNS, you pay per zone, per month, and then per million queries. The pricing per zone changes depending on the zone. Private domain support is currently in a preview state

- **Traffic Manager** – It is a global traffic router that distributes DNS-based traffic to services across the Azure region to get the best available endpoint, providing high availability and responsiveness. It supports four routing methods: priority, weighted, geographic, and performance. The traffic will be sent depending on the routing method and health checks. It can be used to build multi-region architecture like web applications

- **Content Delivery Network (CDN)** – This provides users with high bandwidth content. CDNs save cached content on edge servers at PoP (Point of Presence) locations near end-users to reduce latency. Edge servers are the smaller data centers. It is mainly used for static assets like media, images, etc. It also supports Dynamic Site Acceleration by optimizing the route between the requester and the origin for dynamic content because it does not cache the dynamic content on the edge servers. In Azure, CDN is provided by Akamai and Verizon. The billing is based per GB outbound per month, and the rates can change on a zone basis

- **Express Route** - ExpressRoute allows you to extend your on-premises networks to Microsoft Cloud by a connectivity provider's private connection. This is a private connection. There is no traffic going on the internet. Connections to cloud services such as Microsoft Azure, Office 365, and Dynamics 365 can be built with ExpressRoute through stable high bandwidth connections. The dedicated link is up to 10Gbps. With that, you have two options: connectivity to MPLS (Multi-Protocol Label Switching) or the on-premises network. This is good for DR (Disaster Recovery) or hybrid cases

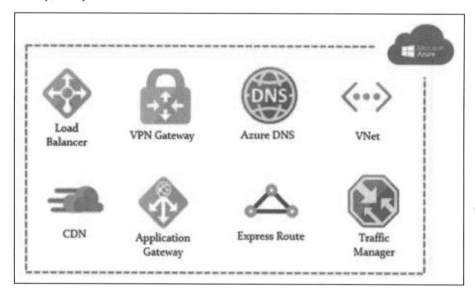

Figure 1-14: Azure Networking

Storage

Azure Storage is a cloud storage system from Microsoft that helps store up-to-date files. It offers an extremely scalable data object store, a cloud file system service, a reliable message store, and a NoSQL store. Azure Storage is secure, highly available, durable, scalable, managed, and accessible. You must first create an account in Azure to use any kind of storage there; the storage account is the parent object. You can move your data to and from your storage account after your account has been established. You can also build a storage account for up to 500TB of cloud data because it has a limit of 500TB per storage account. Use a Blob storage account and hot or cold access tiers to manage your expenses depending on

how often the object data is accessed. A storage account can be of two types: Standard and Premium accounts.

In Azure Storage, there are multiple types of replications: Locally Redundant Storage (LRS), Zone Redundant Storage (ZRS), Geo-Redundant Storage (GRS), and Read Access Geo-Redundant Storage (RA-GRS). In Azure Storage, there are also various tiers of Storage: Archive (for blob only), Cool Storage (for infrequently accessed data), and Hot Storage (for frequently accessed data).

- **Blob Storage** - Azure Blob Storage is Microsoft's cloud object storage solution. Blob storage is for the storage of large volumes of unstructured data, like text or binary data. It is an internet-accessible Object Store via HTTP or HTTPS. In that, you have the option to make your data either public or private. The hierarchy is: Storage Account -> Containers -> Blobs. A blob is an object which is in the container. It also has an archiving tier available

- **Queue Storage** – Azure Queue Storage is a data store for queuing and for the reliable provisioning of messages. It is a managed queuing service through which you get secure storage for communication between apps based on the message. Messages in the queue can be up to 64 KB, and millions of messages can be stored in a single queue. A queue is generally used to store asynchronous lists of messages. It is useful for decoupling applications. The lifetime of a message in the queue is seven days

- **File Storage** - Azure File Storage makes use of a regular SMB (Server Message Block) to set up a highly available network of file shares. You also can read files via the REST interface or libraries for the storage client. The cloud or on-site implementations of Windows, Linux, and macOS install Azure file shares concurrently. Azure file shares can also be cached with Azure file sync on Windows Servers for easy access close to the data point. You can use it as a shared file system for the apps that lift and shift into the cloud. The maximum file share size is 5TB

- **Table Storage** - Azure Table Storage is a service that stores NoSQL unstructured data in the cloud and offers a schema-less design for providing a key/attribute database. Since table storage is schema-less, the development of your application will make it easy for you to adapt your data. There can be as many entities and tables as you like in table storage. The maximum entity size can be up to 1MB. Access to table storage data for many types of applications is fast, cost-effective, and typically lower than conventional SQL for similar data volumes. A new Azure Cosmos DB Table API is introduced in addition to the Azure Table storage service, which offers tables, global distribution, and automated secondary indexes. It has now become a part of Cosmos DB

- **Disk Storage** – Azure Disk Storage provides a managed or unmanaged disk for your VMs. Managed disk takes care of the storage account and disks, while you only pay for what you provisioned. You have to manage the disk in the un-managed disk, paying for what you use. It has 99.999% availability with three replicas. The available types of disk storage are Ultra-Disks, Premium Solid-State Drives (SSDs), Standard SSDs, and Standard Hard Disk Drives (HDDs). In premium, you have an option of disk IOPS (input/output operations per second) that are provisioned, and these are mapped on disks, not on VMs. However, not all VM families support the premium disk type. In Standard Disk, the IOPS are not provisioned via disk as it varies with VMs. The size for the disk storage is from 32 GB to 4 TB, but you have the option to attach multiple disks to a VM

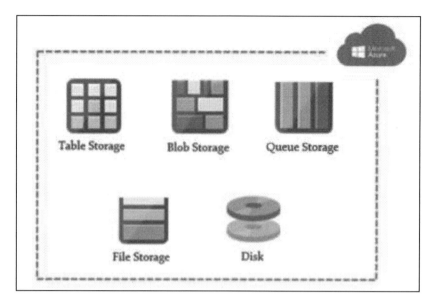

Figure 1-15: Azure Storage

Data and Analytics

Data is available in all sizes and formats. Big Data refers to large volumes of information, such as the hundreds of gigabytes of data produced by weather systems, communications systems, genome analysis, imagery platforms, etc. The volume of data makes it difficult to interpret and determine. It is often so large that it is no longer appropriate to use traditional processing and analysis methods.

To cope with these large data sets, Open-Source cluster technologies have been developed. Microsoft Azure offers a wide range of Big Data and analytics tools and services.

- **HDInsight** – This is an open-source, fully managed analytic service. It processes huge amounts of data in the cloud with managed Hadoop clusters. The 99.9 % SLA for your business is given by this. It is basically a Hadoop component from HDP (Hortonworks Data Platform). It is used to run streaming and historical data analytics. The open framework for HDInsight includes Hive, Spark, Kafka, Storm, etc. The use cases for this service are batch processing, data science, etc.
- **Event Hub** – This large-scale telemetry ingestion allows you to run millions of events per second. You can use it to load a large amount of data into the cloud in real-time. It captures data into the Azure Blob or Data Lake; publishers send it to the event hub. From these hubs, the consumer reads data. The retention period of an item in the hub is seven days
- **Data Lake Store and Analytics** - Azure Data Lake provides all the capabilities to make storing data of any scale, shape, speed, processing, and analytics across platforms and languages simple for developers, data scientists, and analysts. This eliminates the complexity of ingesting and processing all your data and makes the process of batching, uploading, and immersive analysis easier. Data Lake Store is a repository for the analytics workload, is HDFS compatible, and can integrate with HDInsight. It has no data storage limit. Data Lake Analytics is a completely managed pay-per-job analysis service with corporate security, auditing, and support. It uses U-SQL language, specifically designed for Data Lake Analytics, combining SQL and using C# code to perform analytics. Data Lake Analytics can work with Data Lake Store and others.
- **Data Factory** – It is a fully managed cloud-based data integration service. Big data demands the service to organize and operationalize processes and refine these huge raw data stores into operational business insights. This is an integrated cloud service for complex hybrid Extract,

transform, and load (ETL), Extract, load, and transform (ELT), and data integration projects. It is a service that automates the data movement along its process through various systems. SQL Server Integration Service built-in V2 of Data Factory is in preview, which is the transformation process of ETL

- **Azure Analysis Service** – This is an analytic engine as a service for enterprise-grade. It uses advanced computing and mashup to combine data from several data sources, set metrics, and secure data in an advanced single table of the semantic data model for query purposes. The data model makes searching vast volumes of data for ad hoc data analysis easier and quicker for users. It supports a hybrid network, and it has a built-in SQL Server Analysis Service

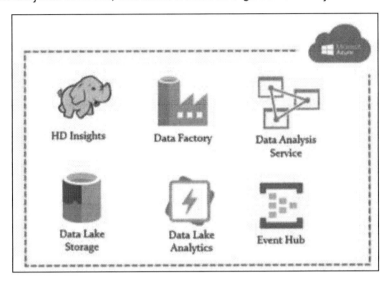

Figure 1-16: Data and Analytics

Databases

Azure Database is a fully managed service. It has business-grade efficiency with integrated high availability that ensures you can easily scale and hit global distribution without needing to worry about costly downtime.

- **SQL DB** – It is a fully managed relational database with high availability and performance data storage for applications. It offers two deployment options: Single DB and Elastic Pools. In Single DB, you pick a single service and scale it up or down in a single database, while in Elastic Pools, a pool of resources is shared across a number of databases. With Elastic Pool, you get better optimization. It has a Database Transaction Unit (DTU) purchasing model. The purchasing model DTU provides a mixture of three levels of computing, storage, and I/O services, supporting light to large databases. SQL DB shares its code base with the MS SQL server, which means that SQL DB gets updated first before rolling out to the MS SQL server; this way, it will be up to date with the feature of an SQL server. It has built-in intelligence via auto-tuning
- **Azure DB for MySQL and Postgre SQL** - Both of the databases are fully managed and relational databases. They both are scalable databases with security and high availability. Both have a pay-as-you-go pricing model
- **SQL Data Warehouse** – It is a managed petabyte data warehouse with complete security at all levels without additional costs. It uses a massively parallel processing technique to run complex queries along with this data. The data is imported into the Data Warehouse by Polybase. The data storage is in columnar storage in a relational database that reduces the query time and

storage. The billing is on compute Data Warehouse Unit (cDWU). There are two performance tiers: one is Elasticity, which is for a short burst and peak activity. The other is Compute Optimized Performance, which uses SDD for frequently accessed data, and is recommended for fast performance requirements. You can map any type of data on SQL Data Warehouse.

- **Cosmos DB** - This is a non-relational database with low latency and high availability. It is a globally distributed and multi-model service that includes SQL, MongoDB, Cassandra, Table, and Germlin (raph). It gives you a guaranteed throughput and within a single region, it gives you 99.99% availability. It also offers you turnkey global replication. Cosmos DB replicates your data transparently wherever your users are. This way, they can interact with a replica of the data closest to them. It offers you five consistency models, from strong SQL to relax NoSQL (the models include strong, bounded staleness, session, consistent prefix, and eventual consistency). It also automatically indexes all your data.

- **Redis Cache** - It is managed in-memory cache service with a quick, scalable, open-source compatible data store for applications. It frequently uses caches and static data to minimize the storage space and latency of the application. It comes in three tiers: a basic tier that comes with a single node and is used for test and dev, and non-critical workloads with a volume of up to 350GB. The standard tier is two replicated nodes in primary and secondary configurations with a high-availability SLA (99.9%) and is managed by Microsoft. The premium tier offers caches with more functionality, and with lower latencies, and higher throughput. Premium tier caches are used on more powerful hardware that performs better than the basic or standard tier. It is useful for snapshots and VNET integration. Its size can be up to 530GB.

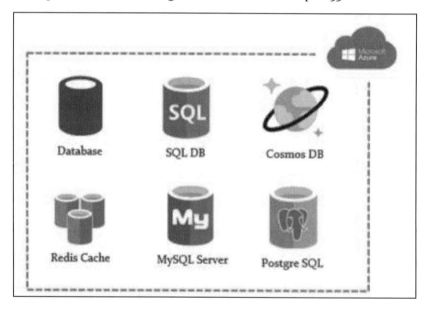

Figure 1-17: Azure Databases

Web and Mobile

Azure provides premium support for creating and managing web applications and HTTP-based web services. Azure builds engaging cross platforms for Android, iOS, and Windows applications with no compromises that will suit your business needs and reach your customers wherever they are. You can power your apps with smart back-end services and simplify your development cycle faster and more confidently.

- **App Service** – It is PaaS in Azure, allowing you to create and host web apps, mobile back ends, and RESTful APIs without network maintenance in the programming language of your choice. It supports both Windows and Linux, automatic deployment from GitHub, Azure DevOps, and any Git repo. It offers high availability and autoscaling. The supported languages are .NET, .NET Core, Ruby, Java, PHP, Node.js, and Python. App Service runs in various "App Service Plans" from free to isolated

- **API Management** - API Management (APIM) creates reliable and functional back-end API gateways. API Management enables companies to publish APIs to external, partner, and internal developers for they to unlock their data and service potential. API Management consists of the following components:
  i. API Gateway has a tunnel feature that accepts the API calls and routes them to the backend. API gateway offers authorization and caching.
  ii. Developer Portal is for developers who are developing the API. It is provided with documentation and different levels or access requirements.
  iii. Azure Portal is for the user to develop the API. Users can import existing APIs and create API products.

- **Media Services** - Cloud-based media workflow platforms allow you to build solutions requiring encoding, packaging, content protection, and live broadcasting of events. The protection of the content is done via encryption. It also has streaming URLs that you provide to the user to download the streaming asset

- **Notifications Hub** – This gives you the ability to send mobile push notifications from any backend service (cloud or on-site) to any platform (iOS, Android, Windows, Kindle, Baidu, etc.). For both corporate and customer applications, the Notification Hubs work well. You can segment the user notification based on tags so that certain notifications are sent to certain users. You can also tailor your notification using the user's language and location. Scheduling of notifications is also available. With this, you can also send silent push notifications to your application

- **Azure Search** - Azure Cognitive Search is the only cloud search service with built-in AI capabilities, enriching all information for easy content recognition and discovery. It also performs a full-text search using simple or lucent query syntax. The data uploaded is in JSON format. It also has the ability to auto-crawl various Azure services to get the data automatically. The supported services are Azure SQL DB, Cosmos DB, and Azure Blob Storage. It supports filter, paging, and sorting for searches. It also has the ability for geo-based searches.

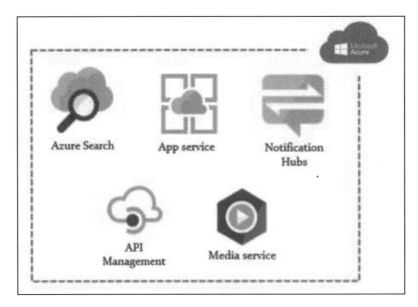

Figure 1-18: Web and Mobile

Security and Identity

It is widely known that safety is an important consideration in the cloud, and it is very important to have accurate and timely Azure Security information. Azure has a wide range of security tools and features that make it the best reason to use for your applications and services. Integrated Azure security services protect data, applications, and infrastructure quickly; this includes unparalleled security intelligence to help in identifying rapidly changing threats earlier, therefore, you can react faster.

You can protect Azure identity and access management solutions for your applications and data on the front door without interrupting productivity. You can defend malicious login attempts and secure passwords through risk-based access controls, identification security tools, and efficient authentication options.

- **Microsoft Entra ID** – It is a cloud-based identity and access management service in Azure and one of its core services. This service allows the user to sign in and access internal or external resources. The access can be role-based and controlled by various resources. With this, you can Single Sign-On (SSO) for multiple clouds-based SaaS applications with your company credentials. You can authenticate your own applications by integrating them with this. You can also integrate your on-premises Windows AD
- **Microsoft Entra ID B2C** – It provides consumer identity and access management for consumer-based applications. Your consumers can use their favorite social, company, or local identity accounts to access your apps and APIs in an SSO interface. It is different from normal AD (Active Directory) as it uses consumers to log in and authenticate. It supports multiple languages
- **Microsoft Entra ID Domain Service** - Microsoft Entra ID Domain Services (Azure AD DS) offer fully Windows Server Active Directory-compatible, managed domain services such as Domain Join, Group policy, Lightweight Directory Access Protocol (LDAP), and Kerberos. There is no need to install, maintain, and patch domain controllers in the cloud. You can use these domain services without a domain controller. It can be used in Cloud Only and Hybrid as well
- **Key Vault** - This is a security service that can be used for key management in encrypted form. When you deploy an application in the cloud, secrets, and keys are needed to access the DB or third-party systems, so you need a service to store them. A key vault is the most secure place for

this. Keys in the key vault are protected by Hardware Security Module (HSM). For your own keys, it uses FIPS 140-2 Level 2 validated HSMs. With this, you can get real-time usage logs of keys.

- **Microsoft Defender for Cloud (Azure Defender)** – It is a centralized network security management system that improves the security position of your data centers and provides advanced threat safety through your hybrid cloud workloads–whether in Azure or on-site. It continuously checks your resources against the policy to inform you about any incident at its earliest. If it finds any incident, it gives you a recommended action in order to resolve the issue. It also gives you a prioritized alert functionality. It comes in two tiers: free or standard, which is $15 per server/month.

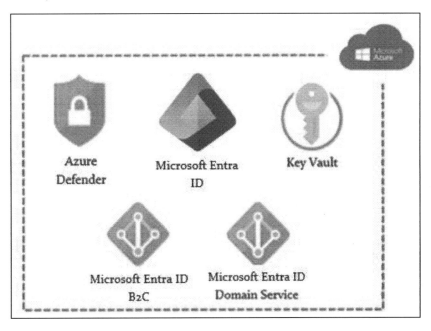

Figure 1-19: Security and Identity

Monitoring and Management

Azure management and governance tools help system managers and developers secure resources and maintain compliance in-house and on the cloud. During the IT cycle, it monitors the infrastructure, software, system provision and set-up, app-updating, vulnerability detection, backup resources, disaster recovery, policy implementation, process automation, and even the management of costs.

- **Azure Policy** - Through this, you can set and manage policies across the resources and monitor compliance
- **Azure Monitor** – This provides basic monitoring of Azure resources, helping you understand how your applications work and recognize challenges and tools that impact them proactively. With this, you can monitor metrics, activity logs, and diagnostic logs
- **Application Insights** - A feature of Azure Monitor, Application Insight is a robust APM (Application Performance Management) tool for Developer and Technical DevOps. You can use it for live application monitoring. This operates with applications on a wide range of different platforms, including .NET, Node.js, and Java EE, hosting on-site, hybrid, and other public clouds
- **Log Analytics** – This collects and visualizes data from various sources like on-premises and cloud. Log Analytics is the primary tool for collecting interactive analysis of log queries within the Azure portal

- **Azure-Site Recovery** – It is a service used for business continuity and DR. It gives highly available, and built-in DR solutions. It has failover and failback capabilities as well
- **Azure Backup** – It is a service in Azure that provides backup against data loss in the cloud and on-premises. For backup, you have multiple options available

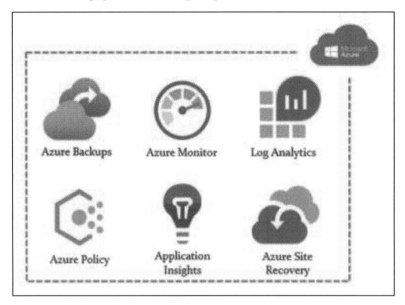

Figure 1-20: Monitoring and Management

Internet of Things

IoT or the Internet of Things, is a network of internet-connected devices communicating with each other (transfer and/or receive information) through embedded sensors via the cloud. Azure IoT is a collection of cloud services managed by Microsoft that connect, monitor, and control tons of IoT assets.

- **IoT Hub** – IoT Hub is a cloud-hosted managed service that functions as the main message hub for bi-directional communication between the IoT solutions and the devices it handles
  The IoT Hub allows for highly secure and efficient connectivity between the IoT solution and its controlled devices. The Azure IoT Hub offers a cloud-hosted backend solution for linking IoT computers. IoT Hub enables you to expand your solution with per-user security, centralized device control, and scaled provisioning from the cloud to the edge
  The Azure IoT Hub facilitates safe and efficient communications between the devices it operates and your IoT solution. A cloud-hosted solution backend for linking devices with per-user authentication, device control, and scaled provisioning is supported by IoT Hub
- **IoT Central** - IoT central is the collection of Microsoft-managed cloud services that can connect, monitor, and control a device. Templates are available to deploy custom IoT Central Solution that requires minimal experience
- **Device Provisioning Service (DPS)** - The Device Provisioning Service (DPS) is a very important service connected with Azure IoT Hub. With this service, you can automate the provisioning service to your devices. It is also called a helper service that enables zero touches and adjusts time provisioning to the right IoT Hub, giving you the ability to provision millions of devices in a scalable and secure way

- **IoT Devices** - IoT devices are connected to the Cloud gateway, or IoT Hub is a managed service hosted within Azure that acts as the bi-directional communicational messenger hub between the devices and the application
- **Azure Sphere** – Azure Sphere is the Microsoft service that lets the vendors enhance and improve the protection and security of the Azure cloud-based environment through continuous monitoring
- **Azure Maps** – It contains a bunch of geospatial services and SDKs that can be used to depict the data in context form for web and mobile applications. Additionally, this service can be used to build and deploy location-based solutions in the Internet of Things (IoT) and Artificial Intelligence (AI) domains

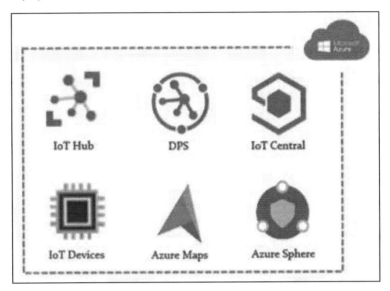

Figure 1-21: IoT Services

How to Interact with Azure

Azure Portal

Azure Portal is the most common way to interact with Azure. It is simply a website where you fill in your Microsoft account ID and password and log in to Azure. With the portal, you get access to all the resources in Azure and all its features. With the Azure Portal, you can build, manage, and monitor everything from simple to complex apps in a single console.

There are many benefits of using the Azure portal, some of which are:

- Personalizing your Azure dashboard, layout, and workflow with colors
- Accurately choosing an access control on all resources to make your management and governance easier
- Cost management keeps an eye on the current and projected cost of resources
- It is like a one-stop-shop with a single portal, and a single login for all of your Azure assets
- It has quick feature updates on products
- It has multi-platforms, available on the web and many other mobile devices

Azure CLI

Azure CLI is another tool that helps you interact with Azure services and features. It is only a text entry tool. In CLI, you need to enter a command to perform any action. Most Azure professionals use Azure CLI frequently. It can be downloaded from the website. The benefits of using Azure CLI are:

- It is stable, meaning commands do not change and can be used reliably
- The commands are structured in a logical way, and all will follow the same pattern
- It is cross-platform, so it can work on Windows, Mac, and Linux
- As the command rarely changes in CLI, you can automate the commands for future purposes
- With CLI, you can keep track of who did what using the CLI command

You can always test the CLI you installed to see if it has the proper version by running the az --version. The CLI is designed to simplify scripting, query details, long-term operations, and more. The current version in use is 2.0.79. To log in to Azure, you first need to write the "az login" command. A browser window will open asking you for login credentials. After logging in, you will see a list of all subscriptions associated with your account.

To install Azure CLI, write the following command in Windows PowerShell.

"Invoke-WebRequest -Uri https://aka.ms/installazurecliwindows -OutFile .\AzureCLI.msi; Start-Process msiexec.exe -Wait -ArgumentList '/I AzureCLI.msi /quiet'"

You can also use the following link to download the CLI:

https://docs.microsoft.com/en-us/cli/azure/install-azure-cli-windows?view=azure-cli-latest

Azure PowerShell

Similar to Azure CLI, PowerShell is pre-installed in your Windows machine, though if it is not, you can simply install it from the internet. PowerShell lets you use the cmdlet, small, lightweight groups of commands, through which you can perform simple tasks by calling a script; for example, to create a VM, you use the command "New-AzVm." With PowerShell, you can also use Azure Resource Manager, just like the Azure portal. It can be used for any other task as well. PowerShell version 5.1 or higher works on Windows, while PowerShell core6.x and later versions work on any other platform. In order to check the PowerShell version, type: $PSVersionTable.PSVersion:

Figure 1-22: Windows PowerShell

Azure Cloud Shell

This is an interactive browser-accessible shell for managing Azure resources. Having shell experience is the best option whether you work in Bash or PowerShell, as it offers flexibility. With Cloud Shell, you can use a fully standalone browser or the portal component to experience Bash, similar to Azure CLI or PowerShell. With Cloud Shell, you get authenticated and secure access to resources using any web or mobile app from anywhere. Choose between Bash (CLI) or PowerShell. Tools included are interpreter, Azure tools, modules, and different language support such as Node.js, Python, or .NET. To persist the data between sessions, it has its own dedicated storage. It also has an integrated file editor.

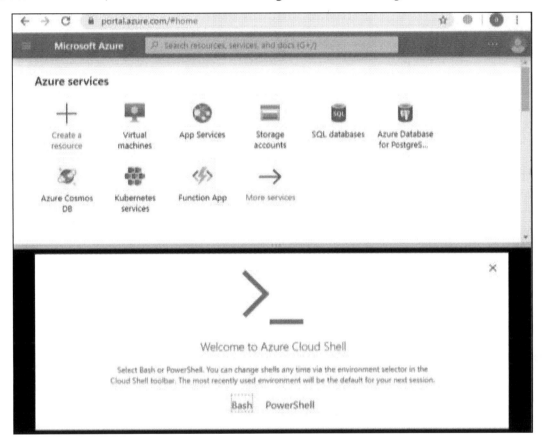

Figure 1-23: Azure Cloud Shell

Creating an Account on Azure

1. You can create an account in Microsoft using your email address. For that, go to **Azure.com**.
2. Click on **Start free**. Now, sign in with your email address.
3. Go to the window of the sign-up process for creating a new account. On the **About You** page, enter all the required details, then click **Next**.
4. Now, enter the number with the country code in **Identity verification by phone**. You will get a message or call option to get the verification code.
5. After verifying the code, enter the card information in **Identity verification by card**.
6. Click **Next**.
7. Now you have an agreement. Select the agreement, then select **Sign-up**.
8. After signing up, click on **Go to Portal**. You will now get a pop-up window, **Welcome to Azure**, with a **Start Tour** or **Maybe Later** options.

9. At the top corner, you also have the **Cloud Shell** button.

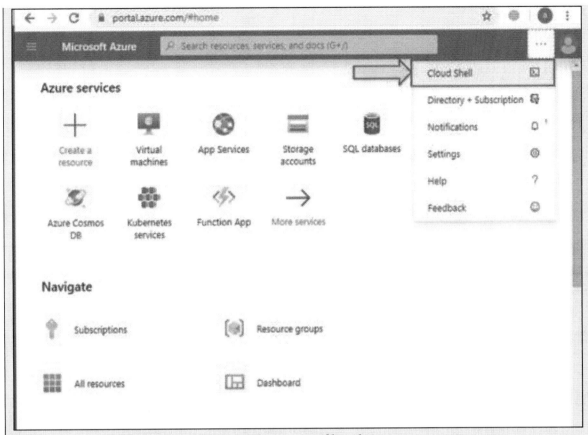

10. You will also find the **Directory and Subscription** filter there.

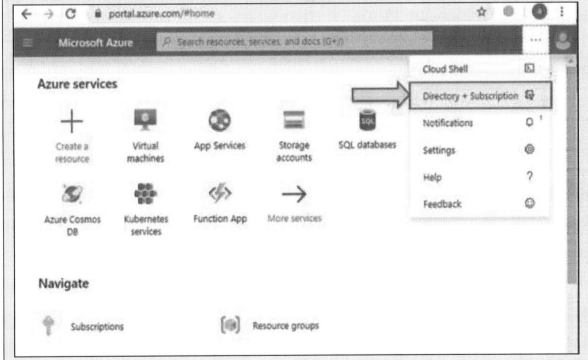

Note: The free Azure Account is limited to free services for 12 months with credit that expires after 30 days.

Mind Map

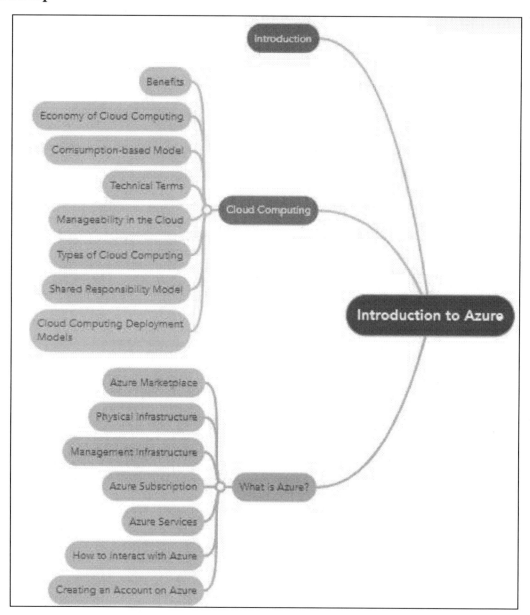

Figure 1-24: Mind Map

Practice Questions

1. Any service that you use on Azure with a consumption component as part of the pricing is known as consumption-based pricing. True or false?
A. True
B. False

2. What does Infrastructure-as-a-Service mean?

A. Services on Azure that are updated automatically to provide a stable infrastructure for your applications
B. The layer of services that enables a complete cloud infrastructure for your business
C. Any hardware service provided by Azure, such as Virtual Machines and Virtual Networks
D. Any service on Azure that you can rent and do not have to buy upfront

3. Which Azure service should you use to correlate events from multiple resources into a centralized repository?
A. Azure Log Analytics
B. Azure Monitor
C. Azure Events Hub
D. Azure Analysis Service

4. What is Cloud Agility?
A. To automatically improve the fidelity of resource usage and utilize the platform better
B. Quickly scale resources as per demand
C. Focus on business rather than provisioning and maintaining resources
D. Using cloud elasticity to increase the return on investment

5. As resource demand increases, Azure can split the demand over more resources and scale the application. True or false?
A. True
B. False

6. In case any resource goes down, instantly replacing it with a new one is known as_____.
A. Scalability
B. Elasticity
C. Fault Tolerance
D. High Availability

7. What is the difference between OPEX and CAPEX?
A. OpEx is the cost for acquiring or maintaining assets. CapEx is the ongoing cost for running a business
B. OpEx has a better return on investment in the short term. CapEx has a better return on investment in the long term
C. OpEx is the ongoing cost for running a business. CapEx is the cost of acquiring or maintaining assets
D. OpEx is the cost of services you do not own, such as cloud computing. CapEx is the cost of ownership

8. What is an Availability Zone?
A. One or more data centers equipped with independent power, cooling, and networking
B. A collection of software that can enable high scalability at short notice
C. A set of data centers close together

D. One of the data centers that are close together to provide backup

9. How many zones must each region have?
A. 2
B. 3
C. 5
D. 6

10. What is Azure Region?
A. One or more data centers equipped with independent power, cooling, and networking
B. A collection of software that can enable high scalability at short notice
C. A set of data centers close together
D. One of the data centers that are close together to provide backup

11. A cloud server is being migrated to Azure. External users can access the web application. Which service would you suggest to reduce the administrative effort needed to manage the web application?
A. IaaS
B. SaaS
C. FaaS
D. PaaS

12. Azure VM resource is a PaaS. True or false?
A. True
B. False

13. For daily operations, Azure resources are needed for every business unit. The same form of Azure services is expected for all businesses. To automate the development of Azure resources, which solution would you suggest?
A. Azure API Management Service
B. Resource Manager Template
C. Management Groups
D. None of the above

14. What is the maximum amount of storage in Azure Storage?
A. 30TB
B. 500TB
C. 500GB
D. 10TB

15. Which Azure Service is relevant to the AWS IAM service?

A. Azure VM
B. Azure Blob
C. Azure MySQL DB
D. Microsoft Entra ID

16. From the following options, what is the best reason to use the Azure CLI?
A. It makes Azure usage cheaper, as you do not have to pay for the Azure Portal
B. You can use products and services that are not available in the Azure Portal
C. It rarely changes, and the commands stay the same for the most part
D. You can use Azure CLI with more than one cloud provider

17. Why would you prefer to use Cloud Shell rather than CLI or PowerShell?
A. The Cloud Shell can be used entirely in a web browser, and can also be used across multiple devices
B. The Cloud Shell gets new features first
C. The Cloud Shell is free for 12 months
D. You can update the Cloud Shell independently of Azure CLI and Azure PowerShell

18. What is the constraint of the Azure free account?
A. Azure free accounts are valid only for certain times of promotion, such as the launch of new services
B. Credit will expire after 30 days, and free resources expire after 12 months
C. Free account resources can only be created when using the USA address
D. You are only allowed to create resources for 30 days

19. What is a PowerShell cmdlet?
A. A PowerShell scripting language specifically for Azure
B. A piece of advice from Microsoft about PowerShell updates
C. A lightweight version of PowerShell that can run on mobile devices
D. A small, lightweight group of commands to perform an action

20. Only products that are available globally can be accessed through Azure Portal. True or false?
A. True
B. False

21. Which of the following services is used to organize and secure resources in Azure?
A. Subscriptions
B. Azure Region
C. Availability zone
D. Azure Resource Manager

22. How can you get authenticated and authorized access to Azure services?

A. Using Multi-Region
B. Azure Marketplace
C. Azure Subscription
D. None of the above

23. How many subscription boundaries exist?
A. Five
B. Three
C. Four
D. Two

24. Which of the following organizes subscriptions and provides the level of scope?
A. Management Groups
B. Resource Groups
C. Tenant
D. Resource

Chapter 02: Compute

Introduction

In advanced computing, computing refers to activities, applications, or workloads that involve processing more resources than memory requirements. In general, compute is used to describe concepts and objects focused on computation and processing. For example, CPUs, APUs, and GPUs are considered compute resources, while graphics processing applications like 3-D rendering and video games are defined as compute-intensive applications.

Compute is commonly encountered in advanced computing concepts such as cloud computing and big data technologies, where resources are used or served in the server and data centers. Concerning Azure, compute is a term that covers all services, enabling computation in the cloud. This chapter will cover topics including Virtual Machines (VMs), Scale Sets, App Services, Container Instances, Kubernetes Services, and Azure Functions.

Microsoft Azure has a variety of Linux-based machines that help you use and explore new ways to run web applications.

Azure Virtual Machines

Microsoft Azure is very flexible; it allows setting functionality as required. Resources can be computed as up and down according to need. You only pay for the resources that you use. Azure Virtual Machine is a cloud-based computing service offered by Azure. It includes a processor, memory, storage, and networking resources. The main benefit of the Azure virtual machine is that you can easily configure this machine and stop the running process when required. Azure portal or Azure CLI configures Azure virtual machine. The web application running on the virtual machine can be operated via the Remote Desktop Protocol (RDP) or Secure Shell (SSH).

Linux-Based Machine in Azure

It is very easy to create a Linux-based virtual machine in Microsoft Azure. The Azure platform has a variety of Linux images that provide you with a way to create virtual machines. These Linux images are built from a variety of Linux distributions like Ubuntu, Red Hat, and others.

Windows-Based Machine in Azure

The Azure virtual machine is a raw server that you get from your cloud service provider. In Azure, this service allows you to scale from tens, hundreds or even thousands of servers. It works on-demand; therefore, you can purchase it whenever required. In addition, many tools in Azure easily allow you to work with virtual machines. The Azure virtual machine provides its own virtual hardware, including the CPU, hard drive, memory, network interface, and other devices. The main advantage of the Windows Azure virtual machine is that you can control your virtual machine by using the Azure portal or with Azure Command Line Interface (CLI).

You can also use Remote Desktop Protocol (RDP), the graphical terminal for remote desktop to connect directly to the Windows desktop User Interface (UI).

Features

Azure provides the following features to deploy virtual machines on its own:

Infrastructure as a Service: Virtual machines are a part of the IaaS offering on Azure, where you can manage everything except the hardware. You have complete control over the operating system, application installation, and maintenance. Additionally, it also provides networking for VM.

Tools: If you want to buy your own hardware and run your own services with Azure, you can add additional tuning to manage up to thousands of VMs. Use the Azure Portal to control your hybrid cloud that includes VMs on Azure and on-premisés.

Compliance: You can ensure virtual machines' compliance with your company guidelines using Azure blueprints; these blueprints give instructions on how to create VMs.

Recommendations: These are recommendations by Azure for improvements to ensure better security, higher availability, lower cost, and greater performance.

Choice: Azure offers running VMs on both Linux and Windows; you can choose the amount of RAM and number of CPUs of your choice.

EXAM TIP: Virtual machines are the core of Azure compute, and are widely used. VM is a machine that you can access exclusively.

Pricing

Azure charges for Virtual Machines on an hourly basis and as per the resources you have used. In simpler words, the more CPUs and RAMs on your VMs, the larger the amount you have to pay per hour.

Use Cases

Before you create a VM, you have all the necessary information regarding the VM, including its pros and cons.

Pros

Control: Before using virtual machines, you need to control all aspects of an environment or machine.

Application: You must install specific applications on your Windows or Linux machines.

Existing Infrastructure: You can move existing resources and virtual machines to Azure from on-premises or another cloud provider.

Cons

Not for Everything: If you want to use a different service on Azure, like hosting a website with an App service, then you do not need a VM.

Maintenance: If you have your VM, a lot of maintenance requirements are involved, such as operating system updates, patches, security concerns, and others.

Scale Sets

Azure virtual machine scale sets allow you to create and manage a group of identical load-balanced VMs. In this, a single VM is provided as a baseline with which you can create VMs instantly. The number of VM instances will automatically increase or decrease in response to demand or a given schedule. Scale

sets make your applications highly accessible, allowing you to manage, configure, and upgrade many VMs centrally. You can create significant services with virtual machine scale sets for areas including computing, big data, and container workloads.

Benefits

Azure virtual machine scale sets provide management capabilities for applications running through multiple VMs, automated resource scaling, and traffic load balancing. The scale sets offer the following key benefits:

Easy to create and manage multiple VMs

- Maintaining a consistent configuration across your environment is important when you have multiple VMs operating your application. The VM size, disk configuration, and device configurations should be the same across all VMs for the reliable performance of your application.
- All VM instances are created from the same base OS image and configuration in the scale set. This approach allows you to easily control hundreds of VMs without additional network management or configuration tasks.
- Scale sets allow the use of the Azure load balancer for basic layer-4 traffic distribution and Azure Application Gateway for advanced layer-7 traffic distribution and SSL termination.

Enables autoscaling to meet resource demands

- Customer demand for your application may change frequently. To fulfill customer demands, scale sets will automatically increase or decrease the number of VM instances according to fluctuations in demand.
- This ability of auto-scaling helps reduce costs and efficiently create Azure resources as required.

Works at large-scale

- Scale sets support up to 1,000 VM instances. If your custom VM images are created and uploaded, the limit is 600 VM instances.
- Azure Managed Disks can be used to achieve the highest performance for development workloads.

 EXAM TIP: Scale sets are identical VMs; they can be activated or deactivated upon demand.

Use Case

Imagine you are running an online store; everyday customers come, browse your shop, and buy your items. As it is with online habits, your traffic usually increases in the evening or on the weekends. Consequently, your sales and traffic increase further. Your part of the online store runs on a VM that processes the data. As demand increases, so does the data you need to process. If you are scaling manually and creating new VMs when needed, you would constantly be doing it, and it would probably be inaccurate. Scale sets would constantly be monitoring usage to make sure you have both enough resources and VMs, and removing them when they are not needed. In effect, you are saving more money.

Examples of when to use VMs

1. Testing and Development:

Scenario: VMs are invaluable during the testing and development phases. They offer a quick and efficient way to create diverse OS and application configurations for testing purposes.

Example: Test and development teams can easily spawn VMs with different environments, conduct testing, and delete VMs once they are no longer needed. This flexibility enhances agility and resource efficiency.

2. Running Applications in the Cloud:

Scenario: Leveraging VMs for running applications in the public cloud provides economic advantages. It is especially beneficial for applications with variable demand, allowing the dynamic scaling of resources.

Example: Applications experiencing fluctuations in demand can benefit from VMs in the cloud. VMs can be shut down during low-demand periods and quickly start up to meet sudden increases in demand, optimizing resource usage and cost-effectiveness.

3. Extending Datacenter Capabilities to the Cloud:

Scenario: Organizations can enhance their on-premises network capabilities by creating a virtual network in Azure and deploying VMs within that network. This extends the data center to the cloud environment.

Example: Running applications like SharePoint on Azure VMs instead of locally can simplify deployment and potentially reduce costs compared to on-premises setups.

4. Disaster Recovery:

Scenario: VMs play a crucial role in disaster recovery scenarios, offering a cost-effective Infrastructure as a Service (IaaS) approach. In case of a primary data center failure, VMs running critical applications can be quickly initiated on Azure.

Example: If a primary data center faces an outage, VMs on Azure can be activated to run essential applications. Once the primary data center is operational again, these VMs can be shut down, providing a resilient and cost-efficient disaster recovery solution.

Moving to the Cloud with VMs:

VMs serve as an excellent choice for migrating from physical servers to the cloud, following a "lift and shift" approach. This involves creating a VM image mirroring the physical server with minimal changes. For example, during the transition from on-premises servers to the cloud, organizations can replicate physical servers as VMs, maintaining familiarity while benefiting from cloud infrastructure. Responsibilities include OS and software maintenance, similar to physical servers.

VM Resource

> **Size**: Choose VM size based on purpose, specifying the number of processor cores and the amount of RAM required.
> **Storage Disks**: Define storage configurations, such as hard disk drives or solid-state drives, to meet performance and capacity needs.
> **Networking**: Configure networking parameters, including the virtual network, public IP address, and port settings, ensuring seamless connectivity and accessibility.

Lab 2-01: Create an Azure Resource

Service Introduction

WorkTrips.com is a Polish company offering a modern platform that optimizes costs, automates processes and provides care during business trips. To handle multiple requests at high speed and to simplify the flow of arranging business travel, it connects various Azure services via Azure Virtual Networking.

Problem

The process is not automated and the users would have to check offers, find the one matching their needs, and send an email to the supervisor to get approval.

Solution

Now, the system can automatically approve the trip if all criteria and limits are met. The superior does not have to be involved. Azure Virtual Machines can be scaled up and down quickly, enabling WorkTrips.com to handle peaks in demand when there are large numbers of requests. The geographical distribution of Azure data centers also gives WorkTrips.com a competitive advantage.

Task 1: Create a Virtual Machine

1. Sign in to the Azure portal.

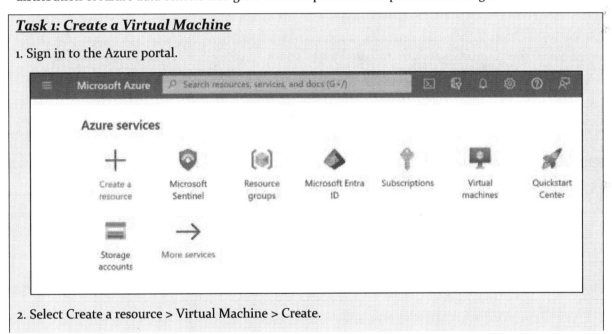

2. Select Create a resource > Virtual Machine > Create.

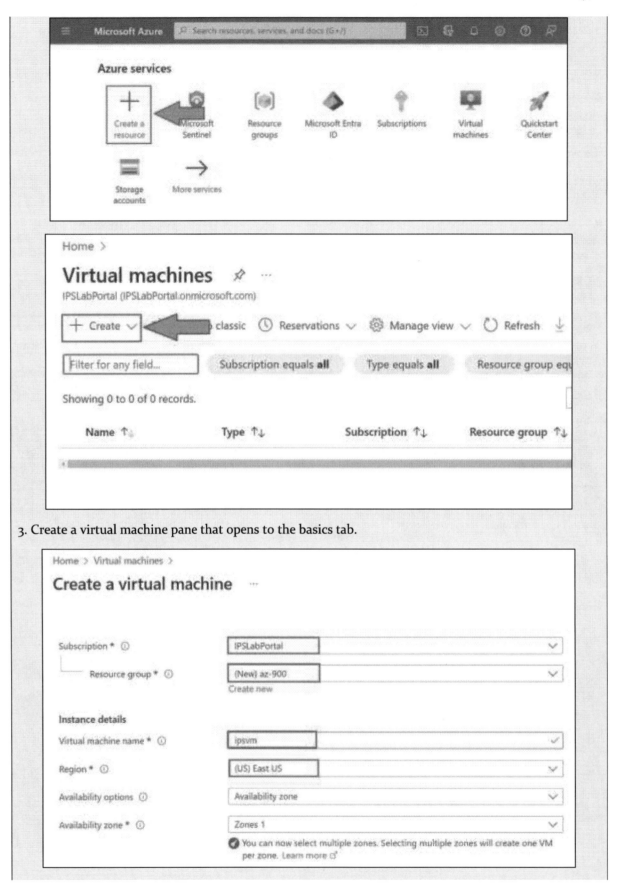

3. Create a virtual machine pane that opens to the basics tab.

4. Verify or enter the following values for each setting. If a setting is not specified, leave the default value.

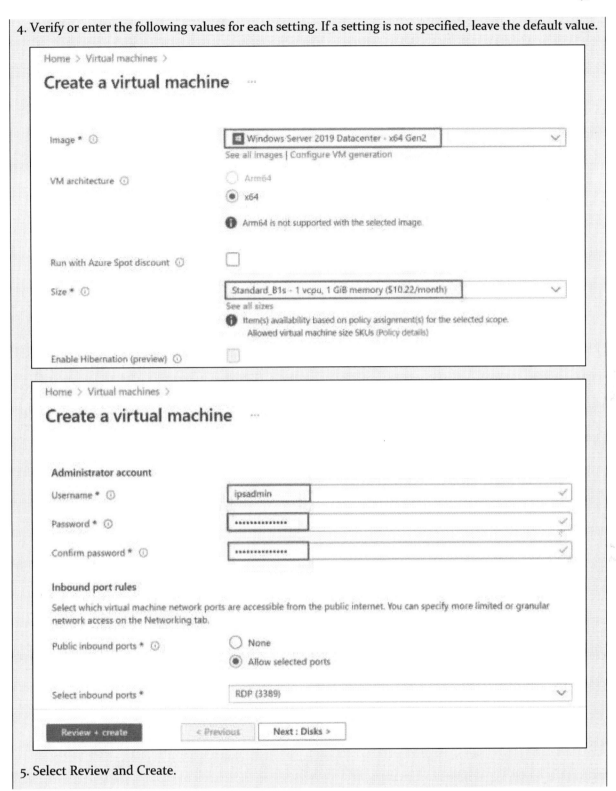

5. Select Review and Create.

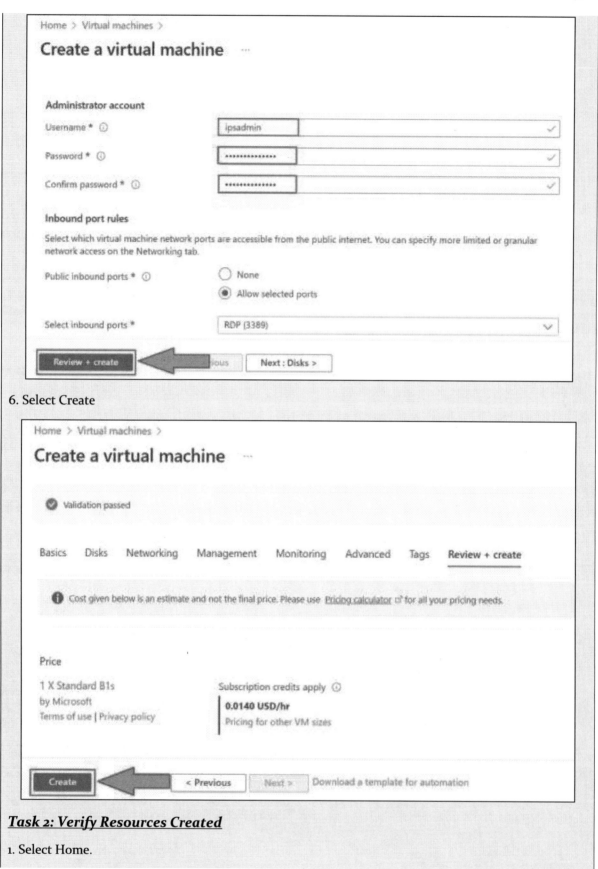

6. Select Create

Task 2: Verify Resources Created

1. Select Home.

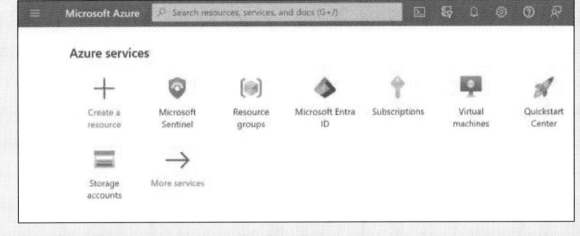

2. Select the resource group and open the vm you created.

Task 3: Create a Linux Virtual Machine and Install Nginx

1. From Cloud Shell, run the command to create a Linux VM:

```
faizan [ ~ ]$ az vm create --resource-group "az-900" --name ipsvm --public-ip-sku Standard --image Ubuntu2204 --admin-
username ipsadmin --generate-ssh-keys
SSH key files '/home/faizan/.ssh/id_rsa' and '/home/faizan/.ssh/id_rsa.pub' have been generated under ~/.ssh to allow
SSH access to the VM. If using machines without permanent storage, back up your keys to a safe location.
{
    "fqdns": "",
    "id": "/subscriptions/797152d3-23c4-499f-bfef-bb103da7d054/resourceGroups/az-900/providers/Microsoft.Compute/virtual
Machines/ipsvm",
    "identity": {
        "principalId": "945e6f5e-aab1-4b76-91d7-a9aac7e36b28",
        "tenantId": "71575372-8592-4097-b688-eb2a4e9abbac",
        "type": "SystemAssigned",
        "userAssignedIdentities": null
    },
    "location": "eastus",
    "macAddress": "00-0D-3A-4F-04-17",
    "powerState": "VM running",
    "privateIpAddress": "10.0.0.4",
    "publicIpAddress": "20.102.60.254",
```

2. Run the following command to configure Nginx on your VM:

```
Bash
faizan [ ~ ]$ az vm extension set --resource-group "az-900" --vm-name ipsvm --name customScript --publisher Microsoft.
Azure.Extensions --version 2.1 --settings '{"fileUris":["https://raw.githubusercontent.com/MicrosoftDocs/mslearn-welco
me-to-azure/master/configure-nginx.sh"]}' --protected-settings '{"commandToExecute": "./configure-nginx.sh"}'
{
  "autoUpgradeMinorVersion": true,
  "enableAutomaticUpgrade": null,
  "forceUpdateTag": null,
  "id": "/subscriptions/797152d3-23c4-499f-bfef-bb103da7d054/resourceGroups/az-900/providers/Microsoft.Compute/virtual
Machines/ipsvm/extensions/customScript",
  "instanceView": null,
  "location": "eastus",
  "name": "customScript",
  "protectedSettings": null,
  "protectedSettingsFromKeyVault": null,
  "provisionAfterExtensions": null,
  "provisioningState": "Succeeded",
  "publisher": "Microsoft.Azure.Extensions",
  "resourceGroup": "az-900",
  "settings": {
```

Azure VMware Solution

Azure VMware Solution is a cloud service offered by Microsoft Azure in collaboration with VMware. It enables organizations to run, manage, and migrate VMware-based workloads in Azure. This solution allows businesses to leverage their existing VMware investments, skills, and tools while gaining the benefits of Azure's scale, flexibility, and hybrid capabilities.

Key features of Azure VMware Solution include:

1. **Seamless Integration:** The service integrates VMware's virtualization technologies with Azure's infrastructure, providing a consistent and familiar environment for VMware workloads.
2. **Hybrid Cloud:** Organizations can extend their on-premises VMware environments to Azure, creating a true hybrid cloud setup. This facilitates workload migration, disaster recovery, and scalability.
3. **Operational Consistency:** Users can use familiar VMware tools, such as vSphere, vCenter, and vSAN, to manage and operate their virtual machines in Azure, ensuring operational consistency.
4. **Scalability:** Azure VMware Solution allows organizations to scale resources up or down based on demand, taking advantage of Azure's vast infrastructure.
5. **Azure Services Integration:** Users can integrate Azure services like Microsoft Entra ID, Azure AI, and Azure IoT with their VMware workloads, enhancing the capabilities of their applications.
6. **Security and Compliance:** The solution provides security features and compliance certifications to meet industry standards and regulatory requirements.

Scale Sets

Azure virtual machine scale sets allow you to create and manage a group of identical load-balanced VMs. In this, a single VM is provided as a baseline with which you can create VMs instantly. The number of VM instances will automatically increase or decrease in response to demand or a given schedule. Scale sets make your applications highly accessible, allowing you to manage, configure, and upgrade many VMs centrally. You can create significant services with virtual machine scale sets for areas including compute, big data, and container workloads.

Benefits

Azure virtual machine scale sets provide management capabilities for applications running through multiple VMs, automated resource scaling, and traffic load balancing. The scale sets offer the following key benefits:

Easy to create and manage multiple VMs

- Maintaining a consistent configuration across your environment is important when you have multiple VMs operating your application. The VM size, disk configuration, and device configurations should be the same across all VMs for the reliable performance of your application
- All VM instances are created from the same base OS image and configuration in the scale set. This approach allows you to easily control hundreds of VMs without additional network management or configuration tasks
- Scale sets allow the use of the Azure load balancer for basic layer-4 traffic distribution and Azure Application Gateway for advanced layer-7 traffic distribution and SSL termination

Allows your application to scale as resource demand changes automatically

- Customer demand for your application may change frequently. To fulfill customer demands, scale sets will automatically increase or decrease the number of VM instances according to fluctuations in demand.
- This ability of auto-scaling helps reduce costs and efficiently create Azure resources as required

Works at large-scale

- Scale sets support up to 1,000 VM instances. If your custom VM images are created and uploaded, the limit is 600 VM instances
- Azure Managed Disks can be used to achieve the highest performance for development workloads

 EXAM TIP: Scale sets are identical VMs; they can be activated or deactivated upon demand.

Use Case

Imagine you are running an online store; everyday customers come, browse your shop, and buy your items. As it is with online habits, your traffic usually increases in the evening or on the weekends. Consequently, your sales and traffic increase further. Your part of the online store runs on a VM that processes the data. As demand increases, so does the data you need to process. If you are scaling manually and creating new VMs when needed, you would constantly be doing it, and would probably be inaccurate. Scale sets would constantly be monitoring usage to make sure you have both enough resources and VMs, and removing them when they are not needed. In effect, you are saving more money.

Application Hosting Options

The first option you might consider if you need to host your application on Azure is a virtual machine (VM) or a container. Both VMs and containers offer excellent hosting solutions. With VMs, you have complete control over the hosting environment and may set it up in anyway you choose. If you are new to the cloud, VMs might also be your most familiar hosting option. Containers can also be a strong and

appealing option because they can isolate and control various components of the hosting solution separately.

Azure App Service is one additional hosting service you may use with Azure.

App Services

Azure App Service is a fully managed Platform as a Service (PaaS). This means servers, networks, storage, and other fundamental infrastructures are all managed and controlled by Azure; you just have to focus on business values and logic.

Azure App Service is an HTTP-based service for hosting web applications, REST APIs, and mobile backends. You can develop it in your favorite programming languages, like .NET, .NET Core, Java, Ruby, Node.js, PHP, or Python. Applications run and scale easily on both Windows and Linux-based environments.

App Service not only adds features of Microsoft Azure to your application, such as security, autoscaling, load balancing, and automated management, but also makes use of its DevOps capabilities, such as continuous deployment from Azure DevOps, GitHub, Docker Hub, and other sources, package management, staging environments, custom domain, and SSL certificates.

 EXAM TIP: Using app services provides an easy way to host and manage your web application.

Features

Some key features of App Service are as follows:

Multiple Languages and Frameworks: App Service has exceptional support for Java, Ruby ASP.NET, ASP.NET Core, Node.js, PHP, or Python. You can also run background services like PowerShell and other scripts or executables.

DevOps Optimization: It helps set up ongoing Azure DevOps, GitHub, BitBucket, Docker Hub, or Azure Container Registry integration and deployment. Encourage updates via environments for testing and staging. You can use Azure PowerShell or the cross-platform Command-Line Interface (CLI) to control the applications in App Service.

Global Scale with High Availability: Scale up or down manually or automatically. Host your apps anywhere in Microsoft's global data center infrastructure, and the App Service SLA assures high availability.

Connections to SaaS Platforms and On-premises Data: Choose from over 50 interfaces for enterprise (such as SAP), SaaS (such as Salesforce), and Web (such as Facebook) applications. Use Hybrid Connections and Azure Virtual Networks to access on-premises data.

Security and Compliance: App Service is compatible with ISO, SOC, and PCI. Authenticate users with Microsoft Entra ID or social login (Google, Facebook, Twitter, and Microsoft). Build limitations on IP addresses and control identities of the service.

Application Templates: Choose from a wide-ranging list of application templates in the Azure Marketplace, such as WordPress, Drupal, and Joomla.

Visual Studio Integration: Dedicated tools in Visual Studio streamline the development, deployment, and debugging work.

API and Mobile Features: App Service provides RESTful API scenarios with turn-key CORS support and simplifies mobile app scenarios by allowing authentication, offline data sync, push notifications, and more.

Serverless Code: Run a code snippet or on-demand script without directly providing or managing resources. Pay only for the compute time your code uses.

App Services Categories

Azure App services are divided into three main categories:

Web Apps

As supported by Azure App Service, Web Apps is a fully managed platform that allows you to create, deploy, and scale Web Apps in seconds to enterprise-grade.

These are the main features:

- Runs on both Windows and Linux environments
- Supports a lot of languages such as .NET, Java, PHP, Node.js, Python, and Ruby
- Has built-in auto-scale and load balancing
- High availability with auto-patching
- Continuous deployment with Git, TFS, GitHub
- Web Apps Gallery: WordPress, Umbraco, Joomla, Drupal

 EXAM TIP: Web Apps are used to host websites and web applications.

Web Apps for Containers

Web Apps for containers allow deploying and running containerized applications in Azure. A container is a self-contained unit of software. All the code programs and applications are shipped inside the container. This means you can deploy your applications anywhere with a consistent experience. Web Apps for Containers allow developers to bring their own Docker formatted container images and easily deploy and run them at scale with Azure. Containers make the software run reliably between environments.

Following are the benefits of using Web Apps for containers:

- Easily deploy and run containerized applications that scale with the business
- Take benefit of built-in autoscaling and load balancing
- Use a fully-managed platform to achieve infrastructure maintenance
- Update CI/CD with Docker Hub, Azure Container Registry, and GitHub

 EXAM TIP: Web Apps for containers can host your existing container images on Azure.

API Apps

API App is an efficient way to connect and expose any backend data you have. API is an Application Programming Interface that does not have a graphical user interface, i.e., no user interface or front-end. API provides the interface to connect other applications programmatically. API Apps offered by Azure App Service provide a rich framework and ecosystem for developing, using, and distributing APIs in the cloud and on-premises.

The main features provided are as follows:

- Incorporate with SaaS and business applications
- Generate client proxies or APIs in your chosen language
- Automate API provisioning and deployment
- Safe APIs through OAuth Active Directory and Single Sign-On
- Exchange APIs internally through corporate galleries

 EXAM TIP: API Apps can host your data backend services and do not have a graphical frontend.

WebJobs

In the same environment as a web app, API app, or mobile app, you can run a program (.exe, Java, PHP, Python, or Node.js) or script (.cmd,.bat, PowerShell, or Bash) using the WebJobs functionality. They can be triggered or programmed to run. In your application logic, background tasks are frequently done in the background using WebJobs.

Mobile Apps

Build a back end for iOS and Android apps easily by using the Mobile Apps functionality of App Service. By performing a few simple steps on the Azure portal, you can:

- Maintain a SQL database in the cloud using data from mobile apps.
- Verify consumer identity against popular social networks, including MSA, Google, Twitter, and Facebook.
- Push notifications to users.
- Custom back-end logic can be implemented in C# or Node.js.

For native iOS and Android, Xamarin, and React native apps, there is SDK support available.

Pricing Tier of an App Service Plan

Azure offers a series of App Service plan pricing tiers. Each tier has several well-defined features like CPU, storage, size, and scale. You can choose the tier according to your requirements and the cost you must pay. The summarized picture of the App Service plan is listed in Table 2-01.

Tier	Storage	Max. Instances	SLA	Apps	Use Cases
Free	1 GB	N/A	N/A	10 apps with 32 bits	Testing and developing the hosting service
Shared	1 GB	N/A	N/A	>100 apps with 32 bits	Low traffic and non-business critical applications

Basic	10 GB	3 Manual	99.95%	Unlimited apps with 32 and 64 bits	Dev/test applications before production
Standard	50 GB	10 Auto	99.95%	Unlimited apps with 32 and 64 bits	Production applications
Premium	250 GB	20 Auto	99.95%	Unlimited apps with 32 and 64 bits	Large-scale and sensitive production applications
Isolated	1 TB	Unlimited	99.95%	Unlimited apps with 32 and 64 bits	High performance, security, and isolation

Table 2-01: Pricing Tiers of App Service Plan

What are Azure Containers?

Containers provide a virtualized environment, similar to running multiple virtual machines on a single physical or virtual host. In contrast to virtual machines, containers do not require managing a full operating system; instead, they encapsulate the application and its dependencies, sharing the host OS kernel. Virtual machines appear as distinct instances of an operating system, each requiring its management, while containers are lightweight and designed for dynamic creation, scaling, and stopping. Unlike traditional virtual machines, containers offer agility and rapid response to changing demands. They are particularly well-suited for scenarios where applications need to be created, scaled, or stopped dynamically. Containers are highly portable, allowing consistent deployment across various environments. When compared to virtual machines, containers are more resource-efficient and faster to start, making them an ideal choice for modern, agile development and deployment practices. Docker is one of the most widely used container engines, and Azure provides robust support for Docker containers. With containers, you can efficiently manage and deploy applications, respond promptly to changes in demand, and enhance overall agility in your development and deployment processes.

To see Important differences between virtual machines and containers, visit Compare Compare Virtual Machine to Container.

Azure Container Instances

In Microsoft Azure, the container is the standardized unit of software, meaning it is a software package that can run reliably and quickly from one computing environment to another. You can easily deploy and manage many complex and sensitive applications in the cloud with containers. Containers require less development overhead, reduced and simplified updates, and a faster startup setup to deploy the applications.

Azure Container Instances (ACI)

Container instance service in Azure is the simplest service for running containers without managing any infrastructure and without having to configure any high-level services.

Azure Container Instances is a great solution for any situation that can be used in isolated containers, including simple apps, task management, and job building.

ACI Features

Manage Application Dependencies

All the dependencies for an application are included in the container image. You can manage the application and its dependencies with confidence.

Less Overhead

Virtual machines require a lot more maintenance and updates. Containers do not have any operating system components that require maintenance.

Increased Portability

Applications running on containers can be deployed easily to multiple different operating systems and hardware platforms.

Efficiency

Containers are much more efficient regarding the development life cycle of deploying and maintaining them. Scaling and patching are much simpler as well.

Consistency

The operations team can rely on containers being the same every time, regardless of where they are deployed.

Container in Azure Workflow

The workflow for using a Container in Azure is as follows:

Software Development Cycle: Develop the desired software application through various processes of the software development cycle. When it is ready, it will go through the container placement phase.

Application Placed in Container: When the software application is ready for deployment or publishing, it is placed in a container image.

Azure Container Instances: When the software application is placed in a container, it can be deployed or published to Azure Container Instances (ACI).

Benefits of ACI

Azure Container Instances (ACI) has the following benefits:

Run containers without managing servers

By running your workloads in Azure Container Instances (ACI), you can concentrate on designing and building your applications instead of managing the infrastructure.

Increase agility with containers on demand.

Deploy unparalleled flexibility and speed containers to the cloud — with a single command. Use ACI to provide additional computation whenever you need challenging workloads.

Secure applications with hypervisor isolation

Gain the security of virtual machines for your container workloads while keeping the efficiency of lightweight containers. ACI provides hypervisor isolation for each container group to ensure that containers operate in isolation without sharing a kernel.

Works with your favorite tools

Azure Container Instances can be accessed using Azure Portal, Azure CLI, or PowerShell, whichever you like the most.

> **EXAM TIP:** Azure Container Instances (ACI) is the container that helps create and manage the containerized application with less resource consumption and requires a small set of commands to build applications.

Azure Kubernetes Service

Kubernetes

Kubernetes is an open-source container orchestration system for automating application deployment, management, and scaling.

Let's briefly understand the above terms;

Open Source: It is an open-source platform, meaning the code is public. Anyone can submit fixes, provision, get involved in, and invest in the product.

Orchestration: It orchestrates a cluster of Azure VMs; Scheduled containers automatically manage service discovery, incorporate load balancing, and track resource allocation. It ensures that all the containers are correctly configured to work properly.

Automatic Application Deployment: Kubernetes deploys more images of containers as demanded by the application.

Automatic Scaling: Automatic monitoring of application load to determine when to increase or decrease the number of containers.

Azure Kubernetes Service

Kubernetes

Kubernetes is an open-source container orchestration system for automating application deployment, management, and scaling.

Let's briefly understand the above terms;

Open Source: It is an open-source platform, meaning the code is public. Anyone can submit fixes, provision, get involved in, and invest in the product.

Orchestration: It orchestrates a cluster of Azure VMs; Scheduled containers automatically manage service discovery, incorporate load balancing, and track resource allocation. It ensures that all the containers are correctly configured to work properly.

Automatic Application Deployment: Kubernetes deploys more images of containers as demanded by the application.

Automatic Scaling: Automatic monitoring of application load to determine when to increase or decrease the number of containers.

Azure Kubernetes Service

Azure Kubernetes Service (AKS) enables the most straightforward deployment of a managed Kubernetes cluster in Azure. AKS eliminates the complexity and operating overheads of Kubernetes management by offloading many responsibilities to Azure. Azure performs essential health monitoring and maintenance tasks for you as a hosted Kubernetes provider. Azure manages the masters of Kubernetes. Only the agent nodes (nodes that run each node in the cluster) are managed and maintained by you. As a managed Kubernetes service, AKS is free; you only pay for the agent nodes within your clusters, not for the masters.

You can build an AKS cluster with Azure CLI or template-driven deployment solutions, such as Resource Manager and Terraform templates, in the Azure portal. The Kubernetes master and all nodes will be deployed and configured for you when you deploy an AKS cluster. Additional features such as advanced networking, integration with Microsoft Entra ID, and monitoring during the deployment process can also be configured.

Azure Container Registry

ACR is a service that keeps track of current valid container images. It manages files and artifacts for containers. When your Azure container instances and Kubernetes service need to create a new container, the images come from ACR. You can also use Azure identity and security features to ensure safe container images.

AKS Cluster Architecture

Azure Kubernetes Service (AKS) cluster architecture is based on the following main components:

Node

You require a Kubernetes node to run your applications and support services. An AKS cluster has one or more nodes, an Azure Virtual Machine (VM) running the components of the Kubernetes nodes and container runtime.

Node Pools

Nodes of the same configuration are grouped into node pools. A cluster of Kubernetes contains one or more node pools. Once you create an AKS cluster, which generates a default node pool, you specify the initial number of nodes and size. This default node pool in AKS contains the underlying VMs that run your agent nodes.

Pods

Kubernetes uses pods to run an application instance. A pod represents a single application instance. Pods usually have a 1:1 container mapping, although there are advanced cases where several containers may be

found in a pod. Such multi-container pods are arranged on the same node together, allowing containers to share similar resources.

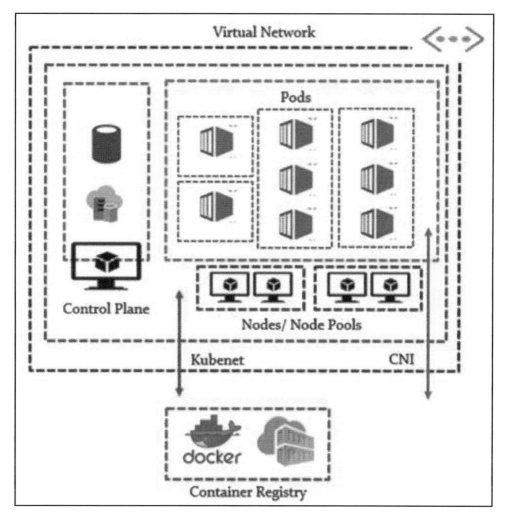

Figure 2-01: AKS Cluster Architecture

AKS supports Kubernetes clusters running multiple node pools to support various operating systems and Windows servers (currently previewed). Linux nodes run a customized Ubuntu OS image, and a modified Windows Server 2019 OS image runs on Windows Server nodes.

As resource demand changes, the number of cluster nodes or pods that run your services can automatically scale up or down. You can use both the horizontal pod auto-scaler and the cluster auto-scaler. This approach to scaling lets the AKS cluster automatically adjust to demands and only run the resources needed.

As the resource demand increases, you can automatically scale up or down the number of cluster nodes or pods running your services. You can use either the pod auto-scaler or the cluster auto-scaler. This scaling approach allows the AKS cluster to adapt to demands automatically and only run the necessary resources.

Applications of Azure Kubernetes Service

Azure Kubernetes Service enables the deployment, configuration, and monitoring of containerized applications using a Kubernetes service in the Azure platform. The container-based workload and containerized applications are ordinary to manage in the cloud. The enterprises and network-developing companies use container-based workloads using the Kubernetes service, which works as an orchestration platform.

AKS allows the flexible migration of projects from on-premises to the cloud. There are two types of migration provided by AKS. One is a "lift and shift" migration that requires setting up features compatible with your demands. The second migration method, the "green field" migration, allows evaluation of the AKS based on the default features.

Many features increase the demand for services provided by Azure Kubernetes. Each feature is enthralled, making you use AKS for your system.

Identity and Security Management

When you are working with an existing Azure resource and want to use Microsoft Entra ID for your project, you can create the AKS cluster that allows you to use the integrated Azure resource and Azure AD with the existing identity and security groups.

Combined Registration and Management

Azure Kubernetes Service (AKS) permits the Azure monitor to continuously monitor the performance of the container instances on your AKS cluster. With custom Kubernetes installation, you can use the monitoring solution that requires installation and configuration for logging and management.

Auto Cluster Node and Pod Scaling

Sometimes, scaling the complex and sensitive containerized application becomes difficult to configure. Therefore, an automatic configuration approach is required to be used in such cases. Azure Kubernetes Service (AKS) offers two auto cluster scaling options.

- Horizontal Pod Autoscaler
- Cluster Autoscaler

Horizontal Pod Autoscaler (HPA)

The horizontal pod autoscaler is one of the scaling options to scale the cluster. It monitors the pod's scale demands and increases or decreases the pod based on the observed CPU utilization and memory consumption to meet the required demand.

Cluster Autoscaler

The cluster autoscaler automatically resizes the cluster node based on the demand of the workload. When the demand is high, it automatically scales out or adds a scheduled node to the system. When the demand goes down, the scaling method automatically scales back the scheduled nodes to their original number. This scaling option increases the availability of your workload when you need it.

Cluster Node Improvement

The cluster node upgrade is necessary to manage and monitor the nodes for the running applications. Minimizing the cluster management task for reliable and fast configuration is very important. AKS monitors the Kubernetes software improvements and the action of cordoning off the cluster nodes and draining the interference of the nodes to active applications. Once AKS completes the monitoring, all the cluster nodes are upgraded successively.

GPU Enabled Nodes

Azure Kubernetes Service supports GPU-enabled nodes to monitor compute-intensive and graphics-intensive workloads.

Persistent Storage

Suppose your running application is stateful and functions as stateless. In such cases, storage volume support is required for persistent storage. AKS supports both static and dynamic storage volumes. Based on the demands of the workload, all the available pods can be attached or reattached to the created storage volumes on different nodes.

Virtual Network (VNet) Support

Another beneficial edge of AKS is that it allows pod-to-pod communication and communication with an on-premises network by deploying the AKS cluster to the existing Virtual Network (VNet).

Access with the Support of HTTP Application Routing

The AKS cluster supports HTTP application routing policies to deploy such AKS containerized applications that are publicly accessible.

Docker Image Support

Azure Kubernetes Service supports the format of the Docker container image that can be used to deploy and develop any workload. The creation of workload is composed in a container, and the container is deployed as a Kubernetes pod.

Private Container Registry

AKS integrates with Azure Container Registry (ACR). It can also be used with other container repositories, either public or private.

> **Note:** All the above-defined features of the Azure Kubernetes Service are used when you create the AKS cluster or use the existing deployment.

Use containers in your solutions

Containers are frequently employed to construct solutions using a microservice architecture, a paradigm that involves breaking down applications into smaller, independent components. In this architectural approach, a solution might be divided into distinct containers, each responsible for a specific function. For instance, a website can be categorized into containers hosting the front end, back end, and storage, creating a modular and scalable structure. The benefit of this containerized microservice architecture lies in the ability to manage, scale, or update individual components independently. Consider a scenario where the back-end capacity of a website has reached its limit while the front-end and storage components remain underutilized. With containers, you have the flexibility to scale the back end separately, addressing performance issues without affecting other parts of the application.

Furthermore, the modular nature of containers allows for independent maintenance and updates. If a change is needed in the storage service or modifications are required in the front end, these adjustments can be made without impacting the functionality of other components. This level of flexibility and isolation provided by containers enhances the agility and efficiency of developing, deploying, and maintaining complex solutions.

Azure Functions

Azure Function is the smallest compute on Azure. It is a single function and an easy way to run small pieces of code or "functions" in the cloud. For the problem at hand, you can write only the code you need without worrying about the whole application or the infrastructure to run it. Functions can make development even more productive, and you can use your development languages of choice, such as C#, Java, JavaScript, PowerShell, and Python. A standard web address URL invokes it. It triggers the events to run at once and then stops.

Azure Functions is a serverless computing service that is hosted on the public cloud of Microsoft Azure. In general, Azure Functions and serverless computing are designed to accelerate and simplify the development of applications. The idea behind serverless computing, also known as function as a service, is to remove the infrastructure for user considerations. A user can create and upload code serverless and then define the triggers or events to execute the code. Triggers may come from a wide variety of sources, including another user's application or other cloud services, such as databases, events, and hubs for notification.

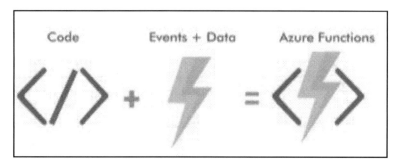

Figure 2-02: Azure Functions

The cloud provider must load the code into a suitable execution environment once a trigger or event occurs, then run the code and release the computing resources. Servers are still involved, but users no longer have to provide or manage instances. In addition, users pay for serverless computing based on the amount of time a function runs in a given billing cycle instead of paying for those compute instances and other associated resources each month.

> **EXAM TIP:** Microsoft Azure Functions is an event-driven, on-demand computation experience that builds on Azure's best offering (PaaS platform).

Use Case

A website named funnyferret lets users upload pictures. These images need both processing and optimization for web display and storage. The Azure Function receives the image when a user uploads a picture on the funnyferret website. The function's job here is to process the image, compress it, and change it into the correct file format. The function then places the image in the online application database for future use.

Features

Here are some key features of Azure Functions:

Choose Language: Write functions using C#, Java, JavaScript, Python, and other languages.

Pricing Model for Pay-per-use: Only pay for the time spent running the code.

Integrated Security: Protects functions enabled by HTTP with OAuth providers such as Microsoft Entra ID, Facebook, Google, Twitter, and Microsoft Account.

Simplified Integration: Azure infrastructure and Software-as-a-Service (SaaS) systems can be easily leveraged.

Open-source: The functions runtime is open-source and available on GitHub.

Azure Virtual Desktop

Azure Virtual Desktop is a cloud-based desktop and application virtualization service. It allows your users to access a cloud-hosted version of Windows from anywhere. It is compatible with apps that let you access distant desktops and apps. Windows, Mac, iOS, Android, and Linux are all supported by Azure Virtual Desktop. Most recent browsers can also be used to access Azure Virtual Desktop-hosted experiences.

For Further Information, visit Azure Virtual Desktop.

Key Features

Simplified Management - Azure Virtual Desktop is an Azure service. Thus, Azure administrators will be familiar with it. To govern resource access, you use Azure AD and RBACs. You may also automate VM deployments, manage VM updates, and provide disaster recovery with Azure. Like other Azure services (Azure AD, Azure VM), Azure Virtual Desktop leverages Azure Monitor for monitoring and notifications. This standardization allows administrators to spot problems using a single interface.

Performance Management – You may load balance users on your VM host pools with Azure Virtual Desktop. Host pools are groups of VMs with the same setup and are shared by multiple users. Load balancing can be configured to happen as users sign in for the optimum performance (breadth mode). Users are sequentially allocated for your workload in breadth mode throughout the host pool. You can save money by configuring your VMs for depth mode load balancing, which allocates all users to one VM before going on to the next. When inbound demand surpasses a certain threshold, Azure Virtual Desktop provides capabilities to provision more VMs automatically.

Multi-Session Windows 10 Deployment - You can use Windows 10 Enterprise multi-session on Azure Virtual Desktop, the only Windows client-based operating system that allows several concurrent users on a single VM. Compared to Windows Server-based operating systems, Azure Virtual Desktop provides a more consistent experience with more application support.

How to Reduce Cost Using Azure Virtual Desktop?

Bring Your License (BYOL)

If you have a Microsoft 365 license that qualifies, you can use Azure Virtual Desktop for free. Pay for the Azure resources that Azure Virtual Desktop consumes.

- Bring your valid Windows or Microsoft 365 license to obtain free desktops and apps for Windows 10 Enterprise and Windows 7 Enterprise.

- Windows Server Remote Desktop Services desktops and apps are accessible at no extra charge if you have a Microsoft Remote Desktop Services Client Access License.

Remote Desktop Protocol (RDP)

Remote Desktop Protocol is the graphical terminal or terminal server used to connect to another computer through a network connection. It listens for TCP on port 3389. RDP allows the client to protect the server from the software interface connection. It can run an application mode that loads the shortcut from the user's desktop and appears as if it is the standard application.

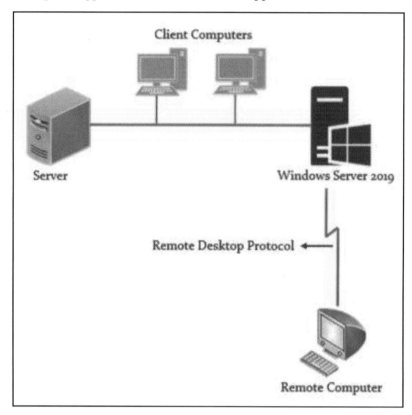

Figure 2-03: Working of Remote Desktop Protocol (RDP)

RDP connection requires an RDP client. Microsoft provides RDP clients for the following operating systems.

- Windows (built-in)
- macOS
- iOS
- Android

Note: Open source Linux client "Remmina" also enables connection to a Windows PC.

Connect Windows Azure VM using RDP

There are two options to connect Azure virtual machines to the on-premises network. One is to connect all Azure virtual machines to a Virtual Network (VNet). All virtual machines should communicate with others over VNet. All VMs have different public IP addresses, which also help them communicate over

the internet. The second option is to create a Virtual Private Network (VPN). This network is especially applicable in communicating the Azure VMs to on-premises machines.

> EXAM TIP: An important thing to remember for the exam is that public IP addresses are often dynamically allocated. It will change when a virtual machine is restarted or newly configured. So, to manage the IP address overhead, it is good to use a static IP address instead of a name to ensure that your VM's IP address will not change.

How to Connect VMs in Azure using RDP?

You can easily connect to RDP when configuring the virtual machine in Azure. You can connect to RDP by choosing the connection option of the configured VM. After that, you will be required to enter the public IP address and give the option to preconfigure the .rdp file.

If you use the static IP address, the .rdp file will remain the same. If you use the dynamic IP address, you will need to use the .rdp file only when your VM runs. If you restart the VMs, you will need to download the .rdp file again.

> EXAM TIP: A direct method to connect the VM in Azure using RDP is to enter the public IP address into the Windows RDP client and click connect.

RDP file is a text file consisting of name/value pairs that define the RDP clients' connection to the remote computer using RDP.

Enhance Security

Azure Virtual Desktop offers centralized security management for user desktops, leveraging Microsoft Enterprise ID for enhanced control. Security measures such as multifactor authentication can be activated to fortify user sign-ins, adding an extra layer of identity verification. Granular role-based access controls (RBACs) provide the ability to finely tailor user access to data, ensuring precise control over permissions. The architecture of Azure Virtual Desktop goes beyond local hardware, separating data and applications from the user's device. By hosting the actual desktops and apps in the cloud, the potential risk of leaving confidential data on personal devices is significantly reduced. Moreover, Azure Virtual Desktop ensures a heightened level of security by isolating user sessions in both single and multi-session environments. This isolation adds an extra layer of protection, preventing unauthorized access and enhancing the overall security posture of the virtual desktop environment.

Multi-session Windows 10 or Windows 11 deployment

Azure Virtual Desktop introduces the capability for a multi-session deployment of Windows 10 or Windows 11 Enterprise. This unique feature allows multiple concurrent users to operate on a single virtual machine (VM), optimizing resource utilization and providing a cost-effective solution. Unlike traditional Windows Server-based operating systems, Azure Virtual Desktop ensures a more consistent user experience and boasts extensive application support. This means that users can enjoy a seamless and efficient environment, benefiting from the familiarity of Windows 10 or Windows 11 while simultaneously maximizing the efficiency of virtual desktop deployments. The multi-session deployment feature aligns with modern computing needs, offering scalability and versatility for organizations embracing cloud-based solutions.

Lab 2-02: Configuration of Windows Virtual Machine in Azure using RDP

Service Introduction

In Azure, deploying a Windows Virtual Machine (VM) enables users to run Windows-based applications and services in the cloud environment. Leveraging Remote Desktop Protocol (RDP), users can securely connect to their Windows VMs, granting them remote access to the desktop interface for configuration, management, and application deployment. This flexibility allows businesses to efficiently scale resources, adjust performance parameters, and optimize workloads to meet specific requirements. The seamless integration of Windows VMs with Azure's ecosystem, coupled with the convenience of RDP, provides a robust and user-friendly solution for hosting Windows workloads in the cloud, enhancing accessibility and facilitating streamlined management processes.

Problem

An organization wants to find a solution to process the data stored in the same format from different applications built on a virtual machine.

Solution

The organization can use the Windows virtual machine and store the incoming data in the same format through the Azure function. This lab is divided into two sections.

- Create and configure a virtual machine in Azure
- Connect Windows Azure virtual machine using Remote Desktop Protocol (RDP)
1. Log in to the **Microsoft Azure portal** and go to the portal menu.

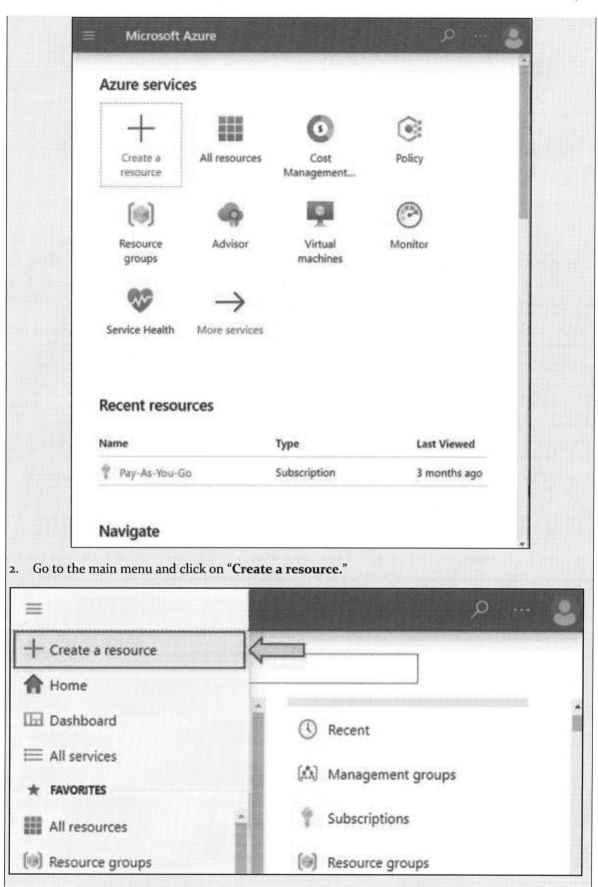

2. Go to the main menu and click on **"Create a resource."**

3. Type "**Windows Server**" in the search box and click "**Enter**."

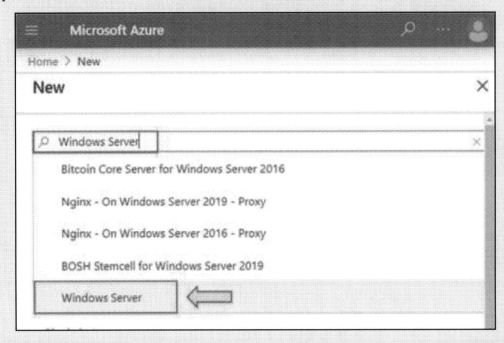

4. Click on "**Select a software plan**" and find "[**smalldisk**] **Windows Server 2019 Datacenter with Containers**" from the list.

Note: You can also use other Windows Server versions to create a virtual machine.

5. Click on "**Create**."

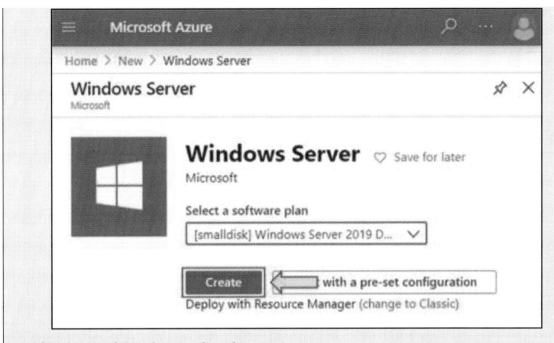

6. After that, configure the virtual machine settings.
7. Choose an available resource group.

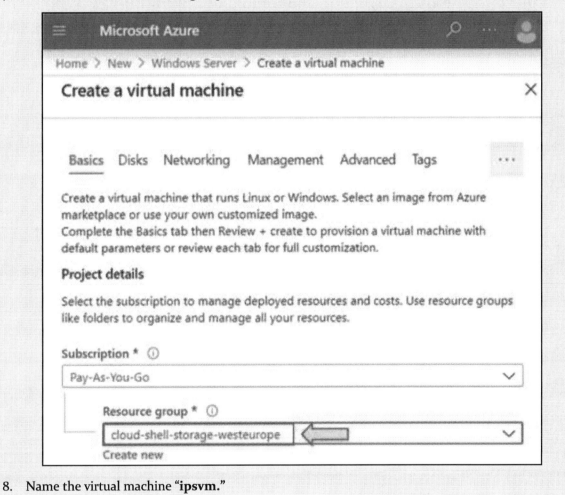

8. Name the virtual machine "**ipsvm.**"

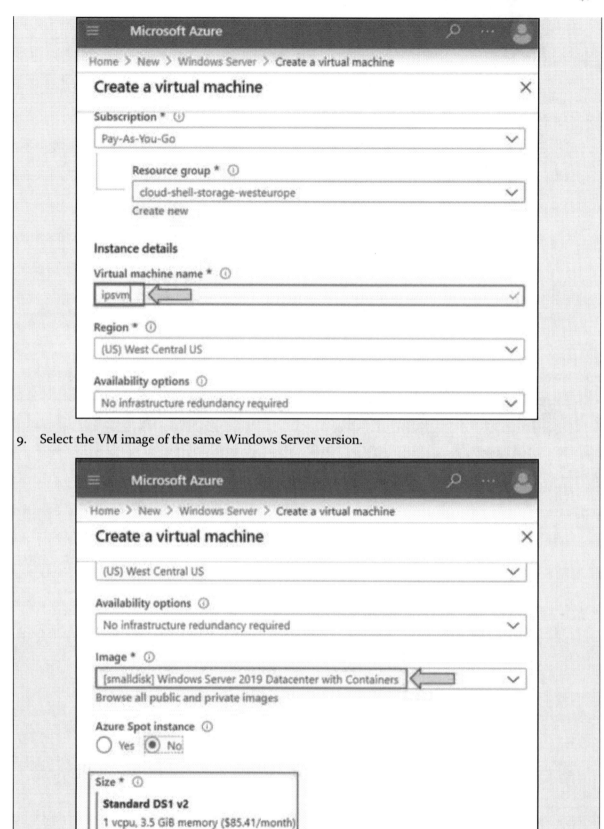

9. Select the VM image of the same Windows Server version.

Note: The size of the VM will be Standard DS1 v2.

10. Fill in the **"Administrator account"** details.

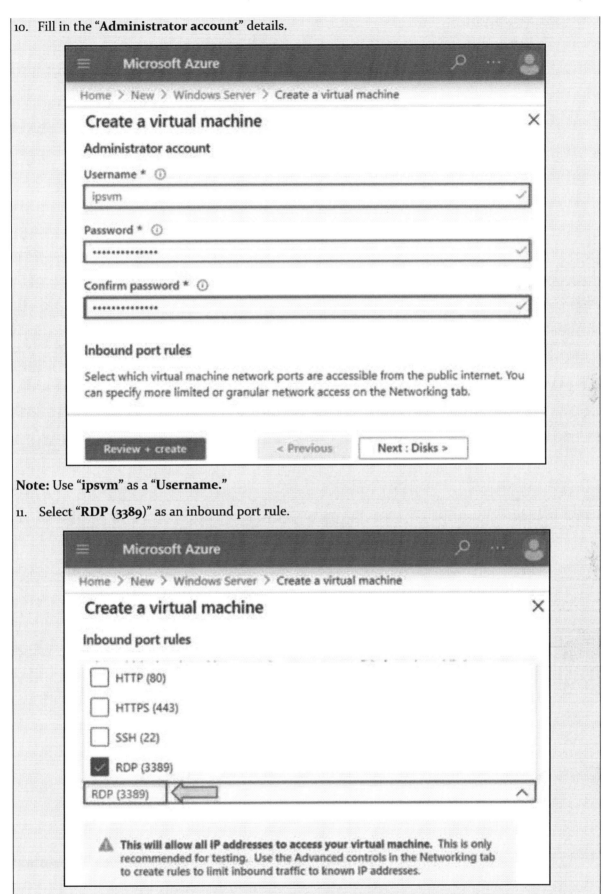

Note: Use **"ipsvm"** as a **"Username."**

11. Select **"RDP (3389)"** as an inbound port rule.

12. Click on **"Next : Disk >."**

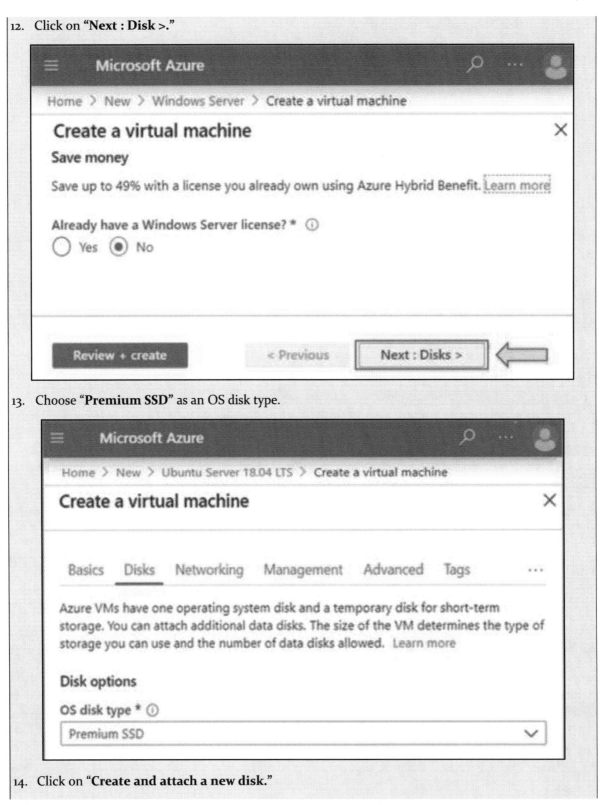

13. Choose **"Premium SSD"** as an OS disk type.

14. Click on **"Create and attach a new disk."**

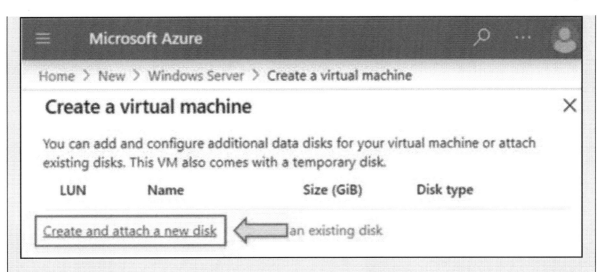

Note: OS disk type will give C: and temporary D: drive. You will have to create and attach a new disk to add a new data drive.

15. Set the name of the new data disk as "**ipsvm_DataDisk_1**".
16. Then, click on "**OK.**"

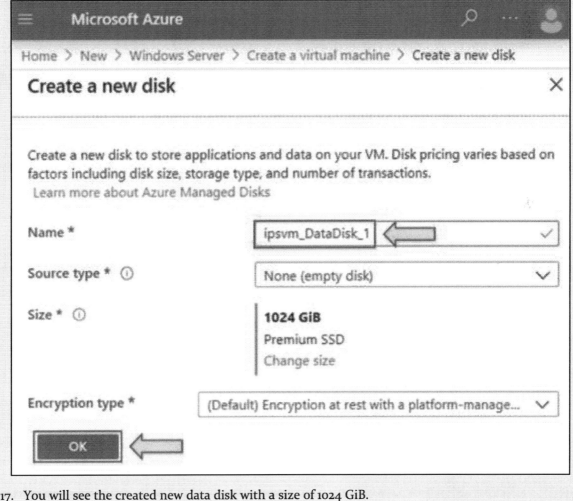

17. You will see the created new data disk with a size of 1024 GiB.
18. Click on "**Next: Networking >.**"

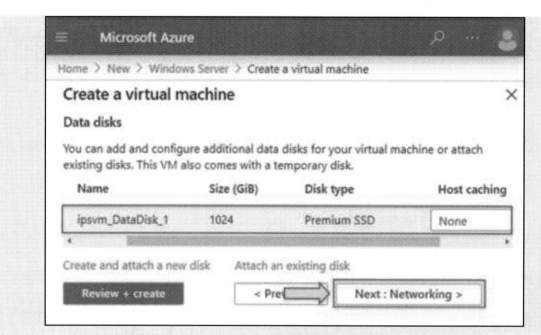

Note: Dedicated data disks are generally considered the best place to store application data files. They can be larger than OS disks, and you can optimize them for the cost and performance characteristics appropriate for your data.

19. Configure a new Virtual Network (VNet).
20. Click on "**Create new.**"

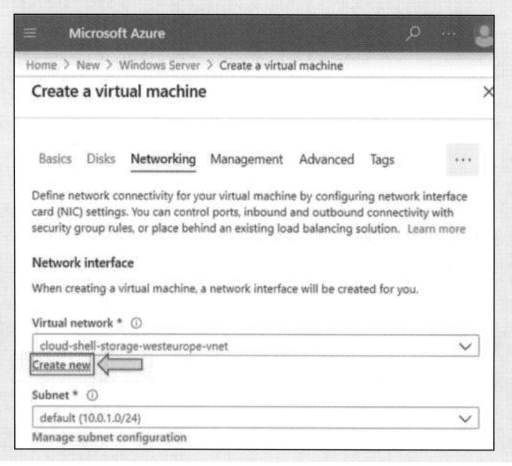

21. Set name as "**ipsvnet.**"
22. Give the address space of "**172.16.0.0/16**".

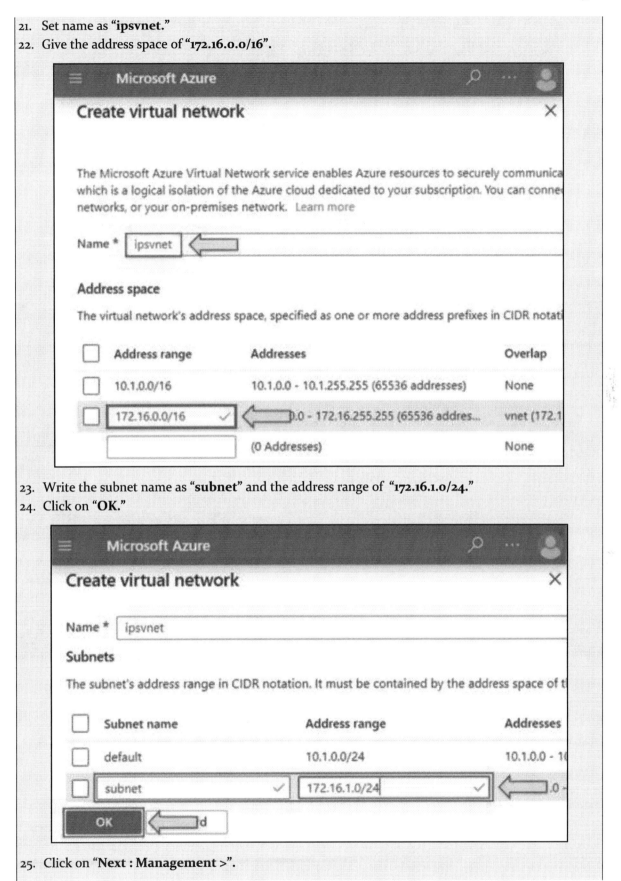

23. Write the subnet name as "**subnet**" and the address range of "**172.16.1.0/24.**"
24. Click on "**OK.**"

25. Click on "**Next : Management >**".

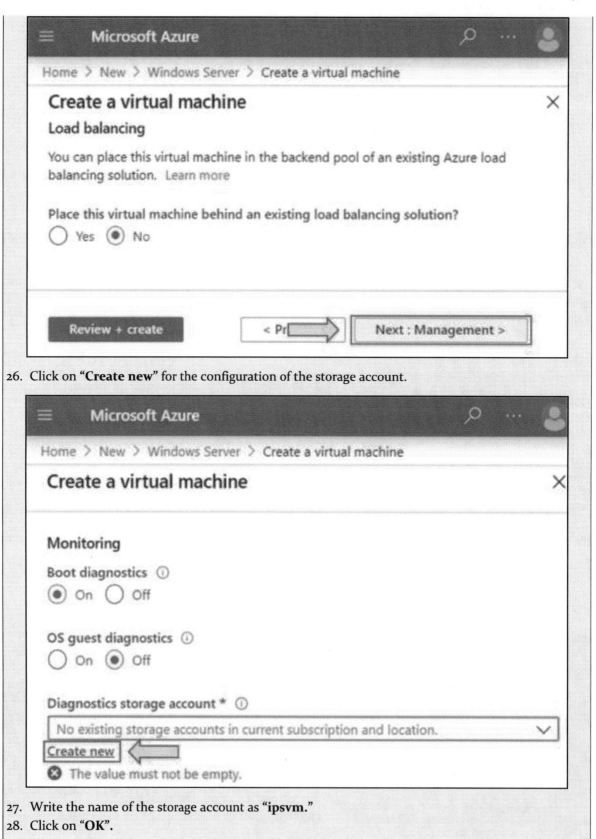

26. Click on **"Create new"** for the configuration of the storage account.

27. Write the name of the storage account as **"ipsvm."**
28. Click on **"OK"**.

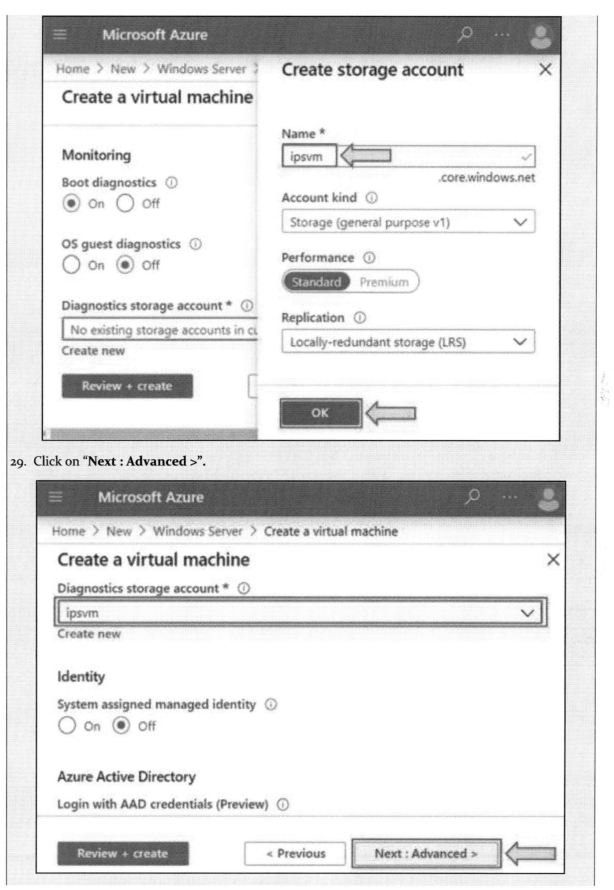

29. Click on "**Next : Advanced >**".

30. Click on "**Next : Tags >**".

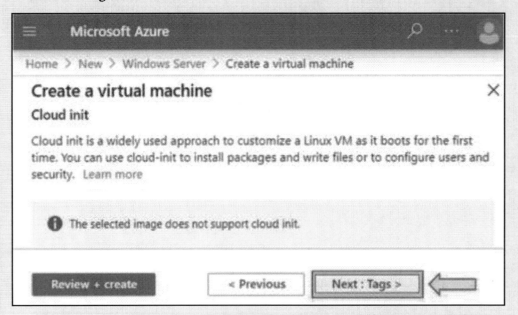

31. When the validation is passed, click on "**Create.**"

32. When all the deployment is done, click on **"Go to resource."**

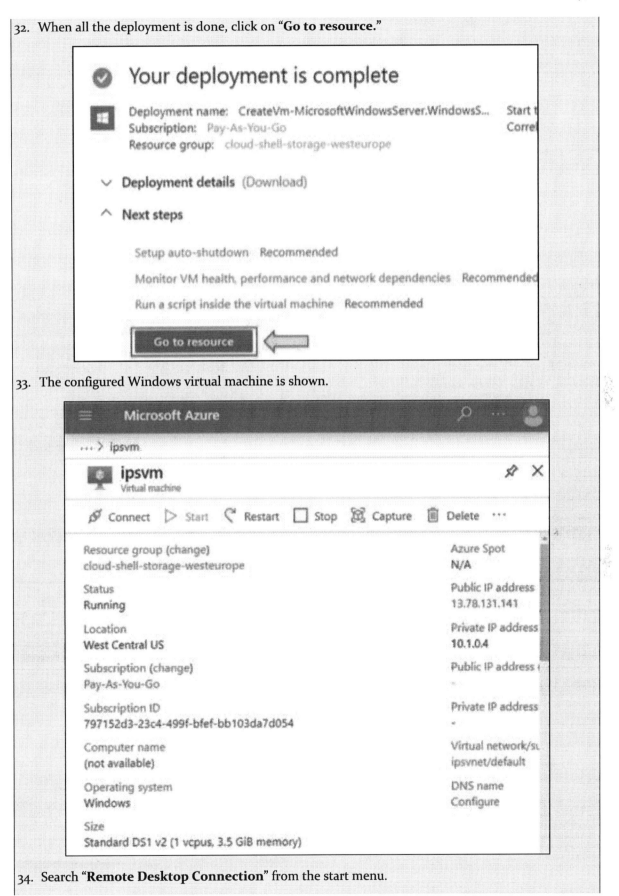

33. The configured Windows virtual machine is shown.

34. Search **"Remote Desktop Connection"** from the start menu.

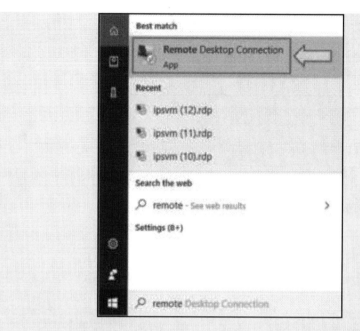

35. Enter the computer name/IP address and username.
36. Enable **"Allow me to save credentials."**
37. Click on **"Save As."**

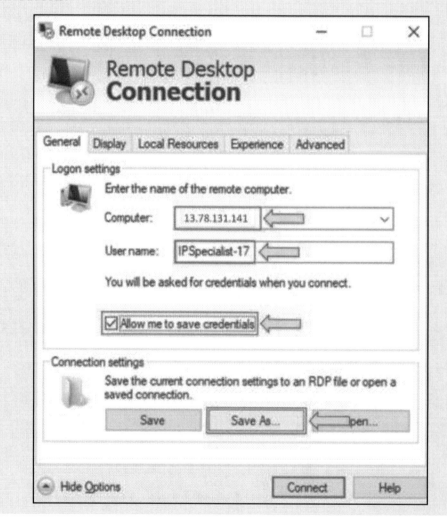

38. Save the file with the name "**ipsvm.**"
39. Click on "**Save**".

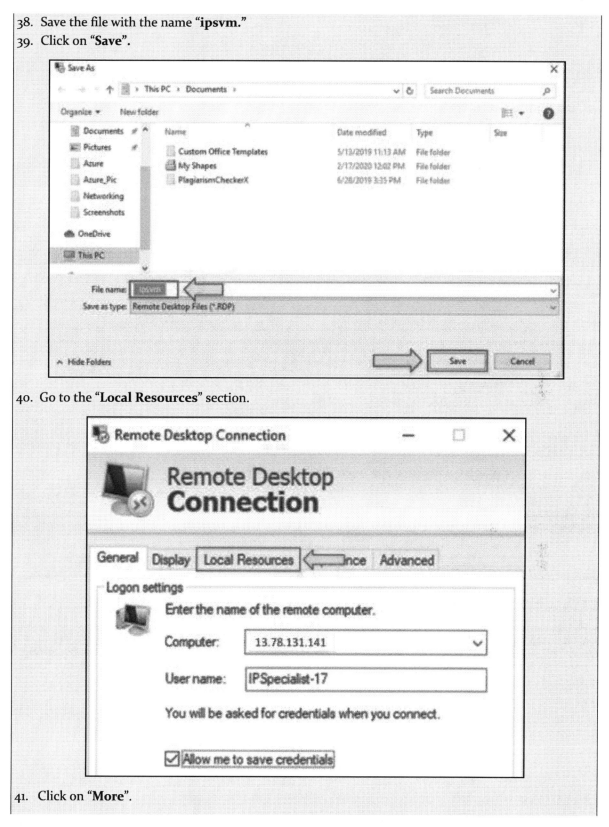

40. Go to the "**Local Resources**" section.

41. Click on "**More**".

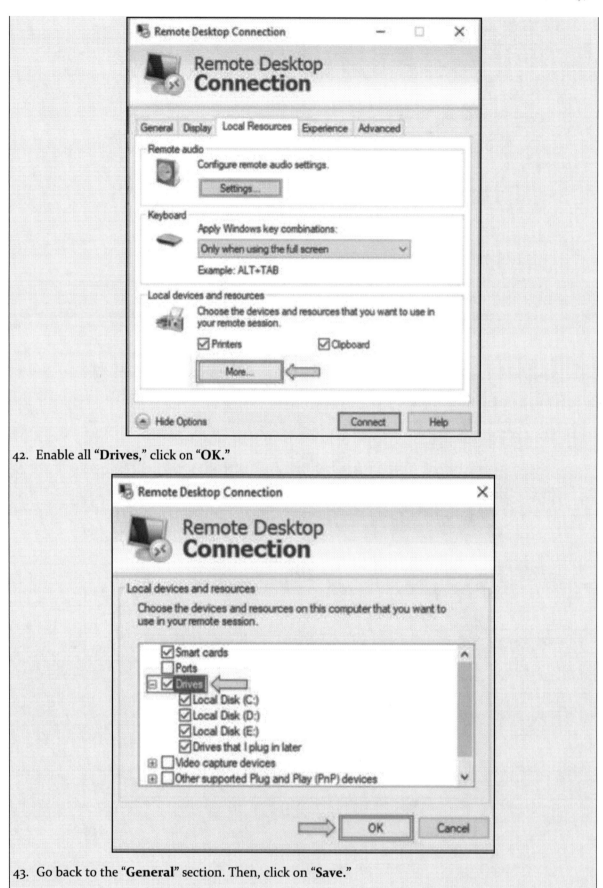

42. Enable all **"Drives,"** click on **"OK."**

43. Go back to the "**General**" section. Then, click on "**Save.**"

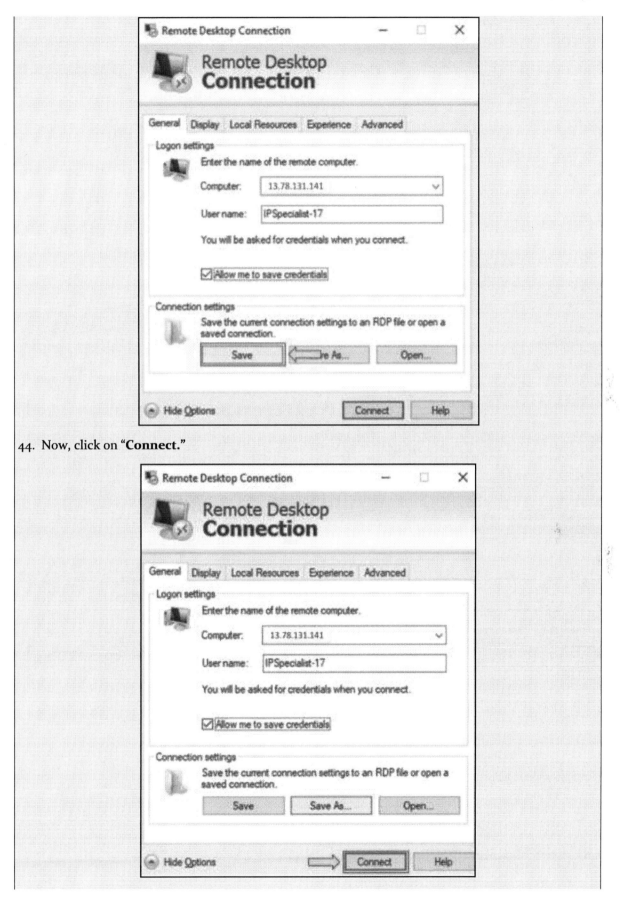

44. Now, click on "**Connect.**"

45. Now, go to the configured Windows virtual machine and click "**Connect.**"
46. Choose the "**RDP**" connection.

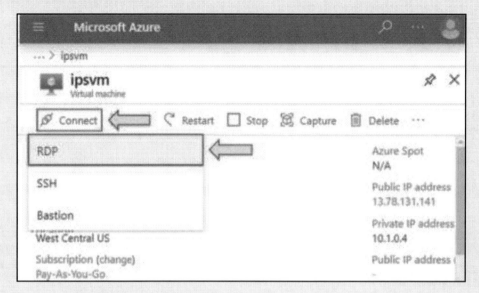

47. Note the IP address and port number.
48. Download the "**RDP**" file.

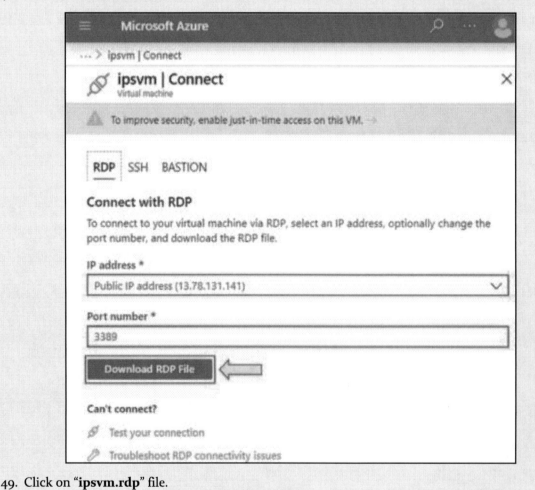

49. Click on "**ipsvm.rdp**" file.

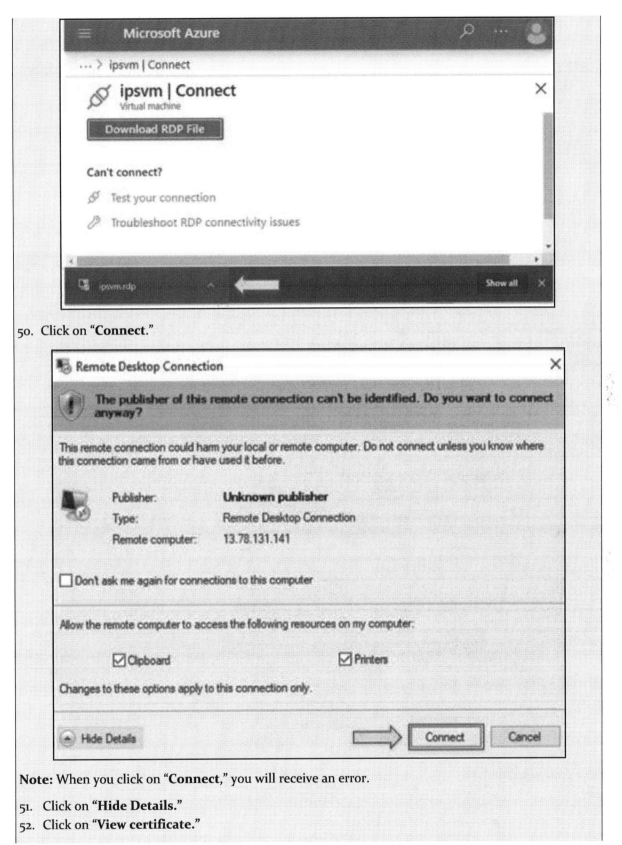

50. Click on "**Connect**."

Note: When you click on "**Connect**," you will receive an error.

51. Click on "**Hide Details**."
52. Click on "**View certificate**."

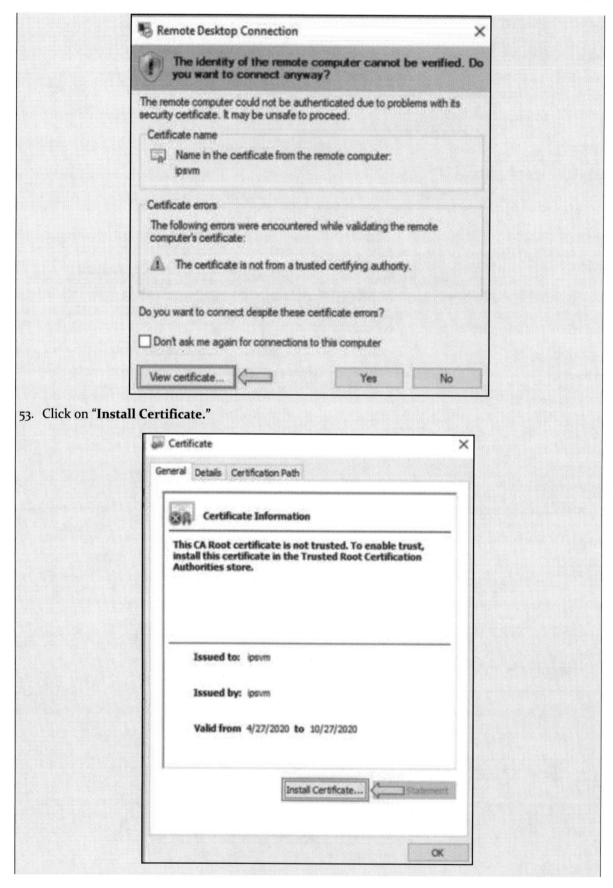

53. Click on "**Install Certificate.**"

54. Click on "**OK**".

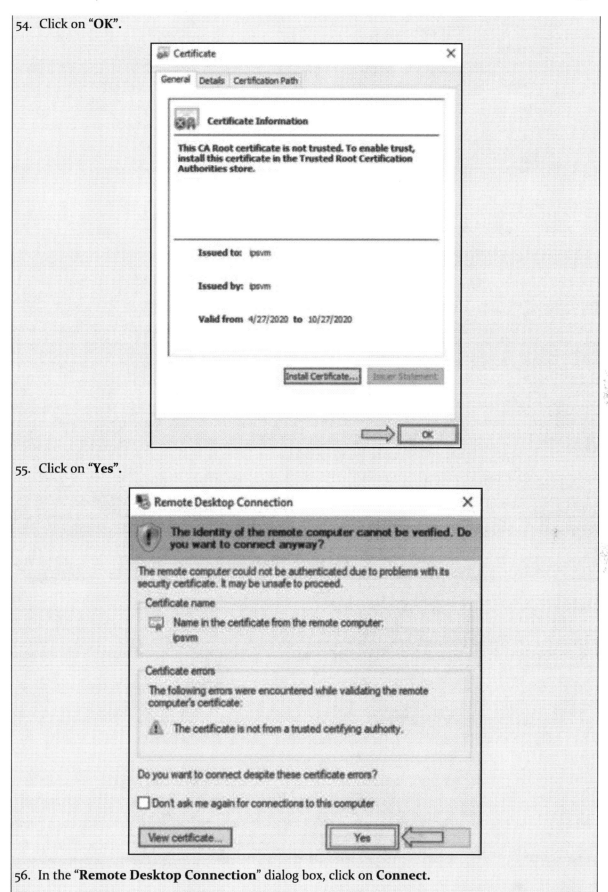

55. Click on "**Yes**".

56. In the "**Remote Desktop Connection**" dialog box, click on **Connect**.

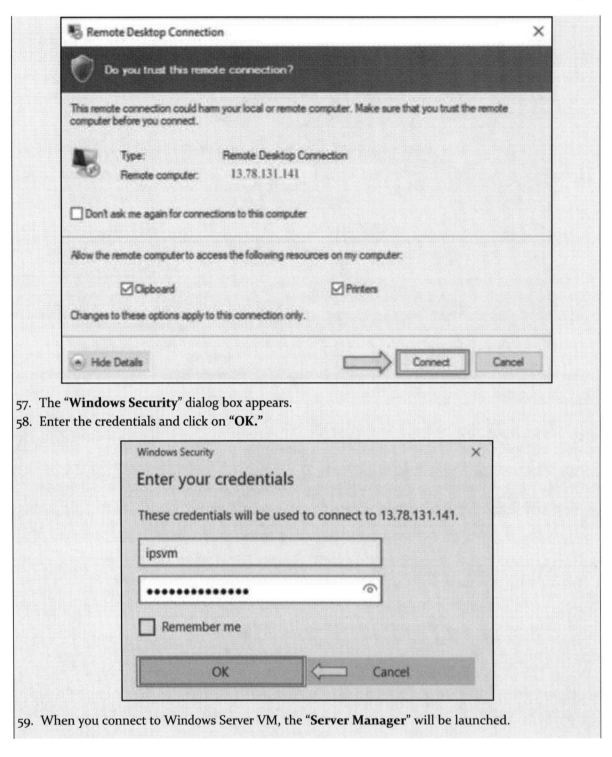

57. The "**Windows Security**" dialog box appears.
58. Enter the credentials and click on "**OK.**"

59. When you connect to Windows Server VM, the "**Server Manager**" will be launched.

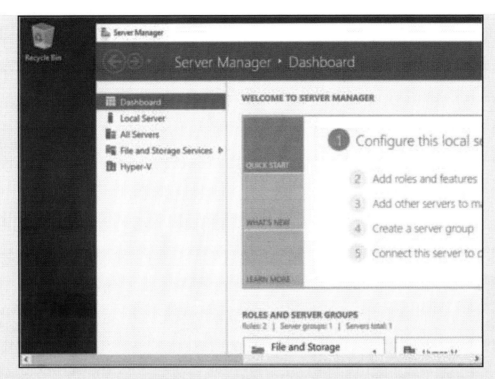

Note: When you connect to the Windows Server VM, you add the Web Server role. This connection will install Internet Information Service (IIS) to block all HTTP requests and enable the FTP server. The FTP server allows access to the folder on the data drive you have added to the VM.

60. Now, go to the start menu and search **"disk management."**

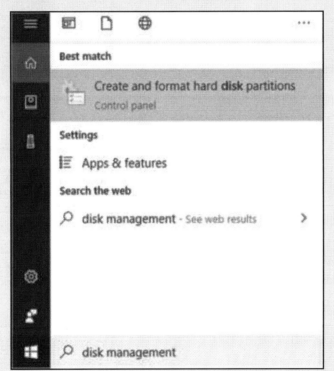

61. Select the number of disks.
62. Enable the style of the selected disk as **"Master Boot Record (MBR)."**

63. Click on "**OK**".

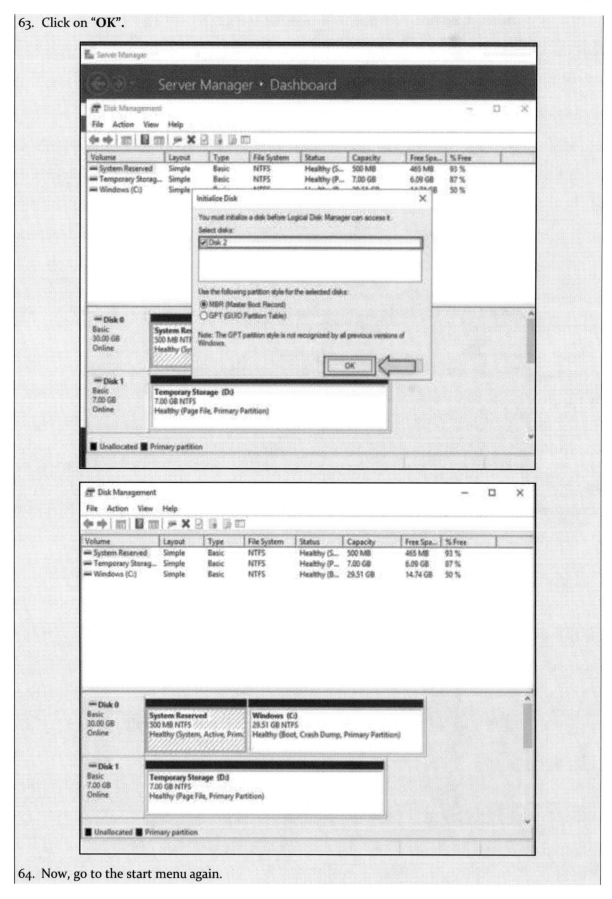

64. Now, go to the start menu again.

65. Search **"File Explorer."**

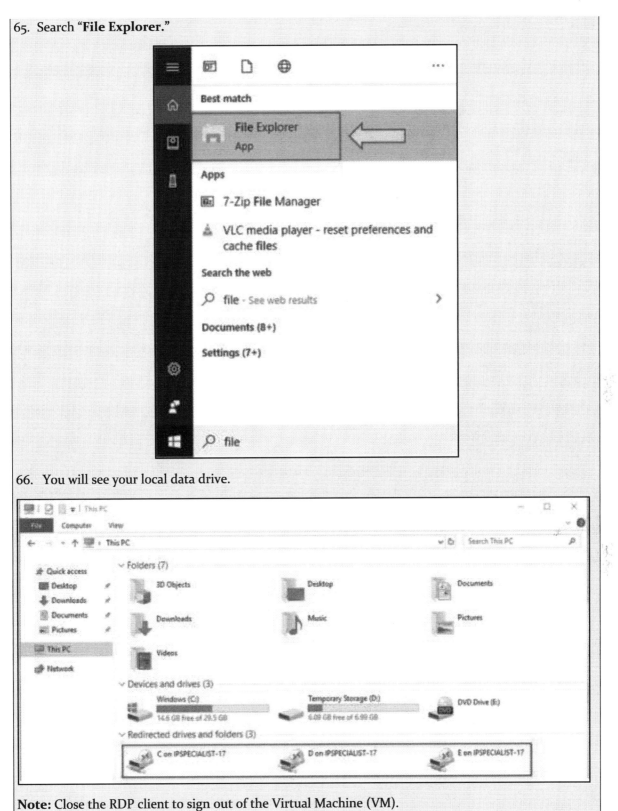

66. You will see your local data drive.

Note: Close the RDP client to sign out of the Virtual Machine (VM).

Lab 2-03: Azure App Services

Service Introduction

Azure App Service is a fully managed platform-as-a-service (PaaS) offering by Microsoft Azure that enables developers to build, deploy, and scale web apps, mobile app backends, and RESTful APIs effortlessly. It provides a robust and flexible environment that supports multiple programming languages, including .NET, Java, Node.js, Python, and more. With features like automatic scaling, continuous deployment, and integrated DevOps capabilities, Azure App Service streamlines the development process and allows developers to focus on coding instead of infrastructure management. Additionally, it offers built-in security features, including authentication and authorization, as well as seamless integration with Azure services like Azure SQL Database, Azure Storage, and Azure Functions, facilitating the creation of powerful and interconnected cloud applications. Overall, Azure App Service is a versatile and efficient solution for deploying and managing modern web and mobile applications in the Azure cloud.

Problem

An organization wants to deploy a web app by using an Azure service that provides a fully managed infrastructure environment for customers and developers to develop and manage applications without having to worry about managing the infrastructure. How can this be done?

Solution

Azure App Service is a fully managed Platform as a Service (PaaS), which means servers, networks, storage, and other fundamental infrastructures are all managed and controlled by Azure. Web Apps allow to creation, deployment, and scale of Web Apps to enterprise grade in seconds.

Step-by-Step Guide

Below are some steps to creating a Web App using Azure App services.

1. Login to **"Azure portal."** Select **"App Services"** from the dashboard.

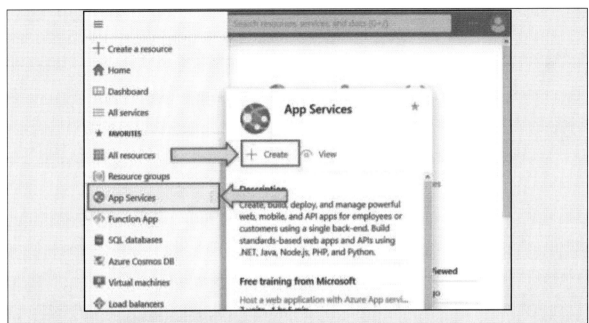

2. Click the "**+ Add**" icon to create a Web App by providing the required details, such as the name of the App, resource group name, etc.

3. When you click on the "**+ Add button**," you will see a screen where you can enter all the information needed to create a web app. All required fields are marked using an asterisk (*) symbol.

4. Select **"Subscription"** and create a resource group.

5. Provide a name to the resource group; we named it **"IPS_appservice."**

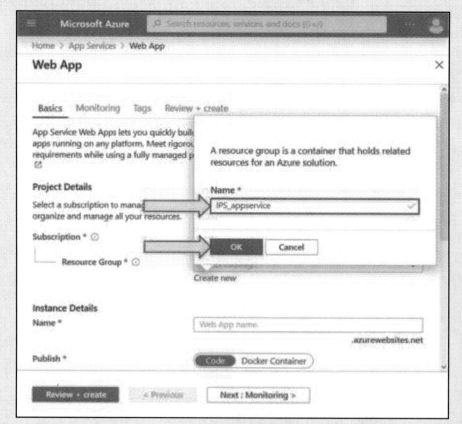

6. Provide instance details such as name, publish, runtime stack, operating system, and region.

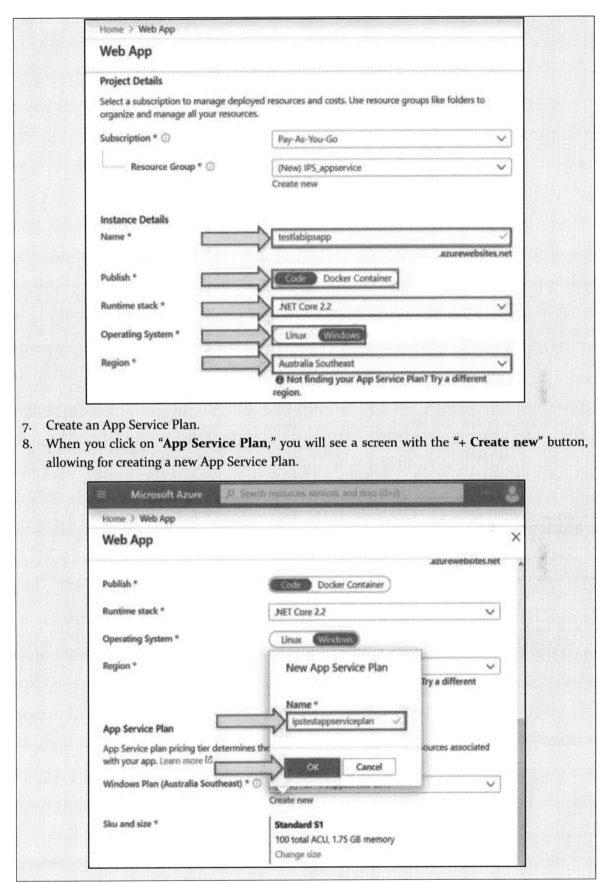

7. Create an App Service Plan.
8. When you click on "**App Service Plan**," you will see a screen with the "**+ Create new**" button, allowing for creating a new App Service Plan.

9. Change the pricing tier.
10. When you click on this option, you will see another screen presenting available features for different tiers. This choice is essential feature-wise and will depend, in most cases, on the environmental characteristics you are planning, such as Dev/Test environments and Production applications.

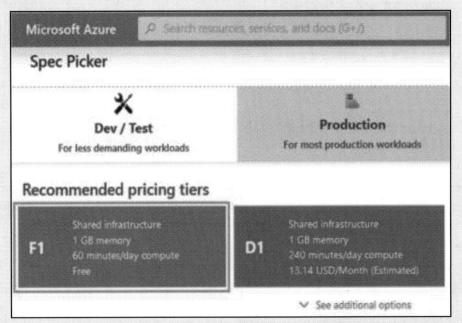

11. The "Dev/Test" category shows F, D, and B tiers (free, shared, and basic). They are designed for simple dev/test scenarios and lightweight web applications that do not need features such as auto-scaling or backups.
12. Select the recommended pricing tiers that are F1.

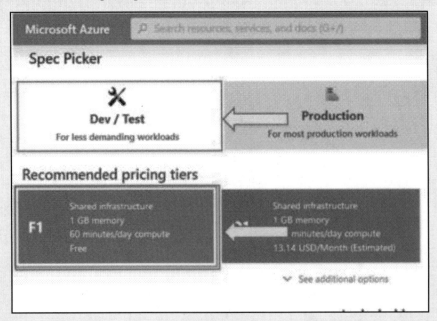

13. The **"Production"** category offers powerful machines and advanced features useful in many realistic scenarios, such as APIs, e-commerce, and popular portals.

14. Select the recommended pricing tiers.
15. After selecting, click the **"Apply"** button.

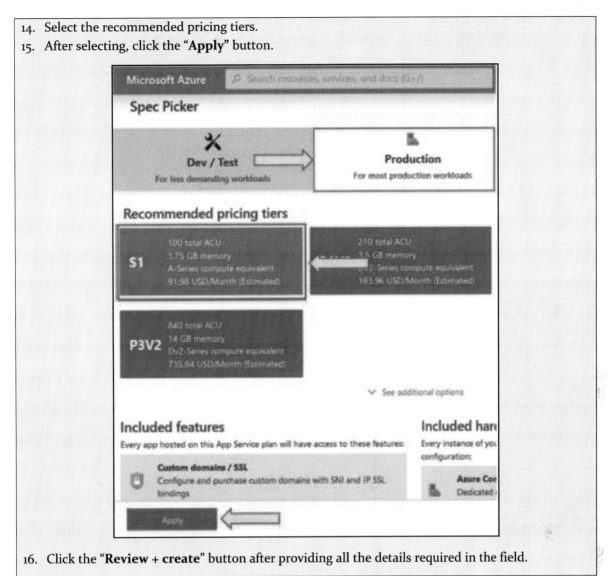

16. Click the **"Review + create"** button after providing all the details required in the field.

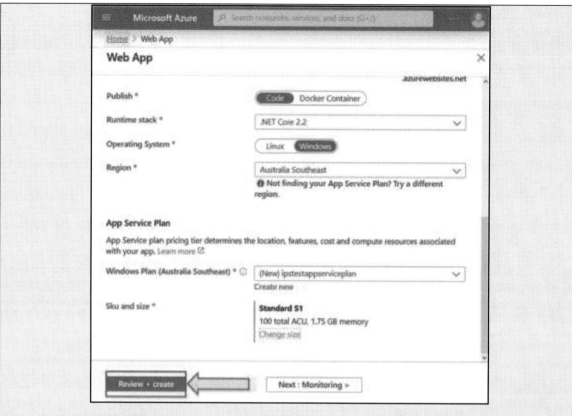

17. After viewing that all the provided details are appropriate on the summary page, click the '**Create button,**' and you will see the notification about deployment initializing.

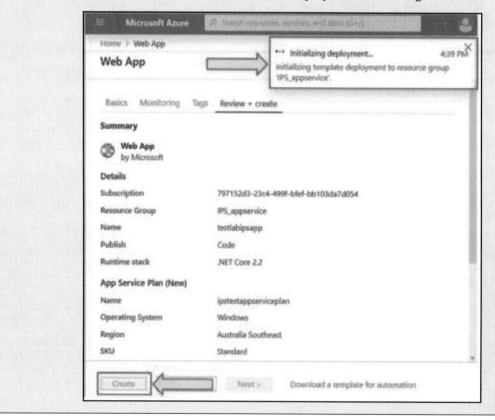

18. When the deployment is completed, click on **"Go to resource."**

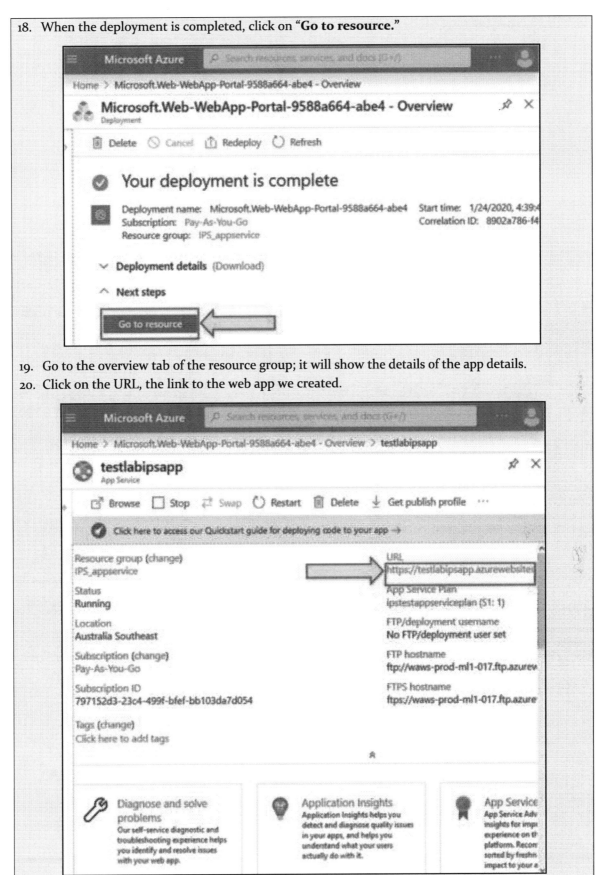

19. Go to the overview tab of the resource group; it will show the details of the app details.
20. Click on the URL, the link to the web app we created.

21. You will be presented with a page when you click on the URL, as shown below.

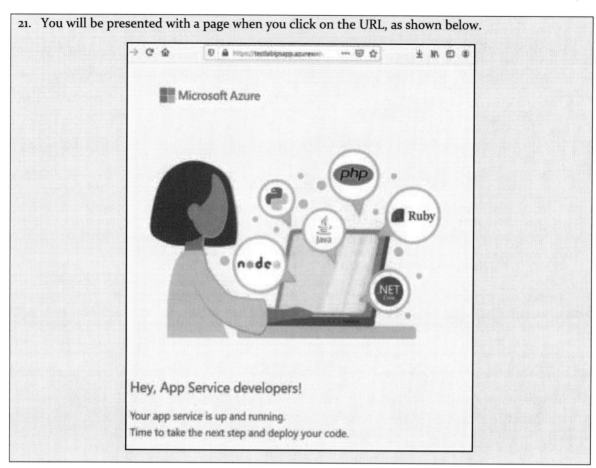

Mind Map

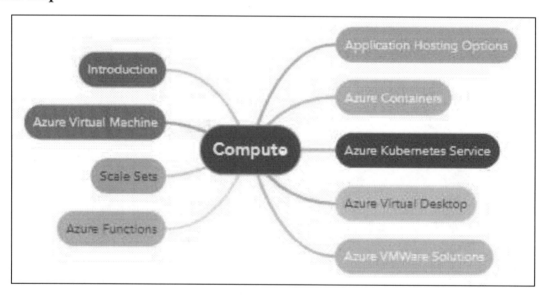

Figure 2-04: Mind Map

Practice Questions

1. Which of the following is the right category to which the Azure Virtual machine belongs?
A. PaaS
B. SaaS
C. IaaS
D. FaaS

2. On which basis will Azure Virtual Machines be charged?
A. Hardware Utilization
B. Resources Utilization
C. Node Utilization on VMs
D. All of the above

3. Which is the simplest and fastest way to run an Azure container without managing any virtual machines and following a higher-level service?
A. App Service
B. Web App for Containers
C. Function Service
D. Azure Container Instances

4. Concerning Azure, compute is a term that covers any service in Azure that enables _____ in the cloud.
A. Migration
B. Calculation
C. Computation
D. Virtualization

5. Which of the following is the right category to which the Azure App services belong?
A. PaaS
B. SaaS
C. IaaS
D. FaaS

6. Scale sets support up to _____ VM instances.
A. 6000
B. 600
C. 50
D. 1000

7. Which of the following programming services is supported by the API app?
A. Backend Service
B. Frontend Service
C. Graphical User Interface
D. All of the above

8. _____ is the preferred way for cloud applications to be packaged, deployed, and managed.

A. Azure Scale Set
B. Azure VM
C. Azure Container
D. Azure Load Balancer

9. Which Azure service is an open-source container orchestration system for automating application deployment, management, and scaling?
A. Azure Functions
B. Kubernetes
C. Azure VM
D. Azure Container Instances

10. On which of the following components is Azure Kubernetes Service cluster architecture based?
A. Node
B. Trigger
C. Node Pools
D. Pods

11. _____ is the serverless computing service that is hosted on the public cloud of Microsoft Azure.
A. Azure Functions
B. Kubernetes
C. Azure VM
D. Azure Container Instances

12. Which would help reduce the administrative effort required to deploy the machines?
A. Azure Functions
B. Kubernetes
C. Azure Scale Sets
D. Azure Container Instances

13. Which solution is great for data processing, systems integration, internet-of-things (IoT) work, and simple APIs and microservices development?
A. Kubernetes
B. Azure Scale Sets
C. Azure Functions
D. Azure Container Instances

14. Which definition best describes compute on Microsoft Azure?
A. A virtual machine
B. An optional component to improve the efficiency of Azure
C. Any service that performs or enables a computation
D. Any serverless service, such as Azure Functions

15. Which cloud service model does Function Service belong to?
A. Platform-as-a-Service

B. Serverless
C. Software-as-a-Service
D. Infrastructure-as-a-Service

16. What is a scale set?
A. A range of sizes of virtual machines ready to take over a workload
B. A set of similar services that all work together for a service or application
C. A pool of identical VMs that can be activated or deactivated as needed
D. A set of virtual machines running in the same data center

17. What is an Azure Function?
A. An add-on to any paid Azure subscription that allows using Azure services as functions in your applications
B. A function to update any resources on Azure
C. A single unit of compute that is triggered by a separate process
D. A foundational component of any Azure infrastructure

18. What is the function of a fully managed platform on Azure?
A. You can pay a monthly fee to have Microsoft look after the maintenance of your applications and services on Azure
B. Servers, networks, storage, and more are all managed by Azure. You focus on your business value and logic
C. Microsoft looks after every part of your Azure services. So you only have to worry about your application development
D. The fully managed platform on Azure is a specific subscription that provides extra support for your Azure services

19. What are the three kinds of App Services? (Choose 3)
A. Web Apps for Containers
B. Event Grid for App Services
C. Web Apps for Linux
D. Web Apps
E. API Apps

20. What are some benefits of using a Virtual Machine on Azure?
A. The much higher performance of applications
B. Owning the hardware while Azure maintains it
C. No maintenance of hardware and only paying for what you use
D. Much cheaper than running your servers

21. Which of the following is a cloud-based desktop?
A. Azure Virtual Desktop
B. Azure Kubernetes Service
C. Azure Functions
D. Azure Cluster

22. Which of the following protocols is a graphical terminal used to connect another computer through a network connection?

A. Transmission Control Protocol

B. Simple Mail Transfer Protocol

C. User DataGram Protocol

D. Remote Desktop Protocol

23. Remote Desktop Protocol (RDP) provides the connection between computers using _____ file?

A. .rtt

B. .rdp

C. .txt

D. .pdf

Chapter 03: Networking

Introduction

Networking is the process of creating long-lasting connections with others. It is the connecting point between the entities for resource sharing or other purposes. In cloud computing, networking is the base. Multiple networks are present in the cloud to provide high-speed connection opportunities for users to use its services, play online games, and use online Photoshop and other applications. Cloud networking enables:

- Cloud computing to develop a network with low latency
- Better security
- Storage capabilities
- Optimized performance

Remember that Microsoft Azure is a PaaS (Platform as a Service) cloud service provider that provides many customer services, as discussed in the first chapter of this course. In this chapter, we will concentrate on getting an overview of Microsoft Azure's networking services when running and building their on-demand applications in the cloud. As all the networking services provide a high-level based service for the customer to fulfill their demands, Azure networking is considered the critical component in building a successful public cloud into Microsoft Azure and its fundamental part. The networking service of Microsoft Azure provides connectivity to users and serves as connectivity between the service elements. Most money bank companies use Microsoft Azure networking services to fulfill the monitoring and management responsibility of the networks.

So, with Networking, you can give your users and customers the best possible experience by connecting the cloud and on-premises infrastructures.

All networking services provided by Microsoft Azure offer various featured services that are discussed in the following sections systematically. Figure 3-01 gives a summarized overview of the networking services offered by Microsoft Azure.

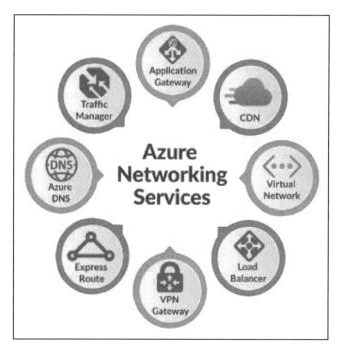

Figure 3-01: Azure Networking Services

Virtual Network

A Virtual Network (or VNet) is used as a networking service to host the infrastructure resources within Microsoft Azure. It is an essential part of the Azure network. It is a logical isolation of the Azure cloud dedicated to your subscription. In Azure, you can use VNets to manage virtual private networks (VPNs).

Azure Virtual Network enables many Microsoft Azure resources, like interMachines (VM), to safely communicate with each other over the internet and on-premises network without any access to the physical hardware. Figure 3-02 shows a simple Virtual Network containing two VMs and the internet.

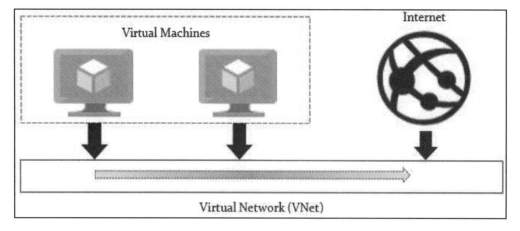

Figure 3-02: Virtual Network

IP Address

When mailing a letter, the letter is sent to the letterbox. After it is processed, the letter is delivered to the correct destination using the address that is already written on the letter. The same procedure is followed

by adding an IP address to the internet. Each traffic has its IP address, ensuring traffic is delivered to the correct destination (server). An IP address serves two principal functions: network interface and address.

A virtual network is similar to a traditional one operating from the data center. VNet consists of four main aspects.

Address Space

An address space is the range of IP addresses. Every resource, service, or connected device on a particular VNet has its IP address within the address space. This way, services in the subnet can communicate with each other. Address space assigned to VNet will automatically get an IP address by each entity present on that VNet.

Subnet

A subnet is a feature that enables segmentation. A virtual network is divided into two or more virtual subnetworks and assigned a range of IP addresses (address space) for each subnet. Therefore, multiple networks can operate simultaneously within the same virtual network.

The significant advantage of subnetting is to make the virtual network more route efficient and reliable. Management control and security groups can also play an important role in securing the individual subnet.

Subnet Regions

Each virtual network within Azure belongs to a single region. Therefore, the resources and services on VM must be physically present in that particular region. VNet can be connected to provide communication across regions.

Subscription

Each virtual network has only one subscription, and every subscription has multiple virtual networks.

The virtual network, including the above-defined features, is shown in Figure 3-03

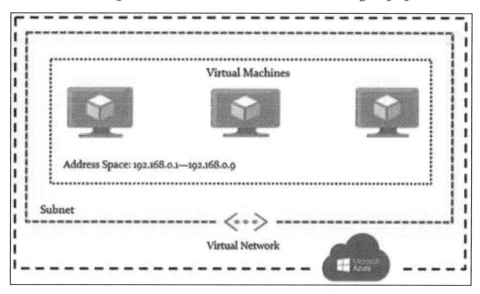

Figure 3-03: Azure Virtual Network

Cloud Advantages

- **Scaling:** Virtual network is the fundamental part of Microsoft Azure. It is also beneficial for scaling due to a wide range of address space that helps in generating more subnets, or you can add more VNets
- **Isolation:** Resources and Services can be managed, organized, and isolated more efficiently in VNets using subnets and network security groups
- **Security:** The inbound and outbound traffic can be controlled by VNets, virtual subnets, and VMs to ensure high security
- **High Availability:** In VNet, the peering feature of the network ensures the high availability of services and resources. Peering means connecting two networks. VNets can communicate via a load balancer or a Virtual Private Network (VPN) gateway

> **EXAM TIP:** VNet is an essential part of Azure infrastructure, responsible for communicating the resources and services in your VNet.
>
> VNet is in a single region and belongs to a single subscription.

Isolation and Segmentation in Azure Virtual Networks

Azure Virtual Network empowers the creation of multiple isolated virtual networks, establishing distinct networking environments. When configuring a virtual network, the definition of a private IP address space involves using either public or private IP address ranges. This IP range exclusively operates within the virtual network, devoid of any internet routability. Further granularity is achieved by dividing this IP address space into subnets, with each named subnet allocated a specific part of the defined address space.

For name resolution, Azure provides a built-in name resolution service. Additionally, configuration options allow the virtual network to utilize either an internal or an external DNS server.

Internet Communications

Incorporating internet connections can be achieved by assigning a public IP address to an Azure resource or placing the resource behind a public load balancer.

Communication between Azure Resources

Enabling secure communication between Azure resources is vital. This can be accomplished in two primary ways:

1. **Virtual Networks:** Beyond connecting Virtual Machines (VMs), virtual networks facilitate connections to other Azure resources, such as the App Service Environment for Power Apps, Azure Kubernetes Service, and Azure Virtual Machine Scale Sets.
2. **Service Endpoints:** Establishing connections to various Azure resource types, such as Azure SQL databases and storage accounts, enables the linkage of multiple Azure resources to virtual networks. This enhances security and optimizes routing between resources.

Communication with On-Premises Resources

Azure Virtual Networks facilitate the linking of resources within both on-premises environments and Azure subscriptions. Three mechanisms support this connectivity:

1. **Point-to-Site Virtual Private Network Connections:** Initiated from a computer outside the organization, these connections establish an encrypted VPN connection to the Azure virtual network.

2. **Site-to-Site Virtual Private Networks:** Connecting on-premises VPN devices or gateways to the Azure VPN gateway, this encrypted connection allows devices in Azure to appear as part of the local network, functioning over the internet.

3. **Azure ExpressRoute:** Offering dedicated private connectivity to Azure, bypassing the internet, ExpressRoute is beneficial for environments requiring higher bandwidth and elevated security levels.

Route Network Traffic

Azure, by default, routes traffic between subnets on connected virtual networks, on-premises networks, and the internet. Additional control and customization options include:

1. **Route Tables:** Allowing the definition of rules governing traffic direction, custom route tables provide control over packet routing between subnets.

2. **Border Gateway Protocol (BGP):** Collaborating with Azure VPN gateways, Azure Route Server, or Azure ExpressRoute, BGP propagates on-premises BGP routes to Azure virtual networks.

Filter Network Traffic

Azure Virtual Networks offer mechanisms to filter traffic between subnets:

1. **Network Security Groups:** These Azure resources contain multiple inbound and outbound security rules, allowing the definition of rules based on factors like source/destination IP address, port, and protocol.

2. **Network Virtual Appliances:** Resembling hardened network appliances, these specialized VMs execute specific network functions, such as running a firewall or performing WAN optimization.

Connecting Virtual Networks

Virtual network peering enables the direct connection of two virtual networks, ensuring private network traffic flows over the Microsoft backbone network, avoiding the public internet. This peering capability facilitates communication between resources in each virtual network, even when located in separate regions, enabling the creation of a globally interconnected network within Azure.

Load Balancer

Consider an example as shown in Figure 3-04. A client introduces an online booking app. The app is working well. At a time, the app is simultaneously accessed by many customers. Initially, only a single virtual machine is responsible for processing the data. As the simultaneous traffic demands increase, the virtual machine becomes overloaded. To overcome this problem, another virtual machine is added. Adding a second virtual machine creates another problem: how traffic is shared between the two VMs. A load balancer is used in front of two VM to access the data before reaching the destination. Therefore, multiple users can access the service at the same time more efficiently.

The load balancer is generally used to distribute the traffic that arrives on the front end to the backend pool as per rules and health status.

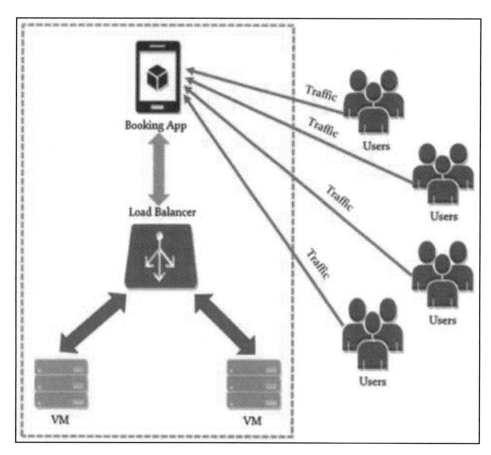

Figure 3-04: Scenario-Load Balancer

Azure load balancer serves the load balancing feature to the connected virtual machines within Microsoft Azure. It operates at the OSI model's transport layer (Layer 4). When multiple VMs serve an application within VNet, a load balancer decides which VM belongs to the particular user.

The two types of load balancers are public and internal. The public load balancer converts the private IP address of the VM to a public IP address for outbound access and internet-facing. In comparison, the internal load balancer can manage the traffic inside the VNet. For example, the load balancer is only used when a private IP address is required. For checking the availability, HTTP and TCP-based probes are used by the load balancer.

Technical Terms of Load Balancer

- **Inbound Flow:** Inbound flow is traffic from the internet or the local network. The load balancer then receives this traffic
- **Outbound Flow:** Outbound flow is used for establishing the connection between the public frontend and virtual machine backend
- **Frontend Pool:** Frontend pool connects clients to the load balancer via IP addresses. It manages traffic to the VM. All the traffic arrives here first
- **Backend Pool:** Backend pool allows the VM to receive traffic from a load balancer
- **Rules and Health Probes:** Rules refer to the load balancer rule for directing the traffic, and health probes ensure that the VM is ready to receive traffic before the load sends any, as the load balancer always sends traffic to a healthy VM. A health probe can be HTTP, HTTPS, or TCP

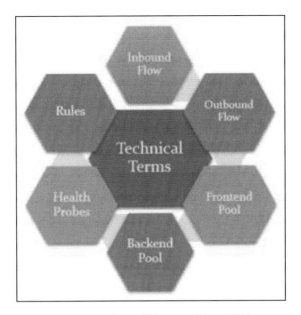

Figure 3-05: Technical Terms of Load Balancer

Benefits of Load Balancer

- **Internet Traffic:** It helps to balance internet traffic when there are many users
- **Internal Network:** Balances the traffic that is generated from internal running applications within Azure
- **Port Forwarding:** Serves as a forwarding point of traffic. We can easily forward traffic to a specific port or specific machine in a backend pool
- **Outbound Traffic:** The load balancer also ensures the outbound connectivity for the VM in the backend pool

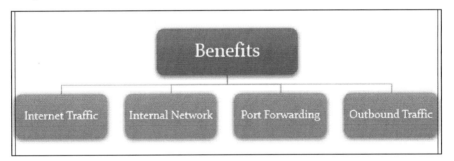

Figure 3-06: Benefits of Load Balancer

Introduction to VPN Gateway

VPN stands for Virtual Private Network. A VPN gateway helps establish the private connection between an Azure resource and an on-premises environment, offices, the cloud, or other premises within the cloud to establish a private and secure connection. In Microsoft Azure, the VPN gateway provides managed services within the cloud.

VPN Gateway

VPN Gateway securely connects the Azure network with the on-premises network. It sends encrypted traffic between the Azure virtual network and on-premises location over the public internet. VPN Gateway provides the encrypted connection between Azure and the on-premises network and allows incoming traffic over a dedicated network and links with different Azure data centers. This way, the VPN gateway securely connects the Azure network in different Azure regions.

In the network, there is only one VPN Gateway. All the bandwidth is shared between the connections to that gateway. The Azure virtual network comprises several virtual machines within the Gateway Subnet, as shown in Figure 3-07. A gateway subnet has a range of IP addresses and VMs within that subnet containing the address under the designed specific range.

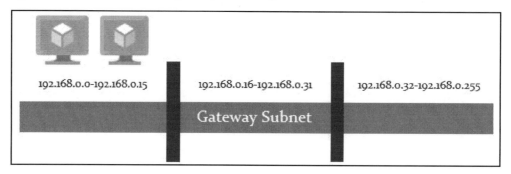

Figure 3-07: Gateway Subnet

The virtual machines in the gateway subnet are created when you create the virtual network gateway. Virtual network gateway VMs are configured to contain routing tables and gateway services specific to the gateway. When you create a VPN gateway, gateway VMs are deployed to the gateway subnet and configured with your specified settings.

Gateway Type

The basic setting required for the gateway configuration is "Gateway Type." It determines how the gateway will function.

For example, for a VPN gateway, the gateway type is "vpn." There are various options available for the deployment of a VPN gateway.

Network-to-Network Connection – This type of connection provides the VPN gateway functionality over IPsec (IKEv1 and IKEv2) VPN tunneling. A tunnel is responsible for providing an encrypted connection between the networks. A typical example of this type of network connection is shown in Figure 3-08.

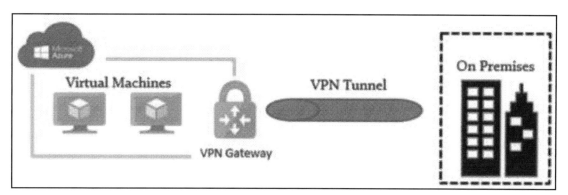

Figure 3-08: Network to Network Connection

Site-to-Site Connection – This type of connection provides the VPN gateway functionality over IPsec/IKE VPN tunneling to communicate between the dedicated Azure network and the on-premises network. A typical example of this type of network connection is shown in Figure 3-09.

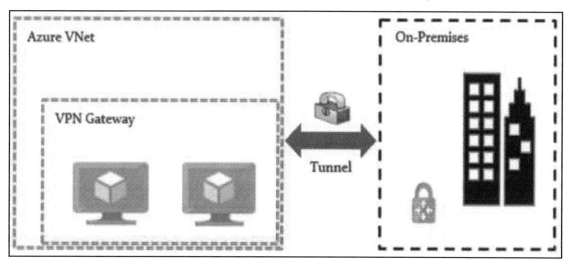

Figure 3-09: Site-to-Site Connection

Point-to-Site Connection – This type of connection provides the VPN gateway functionality over IKEv2 or SSTP and communicates the Azure network with the client computer. A typical example of this type of network connection is shown in Figure 3-10.

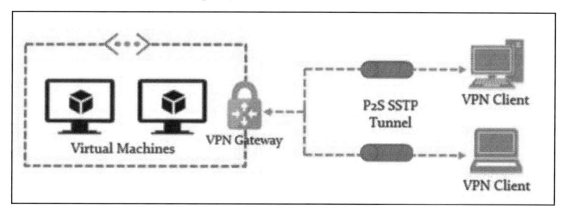

Figure 3-10: Point-to-Site Connection

> EXAM TIP: A VPN gateway can provide efficient cloud computing services within the hybrid cloud infrastructure. VPN gateway is composed of a VNet gateway and a virtual private network.

Create a VPN Gateway

There are two possible options for creating the VPN gateway.

RouteBased – Route-based VPN works on route tunnel interface in the virtual network. This device allows the routing table to direct the traffic to different IPsec tunnels. It routes traffic dynamically over the tunnel interface. This VPN option is commonly used to avoid overlapping subnets and is vital in accessing multiple subnets.

PolicyBased – Policy-based VPN restricts traffic flow to particular network subnets according to the configured policy. It is built on a firewall device and defines the policy of how to encrypt or decrypt the network traffic through an IPsec tunnel. This VPN option is commonly used to access only one subnet or network at the remote site.

High-Availability Scenarios for VPN Gateways

Ensuring the resiliency and fault tolerance of a Virtual Private Network (VPN) configuration is paramount when prioritizing the security of your information. Various strategies can be employed to maximize the availability of your VPN gateway.

Active/Standby Configuration:

By default, VPN gateways are deployed in an active/standby configuration, even when appearing as a single resource in Azure. In this setup, two instances operate, with one as the active gateway and the other as the standby. During planned maintenance or unforeseen disruptions affecting the active instance, the standby instance seamlessly takes over connections without requiring user intervention. While there might be a brief interruption during failover, connections are typically restored within seconds for planned maintenance and 90 seconds for unplanned disruptions.

Active/Active Configuration with BGP Support:

The introduction of support for the Border Gateway Protocol (BGP) allows deploying VPN gateways in an active/active configuration. Each instance is assigned a unique public IP address, and separate tunnels are established from the on-premises device to each IP address. The high availability can be extended by deploying an additional VPN device on-premises.

Azure ExpressRoute

Azure ExpressRoute allows you to have a dedicated private connection from your on-premises network into the Microsoft cloud. With the help of ExpressRoute, you can easily connect to your data center and a Microsoft cloud provider like Azure.

ExpressRoute also provides layer 2 and 3 connectivity to allow private, secure access to the resources deployed in the Azure virtual network.

Figure 3-11 shows the network employing the ExpressRoute connectivity between on-premises and Azure networks. The arrangement between the two networks shows that connectivity is not established via the internet but across the dedicated link called ExpressRoute.

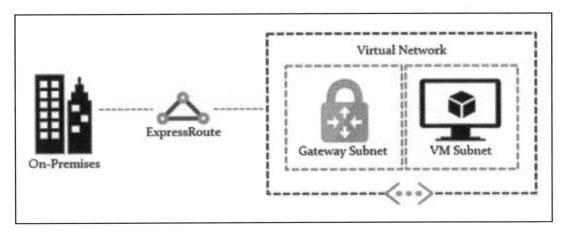

Figure 3-11: Network with Azure ExpressRoute

Advanatges of ExpressRoute

There are several benefits of using ExpressRoute. Some of these are:

- **Bandwidth** – ExpressRoute gives bandwidth options between 50 Mbps to 10 Gbps with dynamic bandwidth scaling
- **Fast Speed** – ExpressRoute delivers throughput that is 100 times faster than the internet
- **Network Privacy** – Compared to VPN, VPN traffic is transiting over the internet. ExpressRoute is a dedicated line between your data center and Azure. This gives you private connectivity. Your traffic does not transit over the internet
- **Low Latency** – As ExpressRoute is not utilizing the public internet, customers can be assured of improved performance and reliability according to the service provider SLA
- **Reliable and Secure** – ExpressRoute provides high security and reliability as compared to any typical connection over the internet
- **Disaster Recovery** – An ExpressRoute service is an excellent option for data migration, business continuity, and Disaster Recovery (DR)
- **Redundancy** – ExpressRoute builds an additional circuit for redundancy
- **Cost-Efficient** – ExpressRoute is one of the best options for transferring data at a low cost
- **Use of BGP** – Express Route makes use of Border Gateway Protocol (BGP) to route the traffic across the internet between two network systems
- **Global Connectivity** – ExpressRoute provides global connectivity to all regions
- **Expansion of Services** – ExpressRoute can increase the route limits, virtual network link per circuit, and global connectivity

Connectivity to Microsoft Cloud Services with ExpressRoute

ExpressRoute provides direct and secure access to a range of Microsoft cloud services across all regions. These services include popular offerings such as Microsoft Office 365 and Microsoft Dynamics 365, as well as core Azure components like Azure Virtual Machines, Azure Cosmos DB, and Azure Storage. This direct connectivity ensures efficient and reliable access to essential cloud resources, allowing for seamless integration of on-premises infrastructure with Microsoft's cloud environment.

Global Connectivity with ExpressRoute Global Reach:

ExpressRoute Global Reach offers a powerful solution to exchange data between on-premises sites by interconnecting ExpressRoute circuits. For instance, if your organization has offices in Asia and a data center in Europe, each equipped with ExpressRoute circuits linked to the Microsoft network, ExpressRoute Global Reach facilitates direct communication between these facilities. By leveraging this capability, data can traverse the connection without being routed over the public internet, enhancing security and efficiency.

Dynamic Routing with BGP:

ExpressRoute employs the Border Gateway Protocol (BGP) for dynamic routing. BGP serves as the mechanism for exchanging routes between on-premises networks and resources hosted in Azure. This protocol enables real-time, adaptive routing between your on-premises network and services operating within the Microsoft cloud. The dynamic nature of BGP ensures optimal and efficient traffic routing, adapting to changes in the network landscape.

Built-in Redundancy for High Availability:

To guarantee high availability, each connectivity provider utilizes redundant devices when establishing connections with Microsoft. This inherent redundancy ensures a robust and reliable network architecture. Moreover, you have the flexibility to configure multiple circuits, further enhancing redundancy and providing additional layers of resilience to meet your specific business needs. This built-in redundancy is fundamental to maintaining continuous and uninterrupted connectivity with Microsoft Cloud services.

ExpressRoute Connectivity Model

There are three ways to connect ExpressRoute:

1. Any-to-Any (IPVPN) Networks
2. Virtual Cross-Connection through an Ethernet Exchange
3. Point-to-Point Ethernet Connection

Layer 3 Connectivity

A routing protocol is required to transfer traffic from one network to another. Microsoft uses a standard dynamic routing protocol called the Border Gateway Protocol (BGP). BGP connects networks across the entire internet. BGP route the traffic between the networks. BGP can be configured in two ways. One is dynamic routing, and the other is static routing. ExpressRoute supports dynamic routing, allowing learning a new route if you set up a new virtual network.

Any-to-any (IPVPN) Networks

In an IPVPN network, Azure is treated as one of the branch offices. For example, if your organization has five data centers in five different locations, all the data centers will be connected to WAN. So if you are connecting to any-to-any IP VPN, the Azure data center will appear as another branch office. The architecture of IPVPN is shown in Figure 3-12.

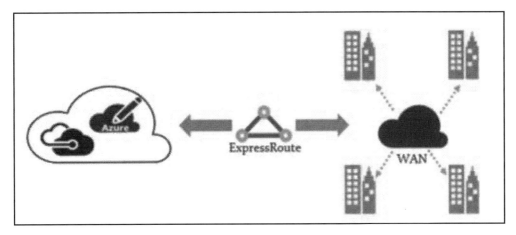

Figure 3-12: IPVPN Network

Virtual Cross-Connection through an Ethernet Exchange

The architecture shown in Figure 3-13 is the cloud exchange co-location. There is an Azure with Microsoft Data center and an exchange provider. The Exchange provider gives the renting facility so that you can rent a facility and co-locate your resources. This type of connectivity is used when people want the output much faster than the internet.

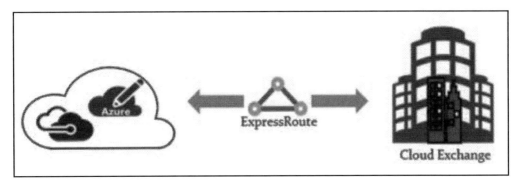

Figure 3-13: Cloud Exchange Co-location

Point-to-Point Ethernet Connection

The Point-to-Point Ethernet connection is shown in Figure 3-14. This connection is useful to provide layer 2 or 3 connectivity between the on-premises network and Microsoft Azure.

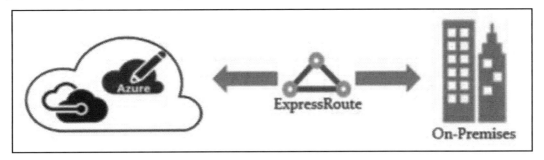

Figure 3-14: Point-to-Point Ethernet Connection

ExpressRoute Failover

In scenarios where high availability is critical, a VPN gateway can be configured as a secure failover path for ExpressRoute connections. While ExpressRoute circuits inherently possess resiliency, they may still be susceptible to physical issues impacting connectivity cables or outages affecting the entire ExpressRoute location. Provisioning a VPN gateway that leverages the internet as an alternative connectivity method ensures a constant connection to virtual networks, mitigating the risk of ExpressRoute circuit outages.

Zone-Redundant Gateways

In regions supporting availability zones, VPN gateways and ExpressRoute gateways can be deployed in a zone-redundant configuration. This approach enhances the resiliency, scalability, and overall availability of virtual network gateways. Deploying gateways across Azure availability zones physically and logically separates them within a region, safeguarding on-premises network connectivity to Azure from failures at the zone level. Notably, these gateways necessitate distinct gateway SKUs and utilize Standard public IP addresses rather than Basic public IP addresses.

Co-location at a Cloud Exchange with ExpressRoute

Co-location involves situating your data center, office, or facility close to a cloud exchange, typically managed by an Internet Service Provider (ISP). When your facility is co-located at a cloud exchange, you gain the advantage of establishing a virtual cross-connect to the Microsoft cloud, facilitated through ExpressRoute.

Security Considerations with ExpressRoute

ExpressRoute offers a secure and private connection, ensuring that your data doesn't traverse the public internet. This eliminates exposure to potential risks associated with internet communications, enhancing the overall security posture of your network infrastructure. The connection established through ExpressRoute serves as a dedicated and private link between your on-premises environment and your Azure infrastructure.

It is important to note that while ExpressRoute mitigates the risks associated with public internet connectivity, certain elements, such as DNS queries, certificate revocation list checking, and Azure Content Delivery Network requests, still utilize public internet routes. Despite these specific scenarios traversing the public internet, the core data transfer between your on-premises infrastructure and Azure remains securely routed through the private ExpressRoute connection. This nuanced approach ensures a balance between security and efficiency in your hybrid cloud connectivity.

Application Gateway

One type of VPN gateway is the application gateway. It is considered the most advanced load balancer that enables the balancing of web traffic to manage web applications using an HTTP request. Because of its services, the gateway is called the layer 7 load balancer within Microsoft Azure. It also supports ADC (Application Delivery Controller) functionality. Figure 3-15 shows a network specifying the contribution of the application gateway. In Figure 3-15, routing decisions are based upon additional characteristics, for example, URI path or host headers of the HTTP request with the application gateway. This request is in the form of data format so that any internet traffic can receive the request. The Uniform Resource Identifier (URI) is the web address, while the host request is the information sent with the request. The

configured network can send a request to a specific web address to a specific machine at the backend pool.

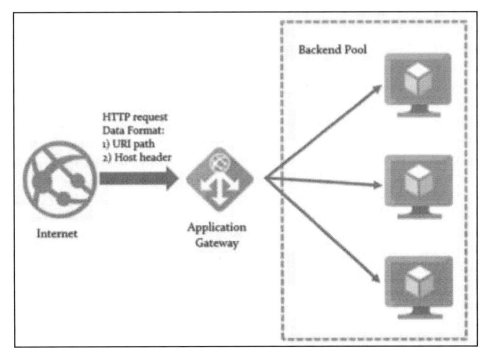

Figure 3-15: Network with Application Gateway

Benefits of Application Gateway

The benefits of the application gateway are as follows;

- **Scaling:** The application gateway can be scaled due to the abrupt change in traffic load
- **High Availability:** The use of a layer 7-based load balancer increases the availability of resources for the web application in Microsoft Azure
- **Encryption:** The application gateway provides end-to-end encrypted communication between the services. You can enable or disable the traffic encryption to the backend pool to improve the processing time
- **Zone Redundancy:** The application gateway supports multiple zones to improve flexibility and fault resiliency
- **Multi-Site Hosting:** By using multi-site hosting, a single application gateway is used for many web applications and provides a secure connection between the entities
- **SSL Offload:** After routing traffic to the correct destination, SSL offloads are supported by the application gateway to provide relief to the webserver
- **Cost-Effective:** As an application gateway, hosting multiple web applications results in saving costs and minimizing complexity
- **Session Affinity:** Application Gateway allows keeping the user on the same web server by directing the user traffic on the same web server
- **Web Socket Support:** The application gateway allows web sockets for client-connected applications. Web socket pushes specific client applications within a browser. Websockets allow you to expose real-time data from your applications. For example, it operates as a bidirectional communications channel using HTTP

- **Web Application Firewall:** Application gateway also provides protection features like web application firewall that protect internet requests and applications

Figure 3-16: Benefits of Application Gateway

> **EXAM TIP:** An application gateway is more efficient in delivering web application services than other gateways.
>
> It works on HTTPS rather than IP address/port.

Content Delivery Network

When a user is far from a data center (online resource) in which they want to get data, one way of getting the data is that the user accesses the data, but that takes much time and provides a low performance of the application due to the distance. Another way of getting the data is using the Microsoft Azure Content Delivery Network (CDN) service. It is a distributed network of servers that can deliver web content close to users. Within Azure, CDN places the duplicates of data at the data center closer to the user side, and users can easily log into the application they want. The data centers closer to the users are called edge nodes/edge servers, containing a cache of files that provide the edge of the internet closest to the users. The information in these edge nodes is limited for a few days because each node has an expiry date. Using edge nodes, users can easily access data from data centers. One problem behind the edge node is how users get informed by the update. The solution for this is that when information is about to expire, the user will get the updated data from the far data center so that the user can create a new data center in which all the updates are available.

The main reason behind using a Content Delivery Network (CDN) is to deliver data to the user with the lowest latency by providing data at edge nodes. The data usually consists of images, files, media, etc. Data content delivery can be improved by using a feature called Dynamic Site Acceleration (DSA). DSA finds the best route for the request of traffic from the user to the server. DSA in Content Delivery Network stores the dynamic content to improve the network's performance.

Figure 3-17 shows the concept of the Content Delivery Network (CDN). The given network is spread over the geographical area, and users from any area can access the data, such as logs of an online application using an edge node. The edge node is the service of Azure CDN.

> **EXAM TIP:** The origin server is the original location of files, such as web applications that hold the master copy of all data.

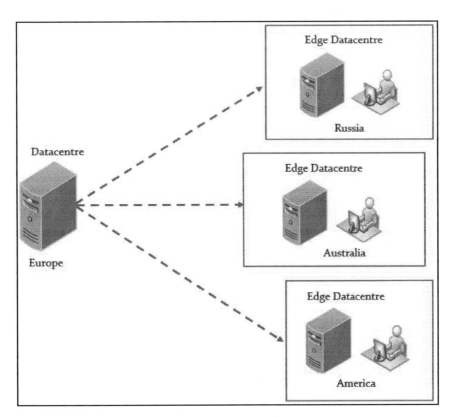

Figure 3-17: Concept of CDN

Benefits of CDN

- **Global Coverage:** Content Delivery Network (CDN) provides global coverage using the multiple edge nodes across the region
- **Better Performance:** Providing optimized performance due to the fast delivery of data and increased user experience
- **Scaling:** CDN can be scaled up or down due to the instantaneous high traffic load and protected by hiding other data from the backend
- **Distribution:** Edge nodes help deliver less content from the main server to the user; all of the request data can be easily achieved by the user from edge nodes

> **EXAM TIP:** A cache is a collection of duplicate copies of a file. The primary purpose of the cache is to provide fast online application services to end-users.

Traffic Manager

The traffic manager manages and monitors the routing traffic globally within the Azure infrastructure. Azure DNS must select the best possible endpoint (internal or external) for routing traffic. The traffic manager distributes the load over multiple regions because of multiple regional web applications.

The traffic manager employs four routing processes, which are:

- Geographic-based routing, in which traffic load is routed over the geographic region, depends on demand
- Priority-based routing that routes the traffic load according to the service requirement
- Weighted routing is used when you want to distribute traffic across a set of endpoints based on their weight

Performance-based routing is beneficial to find the best possible route for directing the traffic load to the backend.

Azure DNS

Microsoft Azure DNS is a Domain Name System hosting domain within Azure. The significant advantage of DNS is that there is no need to host it within DNS providers and Azure. Azure DNS allows monitoring of the DNS records using the same authorization and other support within the Azure service. Azure DNS is also responsible for fast managing the communication between domain and DNS servers. Figure 3-18 shows the utilization of Azure DNS for providing high availability and improved performance.

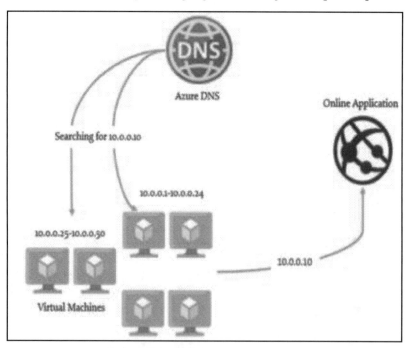

Figure 3-18: Utilization of Azure DNS

Key Benefits of Azure DNS

Azure DNS harnesses the extensive capabilities of Microsoft Azure, offering a range of advantages:

- ➤ Reliability and performance
- ➤ Security
- ➤ Ease of Use
- ➤ Customizable virtual networks
- ➤ Alias records

Reliability and Performance

- ➤ Azure DNS hosts DNS domains on Azure's global network of name servers, ensuring resiliency and high availability.
- ➤ Utilizes any cast-networking for each DNS query, directing it to the closest available DNS server, optimizing performance.

Security

- ➤ Built on Azure Resource Manager, Azure DNS incorporates robust security features.
- ➤ Azure Role-Based Access Control (RBAC) allows precise control over user access, specifying actions within the organization.
- ➤ Activity logs provide detailed monitoring of user actions, aiding in troubleshooting and auditing.
- ➤ Resource locking prevents unintentional modifications or deletions of critical resources within the organization.

Ease of Use

- ➤ Integrated into the Azure portal, Azure DNS simplifies DNS record management for Azure services and external resources.
- ➤ Shares credentials, support contracts, and billing processes with other Azure services.
- ➤ Manageable through the Azure portal, Azure PowerShell cmdlets, and Azure CLI, providing flexibility in administration.
- ➤ Offers REST API and SDKs for seamless integration with applications requiring automated DNS management.

Customizable Virtual Networks with Private Domains

- ➤ Supports private DNS domains, allowing the use of custom domain names within private virtual networks.
- ➤ Provides flexibility beyond Azure-provided domain names, enhancing customization options.

Alias Records

- ➤ Introduces support for alias record sets, enabling references to Azure resources like public IP addresses, Traffic Manager profiles, or CDN endpoints.
- ➤ Ensures seamless updates during DNS resolution if the underlying resource's IP address changes.

Azure DNS stands out as a versatile, reliable, and secure DNS solution within the broader Azure ecosystem, offering a comprehensive suite of features for efficient domain management.

Lab 3-01: Creating a Virtual Network Connection

Service Introduction

Wanderlust Travel, a rapidly growing online travel agency, faced a critical dilemma: their web server hosted on a traditional shared server lacked the security and scalability to handle their increasing booking volume. Frequent outages and data breaches were impacting customer trust and business reputation.

Problem

Their shared server offered limited security controls, leaving them vulnerable to hacking attempts and data breaches, compromising sensitive customer information. The shared server could not handle peak booking times, causing frequent outages and impacting customer experience and revenue generation.

Solution

Wanderlust Travel's story demonstrates the power of Azure Virtual Network and web server hosting for businesses seeking secure, scalable, and cost-effective web hosting solutions. By embracing cloud technology, Wanderlust achieved enhanced security, improved customer experience, and gained a platform poised for continued growth in the competitive travel industry.

1. Log in to the Microsoft Azure portal and go to the portal menu.

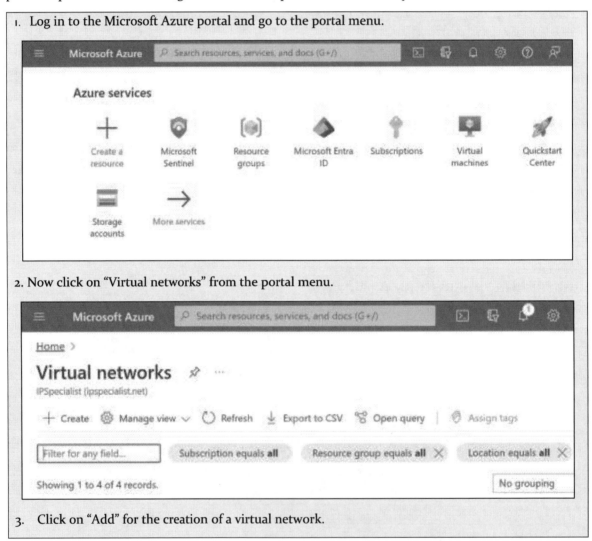

2. Now click on "Virtual networks" from the portal menu.

3. Click on "Add" for the creation of a virtual network.

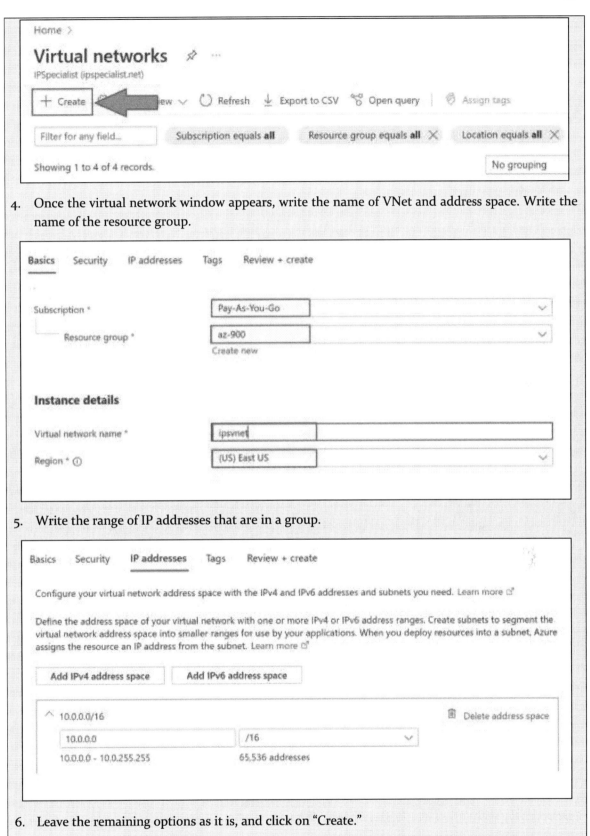

4. Once the virtual network window appears, write the name of VNet and address space. Write the name of the resource group.

5. Write the range of IP addresses that are in a group.

6. Leave the remaining options as it is, and click on "Create."

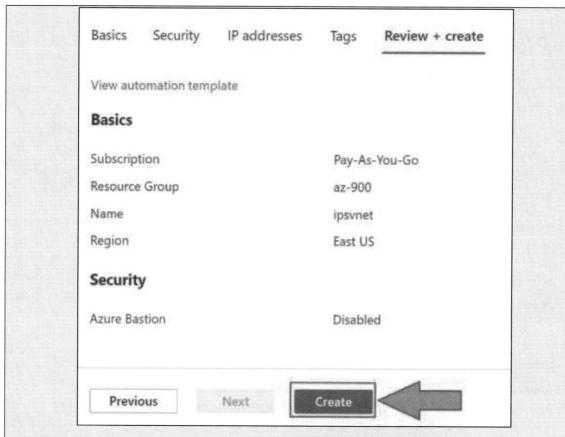

7. Your VNet will now be created; click on "Refresh" to see the created VNet.

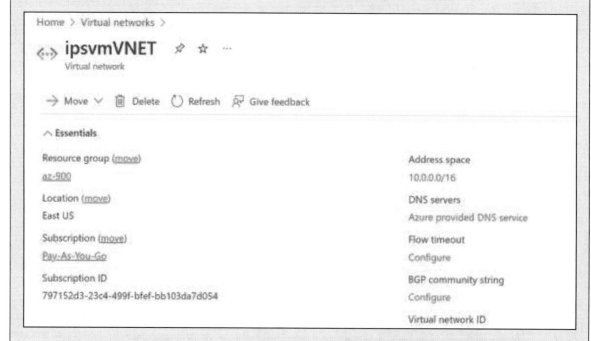

8. To add a virtual machine to VNet, click "Virtual machines." A window will appear; click on "Add" to create a virtual machine for VNet.

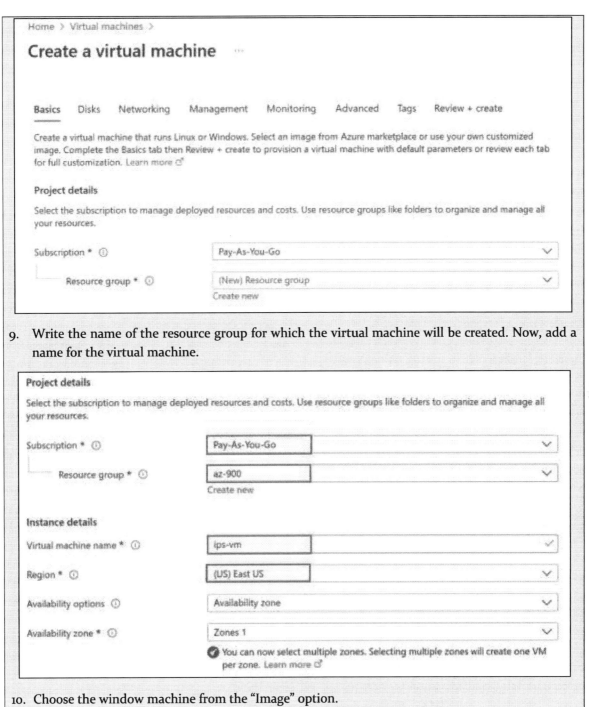

9. Write the name of the resource group for which the virtual machine will be created. Now, add a name for the virtual machine.

10. Choose the window machine from the "Image" option.

Security type ⓘ	Trusted launch virtual machines ⌄
	Configure security features
Image * ⓘ	🔳 Windows Server 2022 Datacenter: Azure Edition - x64 Gen2 ⌄
	See all images | Configure VM generation
VM architecture ⓘ	⚪ Arm64
	⦿ x64
	❶ Arm64 is not supported with the selected image.
Run with Azure Spot discount ⓘ	☐
Size * ⓘ	Standard_B2s - 2 vcpus, 4 GiB memory ($36.21/month) ⌄
	See all sizes
Enable Hibernation (preview) ⓘ	☐
	❶ To enable Hibernation, you must register your subscription. Learn more ❏

11. Add Username and Password.

Administrator account

Username * ⓘ	ipsadmin ✓
Password * ⓘ	•••••••••••••• ✓
Confirm password * ⓘ	•••••••••••••• ✓

Inbound port rules

Select which virtual machine network ports are accessible from the public internet. You can specify more limited or granular network access on the Networking tab.

Public inbound ports * ⓘ	⚪ None
	⦿ Allow selected ports
Select inbound ports *	RDP (3389) ⌄
	❶ All traffic from the internet will be blocked by default. You will be able to change inbound port rules in the VM > Networking page.

12. Leave the remaining options as it is. Click on "Next : Disks >".

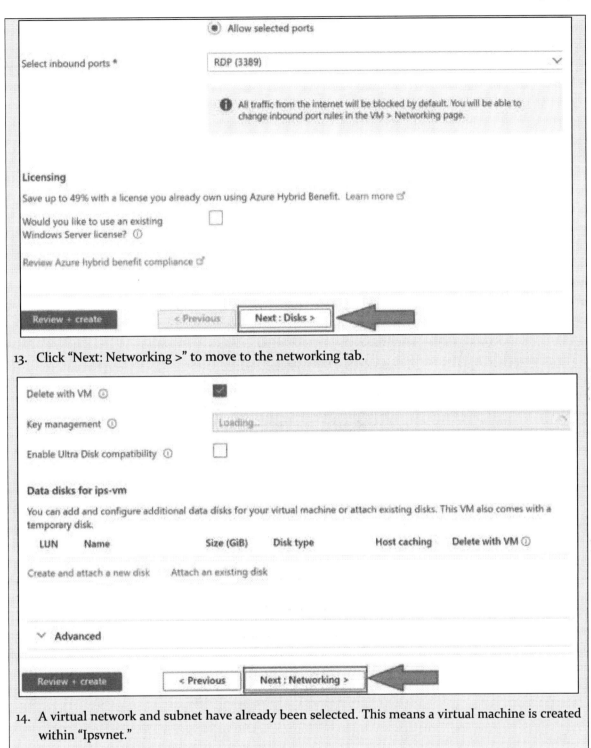

13. Click "Next: Networking >" to move to the networking tab.

14. A virtual network and subnet have already been selected. This means a virtual machine is created within "Ipsvnet."

Network interface

When creating a virtual machine, a network interface will be created for you.

Virtual network * ⓘ	ipsvmVNET ⌄
	Create new
Subnet * ⓘ	ipsvmSubnet (10.0.0.0/24) ⌄
	Manage subnet configuration
Public IP ⓘ	(new) ips-vm-ip ⌄
	Create new
NIC network security group ⓘ	◯ None
	⦿ Basic
	◯ Advanced
Public inbound ports * ⓘ	◯ None
	⦿ Allow selected ports

15. Leave the remaining options as default. Click on "Review + create."

Delete public IP and NIC when VM is deleted ⓘ	☐
Enable accelerated networking ⓘ	☐ The selected VM size does not support accelerated networking.

Load balancing

You can place this virtual machine in the backend pool of an existing Azure load balancing solution. Learn more ⬚

Load balancing options ⓘ   ⦿ None

◯ Azure load balancer
Supports all TCP/UDP network traffic, port-forwarding, and outbound flows.

◯ Application gateway
Web traffic load balancer for HTTP/HTTPS with URL-based routing, SSL termination, session persistence, and web application firewall.

[Review + create] ⟸ vious   [Next : Management >]

16. Once the validation is passed, click on "Create" to create the virtual machine.

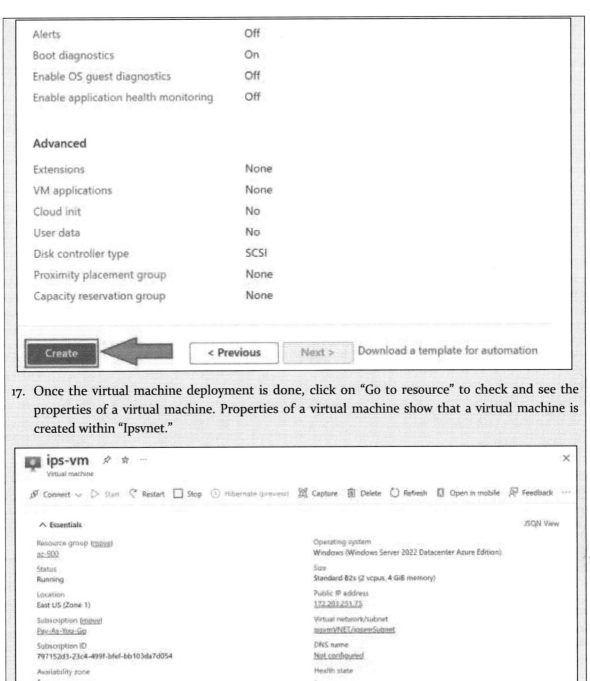

17. Once the virtual machine deployment is done, click on "Go to resource" to check and see the properties of a virtual machine. Properties of a virtual machine show that a virtual machine is created within "Ipsvnet."

EXAM TIP: Resources should be deleted after being used by the customer from the Azure portal. Otherwise, the customer will be highly charged according to the subscription criteria.

Mind Map

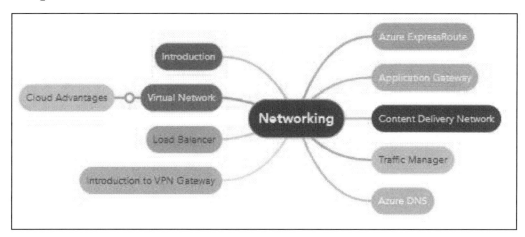

Figure 3-19: Mind Map

Practice Questions

1. What is Azure Networking?
A. A representation of a network in the cloud
B. A network made up of optical fiber
C. It provides 4G connectivity
D. None of these

2. Which Azure networking service is similar to the load balancer service?
A. VPN Gateway
B. Virtual Network (VNet)
C. Application Gateway
D. Traffic Manager

3. Which feature of CDN helps to improve performance?
A. Dynamic Site Acceleration (DSA)
B. Provides data such as images, files, media, etc.
C. Can work with the internet
D. Has resource management capabilities

4. Which networking service launches edge nodes?
A. Azure Load Balancer
B. Azure DNS
C. MPLS Network
D. Content Delivery Network (CDN)

5. If a person wants to use their data on both Azure and on-premises, how can a secure connection between the entities be possible?
A. By using VPN Gateway
B. By adding extra resources to VNet
C. By adding a traffic router
D. By utilizing the cipher key

6. Which problem will be solved by adding the application gateway?
A. Web traffic management
B. Equally balancing the traffic
C. Creating a private connection
D. Performance degradation

7. What information is provided by the Content Delivery Network (CDN)?
A. Encrypted data in binary format
B. Images, files, and media
C. Sequence of alphabets
D. Characteristics of VM

8. What is the purpose of the VPN gateway in Azure?
A. Distributes the traffic load
B. Manages the power of all entities in the network
C. Provides encrypted connection
D. None of these

9. If a virtual network is configured so that it has several subnets, then which additional feature does it possess?
A. Delivers multiple network features
B. Saves power
C. Is cost-effective
D. All of the above

10. Which service is responsible for managing the traffic flow in the network?
A. Traffic Manager
B. Express Route
C. Load Balancer
D. Azure DNS

11. Why do we need the Azure portal?
A. To manage the resources
B. To create VNet with Azure services

C. To configure a network with Azure services
D. All of the above

12. Which of the following provides better security and storage capabilities?
A. Cloud Networking
B. Local Area Network
C. Logical Network
D. None of the above

13. For how many connections can a VPN gateway be used?
A. 2
B. 3
C. 4
D. 10

14. Which of the following services is provided by a VPN gateway?
A. Offers open-source availability
B. Creates multiple layers of service for security purposes
C. It is used in private cloud architecture only
D. Provides a secure connection between Azure resources and the on-premises network

15. Which main resources and services should be present in a VNet?
A. VM, internet, on-premises network
B. 10 internet users only
C. Traffic manager, route finder, and online services
D. All possible gateways

16. Which of the following is not suited for networking service?
A. Network failure
B. Abrupt behavior of VM
C. Scalability
D. Global coverage

17. Which of the following services is offered by a load balancer?
A. Encrypts the incoming traffic among services
B. Provides internet connection for communication
C. Works as a port forwarding point
D. None of these

18. While creating a VNet using the Azure portal, what specific things should be assigned in the network?
A. Username and password
B. Address space, resource group, subnets, and location
C. App services only
D. Compute resources

19. We can add a maximum of two resources in Azure to VNet. True or false?
A. True
B. False

20. How is a load balancer different from an application gateway?
A. Layer 1, layer 5
B. Layer 7, layer 2
C. Layer 4, layer 7
D. Layer 3, Layer 6

21. If a person wants to use their data that is present on both Azure and on-premises, how can a secure connection between the entities be possible?

A. By adding extra resources to VNet

B. By using a VPN gateway

C. By adding a traffic router

D. Utilizing the cipher key

22. Which service is responsible for providing the private connection between Azure and on-premises?

A. Virtual Network

B. Azure VPN Gateway

C. Azure ExpressRoute

D. Load Balancer

23. Which configuration provides the way to connect the on-premises network to the Azure virtual network?

A. Site-to-Site VPN

B. Point-to-Site VPN

C. Multi-Site VPN

D. None of the above

24. How many connectivity models of ExpressRoute exist?

A. 2
B. 5
C. 3
D. 1

25. Which of the following Azure service provides global connectivity?

A. VPN Gateway
B. Network Security Group
C. Virtual Network
D. ExpressRoute

Chapter 04: Storage

Introduction

It is a known fact that to perform any compute, we need some form of storage. We need storage for transient data, data used for a single session, user details, customer data, and orders. This chapter will discuss four ways to create Storage on Azure. These include:

- Blob - It is used in many different scenarios and is incredibly flexible.
- Disk Storage - It is like a disk for storing data
- File Storage – It is a fully managed file storage in the cloud used to the extent of your on-premises storage.
- Archive Storage – A cheap way to store massive archived data.

It would be best if you made the right decision in storage, as it makes your application sufficient. Choosing the right storage option for your required job is one of the most critical steps. Storage is scaling up constantly, and we need modern solutions. Therefore, Microsoft introduced Azure Storage, which provides us with the best solution.

Storing data in the cloud omits the need for any hardware or physical space and makes scaling storage as per requirement very easy. By storing data in the cloud, you can also increase data availability.

Storage Account

Before we go deep into Azure Storage, we must understand what a Storage Account is. A Storage Account is like an access point for Azure Storage. All your Azure Storage Data Objects, like blobs, files, queues, tables, and disks, are on an Azure storage account. The storage account provides a unique namespace for your Azure Storage data, which is available via HTTP or HTTPS from anywhere in the world. Data on your Azure Storage Account are durable, highly accessible, safe, and scalable. The unique namespace means that every storage data has its webpage with its unique name. It is written in the format:

"https://<Storage-Account-Name>.<Storage-type>.core.windows.net.

The name of the storage account must be unique all over Azure. It is a base for all storage types, as we know. The limit size of the Storage Account was already discussed in Chapter 1. All storage accounts are encrypted for data at rest using SSE (Storage Service Encryption). While naming your Storage Account, you must remember two things:

- The name length must be between 3 to 24 characters and may only contain numbers and lowercase letters
- The name of your storage account must be Azure-specific. There can be no two storage accounts with the same name

Two types of storage accounts are available. Users can access Blob Storage, Table Storage, Queue Storage, and File Storage through the "Standard" storage account. The alternative is a "Premium" account, a new option allowing users to save data on SSD drives to boost IO capacity. Five types of storage accounts are available that depend on different features and pricing.

- General-purpose v2 accounts
- General-purpose v1 accounts
- BlockBlobStorage accounts
- FileStorage accounts
- BlobStorage accounts

Azure Storage Redundancy

Your data is always stored in several copies by Azure Storage to safeguard it against both planned and unforeseen occurrences, such as temporary hardware failures, network outages, power outages, and natural disasters. Despite failures, redundancy makes sure that your storage account reaches its availability and durability goals.

Consider the trade-offs between cheaper costs and higher availability when selecting which redundancy option is appropriate for your situation. Which redundancy option you should select will depend on several factors, including:

- How the primary region replicates your data
- To guard against local disasters, consider whether your data is replicated in a second location that is geographically remote from the primary region.
- If the primary region becomes inaccessible, your application needs read access to the duplicated data in the secondary region.

Redundancy in a Primary Region

In the primary region, data in an Azure Storage account is always duplicated three times. In the primary region, Azure Storage provides two choices for data replication: locally redundant storage (LRS) and zone-redundant storage (ZRS).

Locally Redundant Storage (LRS)

Your data is replicated three times within a single data center in the primary region with locally redundant storage (LRS). Over a given year, LRS guarantees at least 11 nines of object durability (99.999999999%).

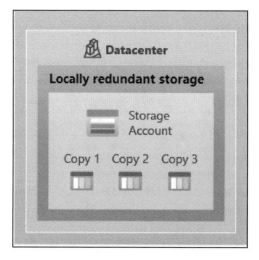

Figure 4-01: Locally Redundant Storage (LSR)

In comparison to other solutions, LRS is the least durable and has the lowest cost of redundancy. LRS protects your data from disk and server rack failures. However, all replicas of a storage account employing LRS could be destroyed or irretrievably damaged if a disaster—such as a fire or flooding—occurs inside the data center. Microsoft advises using geo-redundant storage (GRS), geo-zone-redundant storage (GZRS), or zone-redundant storage (ZRS) to reduce this risk.

Zone-Redundant Storage

Zone-redundant storage (ZRS) replicates your Azure Storage data synchronously across three Azure availability zones in the primary region for Availability Zone-enabled Regions. For data objects stored in Azure Storage, ZRS offers the durability of at least 12 nines (99.9999999999%) over a specific year.

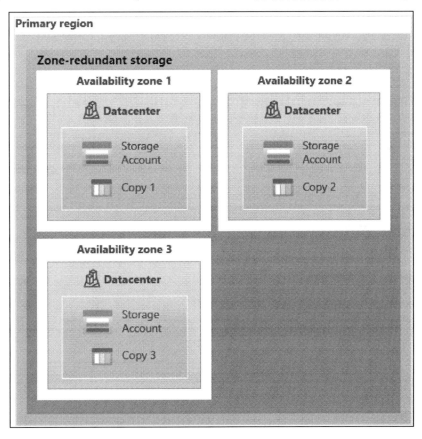

Figure 4-02: Zone-Redundant Storage (ZRS)

With ZRS, your data is still reachable for read and write operations, even if a zone becomes inaccessible. The connected clients do not need to remount Azure file shares. Azure makes networking adjustments, such as DNS repointing, if a zone becomes unavailable. It can be affected if you use your application to access data before these upgrades are finished.

Microsoft advises using ZRS in the main region for high availability scenarios. ZRS also advises limiting data replication inside a nation or region to satisfy data governance needs.

Redundancy in a Secondary Region

For applications that demand exceptional durability, you can also opt to replicate the data in your storage account to a secondary region that is hundreds of miles away from the original region. In the event of a

catastrophic failure that prohibits the recovery of the data in the primary region, if the data in your storage account is transferred to a backup region, your data will still be available.

You choose the account's primary region when you create a storage account. The Azure Region Pairs are the foundation for the paired secondary region and cannot be altered.

Geo-redundant storage (GRS) and geo-zone-redundant storage (GZRS) are two solutions provided by Azure Storage for replicating your data to a separate region. Running GRS in two regions is comparable to running LRS in two regions while running GZRS in one region is comparable to running LRS in one region and ZRS in another.

By default, read and write access to data in the secondary region is disabled unless there is a failover to the secondary region. You might decide to fail over to the secondary region if the original region becomes unavailable. The secondary region becomes the primary region after the failover is finished, enabling data reading and writing once more.

> EXAM TIP: A failure that affects the primary region may result in data loss if the primary region cannot be recovered since data is replicated to the secondary region asynchronously. The recovery point objective (RPO) is the distance between the most recent writes to the primary region and the most recent write to the secondary region. Data recovery is possible up to a point in time indicated by the RPO. There is presently no SLA on how long it takes to replicate data to the secondary region. However, Azure Storage normally has an RPO of less than 15 minutes.

Geo-Redundant Storage

Using LRS, GRS replicates your data three times synchronously within a single physical location in the primary region. The data is then asynchronously copied via LRS to a single physical place in the secondary region (the region pair). For data objects stored in Azure Storage, GRS offers the durability of at least 16 nines (99.99999999999%) over a specific year.

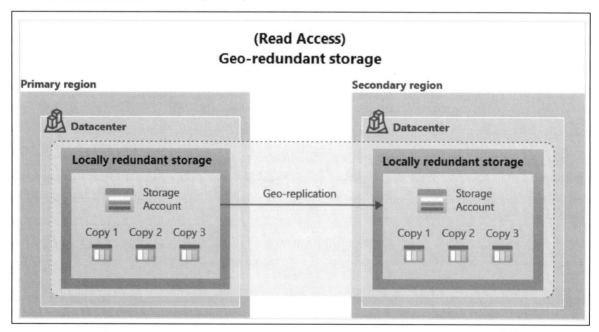

Figure 4-03: Geo-Redundant Storage (GRS)

Geo-Zone-Redundant Storage

Geo-replication and availability zone redundancy work together to give GZRS with both high availability and protection from regional failures. In a GZRS storage account, data is replicated to a secondary geographic region using LRS for protection against local disasters, and it is copied across three Azure availability zones in the primary region (equivalent to ZRS). Microsoft suggests using GZRS for applications that call for the highest levels of consistency, durability, and availability, as well as good performance and resilience for disaster recovery.

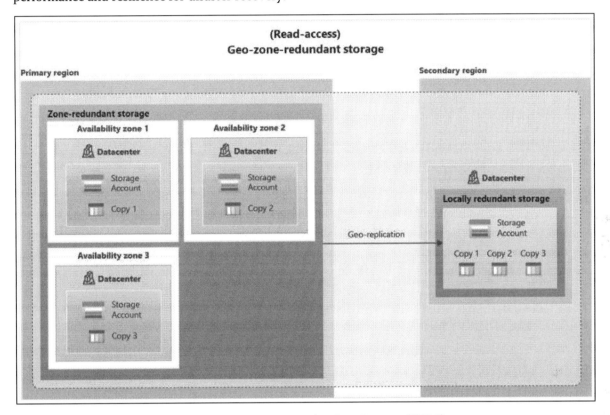

Figure 4-04: Geo-Zone-Redundant Storage (GZRS)

GZRS is made to guarantee an object's longevity for at least 16 nines (99.99999999999999%) over a specific year.

Read Access to Data in Secondary Region

To guard against regional failures, geo-redundant storage (with GRS or GZRS) duplicates your data to a different physical location in the secondary region. However, that information may only be viewed if the customer or Microsoft starts a failover from the primary to the secondary region. However, even when the primary region is operating at peak performance, your data is always accessible if you grant read access to the secondary region. Enable read-access geo-redundant storage (RA-GRS) or read-access geo-zone-redundant storage for read access to the secondary region (RA-GZRS).

Azure Storage

Azure Storage is a Microsoft Cloud storage for storing data. It is a highly scalable object store and a message store for messaging. It also offers a file system service. It is a NoSQL store that provides many benefits:

- **Durability and High Availability** - In case of any hardware failure, it provides you with replicas by placing the data in a replicated form in different geographical locations. So your data is always highly secure and available
- **Security** - The data stored in Azure Storage cannot be accessed as it provides encryption of all data stored in storage. It has restricted access to the data
- **Accessibility** - The data stored in Azure Storage can be accessed from anywhere in the world over HTTP or HTTPS
- **Scalability** - It can easily scale to meet the performance requirements

EXAM TIP: You must first create an account in Azure to use any storage; the storage account is the parent object.

Blob Storage

Blob means Binary Large Object, which stores binary or text data. It is used to store vast amounts of data. Inside the storage account, these blobs are stored in a container. A container is a place for organizing a set of blobs. Within the storage account, you have unlimited containers with unlimited capacity for storing blobs. As we have seen earlier, each object has its unique address, so the individual blob also has its unique address here.

In different scenarios, you can use blob storage to store images in different sizes and formats for storing all kinds of files with distributed access to them via Azure Storage. It can be used for streaming audio and video directly from blob storage, for writing log files regardless of the size and frequency of writing, storing backup data, restoring, DR or any other archiving, and much more.

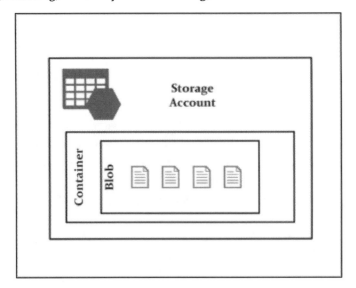

Figure 4-05: Blob Storage

In Azure, three types of Blobs are supported;

1. Block blobs store text and binary data up to 4.7TB. It is made up of blocks of data that can be managed individually. In one block blob, you can have 50,000 blocks.
2. Append blobs are used for log data and can be up to 195GB. It is usually used for optimizing the append operation.
3. Page blobs are used for frequent read and write operations on data. It has a size up to 8TB. The files stored in page blobs can be accessed with any part of the file at any time. It is used for storing virtual hard drives and then serves as a disk for the virtual machine.

During the creation time, you must select the storage account type based on different pricing options.

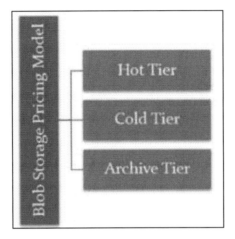

Figure 4-06: Pricing Model

1. **Hot Tier** - It is for frequently accessed data and is the most optimized. The access costs are low (read-write), but storage costs are the highest.
2. **Cool Tier** - It is for data that is not frequently accessed. Data is stored in the cool tier for 30 days. Its storage cost is low, but accessing cost is high. It is used for short-term backup or telemetry data.
3. **Archive Tier** - It is used to store rarely accessed data and has the lowest storage cost but the highest access cost.

The archive tier can be set to blob only while the Hot/Cool tier is enabled at the storage account or blob level. All three levels of storage access can be found in the same storage account, and a blob default level is inherited from the account level setting. However, a blob-level tier can be used to set the level of the object.

The various access tiers should be taken into account:

- Only the hot and cool access tiers are programmable at the account level. At the account level, the archive access tier is not accessible.
- Tier settings for hot, cool, and archives can be made at the blob level before or after upload.
- Although data availability in the cold access tier can be significantly lower, it still needs good durability, short retrieval time, and high throughput. Compared to hot data, cold data offers an acceptable trade-off between cheaper storage costs, a somewhat poorer availability service-level agreement (SLA), and higher access prices.
- The least expensive form of data storage is archive storage, which also has the highest access and rehydration fees.

The choice between the hot and cold access tiers on a general-purpose storage account is shown in the following example:

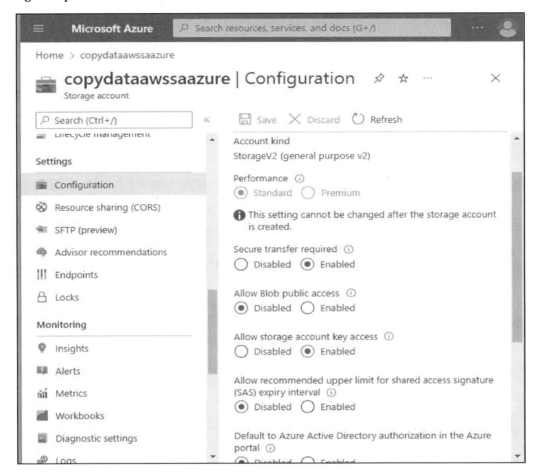

Figure 4-07: Account Configuration

> **EXAM TIP:** Blob Storage is a general kind of storage in which you can store data. Mainly, it has three pricing tiers: Hot, Cool, and Archive.

Disk Storage

Azure Disk storage, also known as Azure managed disks, provides block-level storage volumes managed by Azure and intended for use with the Azure Virtual Machines (VMs). These virtualized disks offer a level of resiliency and availability superior to physical disks. Provisioning a disk is a straightforward process, and Azure takes care of the management aspects.

A managed disk is the disk that is attached to your VM. It is a disk on which you can store your data. Here, managed means Azure will look after this disk for you and manage the uptime and backup. You also do not need to take care of the size and performance, as it is a part of the agreement with Microsoft Azure. With disk storage, you can easily upgrade the disk size and type. Managed disks provide you with two kinds of encryptions: Storage Service Encryption and Azure Disk Encryption.

There are four different types of disks.

- **HDD** – It is a spinning hard drive. HDD is a low-cost storage option for data that are accessed infrequently. It is suitable for backups and testing.
- **Standard SSD** - It is generally for the production environment. Standard SSD gives you a lower latency than HDD with improved reliability and better scalability.
- **Premium SSD** - It is super-fast and high-performance storage for critical workloads. Having low latency, a premium SSD is recommended for database installation. It is better than the standard SSD. Only VM series that are compatible with premium storage can use premium SSDs
- **Ultra Disk** - It is for the most demanding and data-intensive workload. Ultra Disk provides exceptionally scalable performance with sub-millisecond latency. It can be up to 64TB in size. It is recommended for analytical models, gaming, etc.

Comparison between all disk types:

	Ultra disk	Premium SSD	Standard SSD	Standard HDD
Disk type	SSD	SSD	SSD	HDD
Scenario	IO-intensive workloads such as SAP HANA, top-tier databases (for example, SQL, Oracle), and other transaction-heavy workloads	Production and performance-sensitive workloads	Web servers lightly used enterprise applications and dev/test	Backup, non-critical, infrequent access
Max Disk Size	65,536 gibibyte (GiB)	32,767 GiB	32,767 GiB	32,767 GiB
Max Throughput	2,000 MiB/s	900 MiB/s	750 MiB/s	500 MiB/s
Max IOPS	160,000	20,000	6,000	2,000

Table 4-01: Comparison between Disk Storage Types

File Storage

We know that most companies have file storage where they store the company's assets. To work with these files, they can upload, delete, synchronize, and more. But on-premises storage can have issues like disk limitation for storage amount. You also need to configure and maintain backups. Data security at on-premises storage is also challenging to maintain, and you may need to hire security specialists. Also, file sharing across the team and organization becomes difficult. Therefore, by using file storage, all of these issues can be resolved. With File Storage, you get the following benefits:

- Share files across multiple Azure machines and be able to connect with the on-premises infrastructure
- It is fully managed, and you do not need to worry about OS or hardware
- Highly available with super resistance against outages
- It has built-in redundancy

Some common scenarios in which you can use file storage are:

- In a hybrid network where your on-premises storage is out of space
- For lift and shift of existing file storage to Azure
- It can also be a centralized location for monitoring logs and configuration files.

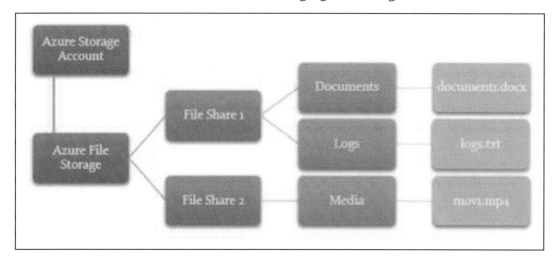

Figure 4-08: File Storage System

 EXAM TIP: File Storage mitigates the on-premises file storage system.

Key Benefits of Azure Files

➢ Azure Files offers several significant advantages for seamless file sharing and management. One notable benefit is the support for industry-standard SMB and NFS protocols, ensuring smooth integration with existing on-premises file shares. This compatibility eliminates concerns about application adaptability when transitioning to Azure file shares, providing a shared access solution that is both versatile and familiar.

➢ Another crucial aspect is that Azure Files are fully managed, eliminating the need for users to handle hardware or operating system management. This translates to simplified operations, as there is no requirement to deal with tasks such as patching server OS for security updates or replacing faulty hardware components.

➢ The availability of scripting and tooling options, including PowerShell cmdlets, Azure CLI, Azure portal, and Azure Storage Explorer, facilitates efficient creation, mounting, and management of Azure file shares. This not only streamlines administrative tasks but also provides users with flexibility in choosing the tools that align with their preferences and workflows.

➢ Azure Files also brings resiliency to the forefront, designed to ensure constant availability. By replacing on-premises file shares with Azure Files, users can mitigate concerns related to local power outages or network issues, contributing to a more reliable and hassle-free file-sharing environment.

➢ Moreover, Azure Files maintains a familiar programmability model. Applications in Azure can access data in the share through file system I/O APIs, allowing developers to leverage existing code and skills during the migration of applications. Additionally, Azure Storage Client Libraries or the Azure Storage REST API provide alternative avenues for seamless integration and interaction with Azure Files.

Archive

Azure Archive Storage is generally used for archiving data and paying less for the process. For most of the company's policies, legislations, and recovery scenarios, storing a large amount of archive data is required. Azure Archive service can prove to be handy for them. It is one of the lowest-priced storage in Azure, which means you can store terabytes of data for just a few dollars per month; with Azure Archive, growth in business data does not necessarily have to mean that there should be a growth in the cost of storage. It is a good storage option for data that are not needed frequently; it is durable, encrypted, and stable. You can free up the most crucial storage on-premises with the archive storage option. It is secure for storing personal data like banking, medical, etc. It secures data at rest with 256-bit AES keys.

In the first chapter, we mentioned that archive storage is blob storage, so the tools that work for blob can even work for archive data.

Use cases for Archive Storage are:

- Security and public safety data retention
- Magnetic tape replacement
- Healthcare Data Archiving
- Long-term backup retention
- Digital media content retention

Queue Storage

Azure Queue storage is a powerful service designed for the storage of large volumes of messages. These messages can be accessed globally through authenticated HTTP or HTTPS calls. A queue can store as many messages as your storage account can accommodate, potentially reaching millions. Each message can be up to 64 KB in size. Queues are frequently employed to establish a backlog of tasks, allowing for asynchronous processing.

Additionally, Azure Queue storage seamlessly integrates with compute functions such as Azure Functions. This integration enables the execution of actions in response to received messages. For instance, if you wish to perform an action when a customer submits a form on your website, you can configure the submit button to trigger a message to the Queue storage. Subsequently, Azure Functions can be employed to execute specific actions upon message reception.

Table Storage

Azure Table storage is designed for the storage of large quantities of structured data. Functioning as a NoSQL datastore, it accepts authenticated calls both within and outside the Azure cloud, making it suitable for building hybrid or multi-cloud solutions with constant data availability. Azure tables are particularly well-suited for storing structured, non-relational data, providing flexibility for diverse data storage needs.

Benefits of Azure Storage

Azure Storage services deliver a range of advantages for both application developers and IT professionals, ensuring robust data management and accessibility:

Durable and Highly Available:

> ➤ Redundancy mechanisms safeguard your data against transient hardware failures.
> ➤ Data replication options across data centers or geographical regions enhance protection, ensuring availability even in the face of local disasters or unforeseen outages.

Secure_:_

> ➤ All data written to an Azure storage account is encrypted, providing a secure storage environment.
> ➤ Fine-grained access control enables precise management of data access, allowing you to control who has permission to interact with your data.

Scalable:

> ➤ Azure Storage is architected for massive scalability, capable of meeting the evolving data storage and performance requirements of modern applications.
> ➤ The scalable nature of Azure Storage ensures that it can grow seamlessly with your application's demands.

Managed:

> ➤ Azure takes care of hardware maintenance, updates, and critical issues, relieving you of the operational burden associated with infrastructure management.
> ➤ This managed service approach allows you to focus more on developing and deploying your applications without the distraction of infrastructure concerns.

Accessible:

> ➤ Azure Storage enables global accessibility of your data through HTTP or HTTPS from anywhere in the world.
> ➤ Microsoft provides client libraries for Azure Storage in various programming languages, such as .NET, Java, Node.js, Python, PHP, Ruby, Go, and more.
> ➤ A mature REST API is available for direct integration, and scripting is supported in Azure PowerShell or Azure CLI.
> ➤ User-friendly tools like the Azure portal and Azure Storage Explorer offer intuitive visual interfaces for efficient data management.

Identify Azure Data Migration Options

It is crucial to comprehend how to enter data and information into Azure. Azure enables asynchronous data movement using Azure Data Box and real-time data migration using Azure Migrate for infrastructure, apps, and data.

Azure Migrate

You can move from an on-premises environment to the cloud using the Azure Migrate service. Your on-premises data center's assessment and migration to Azure can be managed with the aid of Azure Migrate, which serves as a hub. The following is provided:

Unified migration platform - A single interface to launch, manage, and follow your Azure migration.

Range of tools - A variety of instruments for migration and assessment.

Server Migrations - Azure Migrate interfaces with other Azure tools, services, and solutions from independent software vendors (ISVs).

Assessment and migration - Using the Azure Migrate hub, you can evaluate and move your on-premises infrastructure to Azure.

Integrated Tools

Along with working with ISV-provided tools, the Azure Migrate hub also has the following tools to facilitate migration:

Azure Migrate: Discovery and assessment. To prepare for the move to Azure, identify and evaluate on-premises servers running on VMware, Hyper-V, and physical servers.

Azure Migrate: Server Migration. Transfer physical servers, other virtualized servers, VMware VMs, Hyper-V VMs, and VMs from public clouds to Azure.

Data Migration Assistant. The standalone utility Data Migration Assistant is used to evaluate SQL Servers. It aids in identifying potential issues that might prevent migration. It identifies features that are not supported, new features that may be useful to you after migration, and the best course of action for database migration.

Azure Data Migration Service. Move databases currently on-premises to Azure VMs running SQL Server, Azure SQL Database, or SQL Managed Instances.

Web App Migration Assistant. An independent tool called "Azure App Service Conversion Assistant" evaluates on-premises websites for migration to Azure App Service. Utilize Migration Assistant to move PHP and.NET web applications to Azure.

Azure Data Box. To transfer substantial amounts of offline data to Azure, use Azure Data Box products.

Azure Data Box

Large amounts of data may be moved quickly, affordably, and reliably with the help of Azure Data Box, a physical migration service. Your exclusive Data Box storage device, which has a maximum usable storage capacity of 80 terabytes, is shipped to you to speed up secure data transmission. A local carrier ship the Data Box to and from your data center. A tough casing shields the Data Box and keeps it safe during transit.

You can order the Data Box device through the Azure interface to import or export data from Azure. After receiving the device, you can simply configure it through the local web UI and link it to your network. Simply return the Data Box after transferring the data (into or out of Azure). Once Microsoft receives the Data Box back, the data is immediately uploaded if you transfer data into Azure. The Data Box service in the Azure interface keeps track of the procedure from beginning to conclusion.

Use Cases

When there is no or little network connectivity, the Data Box is well suited to transfer data quantities greater than 40 TBs. The data transmission might be one-time or repeated, or it can start as a bulk data transfer and then continue with periodic transfers.

The several situations where Data Box can be used to import data to Azure are listed below.

- Onetime migration - the transfer of a sizable amount of on-premises data to Azure.
- Creating an online media library by moving a media library from offline tapes into Azure.
- Moving your SQL server, applications, and VM farm to Azure.
- Transferring historical data to Azure for HDInsight-based analysis and reporting.
- Initial bulk transfer - When a Data Box (seed) is used to do an initial bulk transfer before additional network transfers are made.
- Periodic uploads - when a lot of data needs to be transferred to Azure regularly.

The different situations where Data Box can be used to export data from Azure are listed below.

- Disaster recovery is the process of restoring an on-premises network with a copy of the data from Azure. A substantial volume of Azure data is typically exported to a Data Box in a disaster recovery scenario. Microsoft will then deliver this Data Box, and the data will be quickly recovered on your premises.
- Security demands - when you must be allowed to export data from Azure because of legal or security demands.
- Return to on-premises or switch to another cloud service provider: Export data via Data Box to relocate workloads when you want to return to on-premises or switch to another cloud service provider.

The disks on the device are completely erased in compliance with NIST 800-88r1 guidelines when the data from your import order is uploaded to Azure. Once the device reaches the Azure data center, the disks are wiped for an export order.

Identify File Movement Options

Azure includes tools that enable you to migrate or interact with single files or small file groups in addition to big-scale migration using services like Azure Migrate and Azure Data Box. AzCopy, Azure Storage Explorer, and Azure File Sync are a few of these utilities.

AzCopy

You can copy blobs or files to or from your storage account using the command-line tool AzCopy. You can synchronize files and upload, download, and copy them between storage accounts with AzCopy. AzCopy can also be set up to cooperate with other cloud service providers to facilitate file transfer between clouds.

EXAM TIP: AzCopy only performs one-direction synchronization when synchronizing blobs or files. AzCopy will copy files or blobs in the direction you specify when you synchronize the source and destination. There is no bi-directional synchronization based on timestamps or other metadata.

Storage Explorer

A standalone software called Azure Storage Explorer offers a graphical interface for managing the files and blobs in your Azure Storage Account. AzCopy handles all file and blob management functions on the backend and is compatible with Windows, macOS, and Linux operating systems. You can upload to Azure, download from Azure, or switch between storage accounts using Storage Explorer.

Azure File Sync

By using Azure File Sync, you can consolidate your file shares in Azure Files while maintaining the adaptability, speed, and compatibility of a Windows file server. It is like creating a small content delivery network on your Windows file server. As soon as you install Azure File Sync on your local Windows server, your files in Azure will automatically remain in bi-directional sync.

Azure File Sync allows you to:

- Use any Windows Server-compatible protocol, such as SMB, NFS, and FTPS, to access your data locally
- Create as many caches as necessary worldwide
- Install Azure File Sync on a fresh server inside the same data center can replace a failed local server
- Create a cloud tiering configuration that keeps seldom-used data in the cloud until needed while replicating commonly used files locally

Lab 4-01: Creating a Storage Account

Service Introduction

Azure Storage Account is a foundational service within the Microsoft Azure cloud platform, designed to provide scalable and secure storage solutions for a variety of data types. It offers a range of storage services, including Blob storage for unstructured data, Table storage for NoSQL data, Queue storage for messaging between application components, and File storage for traditional file shares. Azure Storage Account ensures high availability and durability by replicating data across multiple data centers, offering options such as locally redundant storage (LRS), geo-redundant storage (GRS), and zone-redundant storage (ZRS). It supports both hot and cool storage tiers, allowing users to optimize costs based on their data access patterns. With features like Azure Storage Explorer for easy management, encryption at rest, and robust access controls, Azure Storage Account provides a reliable and scalable foundation for building cloud-based applications and services.

Problem

John has an organization for which he wants storage in Azure Cloud to store essential documents. Which storage option can he used to store the documents?

Solution

By using Azure Storage, he can store his organization's vital documents.

1. Log in to the **Azure** portal and go to the **"Storage Account"** service.

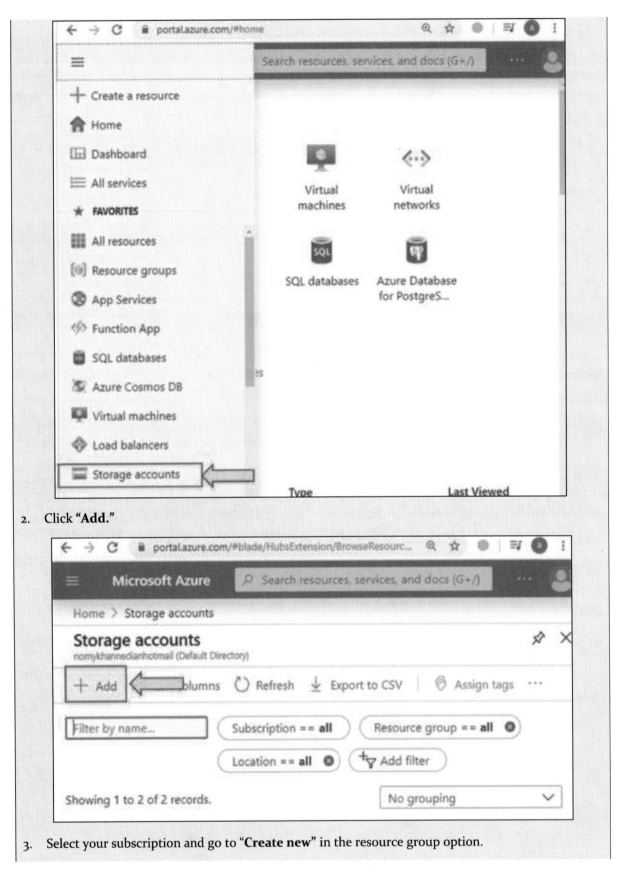

2.   Click "**Add.**"

3.   Select your subscription and go to "**Create new**" in the resource group option.

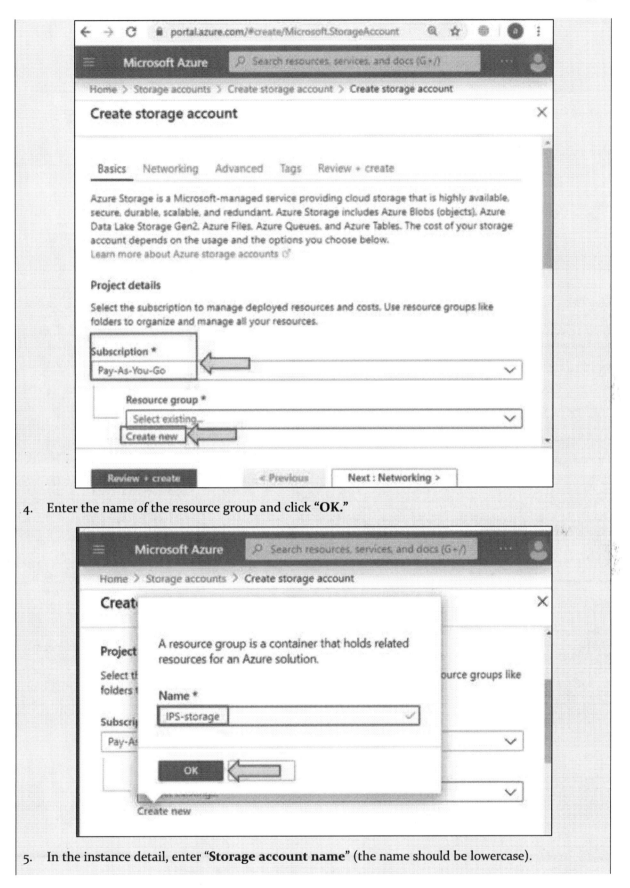

4.   Enter the name of the resource group and click **"OK."**

5.   In the instance detail, enter **"Storage account name"** (the name should be lowercase).

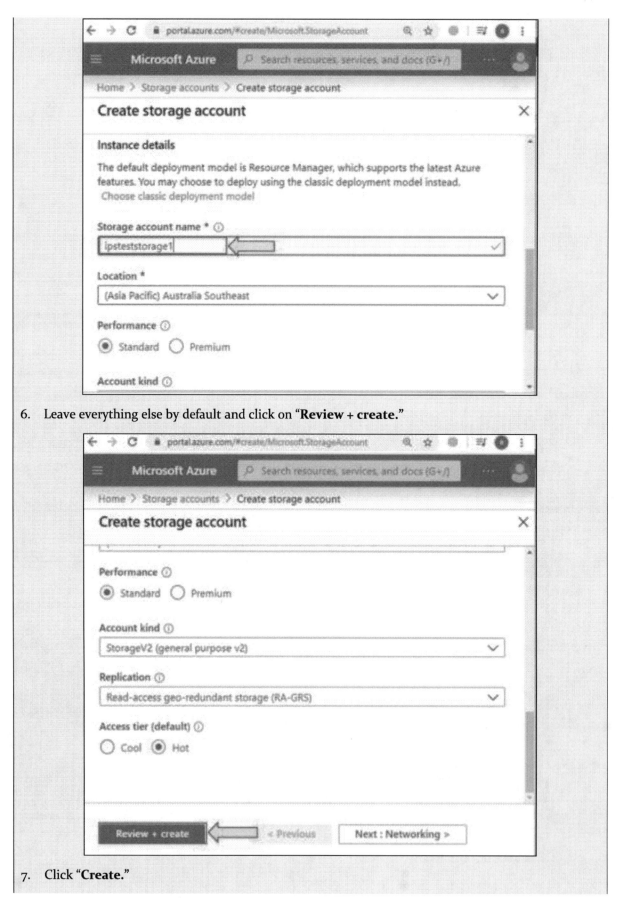

6. Leave everything else by default and click on "**Review + create.**"

7. Click "**Create.**"

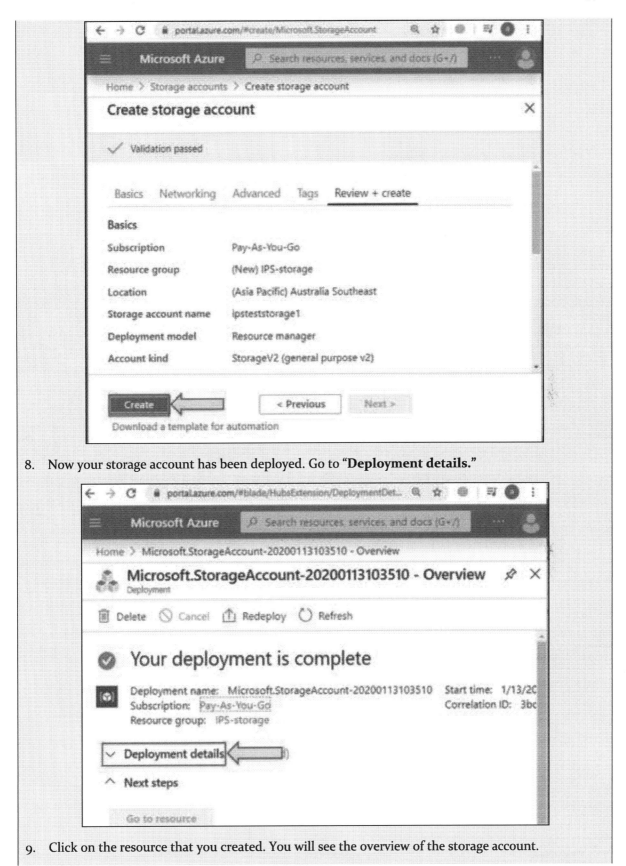

8. Now your storage account has been deployed. Go to **"Deployment details."**

9. Click on the resource that you created. You will see the overview of the storage account.

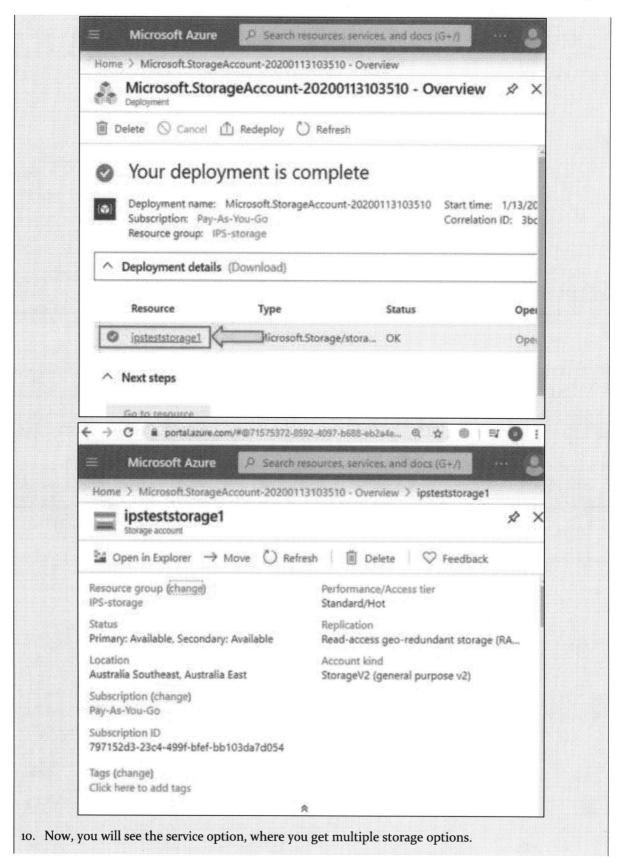

10. Now, you will see the service option, where you get multiple storage options.

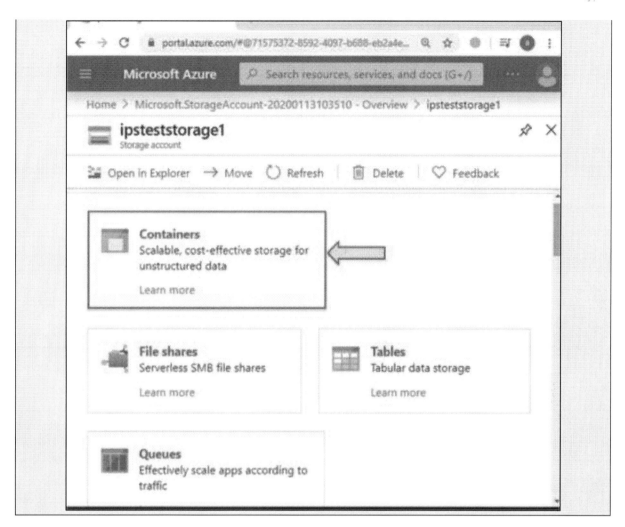

Lab 4-02: Create a Storage Blob

Service Introduction

MediaStream, a rapidly growing streaming service provider, faced a critical challenge: their on-premises storage system couldn't handle the explosive growth of user content and video libraries. Lagging playback, buffering, and server crashes threatened their reputation and user experience.

Problem

MediaStream's existing storage infrastructure couldn't keep up with the rising volume of video content uploaded by users and creators. This led to frequent capacity bottlenecks and performance issues.

Solution

Recognizing the necessity for a robust and scalable solution, MediaStream partnered with a cloud provider to migrate their entire video library and user content to Azure Blob Storage. Azure Blob Storage effortlessly scales to accommodate any video content volume, eliminating capacity constraints and future worries about growth.

Task 1: Create a Storage Account

to the Azure portal.

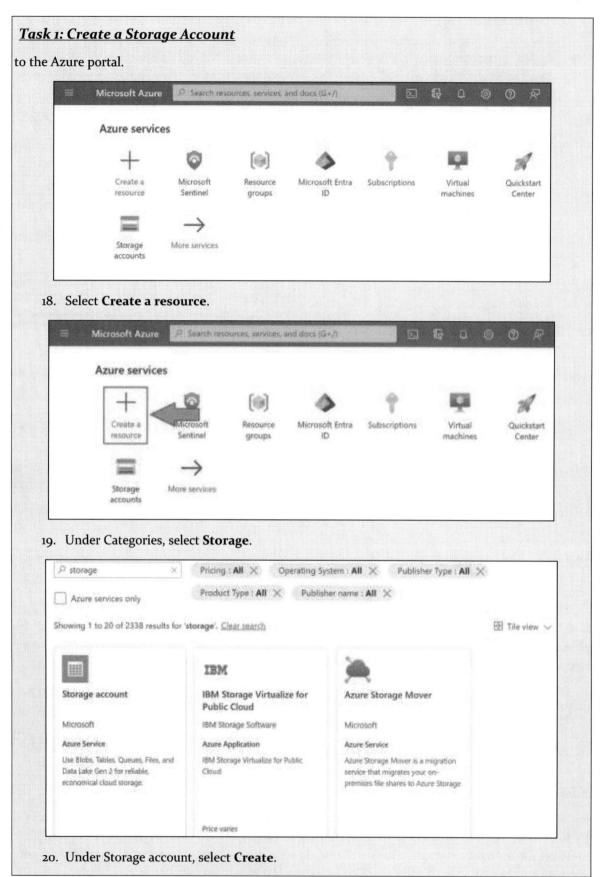

18. Select **Create a resource**.

19. Under Categories, select **Storage**.

20. Under Storage account, select **Create**.

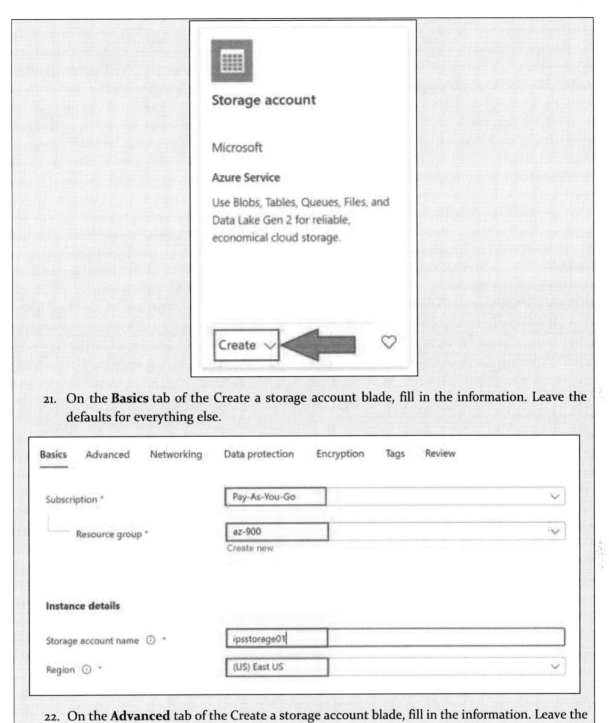

21. On the **Basics** tab of the Create a storage account blade, fill in the information. Leave the defaults for everything else.

22. On the **Advanced** tab of the Create a storage account blade, fill in the information. Leave the defaults for everything else.

Basics   **Advanced**   Networking   Data protection   Encryption   Tags   Review

ⓘ Certain options have been disabled by default due to the combination of storage account performance, redundancy, and region.

Security

Configure security settings that impact your storage account.

Require secure transfer for REST API operations ⓘ   ☑

Allow enabling anonymous access on individual containers ⓘ   ☐

23. Select **Review** to review your storage account settings and allow Azure to validate the configuration.

Basics   **Advanced**   Networking   Data protection   Encryption   Tags   Review

ⓘ Certain options have been disabled by default due to the combination of storage account performance, redundancy, and region.

Security

Configure security settings that impact your storage account.

Require secure transfer for REST API operations ⓘ   ☑

Allow enabling anonymous access on individual containers ⓘ   ☐

Review   < Previous   Next : Networking >

24. Once validated, select **Create**.

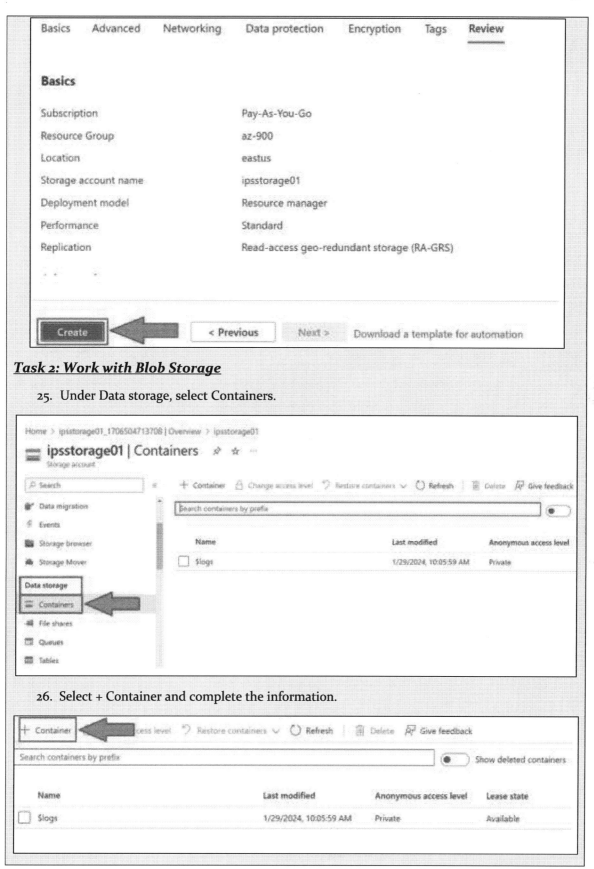

Task 2: Work with Blob Storage

25. Under Data storage, select Containers.

26. Select + Container and complete the information.

27. Select Create.

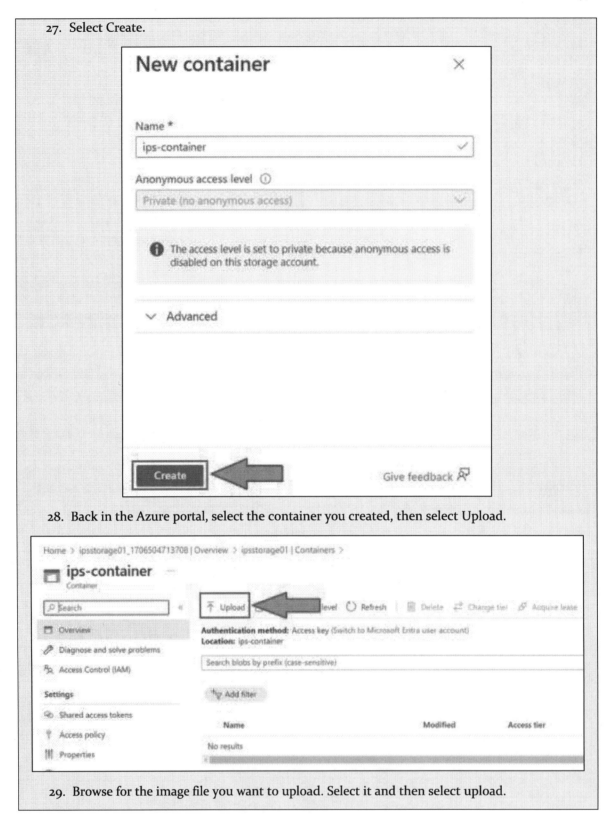

28. Back in the Azure portal, select the container you created, then select Upload.

29. Browse for the image file you want to upload. Select it and then select upload.

30. Select the Blob (file) you just uploaded. You should be on the properties tab.

31. Copy the URL from the URL field and paste it into a new tab.

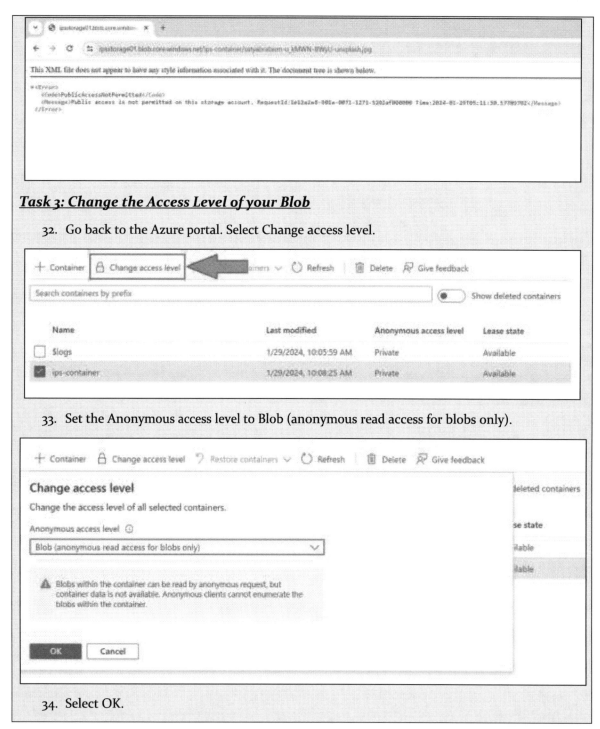

Task 3: Change the Access Level of your Blob

32. Go back to the Azure portal. Select Change access level.

33. Set the Anonymous access level to Blob (anonymous read access for blobs only).

34. Select OK.

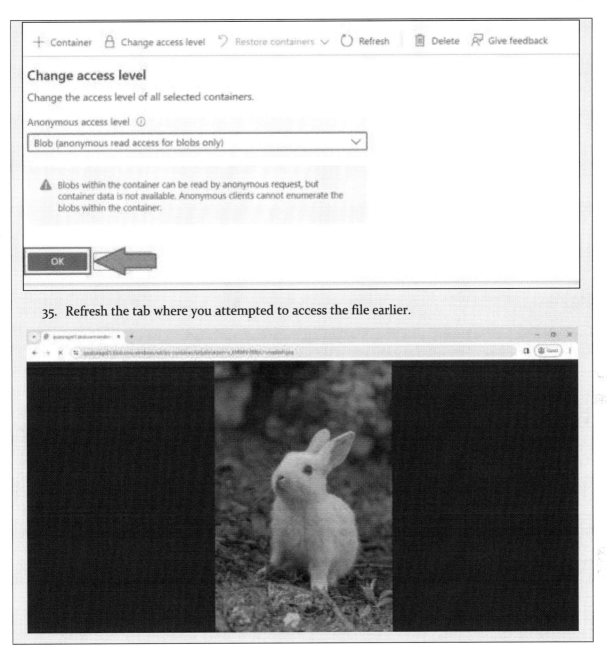

35. Refresh the tab where you attempted to access the file earlier.

Mind Map

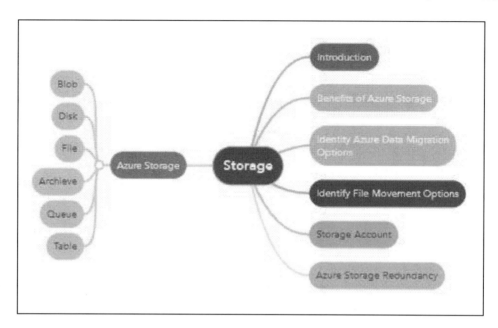

Figure 4-09: Mind Map

Practice Questions

1. To create a VM, you need a storage service that stores the data of a VM disk. Which storage option should you use?
A. Blob
B. File
C. Queue
D. Disk

2. In a blob container, what type of data can you store?
A. Only known binary format
B. Binary files that comply with the Azure data types defined for the storage type
C. Any sort of binary files
D. The binary file that is less than 500KB

3. A network drive will be mapped from multiple computers running Windows 10 to Azure Storage. You need to create a storage solution in Azure for the planned mapped drive. Which storage option is suitable for this?
A. Blob
B. File
C. Queue
D. Disk

4. From the following options, which storage is also known as Archive storage?
A. File Storage
B. Blob Storage
C. Archive its own
D. Disk Storage

5. The name must contain a capital letter and special characters when creating a storage account. True or false?
A. True
B. False

6. When creating an Azure storage account, what is the most significant?
A. The name you give the storage account becomes the main web address for accessing its files. It must be unique across all of Azure
B. The name you give the storage account becomes the main web address for accessing its files. It must be unique within your Azure subscription
C. Each storage account name is linked to a set of users that can access it
D. No significance. You can name a storage account as you want

7. Which storage solution can you use as an extension to your on-premises storage from the following options?
A. Blob
B. Queue
C. File
D. Disk

8. From the following, what are the types of disk storage? (Choose 2)
A. Slow HDD
B. Ultra Disk
C. Premium HDD
D. Standard HDD

9. In the storage account, data at rest is encrypted via RSA. True or false?
A. True
B. False

10. Which type of blob can you use to store log data?
A. Page Blob
B. Fast Blob
C. Block Blob
D. Append Blob

11. Which pricing model of blob storage can you use to store the most frequently accessed data?
A. Cold
B. Hot
C. Archive
D. All of the above

12. Which disk storage type gives super-fast and high-performance storage for critical workloads?
A. Standard HDD
B. Standard SSD
C. Premium SSD
D. Ultra Disk

13. What URL format can Blobs be accessed from?
A. http://<storage account>.blob.core.windowsazure.net/<container>/<blob>
B. http://<storage account>.core.windows.net/<container>/<blob>
C. http://<storage account>.blob.core.windows.net/<container>/<blob>
D. http://<storage account>.core.windowsazure.net/<container>/<blob>

14. Before using any Azure Storage option, you must create a storage account first. True or false?

A. True
B. False

15. The maximum size of data that you can store in block blob storage is _____.
A. 10TB
B. 15TB
C. 45TB
D. 4.7TB

Chapter 05: Databases

Introduction

In modern business, managing data is much more critical as a tremendous amount of data is collected from various sources, and you want this data stored safely in a database. Azure has a service known as Azure Databases that fulfills your business requirements. This chapter will discuss some keys that Azure databases offer, which are essential from the exam perspective. We will discuss Cosmos DB, which scales globally and is a fully managed database service. It has a fast read and write capability. Azure SQL is a managed database that will also be discussed in this chapter. We also learn about MySQL database, one of the most popular community databases. We will discuss PostgreSQL, an open-source database with some unique features.

Furthermore, we will learn about the migration of databases to Azure by using Database Migration Services. With the database, your data will be organized to get precisely the data you want within no time.

Databases

Microsoft Azure helps you unlock your potential wherever you have your data. You can support rapid growth and save innovation time by supporting open-source database engines with a secure, corporate-grade, fully managed database service. Azure provides a variety of data types and volume storage facilities. In addition, this data is available to users immediately via global connectivity. Azure helps you get it to the market quickly, distribute it widely, and handle it with ease and confidentiality no matter what you create. There are multiple Azure Database Services provided by Azure, which include:

- Cosmos DB
- Azure SQL
- Azure Database for MySQL
- Azure Database for Postgre SQL

> 💡 EXAM TIP: Users can create multiple databases on a single MySQL server, and there is no limit to the number of databases that can be created.

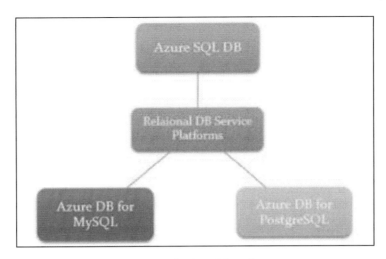

Figure 5-01: Relational Database

Cosmos DB

Cosmos DB is a global service. With Cosmos DB, you can put the data closest to the user. This is one of the key features of a great user experience. Putting the databases at multiple locations with synchronization can be a tricky thing. With Cosmos DB, Azure takes care of this synchronization. You can add your Cosmos DB to more regions with a single click. Then, Azure takes care of storing that data and keeping it in Sync with other regions. Cosmos DB's pricing depends on the throughput and consumed storage per hour.

All the data stored in Cosmos DB are encrypted at rest or in motion.

Multi-data templates can be provided with one backend. It is, therefore, ideal for documents, key values, relational, and graph models. It is a NoSQL database, more or less, because it does not rely on schemas (describes the structure of ARM templates and languages). Nonetheless, as it has SQL-like query language and can easily support ACID transactions, some people have categorized it as a NewSQL database type.

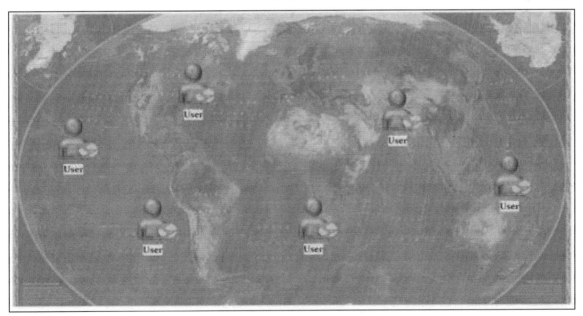

Figure 5-02: Globally Distributed

Latency

We all know that latency is the time the data takes to travel. The higher the latency, the longer the data reaches the user. With Cosmos DB, the latency is limited to a single digit millisecond (0-9) to anywhere in the world.

Scalability

With Cosmos DB, you can automatically scale your database to infinity when the requirement goes up to meet the resources. When you add more resources, there is no limit on the number of users it can support. Scaling is automatic, but you only need to pay for what you use, which means it is available at the lowest price.

Connectivity

With Cosmos DB, you can work in various ways; for example, if you are a developer, you can choose from multiple built-in ways to connect to Cosmos DB, such as SDKs or APIs. You can also use different languages such as C#, Java, or Node.js. It can also be integrated with SQL, MongoDB, or Cassandra.

EXAM TIP: A disadvantage with Cosmos DB is that it gets costly even though you have to pay for what you use. As the Cosmos DB scales up, the cost automatically increases.

When you have embedded data in Azure Cosmos DB, then treat your data as a self-contained document in JSON.

Azure SQL

Azure SQL database was launched in 1989 and is now one of the most stable products. It is a managed Azure SQL service. SQL Database can be a good choice for a wide range of hybrid cloud applications because it helps you handle relational and non-relational data structures like graphs, JSON, spatial, and XML. It is a managed Database as a Service, as another service in Azure takes care of hardware and IaaS levels. Azure SQL is on top of this and provides you with fundamental business logic and functions as per requirement. A cloud-based Database Management System (DBMS) is provided in the Microsoft Azure SQL Database. With Azure SQL, you can easily migrate your on-premises SQL database to Azure SQL and benefit from that. This is done without any code change and with a frictionless process. This technology allows on-site and cloud apps to store data in Microsoft data centers. Like other cloud-based services, a company pays for only what it requires, increasing and reducing usage and cost as per requirements. Therefore, a cloud service helps capital expenditure, such as storage and DBMS investment, translate into operating costs. With Azure SQL, you can store 100TB of data within a minute.

Integration with ML

With Azure SQL, you can also use integrated Machine Learning tools. Database optimization and performance improvement suggestions are given depending on the usage pattern. With ML, you get notified whenever there is degradation or anything terrible happening in your database.

Scalability

Azure SQL Database enables you to scale your database by adding more compute power (scale-up) or more database units (scale-out). As it is a cloud-based service, it also offers excellent scalability through which you get high availability. And it gives 99.995% availability.

Security

With Azure Cloud Platform, security is a built-in feature that gives you benefits in terms of the security of your data. With this service, you can get improved data security in a single glass Window, including discovery and authentication of files, vulnerability identification, and automated threat detection. You can get continuous security from the Microsoft Defender for Cloud with deeper insights.

Lab 5-01: Create Cosmos DB and SQL Database

Service Introduction

The Social Scoop, a rapidly growing social media platform, faced a data dilemma. Their existing relational database struggled to handle the explosive growth of user data, leading to sluggish performance and hindering user engagement. At the same time, their desire for real-time analytics and flexible data structures required a more agile solution.

Problem

Their relational database could not keep up with the high volume of user activity, resulting in slow loading times, lagging updates, and frustrated users. The rigid schema of their relational database limited their ability to store and analyze new data types, like user sentiment and network connections.

Solution

The Social Scoop partnered with a cloud solutions provider to implement a hybrid data solution leveraging both Azure Cosmos DB and Azure SQL Database. The Social Scoop's success demonstrates the power of a hybrid approach using Azure Cosmos DB and SQL Database. By leveraging the strengths of each service, they achieved a balance between speed, scalability, flexibility, and security, paving the way for continued growth and innovation in the competitive social media landscape.

I. Login to **Portal** and go to the "**Azure Cosmos DB**" service.

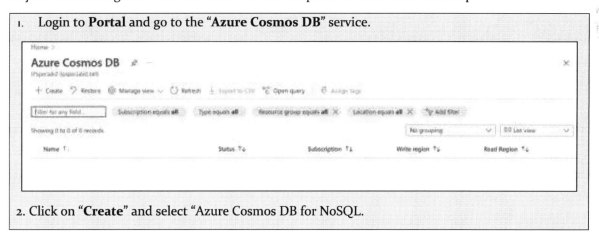

2. Click on "**Create**" and select "Azure Cosmos DB for NoSQL.

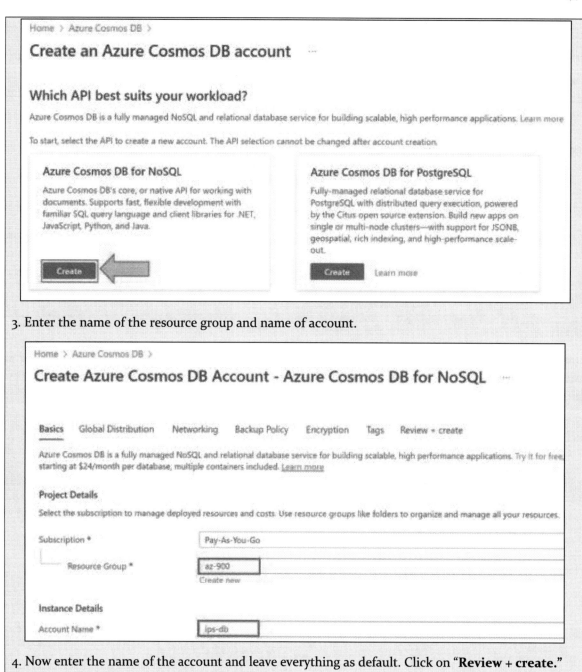

3. Enter the name of the resource group and name of account.

4. Now enter the name of the account and leave everything as default. Click on "**Review + create.**"

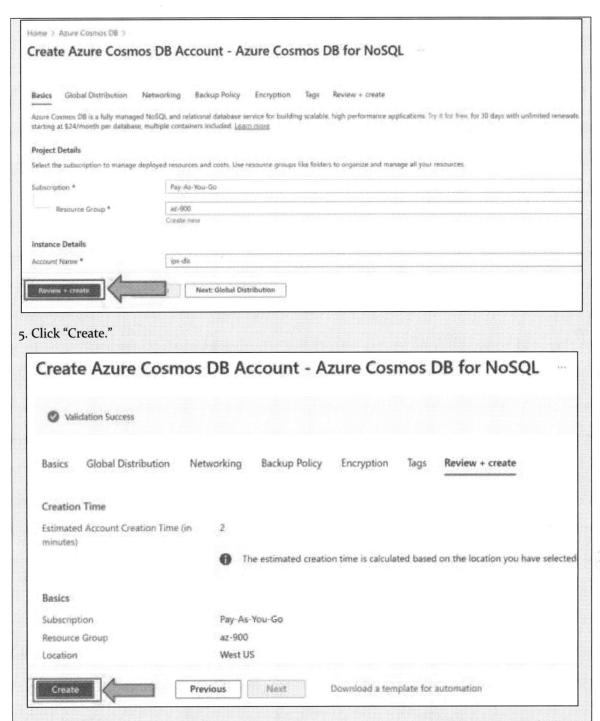

5. Click "Create."

6. Once the deployment is complete, click on **"Go to resource."** You can see the URL here, which you can use to access the data in Cosmos DB if accessing outside Azure.

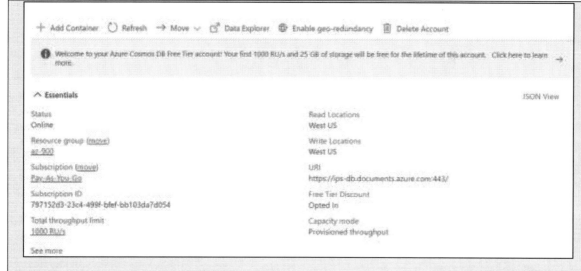

7. Now, click on "Replicate Data Globally."

8. Here, you can enable more data centers. The blue ticks on the map indicate where your actual data center is.

9. Now, click on the region where you want to replicate the data, then click **"Save."**

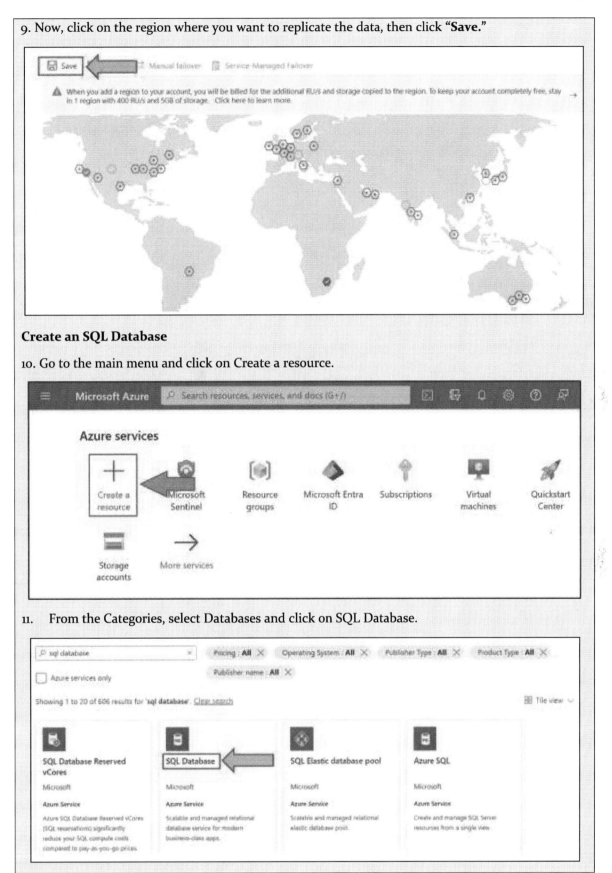

Create an SQL Database

10. Go to the main menu and click on Create a resource.

11. From the Categories, select Databases and click on SQL Database.

12. First, select your Azure subscription and resource group to configure the SQL server.

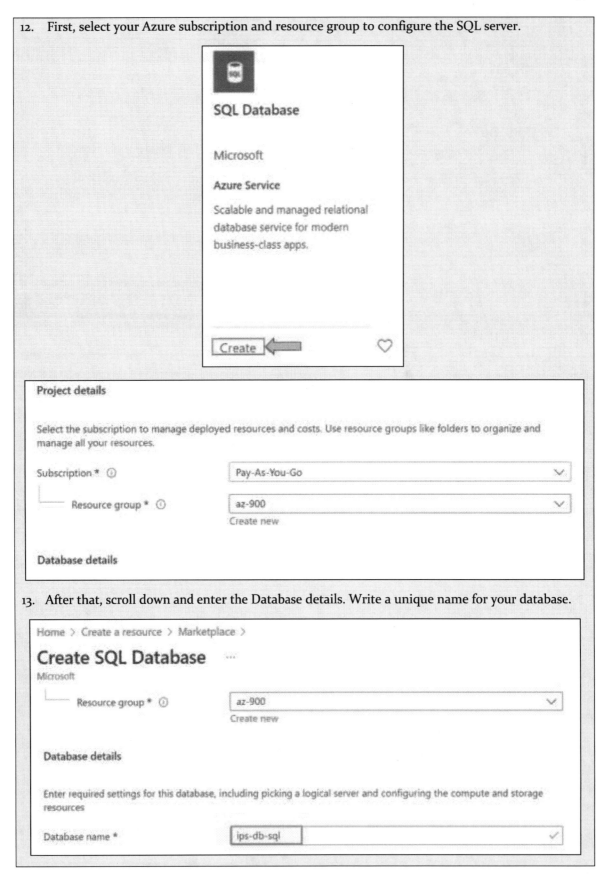

13. After that, scroll down and enter the Database details. Write a unique name for your database.

14. Click on Create new to create a new SQL server.

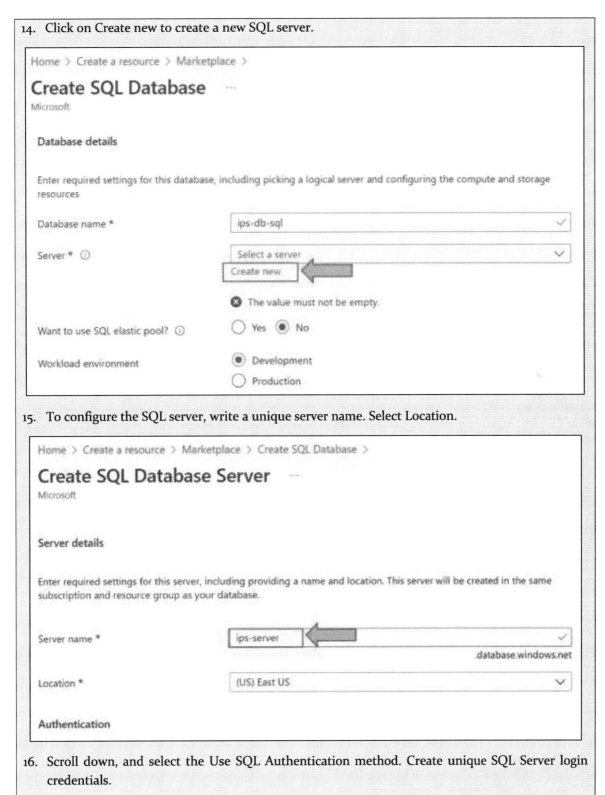

15. To configure the SQL server, write a unique server name. Select Location.

16. Scroll down, and select the Use SQL Authentication method. Create unique SQL Server login credentials.

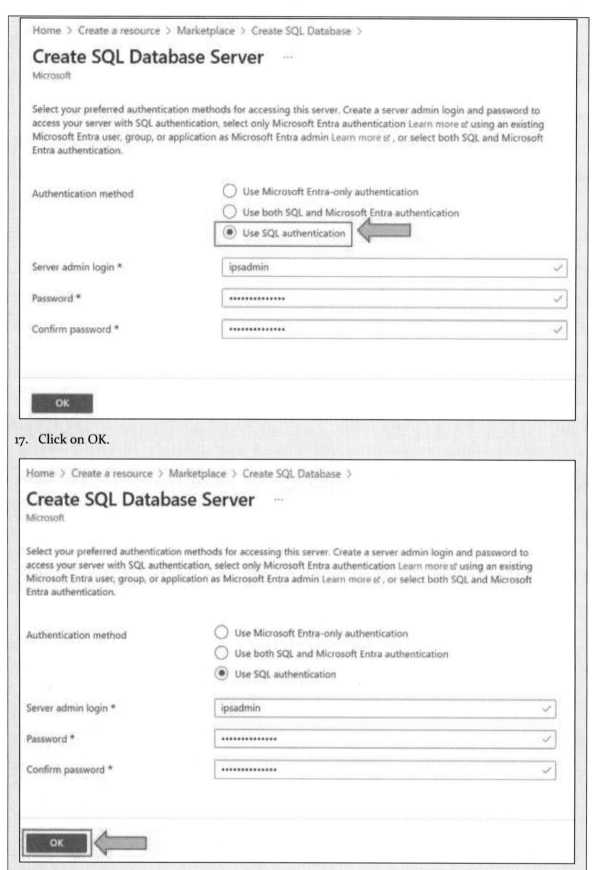

17. Click on OK.

18. Select No option for SQL elastic pool.

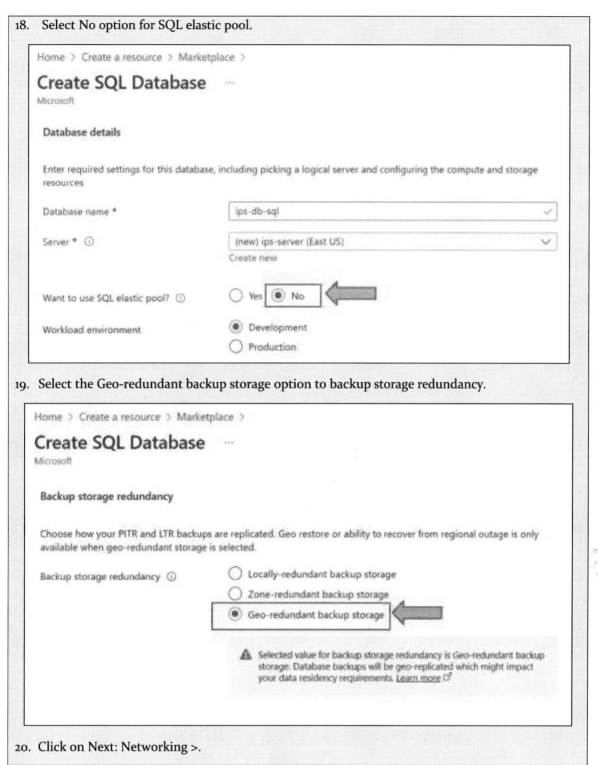

19. Select the Geo-redundant backup storage option to backup storage redundancy.

20. Click on Next: Networking >.

Home > Create a resource > Marketplace >

Create SQL Database ···
Microsoft

Backup storage redundancy

Choose how your PITR and LTR backups are replicated. Geo restore or ability to recover from regional outage is only available when geo-redundant storage is selected.

Backup storage redundancy ⓘ
- ○ Locally-redundant backup storage
- ○ Zone-redundant backup storage
- ◉ Geo-redundant backup storage

⚠ Selected value for backup storage redundancy is Geo-redundant backup storage. Database backups will be geo-replicated which might impact your data residency requirements. Learn more ☐

[Review + create]   [Next : Networking >] ⬅

21. In the Networking section, select Public endpoint for Network connectivity.

Home > Create a resource > Marketplace >

Create SQL Database ···
Microsoft

Basics   **Networking**   Security   Additional settings   Tags   Review + create

Configure network access and connectivity for your server. The configuration selected below will apply to the selected server 'ips-server' and all databases it manages. Learn more ☐

Network connectivity

Choose an option for configuring connectivity to your server via public endpoint or private endpoint. Choosing no access creates with defaults and you can configure connection method after server creation. Learn more ☐

Connectivity method * ⓘ
- ○ No access
- ◉ Public endpoint ⬅
- ○ Private endpoint

22. Select the Minimum TSL version.

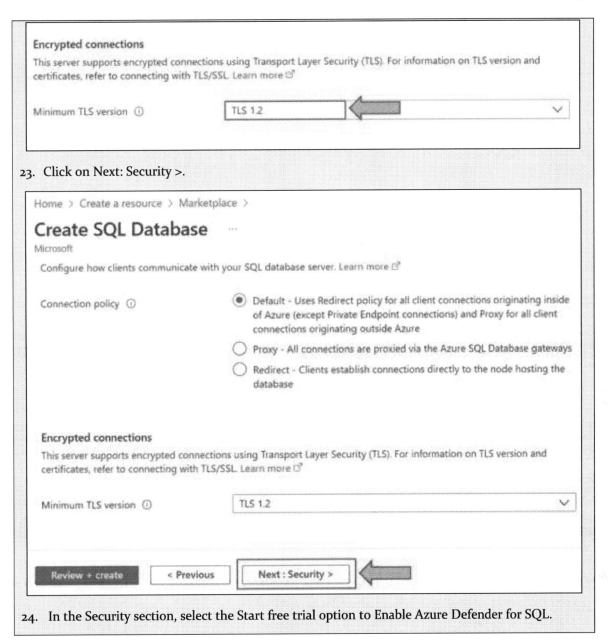

23. Click on Next: Security >.

24. In the Security section, select the Start free trial option to Enable Azure Defender for SQL.

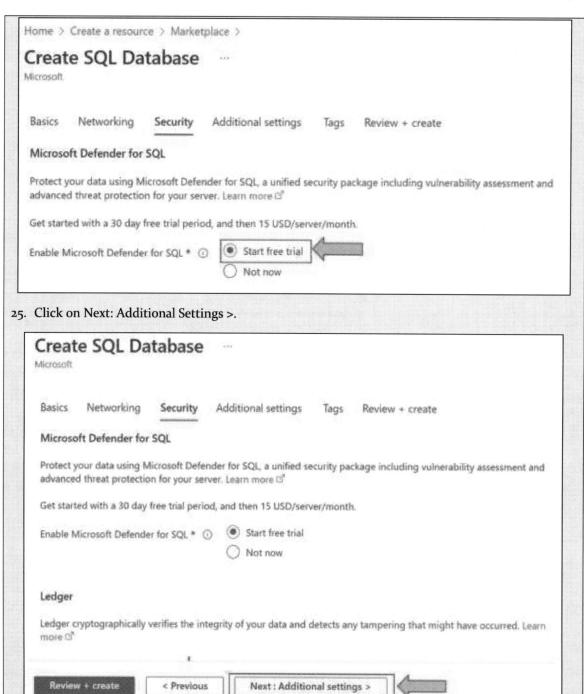

25. Click on Next: Additional Settings >.

26. In the Additional Settings section, use the Sample option for Use exiting data.

27. Click on Review + create.

28. Once the validation is passed, click on Create.

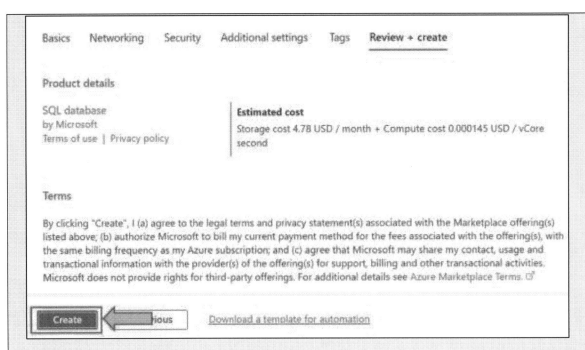

29. Verify the configuration details from the Overview page. Now, click on Set server firewall present on the top given options.

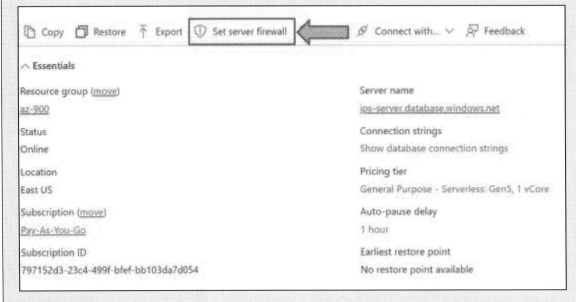

30. Select the Yes option to Allow Azure services and resources to access this server.

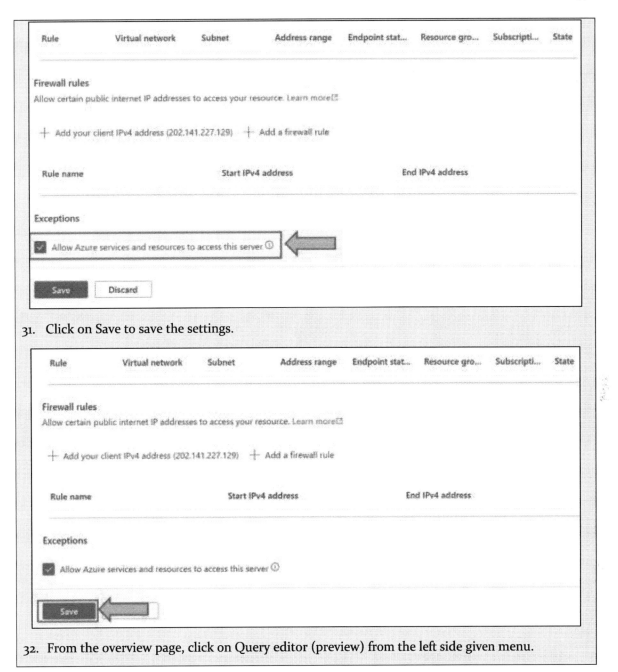

31. Click on Save to save the settings.

32. From the overview page, click on Query editor (preview) from the left side given menu.

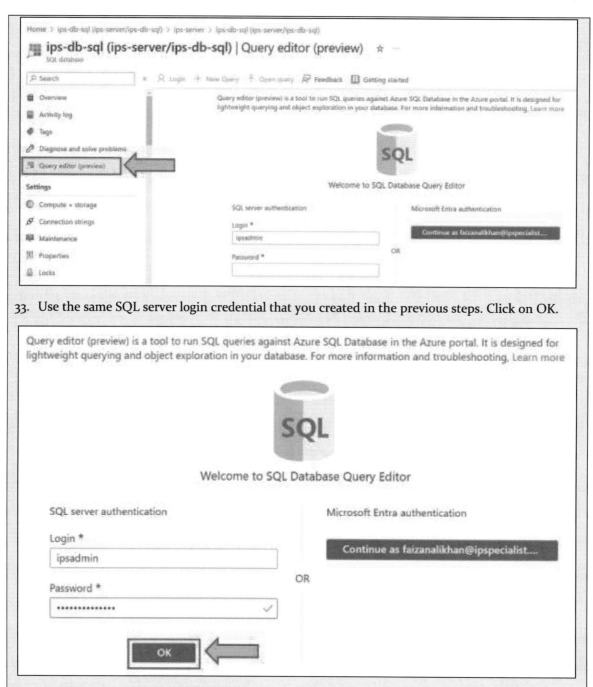

33. Use the same SQL server login credential that you created in the previous steps. Click on OK.

34. The following error will appear if your server is not allowed to access from a client IP address.

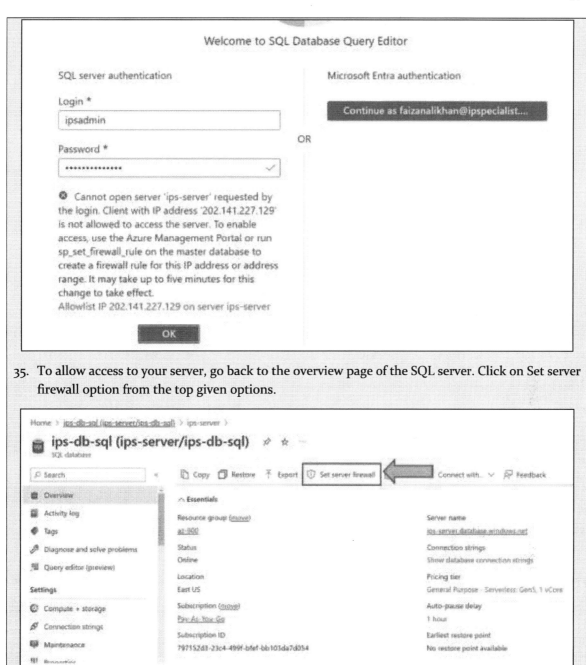

35. To allow access to your server, go back to the overview page of the SQL server. Click on Set server firewall option from the top given options.

36. Click on + Add client IP.

37. Add ClientIPAddress with the same IP address as defined in error.

38. Click on Save to save the settings.

39. Now, go to the Query editor (preview) option again and log in with the same SQL service credential.

40. The query editor will successfully open now.

41. Inside the Query 1 section, enter the following code and click on Run.

```
1  SELECT TOP 20 pc.Name as CategoryName, p.name as ProductName
2  FROM SalesLT.ProductCategory pc
3  JOIN SalesLT.Product p
4  ON pc.productcategoryid = p.productcategoryid;
```

42. Explore the results with Query succeeded statement.

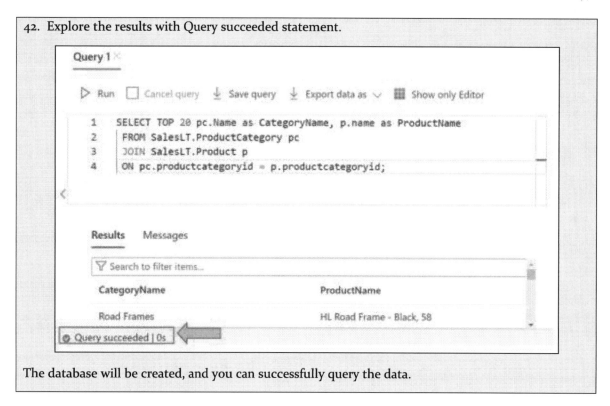

The database will be created, and you can successfully query the data.

Azure Database for MySQL

Azure Database for MySQL is the database built-in by the community, while Azure SQL is Microsoft's product. MySQL is an open-source project where anyone can contribute to the community. It is a relational database like SQL, meaning that data is related to itself or other connections via defined connections. Currently, millions of MySQL databases are used as it is a mature and proven architecture for stability.

Azure MySQL platform provides a full-managed, business-ready MySQL cloud database. The MySQL Community Version quickly upgrades and migrates into the cloud with the choice of your language and framework, of which some of the most popular are PHP or WordPress. Therefore, high flexibility and robust scaling are built to help you adapt easily to changes in customer requirements. The protection and security, including the Azure IP advantage and the leading market scope of Azure, are incomparable. With a transparent price model, you can pick services without any hidden costs for your workload. Azure Server for MySQL was designed to provide high availability with 99.99% SLA and does not require additional setup, replica features, or costs to guarantee that your apps run as necessary. It has automated batching and backup with monitoring. All of these are included without any cost.

Azure Database for MySQL is PaaS, which Microsoft manages. Using this, you can focus on developing the business strength rather than managing servers or networks.

You can also use all security features of Azure with Azure Database for MySQL, like advanced threat protection, monitoring, and identity management.

Use Cases

- Web Application
- E-Commerce

- Mobile Application
- Digital Marketing
- Finance Management
- Gaming

Azure Database for Postgre SQL

It is an open-source relational database similar to MySQL. The first version of this database is based on ingress, and the latest version can post; that is why it is named PostgreSQL. SQL is the language used to query the data in the database. PostgreSQL has been in the market since 1996, and it is free. It is a default database from MacOS. It is suitable for mission-critical workloads with predictable performance, security, high availability, and dynamic scalability. It is deployed as a single server and as a Citus cluster. The Hyperscale (Citus) choice horizontally scales queries through multiple sharding tools and offers more scaled and productive applications.

Features

- You can integrate this database with many extensions like JSONB (Binary version of JSON), geospatial functions, rich indexing, and integration with code like Ruby, Python, etc.
- With this, you can perform horizontal scaling, which gives you a very high performance to access the distributed data sets across many PostgreSQL instances. You can also scale up to 100 nodes with no application reads and writes
- The performance recommendation in this is based on the usage of data on the database. It has a feature that detects the disruptive events that affect performance on which you can perform actions
- Similar to Azure Database for MySQL, it also offers fully managed database services like automatic patching, automatic backups, and built-in monitoring

Use Cases

- Financial Applications - it is suitable for online transactions and integrates with mathematical software such as MATLAB
- For geometric data (GIS), the government mainly uses Postgres. PostGIS is the GIS extension that gives hundreds of functions to process geometric data in multiple formats
- It provides automatic failover or full redundancy, which is suitable for manufacturing purposes

Database Migration Service

We already know that we can migrate our data server, in particular Azure SQL servers, and this can be done using Database Migration Services. In Azure, you have a dedicated tool for migrating databases from on-premises to Azure. You can move your existing SQL server; there is no need to use multiple tools. To do that, you have step-by-step documentation. There is also complete documentation for non-Microsoft database migration. The Azure Server Migration Service is a fully managed program that permits smooth migration to Azure Data systems with minimal downtime from various service providers. The service is currently available in general, with ongoing efforts for growth focused on the following:

- Reliability and performance
- Addition of source/target pairs
- For friction, free migration is used for continuous investment

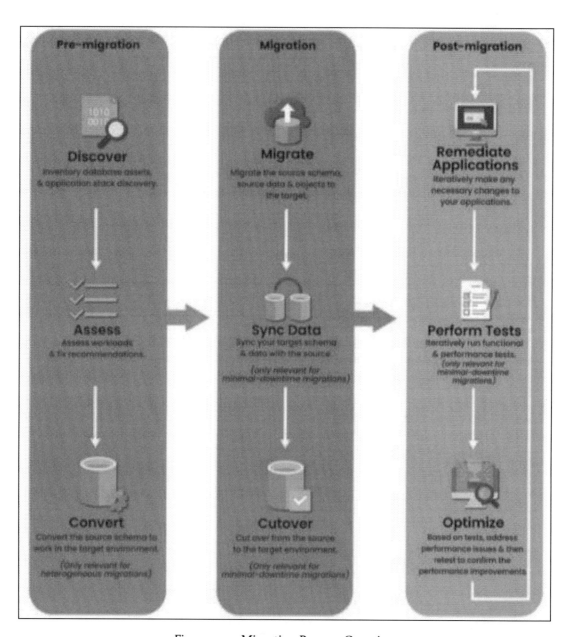

Figure 5-03: Migration Process Overview

Use Case

Consider a company that has everything on its on-premises location. The current database is Microsoft SQL. Using Database Migration Services; you can easily move your SQL server to a managed Azure SQL instance in the cloud. Similarly, if you have a MySQL server, you can also move that.

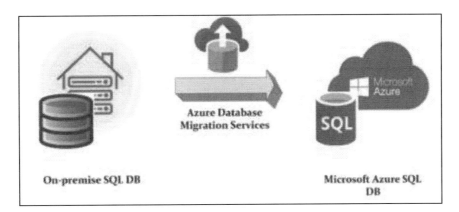

Figure 5-04: Azure DMS

Azure Big Data and Analytics

Big data is the field of technology that helps with extracting, processing, and analyzing information that is too large or complex to deal with traditional software. Therefore, Azure provides a wide range of technologies and services to handle large and complex datasets. The most commonly used services are:

- Azure Data Lake Analytics
- Azure Databricks
- Azure Synapse Analytics
- Azure HDInsights

Azure Data Lake Analytics

Azure Data Lake functions typically in two modes – data storage and data analytics. Business owners use Azure Data Lake to run big data applications. Azure Data Lake Storage is a service specifically designed for big data analytics of data stored on Azure blob storage. Data Lake Storage allows storing relational and non-relational data from any device, video, or web application.

Azure Databricks

Databricks is the data analytics service used in the cloud-based platform. Azure Databricks promises fast data transformations in the cloud, whether steam, data batch, or experiments related to data science. It also allows a collaborative working environment for data processing and implementation.

Azure Synapse Analytics

Azure Synapse is a data warehouse that blends data, big data analytics, and data integration into a unified service that provides end-to-end analytics at a cloud-scale. It stores big data with a size of petabytes and runs queries on relational and non-relational data.

Azure HDInsights

Azure HDInsights is a fully-managed open-source analytics service with many supported frameworks and tools like Hadoop, Spark, Kafka, etc. The primary purpose of this analytics service is to allow you to provision clusters with multiple services to perform a specific task efficiently.

Mind Map

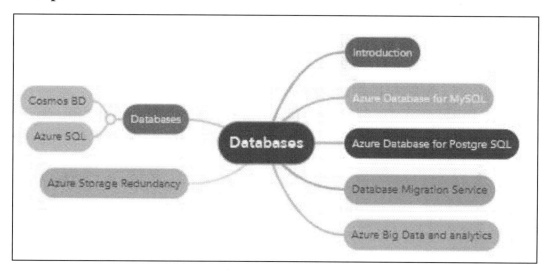

Figure 5-05: Mind Map

Practice Questions

1. Cosmos DB is a Relational DB. True or false?
A. True
B. False

2. Latency is the time taken when you keep inserting data until the complete data is uploaded. True or false?
A. True
B. False

3. How much latency is guaranteed by CosmosDB?
A. Single-digit milliseconds
B. Two-digit milliseconds
C. Single-digit second
D. Single-digit minutes

4. From the following DBs, which is best suited for migrating on-premises DB to Azure DB with all benefits?
A. Cosmos DB
B. Azure DB for MySQL
C. Azure DB for PostgreSQL
D. Azure SQL DB

5. How much data can you store with Azure SQL DB in a minute?

A. 100GB
B. 100MB
C. 100TB
D. 10TB

6. With Azure SQL DB, you can get the benefits of ML. True or false?
A. True
B. False

7. Azure DB for MySQL provides high availability with SLA _____ .
A. 99.9%
B. 99.95%
C. 99.89%
D. 99.99%

8. From the following options, which one is an open-source database in Azure?
A. Cosmos DB
B. Azure SQL
C. Azure DB for MySQL
D. None of the above

9. Azure database for MySQL is _____ , which is managed by Microsoft.
A. IaaS
B. FaaS
C. PaaS
D. SaaS

10. From the following, which one is the default database for macOS?
A. SQL
B. PostgreSQL
C. MySQL
D. None of the above

11. From the following options, which is the best reason to choose a database for data storage?
A. You can store more data in less space due to the compression algorithms used by databases
B. Databases are more secure for storing data than regular Azure Storage
C. You can manage access to data in a database more granularly than for any other type of storage
D. It is a compelling way of getting the data out in the exact format you want

12. Cosmos DB offers very low latency and can work with many tools like SDKs, APIs, etc. True or false?

A. True
B. False

13. From the following options, which are the targets for DMS?
A. HDInights
B. Azure Data Lake
C. Azure SQL
D. Microsoft SQL Server

14. How many methods of configuring Azure DB for MySQL are there?
A. 2
B. 3
C. 4
D. 5

15. From the following, which database is used for geometric data?
A. SQL
B. MySQL
C. PostgreSQL
D. All of these

16. If you want to store frequently accessed data, which data storage layer would you use?
A. Data Warehouse
B. Data Lake
C. Azure Cosmos DB
D. All of the above

17. Which of the following analytic services stores big data of petabytes?

A. Synapse
B. Data Lake
C. HDInsights
D. Databricks

Chapter 06: Authentication and Authorization

Introduction

Any technology service with IT applications that control data access from illegal users is essential to provide a secure environment. In addition, it is also very critical to find which user accesses which part of the infrastructure. This chapter will discuss the fundamentals of authentication and authorization of users in Azure. Both of them are two significant steps for ensuring network security. Authentication is a way of determining whether the user exists in the database. Once the user is found from the database user ID and password, the next step is to ensure the user can access how many services.

Authentication and Authorization in Azure includes:

- **Identity Services:** Identity services identify the platform for the user and ensure user validations for the application
- **Microsoft Entra ID:** This service can provide access and control of access to users with different directory services
- **Multi-Factor Authentication:** Provides security features by getting multiple information about the user for authentication

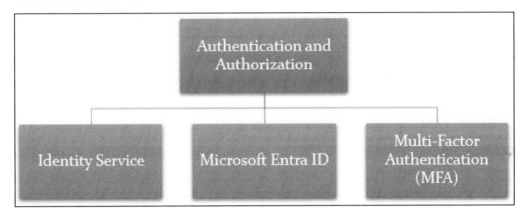

Figure 6-01: Azure Authentication and Authorization

Identity Services

When a user uses an online service with no privacy criteria, the user requires at least a username (the User ID) and password. Identity services include authentication, authorization, and access management policies.

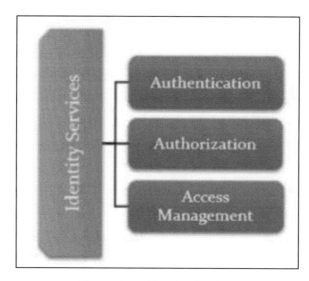

Figure 6-02: Identity Services

Authentication

Authentication is a way of identifying the user with the help of a user ID and password from the database. For example, if a user wants to use the Yahoo mail service, they cannot just access it easily by opening the Yahoo mail page. The user must have a valid ID and password to log in to the Yahoo mail page, and then they can use its services such as view Newsbeat, send an email, etc. In short, Authentication confirms the validity of the user by using their ID and password for the desired application.

Authorization

Authorization is the process that is conducted after authentication. When the user is authenticated, the next step is to find which data access is available for the authenticated user. For example, an Azure user is restricted to using limited resources and services such as SQL Database, Virtual Network, or Virtual Machine. If that Azure user tries to use those resources they are not authorized for, Azure will not give access to that resource. Likewise, if a diabetic person visits an online shopping app, the Azure service has the profile of the diabetic person. According to their profile, they are only allowed to purchase sugar-free items. That is, a person is authorized to buy only sugar-free items.

The process of identity service is clearly shown in the scenario defined in Figure 6-03.

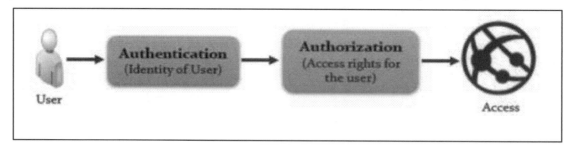

Figure 6-03: Process of Identity Management

Authentication vs. Authorization

Authentication and authorization have very little difference. The summarized table shows the difference between these two entities.

Authentication	Authorization
The first step toward accessing resources	A person can be authorized only when their authentication has been done
A way to verify the customer or user's identity	Authorization allows authenticated users to access files, databases, mail, etc.
Typically, a user can be authenticated using a user ID and password	Controls user access
Factor-based authentication is usually preferred for security purposes	Authorization is the granular part of identity services

Table 6-01: Authentication vs. Authorization

EXAM TIP: Authentication is the process of verifying users using the user ID and password. Authorization is the method of providing rights to authenticated users.

Access Management

Access management is a critical part of any cloud infrastructure as it ensures the restriction of access to service toward other users. It provides confidentiality, integrity, and availability. This means that access to any online application should be confidential for an unauthorized user and immediately available to authorized users. Access management policies should also be responsible for the following:

- **Authentication and Authorization:** The user must be authenticated first, then authorized for the particular application
- **Faraway from Unauthorized Users:** Access management policies must be designed so that no unauthorized person can access the information. Azure provides several ways to access management depending on the application.

Microsoft Entra ID

Microsoft Entra ID is the primary tool used to manage and monitor the dedicated users' information in Microsoft Azure.

Active Directory

Active Directory (AD) is a directory service created by Microsoft for storing information about users, resources, and other networked objects. Offices, educational institutions, and management departments all employ AD.

- **Limitation of Active Directory:** Active Directory provides information for authentication and authorization, but it has some limitations;
  - **Traditional Use Only:** Active Directory provides directory services for physical access only. It is most commonly used in the on-premises network
  - **Not Permitted for Web Applications:** Active Directory is not applicable to serve its services for web applications
  - **Authentication:** Active Directory provides such directory services for authentication not available on Azure

Figure 6-04 shows the conceptual view of the Microsoft Active Directory (AD) services.

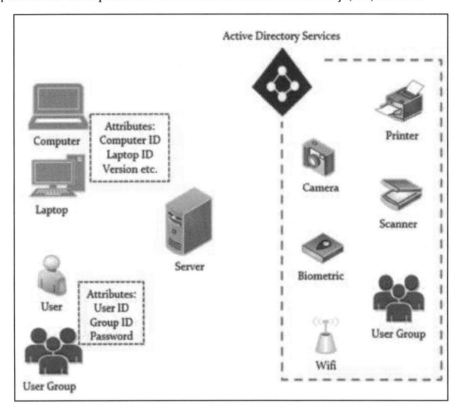

Figure 6-04: Active Directory Services

Describe Microsoft Entra ID

Microsoft Entra ID is a cloud-based identity and access management service provided by Microsoft. It enables users to sign in, access Microsoft Cloud applications, custom-developed cloud applications and assists in maintaining on-premises Active Directory deployments. The service supports IT administrators, app developers, and users, offering functions such as authentication, single sign-on, application management, and device management.

Microsoft Entra ID

Microsoft Entra ID serves as a comprehensive directory service facilitating sign-in and access to both Microsoft cloud applications and custom-developed cloud applications. It extends support for maintaining on-premises Active Directory deployments while offering cloud-based identity and access management. In essence, Microsoft Entra ID puts you in control of identity accounts, with Microsoft

ensuring global availability. For those familiar with Active Directory, Microsoft Entra ID presents a seamless transition.

Users and Usage

Microsoft Entra ID caters to a diverse user base, including IT administrators, app developers, general users, and subscribers to Microsoft 365, Microsoft Office 365, Azure, and Microsoft Dynamics CRM Online. It empowers IT administrators to control access, enables app developers to incorporate standardized functionalities, allows users to manage identities, and serves as the authentication mechanism for various Microsoft services.

Key Functions

Microsoft Entra ID delivers essential services like authentication, single sign-on (SSO), application management, and device management. Authentication encompasses identity verification, password reset, multifactor authentication, banned passwords list, and smart lockout services. SSO simplifies access across multiple applications with a single identity, while application management and device management contribute to a holistic identity and access management experience.

Connecting On-Premises AD

Microsoft Entra ID supports connecting with on-premises Active Directory, ensuring a consistent identity experience across cloud and on-premises environments. Microsoft Entra Connect facilitates the synchronization of user identities, enabling features such as SSO, multifactor authentication, and password reset under both identity systems.

Microsoft Entra Domain Services

Microsoft Entra Domain Services offers managed domain services, including domain join, group policy, LDAP, and Kerberos/NTLM authentication. This service eliminates the need to deploy, manage, and patch domain controllers in the cloud. It is particularly beneficial for running legacy applications in the cloud, providing domain services without maintaining the underlying infrastructure.

Working Mechanism

Upon creating a managed domain with Microsoft Entra Domain Services, a unique namespace (domain name) is defined. Two Windows Server domain controllers are deployed in the selected Azure region, forming a replica set. These domain controllers are fully managed by Azure, including backups and encryption at rest using Azure Disk Encryption. The managed domain performs one-way synchronization from Microsoft Entra ID to Microsoft Entra Domain Services, ensuring a smooth integration without the need for manual configuration.

Microsoft Entra ID and Microsoft Entra Domain Services collectively offer a robust identity and access management solution, supporting a wide range of users and scenarios with a focus on simplicity, security, and seamless integration.

Tenant

A tenant is the representation of an organization in Azure. A tenant is a dedicated instance of AAD service. It is the first ADD service when a user creates an account in Azure. Each AAD tenant is separate from other AAD tenants. A single user belongs to one tenant only. Each tenant contains a user or group of users. All users and tenants are a part of the AAD instance. Users may become a guest for other tenants for some duration.

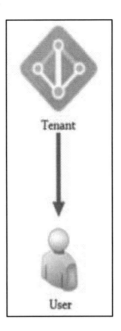

Figure 6-05: Concept of Tenant

EXAM TIP: Tenant is a particular instance of AAD. It is the first AAD instance generated when a user creates an Azure account. Each user belongs to a single tenant at a time.

Subscription

All Azure services require a subscription to access Azure resources and services.

- **Billing Entity:** All the resources used by the user in Azure are charged according to the subscription criteria
- **Cost:** A user can have multiple subscriptions within a single tenant to pay separately
- **Subscription Blockage:** The subscription of the Azure user may be blocked for a time until they pay the bills

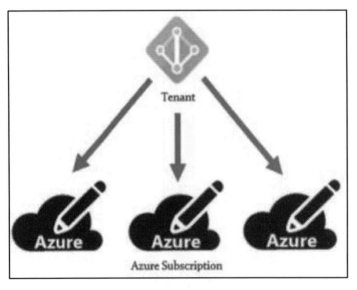

Figure 6-06: Azure Subscription

Hybrid Cloud Architecture

Within a hybrid cloud architecture, some services are on-premises, and some are hosted on the cloud. When a user wants to set the hybrid cloud infrastructure, the AAD instance can be used in hybrid cloud architecture. AAD can help users manage services on the on-premises network and the cloud. It is considered a significant part of hybrid cloud infrastructure and is allowed for any organization. There are several services that AAD uses on Azure for management purposes.

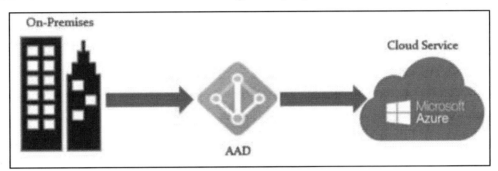

Figure 6-07: Hybrid Cloud Architecture

> 💡 EXAM TIP: Hybrid cloud architecture can be achieved using an AAD instance, which connects Azure and on-premises networks.

Azure External Identities

A person, thing, service, etc., external to your business is known as an external identity. All the secure communication channels you can utilize with users outside your business are Azure AD External Identities. You can share your resources and specify how internal users can access other businesses if you wish to work with partners, distributors, suppliers, or vendors. Developers who make consumer-facing apps have control over their users' identity experiences.

Single sign-on may sound similar to external identities. External users can "bring their own identities" with the help of External Identities. They can sign in using their credentials regardless of whether they have a digital identity granted by a company, the government, or an unmanaged social identity like Google or Facebook. To safeguard your resources, the external user's identity provider handles their identity while you control access to your apps using Azure AD or Azure AD B2C.

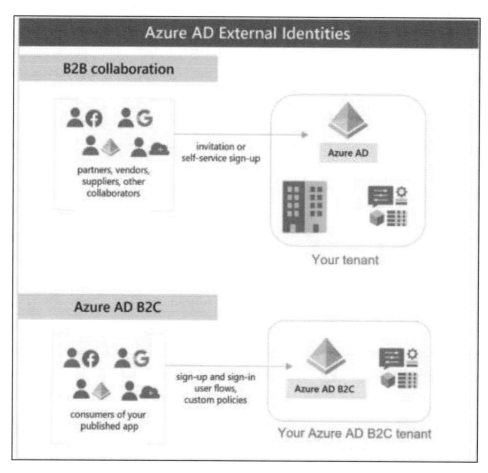

Figure 6-08: Azure AD External Identities

External Identities include the following abilities:

- **Business-to-business (B2B) collaboration** - Enable external users to sign in to your Microsoft applications or other enterprise applications using their preferred identity (SaaS apps, custom-developed apps, etc.). Users participating in B2B cooperation are represented in your directory, often as guests

- **B2B direct connect** - For smooth collaboration, create a mutual, two-way trust with another Azure AD company. Currently, Teams shared channels are supported by B2B direct connect, allowing other users to access your resources from within their personal instances of Teams. Although B2B direct connect users are not listed in your directory, they may be seen in Teams shared channels and tracked in admin center reports

- **Azure AD business to customer (B2C)** - Use Azure AD B2C for identity and access management while publishing contemporary SaaS apps or custom-developed apps (apart from Microsoft apps) to users and customers

You can employ a combination of these capabilities, depending on how you wish to communicate with other organizations and the kinds of materials you need to share.

Using the Azure AD B2B functionality, you can quickly allow collaboration across organizational boundaries with Microsoft Entra ID (Azure AD). Administrators or other users may invite visitors from other tenancies. Additionally, social identities like Microsoft accounts are covered by this feature.

Additionally, it is simple to guarantee that visitors have the proper access. You can ask the visitors to take part in an access review and recertify (or testify) to the visitors' access, or you can ask a decision maker. Based on recommendations from Azure AD, the reviewers can offer their opinions regarding each user's necessity for continued access. Once an access assessment is complete, you can make adjustments and deny access to those who no longer require it.

Lab 6-01: Azure Entra ID

Service Introduction

CloudHealth, a leading cloud management platform provider, faced a growing challenge: managing complex access across multiple cloud providers and on-premises infrastructure. Their existing identity system, fragmented and manual, hindered collaboration, created security risks and slowed down onboarding.

Problem

CloudHealth's existing system relied on a patchwork of on-premises directories and disparate cloud provider solutions, making access control inconsistent and difficult to manage. The complex process of adding users and granting access hampered collaboration and slowed down new customer acquisition.

Solution

CloudHealth partnered with Microsoft to implement Azure Entra ID, a comprehensive identity and access management (IAM) solution, as their single source of truth for user identities and access control. Azure Entra ID consolidated all identities, from employees to partners, into a single, centralized platform, simplifying management and access control.

Task 1: Create Azure Entra ID

1. Log in to the **Microsoft Azure** portal and go to the portal menu.

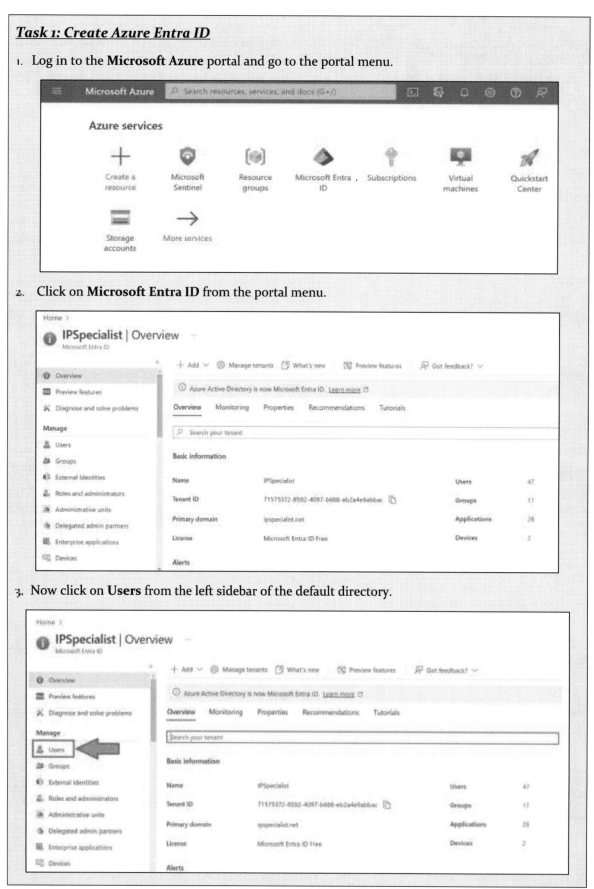

2. Click on **Microsoft Entra ID** from the portal menu.

3. Now click on **Users** from the left sidebar of the default directory.

4. The **Users** tab displays the list of all users currently in the tenant.

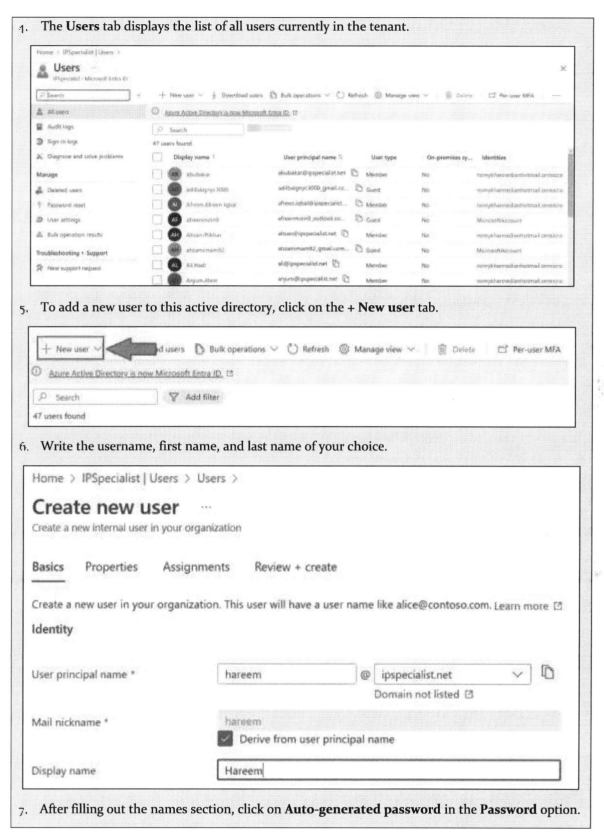

5. To add a new user to this active directory, click on the **+ New user** tab.

6. Write the username, first name, and last name of your choice.

Home > IPSpecialist | Users > Users >

Create new user   ...

Create a new internal user in your organization

Basics   Properties   Assignments   Review + create

Create a new user in your organization. This user will have a user name like alice@contoso.com. Learn more ☑

Identity

User principal name *	hareem	@	ipspecialist.net
			Domain not listed ☑
Mail nickname *	hareem		
	☑ Derive from user principal name		
Display name	Hareem		

7. After filling out the names section, click on **Auto-generated password** in the **Password** option.

Home > IPSpecialist | Users > Users >

Create new user ...

Create a new internal user in your organization

Basics   Properties   Assignments   Review + create

Create a new user in your organization. This user will have a user name like alice@contoso.com. Learn more

Identity

User principal name *   hareem   @   ipspecialist.net   ⌄   ⟐

Domain not listed

Mail nickname *   hareem

☑ Derive from user principal name

Display name   Hareem

Password *   ••••••••••   👁   ⟐

☑ Auto-generate password ⬅

Account enabled ⓘ   ☑

8. Then, click **Create.**

Home > IPSpecialist | Users > Users >

Create new user ...

Create a new internal user in your organization

Basics   Properties   Assignments   **Review + create**

Basics

User principal name   hareem@ipspecialist.net ⟐

Display name   Hareem

Mail nickname   hareem

Password   ••••••••••   👁

Account enabled   Yes

Properties

User type   Member

Assignments

[Create] ⬅   [< Previous]   [Next >]

9. After clicking **Create,** the notification of "Successfully created user" will appears.

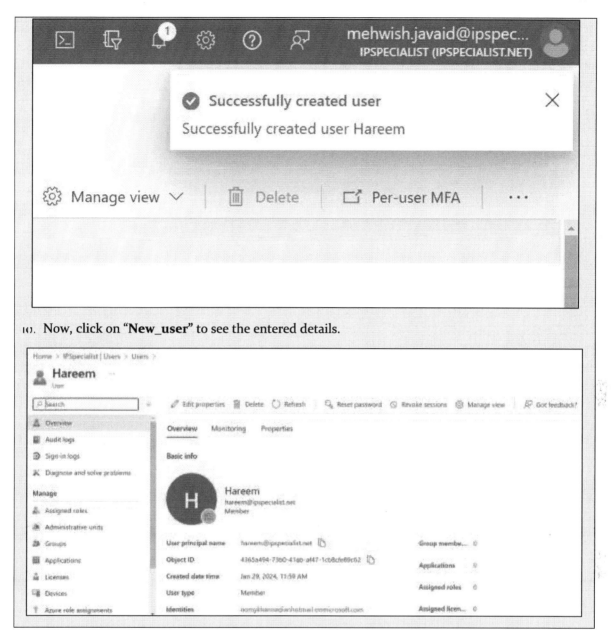

₍₄₎. Now, click on **"New_user"** to see the entered details.

Multi-Factor Authentication

Multi-Factor Authentication (MFA) provides a layer-based authentication using more than one form of authentication. This means if attackers compromise one, then they will still not be able to get in. MFA is recommended as a default. It is a part of AAD that enables other ways to authenticate users. MFA is needed in organizations that have a large number of users, devices, and resources. To avoid any collapse of security breach, extra security is required for protection and efficient throughput.

<u>How does an MFA Work?</u>

Multi-Factor Authentication (MFA) conducts the user's authentication in multiple steps. The first step is to verify the user with a user ID and password. The second step is to send a code to the user's phone for further verification. The third step is biometric verification. This step is optional.

For example, Azure users want to log in to the online booking web app. Many already access that web application due to its efficient throughput and fast response. Using MFA, the simplest way to use the application, requires the user to enter a user ID and password for verification. Once a user correctly enters the ID and password, the second step of MFA verification is to confirm the user's credentials from the database by sending a code to the user's phone. A combination of numbers in the form of a code is sent to the user's phone to confirm the user. When the user gets the code, they must put it in the given area to confirm the validity. Once the code is entered, the authentication of the user is complete. Another way to authenticate the user is biometric verification, but this step is only needed for highly advanced security purposes. Figure 6-09 shows the layer-based services offered by MFA.

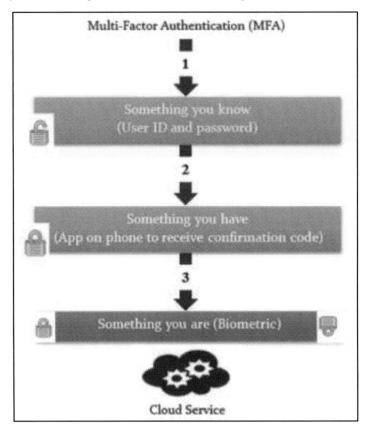

Figure 6-09: Multi-Factor Authentication

> **EXAM TIP**: Multi-Factor Authentication (MFA) provides a combined version of authentication that results in an advanced level of security and protection.

Conditional Access

Microsoft Entra ID employs Conditional Access to enable (or restrict) access to resources based on identification signals. These signals include the user's identity, location, and the device from which the user is seeking access.

IT administrators benefit from Conditional Access in the following ways:

- Allow users to be productive wherever and at any time

- Safeguard the company's assets
- Users can also enjoy a more granular multifactor authentication experience with Conditional Access. For example, if a user is at a known location, they may not be asked for a second authentication factor. If their sign-in signals are uncommon or they are at an exceptional location, they may be asked for a second authentication factor

Uses of Conditional Access

- To gain access to the application, you must use multifactor authentication
- Requires only approved client applications to gain access to services
- Requires users to use only managed devices to access your app
- Access from untrustworthy sources, such as unknown or unexpected locations, is blocked

Lab 6-02: Multi-Factor Authentication

Service Introduction

Azure Multi-Factor Authentication (MFA) is a security feature provided by Microsoft Azure that adds an extra layer of protection to user logins. By requiring users to verify their identity through a second authentication method beyond just a password, such as a phone call, text message, or mobile app notification, Azure MFA significantly enhances the security posture of applications and resources. This additional layer helps safeguard against unauthorized access, even if passwords are compromised. Azure MFA can be easily integrated with various Azure services, applications, and on-premises resources, providing a flexible and comprehensive solution for organizations aiming to strengthen their authentication mechanisms and protect sensitive data from unauthorized access.

Problem

The organization has recently shifted its resources from on-premises to the Azure cloud platform. The security and access management department wants to use a service that keeps things simple for users while securing access to data and apps. How would it be possible?

Solution

Using an Azure service called Multi-Factor Authentication (MFA), the organization can easily fulfill the requirement to safeguard access to data and apps. MFA also delivers robust authentication using various simple validation methods and adds security by requiring a second form of verification.

Task: Multi-Factor Authentication

1. Log in to Azure Portal using your credentials.

2. From the home page, select Azure Entra ID. The Default Directory Overview page will appear.

3. From the left side given menu, click on Security under Manage.

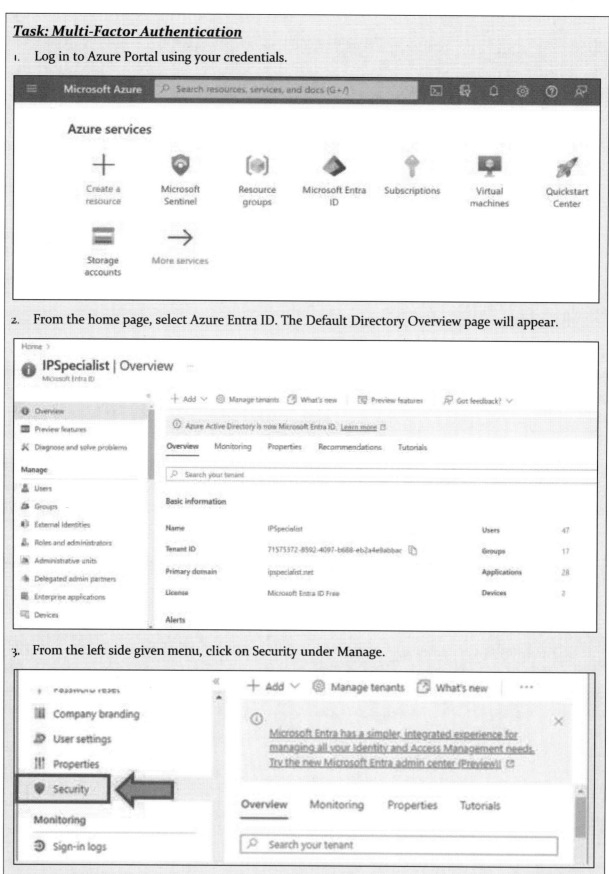

1. From the Getting Started page, select Conditional Access present inside Protect.

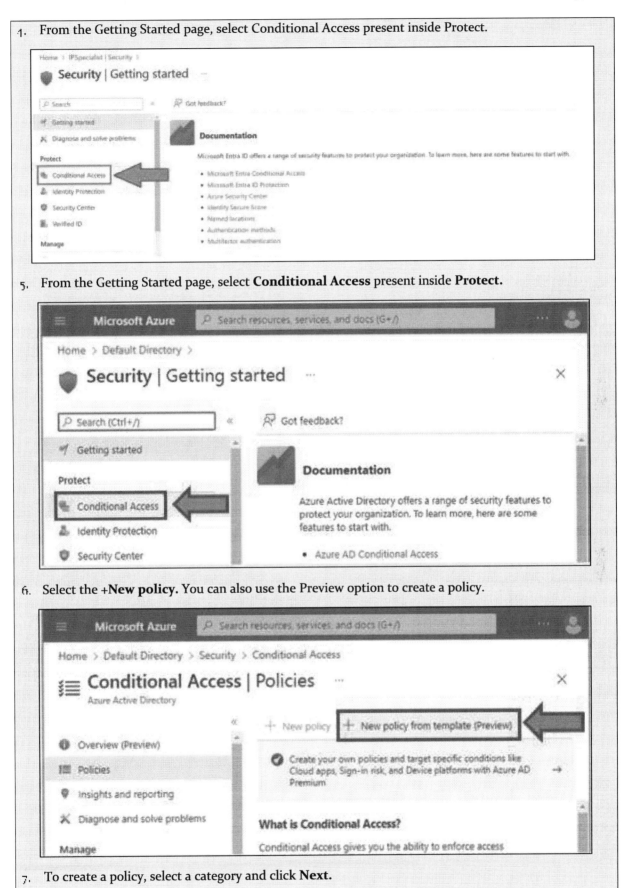

5. From the Getting Started page, select **Conditional Access** present inside **Protect.**

6. Select the +**New policy.** You can also use the Preview option to create a policy.

7. To create a policy, select a category and click **Next.**

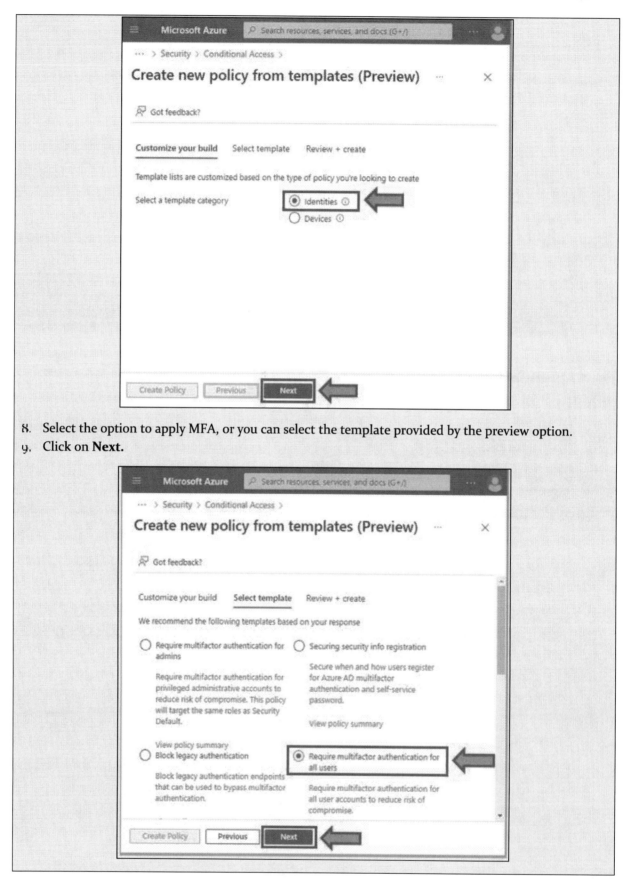

8. Select the option to apply MFA, or you can select the template provided by the preview option.
9. Click on **Next.**

Note: Here, we are enabling MFA for all users.

10. After reviewing the settings, click on **Create Policy.**

Note: Within a few minutes, your policy for MFA will be successfully created.

11. You can restrict access to your account by the given steps. Go to the home page and search and open **Multifactor authentication.**

12. The overview page will appear. Go to the **Block/unblock users** from the Settings section.

13. Click on +**Add** to add a user you want to block.

14. Write the User name and provide a reason to block.

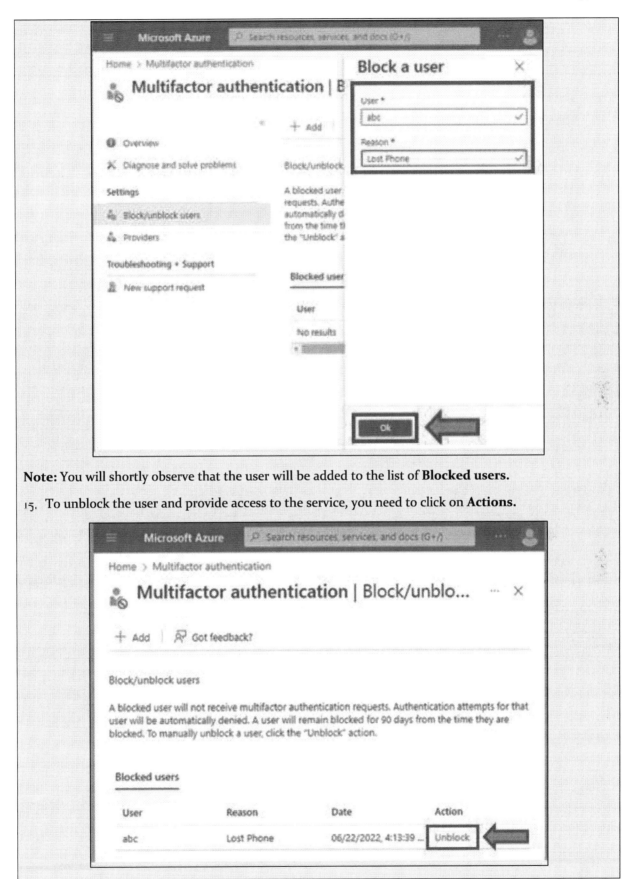

Note: You will shortly observe that the user will be added to the list of **Blocked users.**

15. To unblock the user and provide access to the service, you need to click on **Actions.**

16. Provide a reason to unblock the user and click on **OK**.

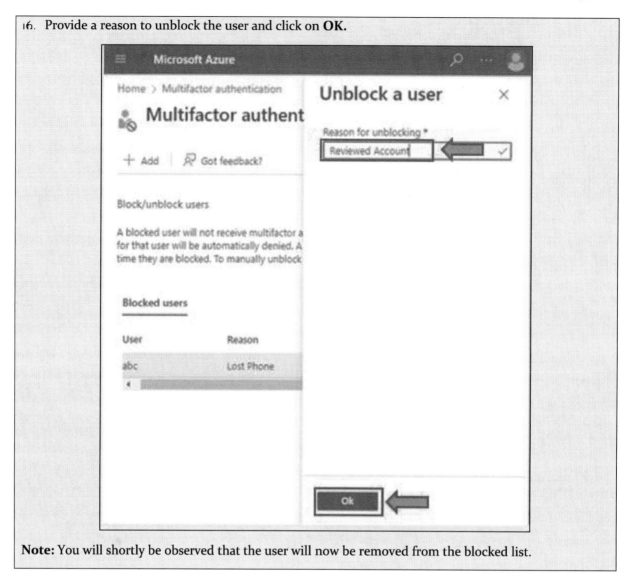

Note: You will shortly be observed that the user will now be removed from the blocked list.

Mind Map

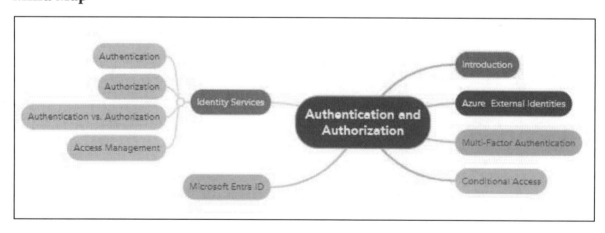

Figure 6-10: Mind Map

Practice Questions

1. Which service is responsible for providing a platform to users for verification?
A. Identity Services
B. Authentication
C. Microsoft Entra ID
D. Multi-Factor Authentication (MFA)

2. The two primary steps toward a secure environment in Azure are _____.
A. Encryption and Decryption
B. Authentication and Authorization
C. Authentication and Encryption
D. All of the above

3. Identity service is responsible for which one of the following?
A. Managing the traffic load
B. Routing Services
C. Subscription and Directory
D. Access Management

4. The identity of a user is called _____.
A. Authorization
B. User profile
C. Authentication
D. None of the above

5. Which term allows an authenticated user to access data?
A. Authentication
B. Authorization
C. Security
D. Microsoft Entra ID

6. Which principle is followed by MFA for providing an advanced level of security?
A. Something you know, you have, you are
B. The code of 6 letters
C. Non-repudiation
D. Keystroke Monitoring

7. The user cannot be authorized until the user has gone through the process of _____.
A. Modulation
B. Encryption
C. Authentication

D. Data Diddling

8. What is the first AAD instance after creating an account in Azure?
A. Tenant
B. Credential
C. Proxy Server
D. None of the above

9. Which directory service is commonly used in traditional offices?
A. AWS Directory Service
B. Google Directory Service
C. Microsoft Directory Service
D. Opera Directory Service

10. If a user has some data on Azure cloud and some present on the on-premises network, which service enables us to build a hybrid cloud architecture?
A. Content Delivery Network (CDN)
B. Multi-Factor Authentication (MFA)
C. Azure DNS
D. Microsoft Entra ID

11. How many authentication ways are provided by MFA?
A. Only one
B. Two or more
C. At least four
D. Depending on the security requirement

12. Which of the following is a granular part of the identity service?
A. Active Directory (AD)
B. Tenant
C. Authorization
D. Cipher key

13. How is AAD different from AD?
A. AD is unable to provide service to web apps
B. Both directory services are the same
C. AAD is easy to use
D. All of the above

14. If the subscription charges are not paid in time, the user will not be able to use Azure resources. True or false?
A. True
B. False

15. Which of the following type of authentication processes are present in MFA?
A. Binary codes
B. Use of the alphabet only
C. The user must say "Security."
D. Biometric

16. Which of the following is responsible for restricting access to the data to unauthorized users?
A. Authorization
B. Access Management
C. Traffic Manager
D. None of the above

17. Which of the following is considered a compulsory service within Azure?
A. Multi-Factor Authentication
B. Azure DNS
C. Microsoft Entra ID
D. Account Creation

18. Which service is responsible for managing users' information?
A. Traffic Manager
B. Microsoft Entra ID
C. Express Route
D. Identity Service

19. Which of the following is the limitation of Microsoft Active Directory (AD)?
A. It is used for traditional offices only
B. It is unable to provide a secure environment
C. It supports administration and control
D. None of the above

20. A single user may belong to how many tenants at a time?
A. Two
B. More than five
C. Only one
D. At least three

Chapter 07: Azure Core Solutions and Management Tools

Introduction

Microsoft Azure is also known as Windows Azure, the public cloud-computing platform used by Microsoft. It provides various cloud services, including computing, analytics, storage, and networking. Users can build and scale new applications in the public cloud or run existing applications from these services. Microsoft Azure offers a Platform as a Service (PaaS) and an Infrastructure as a Service (IaaS).

Azure has a lot of products, features, and services. In this chapter, we will focus on some of the core products of Azure. You will learn about some of the most cutting-edge technologies available today in Azure, which includes the Internet of Things (IoT), Big Data, Artificial Intelligence (AI), serverless computing in Azure, and DevOps. These are all solutions built by Azure to solve their clients' problems.

Choosing the Best Azure IoT Service for Your Application

Internet of Things

The Internet of Things (IoT) is a collection of interconnected computing devices, mechanical and digital machines, objects, or individuals. All of them are equipped with Unique Identifiers (UIDs) and the ability to transfer data over a network without requiring human intervention.

Azure Internet of Things (IoT) is a collection of cloud services managed by Microsoft, connecting, monitoring, and controlling billions of IoT assets. An IoT solution comprises one or more IoT devices and one or more back-end services in the cloud that communicate with each other.

Identify the product options

IoT allows devices to collect and then deliver information for data analysis. Smart devices are decked with sensors that gather data. A few common sensors that measure attributes of the physical world are mentioned below:

- Environmental sensors that capture temperature and humidity levels
- Barcode, QR code, or Optical Character Recognition (OCR) scanners
- Geo-location and proximity sensors
- Light, color, and infrared sensors
- Sound and ultrasonic sensors
- Motion and touch sensors
- Accelerometer and tilt sensors
- Smoke, gas, and alcohol sensors
- Error sensors to identify when there is a problem with the device
- Mechanical sensors that detect anomalies or deformations
- Flow, level, and pressure sensors for measuring gasses and liquids

By utilizing Azure IoT services, devices equipped with sensors connecting to the internet could transfer their information to a specific endpoint in Azure via a message. The message's data is then gathered, aggregated, and converted into reports and alerts. On the other hand, all devices could be modernized

with new firmware to fix issues or add new functionality by relaying software updates from Azure IoT services to each device.

Many services can support and drive end-to-end solutions for IoT on Azure.

IoT Services

There are many IoT-related services that Azure offers to help you out. Two of the main IoT services are described here.

IoT Hub

IoT Hub is a cloud-hosted, managed service that serves as a central hub to collect all devices' data feeds. It is for bi-directional communication between your IoT application and the devices it manages. Using Azure IoT Hub, you can build IoT systems with efficient and secure communication between millions of IoT devices and a cloud-hosted back-end solution. Virtually any computer can be connected to an IoT Hub.

As we know, it supports bi-directional communication from cloud to device and device to cloud. IoT Hub monitoring helps you keep your solution healthy by tracking actions such as device creation, device failures, and device connections.

IoT Hub's features enable you to create scalable, full-featured IoT applications for operating industrial equipment in manufacturing, tracking precious healthcare assets, and monitoring office building usage.

 EXAM TIP: IoT Hub can receive and manage data from millions and even billions of devices.

IoT Hub Features

- **Scaling:** IoT Hub scales to millions of connected devices simultaneously and millions of events per second to support your IoT workloads
- **Securing**: IoT Hub gives you a secure communication channel for your devices to send data
- **PaaS**: It is a Platform as a Service in Azure
- **Integrating**: To build complete, end-to-end solutions, you can integrate the IoT Hub with other Azure services
- **Ease of Deployment:** With an array of built-in features, you can control your devices connected to an IoT Hub

Microsoft Raspberry Pi Simulator

Microsoft has launched a Raspberry Pi Azure IoT online simulator to connect the devices to the Azure IoT Hub.

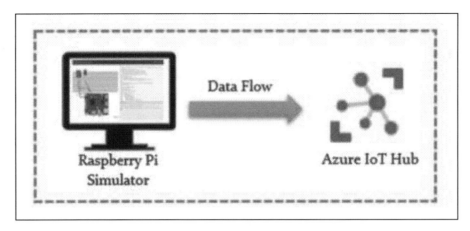

Figure 7-01: Connect Raspberry Pi to IoT Hub

This online simulator is a core tool with three main areas. These are:

- Assembly Area
- Coding Area
- Integrated Console Window

Assembly Area

This area defines the default circuit consisting of a pressuring temperature humidity sensor wired into the virtual Raspberry Pi and a little LED, as shown in Figure 7-02.

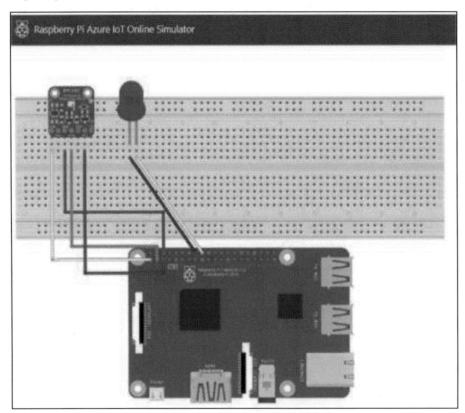

Figure 7-02: Raspberry Pi Simulator-Assembly Area

Coding Area

The coding area contains the built-in code that will connect to an IoT Hub device and send telemetry data and messages.

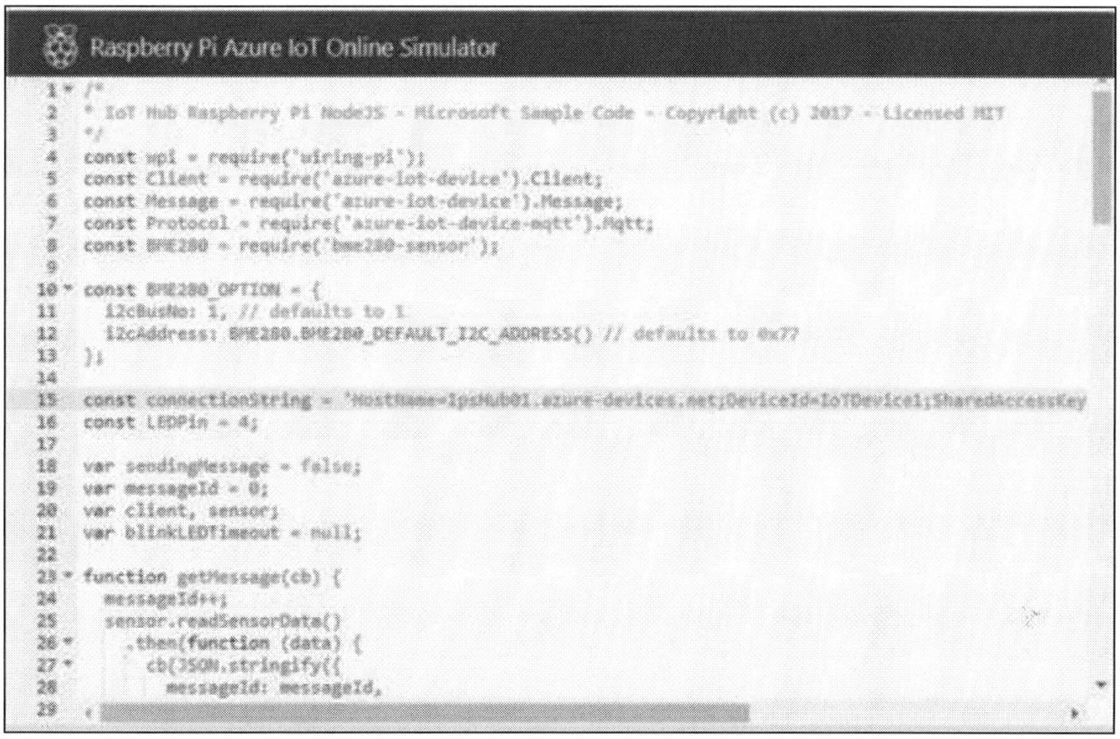

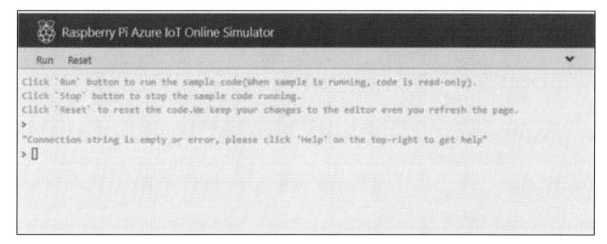

Figure 7-03: Raspberry Pi Simulator-Coding Area

Integrated Console Window

The third area of this online simulator is the command window that shows the output by running the commands. Initially, when you run the command window, you must enter the Azure IoT Hub device connection string.

Figure 7-04: Integrated Console Window

IoT Central

Azure IoT Central is a fully managed, highly scalable IoT SaaS solution that simplifies enterprise-grade IoT systems' development, management, and maintenance. Because it is built using Azure IoT Central, you can focus your time, money, and energy on transforming your company with IoT data rather than on maintaining and upgrading a complicated and continuously evolving IoT infrastructure, as it does not require code to deploy. You will find pre-made connectors in this section that you may utilize in IoT Central.

Its user-friendly interface allows easy monitoring of device requirements, developing guidelines, and managing millions of devices and their data over their life cycle. Additionally, it enables you to act on device insights by extending IoT intelligence into line-of-business applications.

> **EXAM TIP:** IoT Central is a Software as a Service (SaaS) offering templates and dashboards for a quick start.

Therefore, in short, we can say that to start an IoT project, there are two ways: IoT Hub, which is the solution where you need more control over the IoT process, which means collecting and processing. At the same time, IoT Central is the solution that provides all the dashboards your infrastructure needs to create an IoT solution without any cloud or IoT knowledge.

Azure Sphere

For customers, Azure Sphere creates an end-to-end, exceptionally secure IoT solution that includes everything from the device's hardware and operating system to the dependable process of sending messages from the device to the message hub. For internet-connected devices, Azure Sphere provides built-in communication and security features.

Azure Sphere has three parts:

- The first part is the Azure Sphere Micro-Controller Unit (MCU), which is qualified for processing the operating system and signals from attached sensors.
- The second part is a customized Linux Operating System (OS) that manages communication with the security service and can execute the vendor's software.
- The third part is Azure Sphere Security Service, also identified as AS3. Its function is to ensure the device has not been maliciously jeopardized. When the device attempts to connect to Azure, it must first verify itself, per device, by applying certificate-based authentication; if it validates successfully, AS3 checks to guarantee that the device has not been tampered with. After it has confirmed a secure communication channel, AS3 pushes any OS or authorized customer-developed software updates to the device.

After the Azure Sphere system has verified the device's authenticity and confirmed it, it can communicate with other Azure IoT services by transferring telemetry and error information.

Azure IoT Edge

Azure IoT Edge is the cloud-based computing service used to manage and ensure the smooth running of workflow on the edge device. It enables moving cloud analytics and custom business logic to IoT devices. The device can easily process logic directly without pushing data to the cloud.

Functions of Azure IoT Edge

There are several functions of Azure IoT Edge that enable us to:

Fast Communication – The Azure IoT Edge can connect the IoT Hub to the edge device by running the functionality built at the edge. The device will take less time communicating with the edge device and ensure low latency and response time.

Monitor Edge Devices – Azure IoT Edge has a cloud interface and a runtime workflow that lets you control and monitor remotely and easily deliver computing workloads to the edge device through IoT Hub.

Distribute AI and Analytics Workloads – IoT Edge provides easy deployment of runtime modules using Artificial Intelligence and machine learning to run them on edge devices.

Reduce Costs – IoT Edge controls and minimizes costs using filtered data for future analysis. This approach reduces response time and storage costs as well.

Supports Multiple Languages – IoT Edge allows using existing developer skill sets and offers multiple programming languages, like C, C#, Node.js, Java, etc., to run the modules on the edge devices.

Provide an Extra Level of Security – IoT Edge uses various security modules to implement secure and sensitive computing and uses Microsoft Defender for Cloud to ensure the threat protection of end devices.

Operate in Offline Mode – IoT Edge also enables intermittent and offline connectivity between the cloud and edge device and provides functionalities to deliver the computing workloads reliably.

Function as a Gateway – The main advantage of the IoT Edge is that it can efficiently work as a protocol gateway that enables the custom and cloud logic on the edge device.

Working of IoT Edge

The structure of Azure IoT Edge consists of three components. These are:

- IoT Edge Modules
- IoT Edge Runtime
- IoT Edge cloud Interface

IoT Edge Modules

The IoT Edge modules are the units that consist of custom logic or cloud logic like Azure Functions, Azure Stream Analytics, and Azure Machine Learning. These modules can be run with the compatible Docker container if required. They are deployed to the IoT edge devices, and each module executes locally on these devices. You can also create such modules that can easily communicate with each other for data processing.

IoT Edge Runtime

The IoT Edge runtime enables custom logic and cloud logic on the IoT Edge device. It is located on the edge device and executes management and communication operations. It also ensures the state of IoT Edge modules and continuously reports the module's health to the cloud.

The Azure "IoT Edge on Ubuntu" virtual machine is an example of an IoT device. Usually, the Azure IoT devices have IoT Edge runtime installed. The Edge runtime consists of different programs that turn a

device into an Azure IoT Edge device. The runtime is responsible for receiving the program code at the edge and communicating the devices with Azure IoT Hub.

IoT Edge Security Daemon

The background handling procedure starts and bootstraps an IoT Edge device by executing the Azure IoT Edge agent.

IoT Edge Agent

Azure IoT Edge agent is a runtime component of Azure IoT Edge. It smoothly deploys and monitors the modules built in the Azure IoT Edge devices with Azure IoT Hub.

IoT Edge Hub

This component manages and controls the communication between the modules or pre-built modules on the edge devices and between the device and Azure IoT Hub.

The other functions performed by the IoT Edge runtime are:

- Install and update the workloads
- Maintain the IoT Edge underlying security standards
- Control and monitor the communication between downstream devices to the Azure IoT Hub
- Connect to the Azure IoT Hub to facilitate the communication between the edge devices and Azure cloud

Analyze the Decision Criteria

This section will examine experts' guidelines when determining which IoT service to employ for a business requirement. Knowing the criteria can also assist us in better understanding the nuanced distinctions between each product.

Is it critical to ensure that the device is not compromised?

No manufacturers or customers would want their devices to be maliciously jeopardized, but it is more crucial to guarantee an ATM's integrity than a washing machine. When security is a significant factor in our product's design, the most suitable product option is Azure Sphere, which provides a complete end-to-end solution for IoT devices.

As we discussed, Azure Sphere guarantees a reliable communication channel between the device and Azure by controlling everything from the hardware to the operating system and the authentication process. This ensures that the integrity of the device is uncompromised. After a reliable channel is placed, messages can be obtained from the device securely, and messages or software updates can be sent to the device remotely.

Do you need a dashboard for reporting and management?

The next decision will be based on the level of services you want from your IoT solution. Suppose you want to connect to your remote devices to obtain telemetry, occasionally push updates, and do not need any reporting functionality. In that case, you might favor performing Azure IoT Hub by itself. Your programmers can still generate a customized set of management tools and reports by using the IoT Hub RESTful API.

But, if you require a pre-built customizable user interface using which we can observe and manage our devices remotely, you may prefer to start with IoT Central. With this solution, you can control a single device or all devices simultaneously and even install alerts for specific situations, such as a device failure.

IoT Central blends with many Azure products, including IoT Hub, to produce a dashboard with reports and management characteristics. The dashboard is based on starter templates for common industry and usage scenarios. We can apply the dashboard generated by the starter template without changing or customizing it to meet our demands. We can have various dashboards and target them for a diversity of users.

Use IoT Hub

Let us consider an example; the Tailwind Traders senior leadership team has partnered with a leading appliance manufacturer to produce an elite, high-end brand that guarantees a preemptive maintenance service agreement. To create a strong brand standing, the appliances will transmit telemetry information to a centralized location, which can be examined and scheduled for maintenance. This novel characteristic would distinguish Tailwind Traders appliances in a crowded, competing market. This characteristic also makes the brand profitable because an annual subscription would be needed.

The devices will not need a remote control. They will only be transferring their telemetry data for analysis and proactive maintenance.

Because Tailwind Traders already has software for handling appliance maintenance requests, the company aspires to combine all functionality into this existing system.

Which service should you choose?

Let's implement the decision criteria we discussed previously.

First, is it critical to ensure that the device or, in this case, each appliance is not compromised? It is favored but not significant that the devices are not jeopardized. The most dangerous thing that could happen is that a hacker learns the current temperature of the customer's refrigerator or the number of laundries the washing machine has done.

A technician could reset or renew the microcontroller even if the customer calls and states unfamiliar behavior with their appliance. It might not justify the extra expense or engineering support needed to employ Azure Sphere.

Second decision criterion: do I need a dashboard for reporting and management? In this situation, no. Tailwind Traders requires to combine the telemetry data and all other functionality into an existing maintenance request system. In this circumstance, Azure IoT Central is not needed.

So, given the responses to the decision criteria, Azure IoT Hub is the most suitable choice in this situation.

Why not use Azure IoT Central?

Azure IoT Central presents a dashboard that enables companies to control IoT devices separately and aggregate, view reports, and install error notifications through a GUI. But, in this situation, Tailwind Traders wants to combine the telemetry it accumulates and other analysis functionality into an existing software application. Moreover, the company's appliances will be collecting data by sensors only and do not require the capacity to update settings or software remotely. Consequently, the company does not require Azure IoT Central.

Why not use Azure Sphere?

Azure Sphere presents a complete solution for situations where security is important. In this situation, security is favored but not significant. The appliances cannot be updated with new software remotely. The sensors list usage data. In conclusion, Azure Sphere is not required.

Use IoT Central

Let us consider an example where Tailwind Traders keeps a fleet of delivery vehicles that move products from warehouses to distribution centers to stores and homes. The company aims for a complete logistics solution that takes data shipped from an onboard vehicle computer and turns it into actionable information.

Moreover, shipments can be equipped with sensors from a third-party vendor to collect and control ambient conditions. These sensors can accumulate information such as temperature, humidity, tilt, shock, light, and shipment location.

A few objects of this logistics system are as follows:

- Shipment monitoring with real-time tracing and tracking
- Shipment integrity with real-time ambient condition monitoring
- Protection from theft, loss, or damage of shipments
- Geo-fencing, route optimization, fleet management, and vehicle analytics
- Forecasting for predictable departure and arrival of shipments

The company would favor a pre-built solution to accumulate the sensor and vehicle computer data and present a graphical user interface that presents reports about shipments and vehicles.

Which service should you choose?

We will implement the decision criteria that we learned about previously.

First, is it crucial to ensure that the device or, in this instance, each appliance is not compromised? Ideally, each sensor and vehicle computer would be impervious to interference. However, security is not named as a critical matter at this point. A third-party vendor creates vehicle computers and sensors. Unless Tailwind Traders needs to build its own devices (which they do not), the company will be limited to using hardware already prepared.

Second, does Tailwind Traders require a dashboard for reporting and management? Yes, a reporting and management dashboard is a must.

Based on these responses to the decision criteria, Azure IoT Central is the most suitable choice in this situation. The Connected Logistics starter template presents an out-of-box dashboard that will meet many of these conditions. This dashboard is preconfigured to showcase the significant logistics device operations activity. The dashboard might require reconfiguring to remove sea vessel gateways, but the truck gateway functionality would be almost exactly what Tailwind Traders needs.

Why not use IoT Hub?

If Tailwind Traders employs IoT Central, the company will adopt an IoT hub that is preconfigured for its particular needs using the Connected Logistics starter template. Otherwise, the company would require a lot of custom development to build its cloud-based dashboards and management systems on top of Azure IoT Hub.

Why not use Azure Sphere?

Azure Sphere provides a comprehensive solution for situations where security is crucial. In this situation, security is ideal but not a significant preference. Even though Azure Sphere presents an end-to-end solution that includes hardware, Tailwind Traders will use hardware from a third-party vendor. So, in this situation, Azure Sphere is not needed.

Use Azure Sphere

Let us consider an example; Tailwind Traders requires to perform a touchless point-of-sale solution for self-checkout. The self-checkout terminals should be, above all else, safe. Each terminal must be invulnerable to malicious code that could produce false transactions, make the company take the systems offline during a heavy shopping period, or transmit transactional data to a spying organization. The terminals should also report essential information on the company's health and remotely allow secure updates to its software.

After evaluating many potential solutions during a request for proposal process, Tailwind Traders concludes that it requires characteristics that vendors have yet to achieve. Instead of using an existing solution, the company elects to operate with a leading engineering firm concentrating on IoT solutions. This strategy enables the company to formulate a uniquely secure terminal that gives it a retail platform to build on.

Although most of the company's focus is on the terminal itself, Tailwind Traders recognizes that it wants a solution that can assist it in making sense of all the data produced by these terminals across all its retail stores. And it wants an easy way to push software updates to its terminals.

Which service should you choose?

We will implement the decision criteria as we have been doing.

First, is it critical to ensure that the device or, in this case, each point-of-sale terminal is not compromised? Device security is the main requirement.

Next, does Tailwind Traders require a dashboard for reporting and management? Yes, the company needs a reporting and management dashboard.

So, given the answers to the decision criteria, the IoT engineering firm will make a platform on top of both Azure IoT Central and Azure Sphere. Even though no specific starter template is possible in Azure IoT Central for this situation, one can easily be adapted to support the kinds of reports the company wants to see and the management actions it wants to execute.

Why not choose IoT Hub?

By using IoT Central, Tailwind Traders would also be utilizing Azure IoT Hub behind the scenes.

Big Data

Big Data is a term used to describe the collection of millions of large amounts of data and keeps growing exponentially over time. Although collecting data from many sources is not difficult, getting any value from any of these data is difficult. That is why Big data is ideal here. It combines structured, semi-structured, and unstructured data collected by companies that can be stored for information and used in predictive modeling, machine learning projects, and other advanced analytics applications. Systems that

process and store big data have become a common component of data management architectures in organizations. In terms of business value, big data is used for better service, products, and profits.

In Azure, many services and tools deal with Big Data. Some of them are defined below:

 EXAM TIP: The value of big data keeps changing as the industrial processes more and more data.

Azure Data Lake Analytics

Azure Data Lake Analytics is an on-demand job analytics service that simplifies big data. The data lake is a large body of data on which you can perform analytical procedures. In Data Lake analytics, there is parallel processing, meaning that two or more processors process the same data simultaneously. Instead of hardware tuning, deploying, and configuring, you write queries to transform the data and valuable abstract insights.

Data Lake Analytics works for the highest performance, throughput, and parallelization with Azure Data Lake Storage and works with Azure Storage blobs, Azure SQL Database, and Azure Warehouse.

HDInsight

Azure HDInsight is Microsoft's cloud-based big data analytics service, which helps organizations process large amounts of streaming or historical data. Azure HDInsight allows storing massive amounts of data easily, efficiently, and cost-effectively. It is similar to Azure Data Lake Analytics but uses the most popular open-source frameworks such as Hadoop, Spark, Hive, LLAP, Kafka, Storm, R, and more. A wide range of scenarios such as Extracting, Transforming, and Loading (ETL), data warehousing, machine learning, and IoT can be enabled with these frameworks.

Azure Databricks

Azure Databricks is an analytics platform based on Apache Spark, an open-source cluster computing framework to enhance the Microsoft Azure platform. Databricks is integrated with Azure to provide a one-click configuration, an open workspace, and streamlined workflows that enable data scientists, data engineers, and business analysts to collaborate. Databricks run and process a dataset on many computers simultaneously. When using Databricks, you do not need a lot of computers or their maintenance. Azure provides all the computing powers and the integration with other Azure Storage Services, such as Azure Data Lake Storage, Azure Blob Storage, Azure SQL Data Warehouse, or Azure Cosmos DB. The data from all these storages are used to find insights and analyze the data in Apache Spark.

Big Data Outcomes

Collectively, big data services can bring the following outcomes for you.

Speed: Speed and efficiency for processing a large amount of data, provided by the big data on Azure, is the real value. You can find trends and insights to act accordingly.

Cost Reduction: Big data technology, such as cloud-based analytics, brings significant cost advantages when storing a large amount of data.

Better Decision Making: Faster and better decision-making with the speed of in-memory analytics combined with the ability to analyze new data sources.

New Products and Services: Understand customer demands and provide them with better products and services.

Lab 7-01: Explore the Azure IoT Hub and Register a Device

Service Introduction

GreenGrid Farms, a pioneering vertical farming company, faced a crucial challenge: maximizing crop yield and resource utilization while minimizing environmental impact. Their existing data collection system, relying on disparate sensors and manual data analysis, lacked the real-time insights and centralized control needed for optimal efficiency.

Problem

GreenGrid's sensor data was scattered across individual greenhouses, hindering centralized monitoring and analysis. Manual data collection was time-consuming and prone to errors. The manual analysis process limited GreenGrid's ability to translate data into actionable insights for optimizing irrigation, temperature, and nutrient levels, leading to suboptimal yields.

Solution

GreenGrid Farms' success story showcases the power of Azure IoT Hub for organizations seeking to leverage the IoT for data-driven decision-making and operational efficiency. By centralizing data, gaining real-time insights, and automating actions, GreenGrid achieved higher yields, reduced environmental impact, and optimized its operations, solidifying its position as a leader in the sustainable agriculture industry.

1. Log in to **Azure** Portal and go to the portal home page. Click on **IoT Hub**.

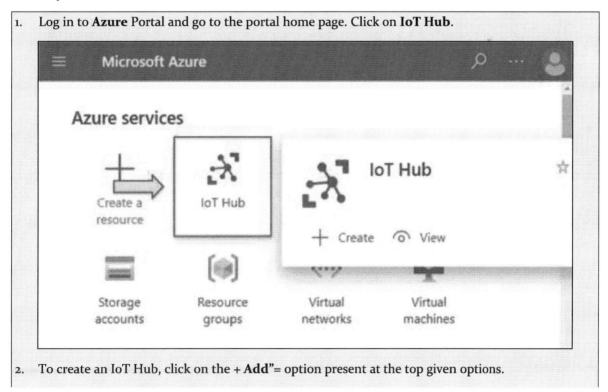

2. To create an IoT Hub, click on the + **Add**"= option present at the top given options.

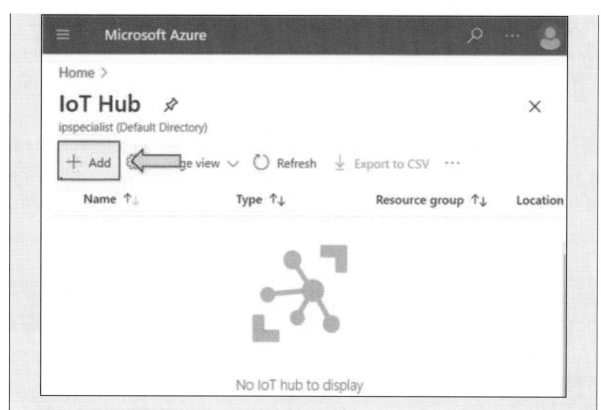

3. Now, enter the **Basics** details. Inside the **Project details,** select your subscription and create a new resource group, **ipsrg.**
4. Select your nearest region.
5. Write the unique name of the IoT Hub.
6. Click on **Next: Networking >.**

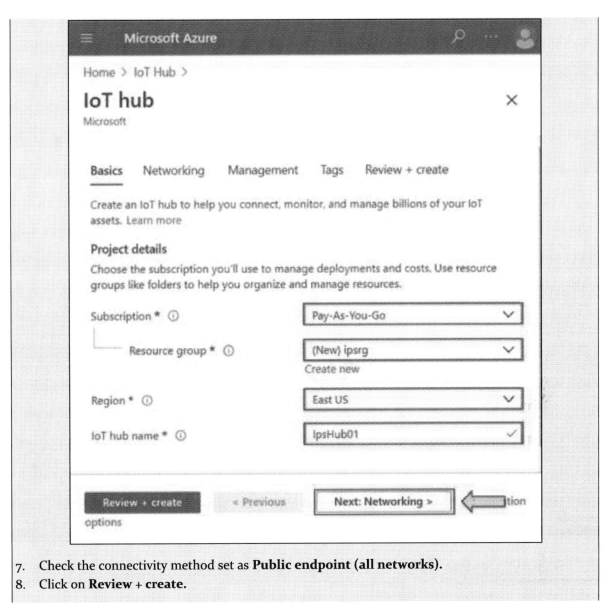

7. Check the connectivity method set as **Public endpoint (all networks)**.
8. Click on **Review + create.**

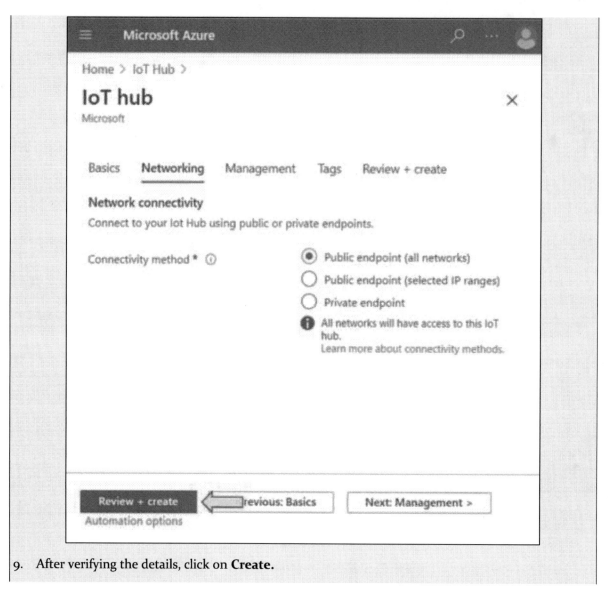

9. After verifying the details, click on **Create.**

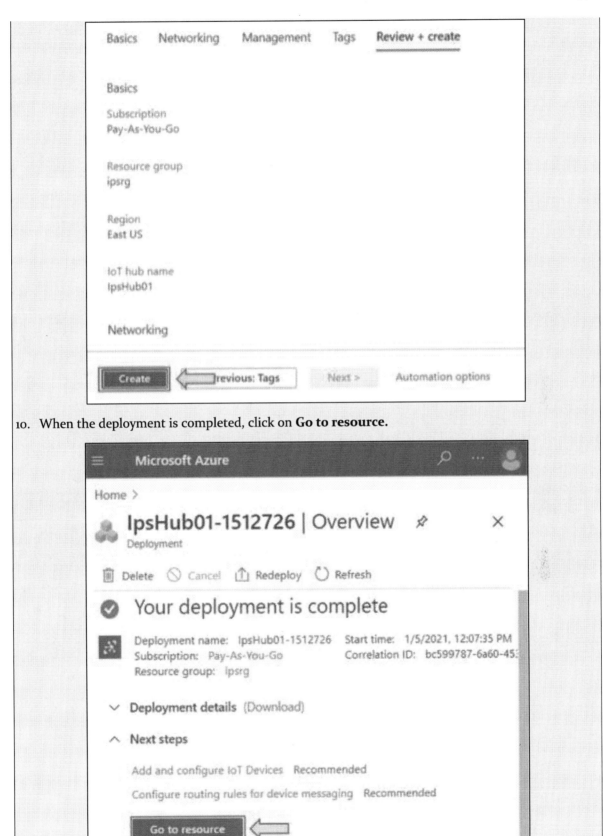

10. When the deployment is completed, click on **Go to resource.**

11. The overview page will appear, containing all the configuration details entered during the creation of the IoT Hub.

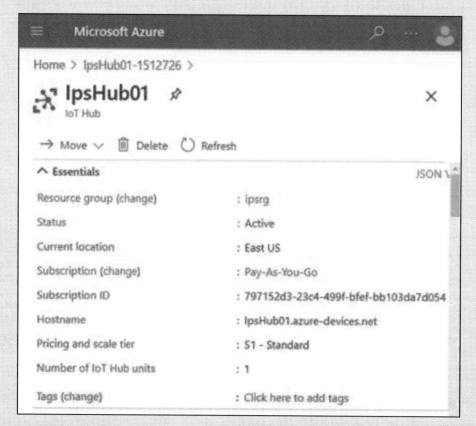

12. To register a device in this IoT Hub, go to the left side of the given menu and click on **IoT devices** present inside **Explorers.**

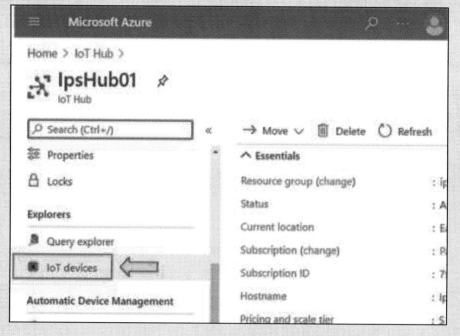

13. To create a new device, click on the + **New** option at the top of the page.

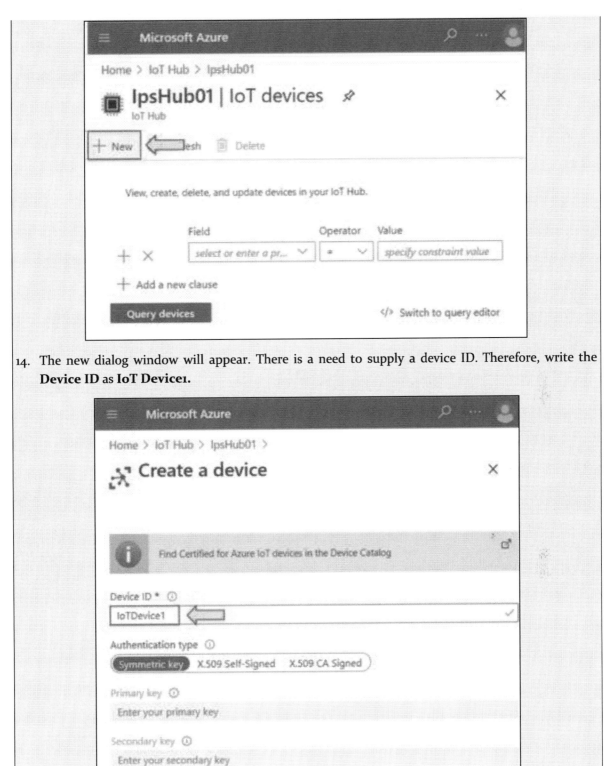

14. The new dialog window will appear. There is a need to supply a device ID. Therefore, write the **Device ID** as **IoT Device1**.

15. For **Authentication type,** there are different methods available to choose from. You can use **X.509 Self-Signed certificate** for a custom solution.

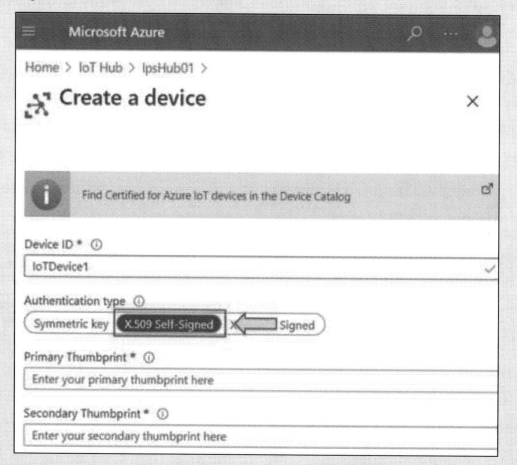

Note: Usually, SSL/TSL certificates are self-signed certificates. These certificates are not useful for public-facing applications.

16. If you want to use the public key certificate signed by Certificate Authority (CA), you can use the **X.509 CA Signed** option.

17. In this case, we will use **Symmetric Keys** as the **Authentication type.**
18. Enable the **Auto-generated keys** option. Leave the remaining options as default.
19. Click on **Save.**

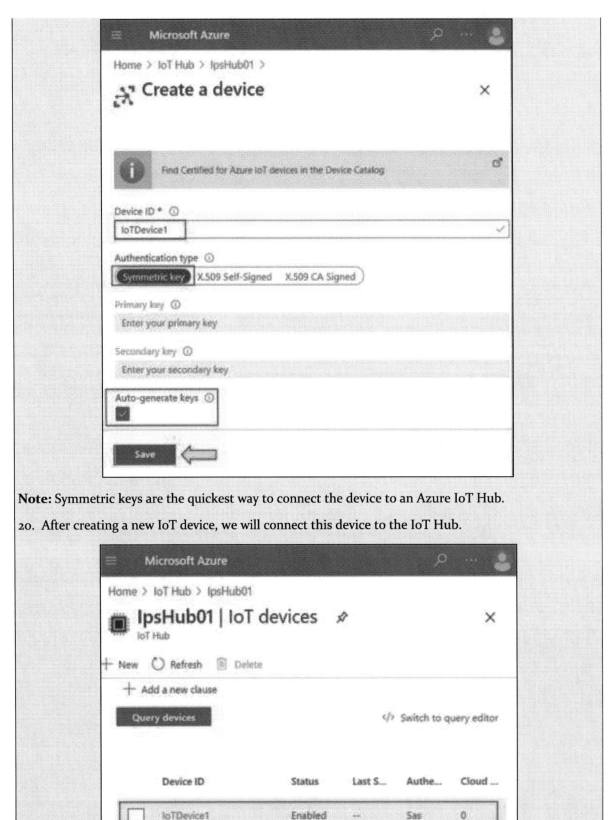

Note: Symmetric keys are the quickest way to connect the device to an Azure IoT Hub.

20. After creating a new IoT device, we will connect this device to the IoT Hub.

21. A simulated device is required to get the device talking to the Azure IoT Hub. In this lab, we will use the Microsoft Raspberry Pi simulator.

22. The online simulator is shown below.

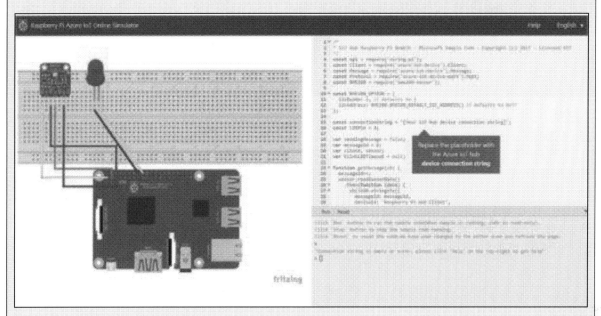

Note: When you click on the **Run** option, it will require a connection string to run.

23. Go back to the IoT devices page to connect to the Azure IoT Hub. Click on your recently created device.

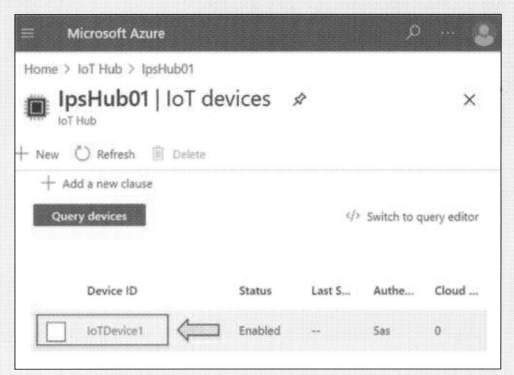

24. The details of the device will appear.

25. The primary and secondary keys will be auto-generated, which means that the primary and secondary connection strings also exist in the device registry.

26. Copy the **Primary Connection String.**

27. Go to the Raspberry Pi online simulator, and paste that connection string in place of the **connectionString** command into the coding area.
28. Click **Run** on the console window.

```
⌗ Raspberry Pi Azure IoT Online Simulator

1 * /*
2  * IoT Hub Raspberry Pi NodeJS - Microsoft Sample Code - Copyright (c) 2017 - Licensed MIT
3  */
4  const wpi = require('wiring-pi');
5  const Client = require('azure-iot-device').Client;
6  const Message = require('azure-iot-device').Message;
7  const Protocol = require('azure-iot-device-mqtt').Mqtt;
8  const BME280 = require('bme280-sensor');
9
10 * const BME280_OPTION = {
11    i2cBusNo: 1, // defaults to 1
12    i2cAddress: BME280.BME280_DEFAULT_I2C_ADDRESS() // defaults to 0x77
13 };
14
15 const connectionString = 'HostName=IpsHub01.azure-devices.net;DeviceId=IoTDevice1;SharedAccessKey
16 const LEDPin = 4;
17
18 var sendingMessage = false;
19 var messageId = 0;
20 var client, sensor;
21 var blinkLEDTimeout = null;
22
23 * function getMessage(cb) {
24    messageId++;
25    sensor.readSensorData()
26 *     .then(function (data) {
27 *       cb(JSON.stringify({
28         messageId: messageId,
29

Run ⇦

Click "Run" button to run the sample code(When sample is running, code is read-only).
Click "Stop" button to stop the sample code running.
Click "Reset" to reset the code.We keep your changes to the editor even you refresh the page.
>
"Connection string is empty or error, please click 'Help' on the top-right to get help"
> ⛶
```

29. Within a few seconds, you can see the statement about sending the telemetry data to your Azure IoT Hub.

```
 1 ▾ /*
 2    * IoT Hub Raspberry PI NodeJS - Microsoft Sample Code - Copyright (c) 2017 - Licens
 3    */
 4    const wpi = require('wiring-pi');
 5    const Client = require('azure-iot-device').Client;
 6    const Message = require('azure-iot-device').Message;
 7    const Protocol = require('azure-iot-device-mqtt').Mqtt;
 8    const BME280 = require('bme280-sensor');
 9
10 ▾  const BME280_OPTION = {
11      i2cBusNo: 1, // defaults to 1
12      i2cAddress: BME280.BME280_DEFAULT_I2C_ADDRESS() // defaults to 0x77
13    };
14
15    const connectionString = 'HostName=IpsHub01.azure-devices.net;DeviceId=IoTDevice1;SI
16    const LEDPin = 4;
17
18    var sendingMessage = false;
19    var messageId = 0;
20    var client, sensor;
21    var blinkLEDTimeout = null;
22
```

Run   Reset   ∨

```
>
Sending message: {"messageId":1,"deviceId":"Raspberry Pi Web Client","temperature":25.94370
>
Message sent to Azure IoT Hub
>
Sending message: {"messageId":2,"deviceId":"Raspberry Pi Web Client","temperature":30.61230
>
Message sent to Azure IoT Hub
>
Sending message: {"messageId":3,"deviceId":"Raspberry Pi Web Client","temperature":28.86444
>
Message sent to Azure IoT Hub
>
```

30. Furthermore, you will see the LED blinking in response to the code.

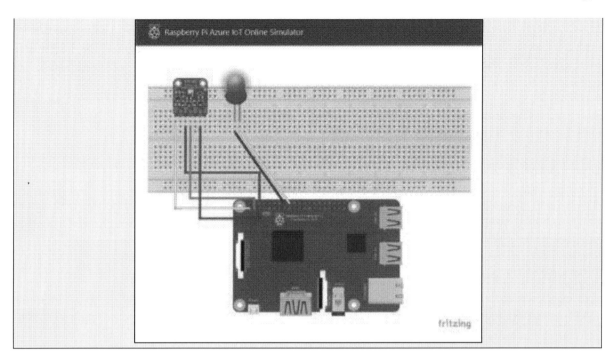

Choosing the Best AI Service for Your Needs

Artificial Intelligence

Artificial Intelligence (AI) is the capability of a machine to imitate intelligent human behavior. With AI, machines can analyze images, comprehend speech, interact naturally, and make predictions using data. In Microsoft, AI is often called Machine Learning, or the sub-category of Machine learning, although AI and Machine learning are often placed in the same bucket.

Microsoft focuses on three main parts of how machine learning can be used on the cloud platform.

Models

The definition of your machine learning application is learning - A model is a set of rules defining how to use the data provided. The model finds patterns based on the rules.

Knowledge Mining

Use Azure Search to find existing insights in your data. File relationships, geography connections, and much more.

Built-in Apps

Azure has several built-in apps that you can use for machine learning and AI immediately. These include cognitive services and bot services.

 EXAM TIP: Azure AI uses Rules and Models to train your AI implementation.

Identify the Product Options

AI is a general classification of computing that enables a software system to understand its environment and take action that maximizes its likelihood of completing its goals. AI aims to produce a software system that can acclimate or learn something independently without being explicitly programmed to do it.

There are two primary strategies for AI. The first is to apply a deep learning system modeled on the human mind's neural network, allowing it to explore, learn, and grow through experience.

The second approach is machine learning, a data science method that uses existing data to train a model, test it, and then apply it to new data to determine future behaviors, outcomes, and trends.

> **Note:** Virtually every device or software system that collects textual, visual, and audio data could feed a machine learning model that makes that device or software system smarter about how it functions in the future.

Azure Product Options

At a high level, there are three main product contributions from Microsoft, each of which is intended for a particular audience and use case. Each option presents different tools, services, and programmatic APIs. In this section, we will only scratch the surface of the options' abilities.

Azure AI Service (Formerly Azure Cognitive Services)

Cognitive services make AI accessible to all developers without needing machine learning skills. All you need is one API call to embed the feature to see, hear, speak, search, comprehend, and expedite decision-making into your apps. Azure AI Service may tackle challenges like assessing text for emotional sentiment or analyzing photos to identify items or faces. You do not need any special machine learning or data science experience to use these services. Developers can use APIs to access Azure AI Service and easily incorporate these features with only a few lines of code. The following are the different types of Azure AI Service:

Vision

Identify and recognize the pictures, images, and digital ink automatically.

Decisions

The apps make content-based decisions by detecting the potential offensive languages and IoT anomalies and leveraging data analytics.

Speech

Integrate speech processes into apps and services by converting speech into the text as transcription. It also identifies unique voices and even verifies a speaker based on the speech.

Language Services

Allow your apps to process natural language with pre-built scripts, assess sentiment, and learn how to identify what users require.

Azure Machine Learning

Azure Machine Learning is a platform for making predictions. It has tools and services enabling you to connect to data to train and test models to discover one that will predict a future result most precisely.

After you have run experiments to examine the model, you can deploy and use it in real time through a web API endpoint.

With Azure Machine Learning, you can do the following:

- Create a process that describes how to gather data, manage missing or bad data, divide the data into either a training set or test set, and deliver the data to the training process
- Train and assess predictive models by employing tools and programming languages familiar to data scientists
- Build pipelines that determine where and when to run the compute-intensive experiments that are required to score the algorithms based on the training and test data
- Deploy the best-performing algorithm as an API to an endpoint so it can be consumed in real time by other applications

> 💡 **EXAM TIP:** Opt for Azure Machine Learning when your data scientists need complete control over the design and training of an algorithm using your data.

Azure Machine Learning Studio

The Azure Machine Learning Studio is the machine learning service's top-level tool. It is a visual tool for managing all of your machine-learning requirements. It gives data scientists and developers a centralized area to work with all the artifacts for designing, training and deploying machine learning models.

You can use pre-made modules in this section because they are ready to use immediately. Some Azure Machine Learning Studio applications include Twitter sentiment analysis, movie recommendations, and photo grouping.

Machine Learning Services

1. **End-to-End Service:** The service to use AI and machine learning almost anywhere on Azure.
2. **Tooling:** The Machine Learning service is a collection of tools to help you build AI applications.
3. **Automation:** Azure automatically recognizes trends in your applications and creates models for you.

Azure Bot Service

Azure Bot Service and Bot Framework are platforms for building virtual agents that understand and respond to questions like humans. Azure Bot Service differs slightly from Azure Machine Learning and Azure AI Services because it has a specific use case. Namely, it forms a virtual agent that can intelligently converse with humans. Behind the scenes, the bot you make applies other Azure services, such as Azure AI Services, to learn what their human counterparts are asking for.

Bots can be used to shift simple, repetitive tasks, such as making a dinner reservation or gathering profile information, onto automated systems that might no longer need direct human intervention. Users converse with a bot through text, interactive cards, and speech. A bot interaction can be a quick question and answer or an advanced conversation that intelligently provides access to services.

Analyze the Decision Criteria

This section will examine the criteria experts apply when choosing. Understanding the criteria can also help us understand the nuanced product differences.

Are you building a virtual agent that interfaces with humans via natural language?

Use Azure Bot Service when you want to create a virtual agent to associate with humans by utilizing natural language. Bot Service combines knowledge sources, natural language processing, and form factors to enable interaction across different channels.

Bot Service solutions normally depend on other AI services for such things as natural language understanding or even translation for localizing replies into a customer's favored language.

Before you jump in to create a custom chat experience using Bot Service, it might make sense to seek prebuilt, no-code solutions that cover common situations. For instance, you can use QnA Maker, which is obtainable from Azure Marketplace, to build, train, and publish a sophisticated bot that employs FAQ pages, support websites, product manuals, SharePoint documents, or editorial content through an easy-to-use UI or REST APIs.

Similarly, Power Virtual Agents combines with Microsoft Power Platform to utilize hundreds of prebuilt connectors for data input. You can extend Power Virtual Agents by building custom workflows with Power Automate, and if you feel that the out-of-the-box experience is too restricting, you can still produce more complex interactions with Microsoft Bot Framework.

Do you need a service that can understand the content and meaning of images, video, or audio or translate text into a different language?

Apply Azure AI Services when it comes to general-purpose tasks, such as delivering a speech-to-text, integrating with search, or recognizing the objects in an image. Azure AI Services is general-purpose, meaning that many types of customers can profit from the work that Microsoft has already done to train and test these models and offer them inexpensively at scale.

Do you need to predict user behavior or provide personalized recommendations in your app?

The Azure AI Services Personalizer views your users' actions within an application. You can use Personalizer to predict their behavior and present relevant experiences as it recognizes usage patterns. Here again, you could capture and collect user behavior and design your custom Azure Machine Learning solution to achieve these things, but this method would require much effort and cost.

Will your app predict future outcomes based on private historical data?

Choose Azure Machine Learning when examining data to predict future results. For example, assume you need to examine years' worth of financial transactions to identify new patterns that could help you generate new products and services for your company's clients and propose those new services during routine customer service calls. You must create a more custom-tailored machine-learning model when working with proprietary data.

Do you need to build a model by using your own data or perform a different task than those listed above?

Employ Azure Machine Learning for maximum flexibility. Data scientists and AI engineers can utilize the tools they are familiar with and the data you present to develop deep learning and machine learning models tuned for your particular demands.

Use Machine Learning for decision support systems

For example, the Tailwind Traders e-commerce website permits customers to scan and purchase items that can be transported or picked up from a nearby retail store.

The marketing team is assured that it can improve sales dramatically by recommending add-on products that complement the items in a shopper's cart at the time of checkout. The team could hard-code these recommendations, but it feels that a more organic path would be to utilize its years' worth of sales data and new shopping trends to determine what products to present to the shopper. Additionally, the suggestions could be affected by product availability, product profitability, and other circumstances.

The marketing team's existing data science experts have already done some primary analysis of the problem domain and have concluded that its plan might take months to prototype and probably a year to roll out.

Which service should you choose?

Let's implement the decision criteria you learned about previously to find the best option.

First, is Tailwind Traders building a virtual agent that interfaces with humans through natural language? It is not, so Azure Bot Service is not a suitable competitor for this situation.

Second, does Tailwind Traders require a service that can understand the content and meaning of images, video, and audio or translate text into a different language? No, it does not, so the relevant Cognitive Services will not accommodate the company.

Third, does Tailwind Traders want to predict user behavior or provide users with personalized recommendations? Yes, it does. But, producing recommendations based on user behavior is only part of the condition. Tailwind Traders wants to create a complex model that combines historical sales data, trending sales data, inventory, and more. Azure AI Services Personalizer service can play a role, but it cannot manage the entire breadth of the project alone.

Fourth, will the Tailwind Traders app foretell future results based on private historical data? Yes, and that is why in this situation, Azure Machine Learning is likely the best choice.

The success of this effort would depend principally on the model's capacity to accurately select the right up-sale products to recommend to the shopper. An off-the-shelf model would likely not satisfy because the model would need to be tweaked and tuned over time.

Lastly, it sounds like the marketing team already uses some data science experts, and the team is ready to make at least a year-long commitment to building, testing, and tweaking the models to be used.

Use Cognitive Services for Data Analysis

Let's consider an example where the first generation of the Tailwind Traders e-commerce website was available solely in English. But, when the marketing team sponsored demographics research for the company's brick-and-mortar locations, it determined that, on average, only 80 percent of possible customers speak English. In some neighborhoods, that number drops to 50 percent. The team sees the addition of multiple languages as an excellent chance to assist non-English speakers with the identical online e-commerce experience as English speakers.

Which service should you choose?

As in the previous section, implement the decision criteria you learned earlier to find the right option.

First, is Tailwind Traders building a virtual agent that interfaces with humans via natural language? It is not, so Azure Bot Service is not a valid competitor. But, should Tailwind Traders ever implement a customer service agent, it might want to contemplate using the Translator API to present real-time translation to serve customers who are not English speakers.

Second, does Tailwind Traders require a service to learn the content and meaning of images, video, and audio or translate text into a different language? Yes, it does. Translating textual content from one language into another is a general-purpose task you can simplify using the Azure AI Services Translator service. The service is easy to mix into your applications, websites, tools, and solutions. It permits you to add multi-language user experiences in more than 60 languages, and you can utilize it on any hardware platform with any operating system for text-to-text language translation.

Azure AI Services is possibly the best option for this situation, but let's apply the decision criteria to make sure.

Third, does Tailwind Traders want to predict user behavior or provide users with personalized recommendations? No, it does not, so the Azure AI Services Personalizer is unsuitable.

Finally, will the Tailwind Traders app need to predict future outcomes based on private historical data? No. Although building a Machine Learning model for multi-language translation is probable, it would be expensive and time-consuming for Tailwind Traders to strive to build translation models themselves. The team has neither the deep learning competency nor the linguistic data needed to train the models.

Now that you have considered all the expert criteria, you can confidently select Cognitive Services as the most suitable product option for this situation.

Use Bot Service for Interactive Chat Experiences

The Customer Service team has long requested for a virtual agent to control the vast majority of questions it gets asked. No matter how obvious it makes the answers to the most frequently asked questions on the website, shoppers are anxious and comprehend contact in a chat window, saving them time.

The team wants shoppers to think they are interacting with a real human. The chat session should be assigned to a human when it becomes apparent that the virtual agent cannot provide an answer.

Giving a virtual agent would reduce the time it takes for all shoppers to obtain answers. The virtual agent could answer most questions, freeing human customer service agents to grant support for more complex questions or thorny account-related issues.

Which service should you choose?

Once again, employ the decision criteria you are now accustomed to find the best product.

First, is Tailwind Traders building a virtual agent that interfaces with humans through natural language? Yes, it is. Azure Bot Service should be adopted to implement a virtual agent chat experience. Bot Service could get data from the information on the website's Frequently Asked Questions page and thousands of chat sessions saved between shoppers and customer service representatives. Customer Service supervisors can test and tweak the answers to continue to refine the chat experience.

Even though you have likely found the best option for this situation, keep implementing the decision criteria to see whether any further options might work.

Second, does Tailwind Traders require a service that can understand the content and meaning of images, video, and audio or translate text into a different language? Possibly, yes. Azure AI Services could be

utilized along with Bot Service to build the solution in this situation. To facilitate implementation, the developers could explore using prebuilt solutions, such as QnA Maker (part of Azure AI Services) or Power Virtual Agents. Additionally, any Azure Bot solution could implement several Azure AI Services, such as Language Understanding (LUIS) and possibly Translator, to translate from the shopper's language to English and back again.

Third, does Tailwind Traders need to foretell user behavior or provide users with personalized suggestions? No, it does not. Azure AI Services Personalizer is not a good competitor in this situation.

Finally, will the Tailwind Traders app need to predict future results based on private historical data? No. Although Tailwind Traders does have historical data to supply into a model, which would make it feasible to apply Azure Machine Learning to create a chat solution, another option is already tailored for the chatbot experience.

Choosing the Best Azure Serverless Technology for Your Business Scenario

Serverless

Serverless computing is a critical component of current cloud computing. By removing the requirement for developers to manage infrastructure, the serverless architecture allows them to build applications faster. It is a PaaS at its most extreme. The infrastructure required for running code with serverless apps is automatically offered, scaled, and managed by the cloud service provider.

> **EXAM TIP:** It is important to understand that "serverless" does not mean that no VMs are involved. It simply means that the VM running your code is not explicitly allocated to you, which means you do not manage them. Your code is moved to the VM, it is executed, and then it is moved off.

Benefits of the Serverless Model

No Infrastructure Management: Use fully managed infrastructure - developers can avoid administrative tasks and concentrate on the core business logic. You simply deploy the code with a serverless platform, and it runs with great availability.

Dynamic Scalability: The infrastructure can automatically scale up and down within seconds to match any workload requirements for serverless computing.

Faster Time to Market: Serverless applications decrease the reliance on each development cycle for operations, allowing development teams to generate more features in less time.

More Efficient Use of Resources: Shifting to serverless technology allows companies to reduce TCO and resource reallocation to speed up the pace of innovation.

Identify the Product Options

In this section, we will study two Azure serverless computing services:

- Azure Functions
- Azure Logic Apps

Azure Functions

Azure Functions is the compute component of serverless services offered by Azure. It is called a function, with a single task to perform every time. This means you can use functions to write code without worrying about deploying that code or creating VMs to run your code. The code runs only once for every invocation. Apps using Azure Functions are often referred to as Function Apps. It can run millions of times per second if needed. Using an event-driven model, serverless functions accelerate development with triggers that automatically execute code to react to events and bindings to incorporate extra services seamlessly.

Azure Logic Apps

Azure Logic Apps is a cloud service that connects the systems inside and outside the Azure Platform; you can integrate apps, data, and services or even an entire system across organizations. You can automate and orchestrate business processes, tasks, activities, and workflows with this. Unlike Function Apps, to create some efficient workflows with Logic Apps, you do not have to write the code. Everything is customizable in Azure Portal. Logic Apps simplify how you design and build flexible applications for application integration, data integration, system integration, Enterprise Application Integration (EAI), and Business-to-Business (B2B) communication, whether in the cloud or at the premises, or both.

Use Case

Every time a new order is created in your ordering system, you can create a logic app to record how long it took. It inserts that into a database and sends an email to the requested person. You can also have a conditional path; for example, when an order is over $100, you can send a different email to customer service to ask them to thank the customer. You can connect a ton of applications either manually or using templates, there is no code needed, no service to set up, and you can get started very quickly.

Azure Event Grid

An event is an activity or occurrence that can be identified by a program and has importance for system application in a computing notion. Azure Event Grid makes it simple to create apps based on event-driven architectures. Choose the Azure resource you want to subscribe to first, then deliver the event to the event handler or Webhook endpoint. Events from Azure services, such as storage blobs and resource groups, have built-in support in Event Grid. Custom-made themes are also supported by Event Grid for your events. Because Event Grid is a serverless service, infrastructure administration is not required.

You can use filters to route specific events to different endpoints, multicast to multiple endpoints, and ensure your events are reliably delivered. Azure Event Grid is deployed to maximize availability by native distribution across multiple fault domains in every region and across availability zones. Event Grid connects data sources and event handlers. Event Grid can trigger a serverless function that analyzes images when added to a blob storage container.

Analyze the Decision Criteria

With two viable serverless choices, it can be tough to identify the most suitable one for the job. In this section, we will examine the criteria experts employ when adopting a serverless service to utilize for a given business need. Understanding the criteria will also aid you in comprehending the subtle distinctions between the products.

Do you need to perform an orchestration across well-known APIs?

From the web-based visual configuration to the pricing model, Azure Logic Apps was designed with orchestration in mind. Logic Apps excels in connecting a wide range of services via APIs to pass and process data through a workflow's various steps.

It is probable to create the same workflow using Azure Functions, but it might take a significant amount of time to investigate which APIs to call and how to call them. Azure Logic Apps has already componentized these API calls so that you only provide some details, and the details of calling the required APIs are abstracted away.

Do you need to execute custom algorithms or perform specialized data parsing and lookups?

With Azure Functions, you can utilize the full expressiveness of a programming language in a compact form. This allows you to concisely build complicated algorithms or data lookup and parsing operations. You would be accountable for maintaining the code, handling exceptions resiliently, and so on.

Although Azure Logic Apps can make logic (loops, decisions, and so on), if you have a logic-intensive orchestration that wants a complex algorithm, implementing that algorithm might be more lengthy and visually overwhelming.

Do you have existing automated tasks written in an imperative programming language?

Suppose your orchestration or business logic is expressed in C#, Java, Python, or another popular programming language. In that case, it might be simpler to port your code into the body of an Azure Functions function app than to create it again using Azure Logic Apps.

Do you prefer a visual (declarative) workflow or writing (imperative) code?

Eventually, your decision comes down to whether you favor working in a declarative or imperative environment. Developers with expertise in an imperative programming language might want to think about automation and orchestration from an imperative mindset. IT professionals and business analysts might want to work in a more visual low-code/no-code (declarative) environment.

Use Azure Functions

For example, Data about each product sold at Tailwind Traders is packaged as a JSON message and transferred to an event hub. The event hub spreads the JSON message to subscribers, which enables various systems to be notified.

Tailwind Traders wants to upgrade its e-commerce site to incorporate real-time inventory tracking. Currently, the website updates product availability nightly at 2:00 AM. A Windows service that is written in C# contains all of the necessary logic to do the following:

- Retrieve messages
- Parse the JSON
- Accomplish a lookup across multiple databases to find additional product information
- Possibly, send notifications to the purchasing department so that they can reorder quantities that fall below certain levels

The Windows service runs on a virtual machine that is hosted on Azure.

Most of the time, this system works fine. Nevertheless, some products are in great demand, and some are kept in fewer quantities at each store. Many times a day, customers drive to a store to pick up an item to find that it is no longer in stock.

Rather than running the algorithm nightly, the company aspires to run the inventory updater each time a product is purchased.

Which service should you choose?

Since the Tailwind Traders developers team has already drafted the logic in C#, it would be reasonable to copy the relevant C# code from the Windows service and port it to an Azure function. The developers would bind the function to trigger each time a new message arrives on a specific queue.

Why not choose Azure Logic Apps?

It is reasonable to perform the same logic in Azure Logic Apps. However, because the team has now spent time building the service in C#, it can apply the same code in an Azure function.

Use Azure Logic Apps

Let us consider an example where Tailwind Traders grants its customers an invitation to engage in a customer satisfaction survey randomly after a purchase. Currently, the customer satisfaction results are aggregated, averaged, and charted. However, its customer service department sees an opening to reach out proactively to customers who provide low scores and leave comments with negative feelings.

Ideally, negative customer satisfaction scores would cause a customer retention workflow. First, a sentiment analysis would be generated based on the free-form comments. An email would be sent to the customer with an apology and a coupon code. The message would be routed to the Dynamics 365 customer service team so that it could schedule a follow-up email.

Regrettably, no Tailwind Traders developer resources are available to carry on this project, even though the customer service team works with several cloud and IT professionals who might be able to create a solution.

Which service should you choose?

In this situation, Azure Logic Apps is likely the most suitable solution. A cloud or IT professional could use existing connectors to execute a sentiment analysis by applying the Azure AI Services connector, sending an email using the Office 365 Outlook connector, and creating a new record and follow-up email using Dynamics 365 customer service connector.

Because Azure Logic Apps is a low-code/no-code service, no developers are required. A cloud or IT professional should be able to build and support this workflow.

Why not choose Azure Functions?

Even though it is likely to build the whole solution using Azure Functions, this method might be difficult if no software developers can be allocated to this project.

This is an excellent scenario for Azure Logic Apps. Connectors already exist for each of the steps described in the workflow. It would take quite a bit of study, development, and testing for a developer to formulate a solution that employs all these disparate software systems.

Choosing the Best Tools to Help Organizations Build Better Solutions

DevOps

DevOps is a combination of the development and operations of the term, meant to reflect a collective or cooperative approach to the activities performed by the application development departments of an organization and IT operations. The term DevOps is used in various ways; it is an organizational concept in its broadest sense that promotes better coordination and collaboration between these teams and others within an enterprise to generate a better and more reliable product.

> **EXAM TIP:** DevOps is all about how Developers, Engineers, and System Administrators organize themselves and work as a team to deliver better products faster.

Understand your Product Options

In this section, we will concentrate only on the Microsoft tools that can help achieve some DevOps goals. Alternately, organizations that are not ready to fully welcome the potential of DevOps can assist technical teams in their cloud development activities.

Microsoft offers tools to enable source-code management, continuous integration, and continuous delivery (CI/CD), and automating the creation of testing environments. Sometimes, it seems as though these tools overlap in functionality, so in this section, you will learn about several product choices and when to pick one product over another.

Product options

At a high level, there are three main offerings aimed at a particular audience and use case and provide a diverse set of tools, services, programmatic APIs, and more.

Azure DevOps

Azure DevOps offers developer tools to support teams in preparing projects, working on application creation, and designing and deploying new products.

Azure DevOps provides integrated features that can be accessed via your web browser or client IDE. Depending on your business needs, you may use one or more of the following services:

1. **Azure Boards:** Allows the project manager to keep track of work tasks, timelines, planning and monitoring, code bugs, and issues.
2. **Azure Pipelines:** Provides services to develop and test automatically and continuously.
3. **Azure Repos:** Provides the source control of your code to Git repositories or Team Foundation Version Control (TFVC). It is a store where your code is securely managed.
4. **Azure Test Plans:** Provides various tools for testing the software, including manual/exploratory testing and continuous testing automatically.
5. **Azure Artifacts:** Allows teams to share public and private Maven, Npm, and NuGet packages and incorporate package sharing into your CI/CD pipelines.

GitHub and GitHub Actions

GitHub is arguably the world's most successful code repository for open-source software. Git is a decentralized source-code management tool, and GitHub is a hosted variant of Git that works as the primary remote. GitHub grows on top of Git to present related assistance for coordinating work, reporting and discussing issues, producing documentation, and more. It offers the following functionality:

It is a shared source-code repository containing tools that allow developers to deliver code reviews by appending comments and questions in a web view of the source code before it can be assimilated into the main codebase.

- It expedites project management, including Kanban boards
- It supports issue reporting, discussion, and tracking
- It emphasizes CI/CD pipeline automation tooling
- It comprises a wiki for collaborative documentation
- It can be run from the cloud or on-premises

GitHub Actions allows workflow automation with triggers for various lifecycle events. One such case would be automating a CI/CD toolchain.

A toolchain is a mixture of software tools that help deliver, develop, and manage software applications throughout a system's development life cycle. Typical tool functions range from implementing automated dependency updates to building and configuring the software, delivering the build artifacts to multiple locations, testing, etc. The output of one tool in the toolchain is the input of the next tool in the toolchain.

With such similarities between many GitHub and Azure DevOps characteristics, you might question which product to pick for your organization. Sadly, the answer might not be straightforward.

Although Azure DevOps and GitHub support public and private code repositories, GitHub has a long history with public repositories and is trusted by tens of thousands of open-source project owners. GitHub is a lighter-weight tool than Azure DevOps, with a center on individual developers contributing to the open-source code. Azure DevOps, on the opposite, is more focused on enterprise development, with heavier project management and planning tools and fine-grained access control.

> **Note:** Your choices are not limited to Azure DevOps Services or GitHub and GitHub Actions. In practice, you can mix and match these services as needed. For example, you can use GitHub Repos with Azure Boards for work item tracking.

Azure DevTest Labs

Azure DevTest Labs helps team developers effectively handle Virtual Machines (VMs) and PaaS tools without waiting for approvals. It focuses on environmental management. With this, developers and engineers can create an environment for test and development.

DevTest Labs creates labs that consist of pre-configured bases or templates for Azure Resource Manager. These have all the tools and applications you can use to create environments. You can create environments in minutes instead of hours or days. It is also helpful for cost management as it minimizes the waste of resources in accounts. The creation of an environment can also be automated.

Analyze the Decision Criteria

This section will examine the criteria experts employ when adopting DevOps tools or services to address particular business needs. Understanding the criteria can also help you better understand the nuanced differences between each product.

Do you need to automate and manage test-lab creation?

If you intend to automate the making and administration of a test lab environment, consider choosing Azure DevTest Labs. It is the only one that offers this functionality among the three tools and services we have outlined.

Nevertheless, you can automate the provisioning of new labs as part of a toolchain by applying Azure Pipelines or GitHub Actions.

Are you building open-source software?

Although Azure DevOps can print public code repositories, GitHub has long been the favored host for open-source software. If you are creating open-source software, you would likely choose GitHub for no purpose other than its distinctness and general approval by the open-source development community.

The remaining decision criteria are particular for either Azure DevOps or GitHub.

Regarding source-code management and DevOps tools, what level of granularity do you need for permissions?

GitHub uses a simplistic read/write permissions model for each feature. Meantime, Azure DevOps has a much more granular kit of permissions that enables organizations to define who can make most operations across the entire toolset.

How sophisticated do your project management and reporting need to be regarding source-code management and DevOps tools?

Even though GitHub has work items, issues, and a Kanban board, project management and reporting are where Azure DevOps shines. Azure DevOps is extremely customizable, which enables an administrator to append custom fields to obtain metadata and additional information beside each work item. In contrast, the GitHub Issues characteristic applies tags to support a team in classifying issues.

Regarding source-code management and DevOps tools, how tightly do you need to integrate with third-party tools?

Although we make no particular suggestions about third-party tools, it is necessary for you to know your organization's existing investments in tools and services and to assess how these dependencies might influence your choice. Most vendors that create DevOps tools will likely create hooks or APIs utilized by Azure Pipelines and GitHub Actions. Even so, it is plausibly worth the trouble to verify that theory.

Use Azure DevOps to manage the application development lifecycle

The software development team at Tailwind Traders operates on various diverse projects, both for internal and external usage. The team must give project sponsors and managers executive-level reporting containing burndown charts, track progress against epics, and track customer information that is particular to Tailwind Traders in each work item and bug report.

As Tailwind Traders grows and hires contractors and outside vendors for short-term work, the upper management team aspires to ensure that these individuals have admittance only to the information they require to do their work.

Which services should we choose?

Implement the decision criteria you learned about in the previous section to find the best option.

First, does Tailwind Traders need to automate and manage test lab creation? No. So, in this situation, Azure DevTest Labs is not a competitor because it is not designed for this particular use case.

Second, is Tailwind Traders building open-source software? Though it is not declared explicitly, Tailwind Traders is developing internal and external systems, such as their e-commerce system, which is not open source. So, that is not a factor in this situation.

Third, what level of granularity do Tailwind Traders require for permissions? Previously, we affirmed that Tailwind Traders would employ temporary employees and vendors for short-term work, which makes a granular permissions requirement an essential point for upper management. Based on our account in the previous unit, this characteristic would secure Azure DevOps as a leading candidate. By adopting Azure DevOps, Tailwind Traders administrators would also have a more sound set of options for managing permissions across the complete portfolio of work.

Fourth, does Tailwind Traders want sophisticated project management and reporting solution? Yes, robust project management and reporting characteristics are fundamental considerations. Again, due to the number of work-item customization and reporting the management team wants, Azure DevOps would be a valid choice.

Fifth, does Tailwind Traders want tight integration with any third-party DevOps tools? Tool integration was not registered as a primary concern for this situation. As you studied in the previous unit, most third-party DevOps tools combined with Azure DevOps and GitHub make it plausible that the team will find the tools it requires.

Use GitHub to contribute to open-source software

Tailwind Traders aspires to issue an API that permits third parties to combine their inventories of new and used items. This plan would enable Tailwind Traders to extend a more extensive assortment of products directly from their e-commerce site.

Although the internal implementation of the API is closed source, Tailwind Traders desires to produce a collection of examples that call the API to execute various actions. The team requires a platform to share sample code, gather feedback on the API, permit contributors to report issues, and develop a community around feature requests.

Which service should you choose?

Apply the decision criteria you studied earlier to find the best option.

First, does Tailwind Traders need to automate and manage test lab creation? No. In this situation, Azure DevTest Labs is not a competitor because it is not intended for this use case.

Second, is Tailwind Traders building open-source software? Yes. As we saw in a previous section, developers are used to seeing this content on GitHub. With GitHub, Tailwind Traders developers can publish their code, acquire community contributions to enhance the code examples, receive feedback

and bug reports, and more. Because this scenario includes open-source code, GitHub is a leading candidate.

Third, what level of granularity does the Tailwind Traders team need for assigning permissions? Though it is not declared explicitly, the fact that Tailwind Traders will be receiving community contributions, issuing reports, and usually attempting to create a community of developers around their API examples, the company's permission requirements are basic: users can use either view only or view and write. This is another reason why GitHub would be a great candidate for this situation.

Fourth, does Tailwind Traders want sophisticated project management and reporting solution? Again, because of the status of this project, the team does not require a sophisticated project management and reporting solution. In this situation, the power of Azure DevOps Services is not needed.

Fifth, does Tailwind Traders require tight integration with any third-party DevOps tools? Tool integration was not registered as a principal concern for this situation and did not pass or disqualify either tool.

GitHub is the most suitable option for this situation. Although you could employ Azure DevOps to make the repository public, some of the other characteristics that include the development community, such as feedback or bug reports, would be less available.

Use Azure DevTest Labs to manage testing environments

Tailwind Traders requires being more systematic and precise when it launches new versions of its e-commerce website to production. The company will grow its Quality Assurance (QA) team and utilize the cloud to build and host virtual machines. This method will produce testing environments that match the production environment.

The management team has concerns about the prices of a more automated test environment. For example, it wants to ensure that the QA professionals are not losing time configuring the testing environment to match the production environment. The team desires to ensure that the VMs are destroyed when they are no longer in practice. It wants to restrict the number of VMs each QA professional can spin up. In addition, the team wants to ensure that each environment is configured accurately and compatible with the production environment.

Which service should you choose?

Once again, start by implementing the decision criteria you studied earlier to obtain the correct product.

First, does Tailwind Traders want to automate and control test lab creation? Yes. This looks like a job for Azure DevTest Labs because it can do everything the team requires to achieve in this situation.

We could evaluate the decision criteria, but neither Azure DevOps nor GitHub is required. Recollect that either Azure DevOps or GitHub could be utilized to produce product releases that can automatically be included in any VMs you build for testing purposes.

Choosing the Best Monitoring Service for Visibility, Insight, and Outage Mitigation

Identify your product options

Following are the questions that companies face while using the cloud:

- Are we utilizing the cloud correctly? Can we get more production out of our cloud spending?
- Are we paying more than we need to?
- Do we have our systems correctly secured?
- How resilient are our resources? If we encounter a regional outage, could we failover to another region?
- How can we diagnose and repair issues that occur intermittently?
- How can we quickly ascertain the reason for an outage?
- How can we study planned downtime?
- Fortunately, by applying a mixture of monitoring solutions on Azure, you can:
  - Gain answers, insights, and alerts to help guarantee that you have optimized your cloud usage.
- Determine the root reason for unplanned issues.
- Plan ahead of time for planned outages.

The Product Options

There are three main Azure monitoring offerings at a high level, each of which is aimed at a particular audience and use case and gives a diverse set of tools, services, programmatic APIs, and more.

Azure Advisor

Azure Advisor evaluates your Azure resources and makes recommendations to improve their dependability, security, and performance and achieve operational excellence and lower expenses. The advisor is designed to save you time for cloud optimization. The recommendation service includes actions you can take immediately, postpone, or dismiss.

> **Note:** The recommendations are available through the Azure portal and the API, and you can install notifications to inform you of new recommendations.

When you are in the Azure portal, the Advisor dashboard presents personalized guidance for all your subscriptions, and you can apply filters to choose recommendations for particular subscriptions, resource groups, or services. The recommendations are classified into five categories as follows:

- *Reliability:* Used to secure and enhance the continuity of your business-critical applications
- *Security:* Used to identify threats and vulnerabilities that might drive security breaches
- *Performance:* Used to increase the speed of your applications
- *Cost:* Used to optimize and decrease your overall Azure spending
- *Operational Excellence:* Used to assist you in achieving process and workflow efficiency, resource manageability, and deployment best practices

Azure Monitor

Azure Monitor is a platform for gathering, analyzing, visualizing, and possibly taking actions based on the metric and logging data from your complete Azure and on-premises environment.

The diagram below demonstrates just how extensive Azure Monitor is.

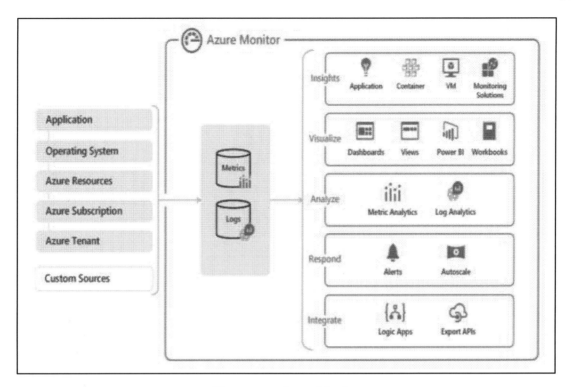

Figure 7-05: Azure Monitor

- On the left is a list of the sources of logging and metric data that can be obtained at every layer in your application architecture, from the application to the operating system and network
- In the center, you can see how the logging and metric data are saved in central repositories
- On the right, the data is used in plenty of ways. You can view real-time and historical performance over each layer of your architecture or aggregate and detailed information. The data is presented at various levels for diverse audiences. You can observe high-level reports on the Azure Monitor Dashboard or create custom views by applying Power BI and Kusto queries

Additionally, you can utilize the data to help you react to crucial events in real-time by alerts delivered to teams through SMS, email, and so on. Or you can implement thresholds to trigger autoscaling functionality to scale up or down to match the demand.

Some popular products, such as Azure Application Insights, a service for transmitting telemetry information from application source code to Azure, use Azure Monitor under the hood. With Application Insights, your application developers can take advantage of the strong data-analysis platform in Azure Monitor to gain deep insights into an application's operations and diagnose errors without waiting for users to report them.

Azure Service Health

Azure Service Health presents a personalized design of the health of the Azure services, regions, and resources you depend on. The status.azure.com website, which presents only the main issues that broadly influence Azure customers, does not present the full picture. But Azure Service Health presents major and minor, localized issues that concern you. Service issues are rare, but it is important to be equipped for the unexpected. You can set up alerts that aid in triage outages and planned maintenance. After an outage, Service Health grants official incident reports, called Root Cause Analyses (RCAs), which you can share with stakeholders.

Service Health assists you in keeping a focus on several event types:

Service issues are problems in Azure, such as outages, that concern you right now. You can drill down to your engineering teams' concerned services, regions, and updates and find ways to share and track the latest information.

Planned maintenance events can influence your availability. You can drill down to the affected services, regions, and details to show how an event will influence you and what you need to do. Most of these events occur without any consequence to you and are not shown here. In the unusual case of a reboot, Service Health enables you to determine when to perform the maintenance to reduce downtime.

Health advisories are issues that need you to act to evade service interruption, including service retirements and breaking changes. Health advisories are declared far in advance to enable you to plan.

Analyze the Decision Criteria

This section will examine experts' criteria when adopting an Azure monitoring service for a particular business requirement. By understanding the criteria, you can better assess the nuanced differences among the products.

Do you need to analyze how you are using Azure to reduce costs? Improve resilience? Harden your security?

Pick Azure Advisor when you want for an analysis of your deployed resources. Azure Advisor examines the configuration and utilization of your resources and gives suggestions on optimizing for reliability, security, performance, costs, and operations based on experts' best practices.

Do you want to monitor Azure services or your usage of Azure?

If you want to keep an eye on Azure itself, particularly the services and regions you rely on, you want to pick Azure Service Health. You can observe the current status of the Azure services you rely on, future planned outages, and services that will be sunset. You can insert alerts that assist you in staying on top of incidents and upcoming downtime without visiting the dashboard regularly.

But, if you want to keep track of the performance or issues related to your specific VM or container instances, databases, applications, and so on, you should visit Azure Monitor and create reports and notifications to help you understand how your services are performing or diagnose issues related to your Azure usage.

Do you want to measure custom events alongside other usage metrics?

Select Azure Monitor when you are required to measure custom events alongside other collected telemetry data. Custom events, such as those attached in the source code of your software applications, could assist in identifying and diagnosing why your application is performing a certain way.

Do you need to set up alerts for outages or when autoscaling is about to deploy new instances?

Again, you would apply Azure Monitor to set up alerts for key events related to your particular resources.

Use Azure Advisor

Let us consider an example Tailwind Traders requires to optimize its cloud cost. Additionally, the organization is concerned about security violations because it saves customer and historical purchase

data in cloud-based databases. As the organization ramps up its cloud expertise, it wants to better understand its use of the cloud and best practices and pinpoint "easy wins" where it can lessen its cloud cost and tighten security measures.

Which service should you choose?

Implement the decision criteria you studied in the previous section to find the best option.

First, does Tailwind Traders need to analyze its Azure usage for optimization in this situation? Yes. Tailwind Traders recognizes that it might be paying too much, is concerned about its security measures, and wants to examine its cloud usage against industry best practices. Hence, Azure Advisor is the ideal option for this situation.

Although you might have found the correct product option, let's continue assessing the decision criteria for this situation.

Second, in this situation, does Tailwind Traders want to monitor Azure services' health that affects all customers or the resources deployed on Azure? This situation is not concerned with operations. However, Azure Advisor does analyze and give recommendations for attaining operational excellence.

Third, does Tailwind Traders want to measure custom events alongside other usage metrics in this situation? No, measuring custom events is not specified as a necessity and is not a factor in this situation.

Fourth, in this scenario, does Tailwind Traders want to set up alerts for outages or when autoscaling is about to deploy new instances? Again, this situation is not concerned with operations. However, Azure Advisor does analyze and provide recommendations for attaining operational excellence.

Azure Advisor is the best product option to help Tailwind Traders properly understand and optimize its cloud spending and security posture. This product might also assist the organization with other areas of its cloud usage.

Use Azure Monitor

For example, the Tailwind Traders e-commerce website is encountering intermittent errors, and the team is uncertain of the reason. Because of the character of the errors, the team speculates that it is either a database or caching problem. What are the events surrounding the errors? Does it occur only during peak usage times? What is the state of the team's Azure SQL instance? What is the state of its Redis caching server? How can it track the issues to a root cause?

Which service should you choose?

As in the previous section, implement the decision criteria you studied earlier to determine the correct option.

First, in this scenario, does Tailwind Traders require an analysis of its Azure usage for optimization? Optimization is not the team's goal, so Azure Advisor is not a nominee.

Second, in this scenario, does Tailwind Traders want to monitor Azure services' health that affects all customers or the resources deployed on Azure? Because this issue occurs intermittently, it is unlikely to influence an entire Azure region or service. It is more probable that a logic problem exists somewhere in their e-commerce website code or another problem is creating database failures or caching locks. In this situation, the team could employ Azure Monitor to pinpoint a particular user session and view the performance of each service involved in the issue.

Third, does Tailwind Traders want to measure custom events alongside other usage metrics in this situation? Yes. Software developers can send supplementary information about the state of the web application through Application Insights to assist in locating the root cause of the issue. Application Insights depends on the Azure Monitor platform to save custom event information.

Fourth, in this scenario, does Tailwind Traders want to set up alerts for outages or when autoscaling is about to deploy new instances? No, alerting is not their goal in this situation.

Azure Monitor is the most suitable option for supporting Tailwind Traders to track this intermittent issue. The team can utilize a wealth of tools to help it gain insight into the application's performance at a high level and dive deep into particular issues.

Use Azure Service Health

Let us consider an example where Tailwind Traders desires to operationalize its cloud environment. Particularly, its cloud operations team desires to let stakeholders understand future planned downtime in advance. The team also needs its solution architects to be alerted about any Microsoft plans to sunset services so it can re-architect its software products respectively.

When outages occur, the team must promptly determine whether the issue is particular to their services or a service interruption that touches many Azure customers. The team also wants to provide key stakeholders with reports that explain how and why the incident occurred, and so on.

Which service should you choose?

Again, implement the decision criteria you studied earlier to obtain the correct product.

First, does Tailwind Traders need to analyze its Azure usage for optimization in this situation? No, so Azure Advisor is not a competitor in this situation.

Second, does Tailwind Traders desire to monitor Azure services' health that affects all customers or the resources deployed on Azure? In this situation, the condition is to stay informed of future planned downtime. Additionally, the team wants to capture official incident reports. For this reason, Azure Service Health is the most powerful candidate to pick for this situation.

Although it is possible that you would prefer Azure Service Health, let's continue assessing the remaining decision criteria.

Third, does Tailwind Traders want to measure custom events alongside other usage metrics in this situation? No, measuring custom events is not mentioned as a condition and is not a concern in this situation.

Fourth, in this situation, does Tailwind Traders need to set up alerts for outages or when autoscaling is about to deploy new instances? Setting up alerts for outages is a condition, but generating alerts for other events, such as autoscaling, is not in scope. Use Azure Service Health to set up alerts that are particular to Azure outages that influence all Azure customers. Adopt Azure Monitor to set up alerts for outages and other events that influence only your particular resources.

In this situation, Azure Service Health is the right option to choose.

Choosing the Best Tools for Managing and Configuring your Azure Environment

Identify the Product Options

There are two general categories of management tools at a high level: visual tools and code-based tools.

Visual tools present full, visually pleasant access to all the functionality of Azure. But, visual tools might not be as beneficial when attempting to set up a huge deployment of resources with interdependencies and configuration options.

A code-based tool is normally the better choice when promptly configuring Azure resources. Although learning the right commands and parameters might take time, they can be stored in files and regularly used as required after access. Also, the code that implements setup and configuration can be saved, versioned, and managed along with application source code in a source code-management tool such as Git. This method of managing hardware and cloud resources, which developers apply when they compose application code, is referred to as infrastructure.

There are two approaches to infrastructure as code: imperative and declarative. Imperative code describes each step that should be implemented to accomplish the desired outcome. In comparison, declarative code details the desired outcome, enabling an interpreter to determine how to accomplish that outcome properly. This difference is necessary because tools based on declarative code can present a more robust approach to deploying dozens or hundreds of resources simultaneously and reliably.

Your product options

Microsoft offers a mixture of tools and services to maintain your cloud environment, each directed at different situations and users.

The Azure Portal

Adopting the Azure portal, a web-based user interface enables you to obtain practically every feature of Azure. The Azure portal presents a pleasant, graphical UI to observe all the services you are utilizing, build new services, configure your services, and view reports. The Azure portal is how most users first experience Azure. But, as your Azure usage grows, you may prefer a more repeatable code-centric way to manage your Azure resources.

The Azure Mobile App

The Azure mobile app gives iOS and Android access to your Azure resources when you are off your computer. By using it, you can do the following:

- Monitor the health and status of your Azure resources
- Inspect for alerts, promptly diagnose and repair issues, and restart a web app or a virtual machine
- Run the Azure CLI or Azure PowerShell commands to handle your Azure resources

Azure PowerShell

Azure PowerShell is a shell with which developers, DevOps, and IT professionals can perform commands called cmdlets (pronounced command-lets). These commands call the Azure Rest API to deliver every conceivable management job in Azure. Cmdlets can be performed independently or merged into a script file and executed together to orchestrate:

- The routine setup, teardown, and management of a single resource or various connected resources
- The deployment of a complete infrastructure, which might include dozens or hundreds of resources from imperative code

Capturing the commands in a script makes the method repeatable and automatable.

EXAM TIP: Azure PowerShell is available for Windows, Linux, and Mac, and you can access it in a web browser via Azure Cloud Shell.

The Azure CLI

The Azure CLI command-line interface is an executable program with which a developer, DevOps professional, or IT professional can perform commands in Bash. The commands call the Azure Rest API to deliver every possible management task in Azure. You can run the commands individually or merge them into a script and execute them together for the routine setup, teardown, and maintenance of a single resource or an entire environment.

In many regards, the Azure CLI is almost identical to Azure PowerShell in what you can achieve. Both run on Windows, Linux, and Mac and can be accessed in a web browser through Cloud Shell.

EXAM TIP: The main difference between Azure CLI and Azure PowerShell is your application syntax. If you are already skilled in PowerShell or Bash, you can use the tool you favor.

ARM Templates

Although it is feasible to put up and pull down one Azure resource or orchestrate an infrastructure containing hundreds of resources using imperative code in Azure PowerShell or the Azure CLI, there is a more reliable approach to accomplish this feature.

You may declare the resources you want to use in a declarative JSON language (ARM templates) using Azure Resource Manager templates. The advantage is that the entire ARM template is checked before any code is executed to ensure that the resources are generated and connected correctly. The template then coordinates the production of those resources in tandem. If you require 50 copies of the same resource, all 50 copies are created simultaneously.

Finally, the developer, DevOps expert, or IT professional must only define each resource's intended state and configuration in the ARM template, and the template will handle the rest. Templates can run PowerShell and Bash scripts before or after the resource is created.

<u>Analyze the decision criteria</u>

In this section, you will examine experts' criteria to help them determine which Azure management tools to employ to meet their business requirements. Understanding the criteria can help you better understand the nuanced product differences.

<u>***Do you need to perform one-off management, administrative, or reporting actions?***</u>

Azure PowerShell and the Azure CLI are Azure management tools that enable you to promptly obtain the IP address of a virtual machine you have used, reboot a VM, or scale an app. You might want to hold

custom scripts for both tools handy on your local hard drive for specific operations you must execute many times.

Opposite to the Azure CLI and PowerShell, Azure Resource Manager templates (ARM templates) determine the infrastructure demands in your application for repeatable deployments. Although ARM templates are not meant for one-off scenarios, they can be used for this purpose. However, for one-off scenarios, you may prefer more agile tools like PowerShell, Azure CLI scripts, or the Azure portal.

Remember that ARM templates can cover both PowerShell and/or Azure CLI scripts, which will give you the knowledge to use scripts for tasks that may not be achievable with the ARM template itself. Combining Azure management tools allows flexibility in choosing the best tool(s) for your precise needs.

The Azure portal can fulfill most if not all, management and administrative actions. Suppose you are just learning Azure and/or need to occasionally set up and manage resources (or prefer a visual interface for viewing reports). In that case, it makes reason to take the help of the visual presentation that the Azure portal offers.

However, relying only on visual scanning and clicking is less effective if you are in a cloud management or administrative position. The Azure CLI or PowerShell will give you the most flexibility for repeatable tasks to immediately locate the settings and information you need to work with.

The last management tool to consider is the Azure mobile app, which you can access through an iOS or Android phone or tablet. Because it is full-featured, it is possibly the most suitable choice when a laptop is not immediately available and you want to view and triage issues instantly.

Do you need a way to repeatedly set up one or more resources and ensure that all the dependencies are created in the proper order?

ARM templates determine your application's infrastructure demands for a repeatable deployment that is prepared logically. A validation step guarantees that all resources can be created in the correct order based on dependencies, in parallel, and idempotent.

By contrast, it is reasonable to use either PowerShell or the Azure CLI to set up all the resources for deployment. But, there is no validation action in these tools. If a script meets an error, the dependency resources cannot be rolled back; deployments happen serially, and only some operations are idempotent.

When you are scripting, do you come from a Windows administration or Linux administration background?

If you or your cloud administrators have Windows administration experience, you may favor PowerShell. If you or your cloud administrators have a Linux administration history, you may favor the Azure CLI. In practice, either tool can fulfill most one-off administration tasks.

Use the Azure Portal to understand and manage your cloud environment visually

Let us consider an example where Tailwind Traders employs Azure largely throughout its entire organization. To ensure that the technical and executive teams are informed of the company's cloud cost, the director of cloud operations will meet weekly with the Chief Financial Officer (CFO) to talk about their cloud spending.

Discussions might begin at a high level, but the two officers might want to jump deep during the meeting to gain insight into how Azure resources are utilized. Ideally, they could see the data presented visually and run custom reports in real-time. Which tool can they apply during their meeting?

Which service should you choose?

Implement the decision criteria you studied in the previous unit to find the best option.

First, does Tailwind Traders need to conduct one-off management, administrative, or reporting actions in this situation? Yes, and given the necessity to view data visually and generate custom reports throughout the meeting, the Azure portal is the most suitable choice. The meeting attendees can promptly find answers to their problems using a wealth of reporting possibilities.

The next two decision criteria do not pertain to this situation because the director of cloud operations and the CFO would not be deploying or configuring any resources.

The Azure portal is the right product option for this situation.

Use Azure PowerShell for one-off administrative tasks

Let us consider an example; Tailwind Traders uses technologists with many diverse skills. A unit of developers and administrators creates and maintains a collection of intranet applications essential to the business. The team members have strong credentials in Windows development and network administration.

The team recognized that managing Azure from the portal takes too much time and is not repeatable. The team migrated its applications to the cloud, and it now requires a way to perform one-off testing, management, and administrative tasks in its intranet environment. Which tool should the company apply for one-off tasks?

Which service should you choose?

Implement the decision criteria you studied earlier to find the best option.

First, does the Tailwind Traders team want to deliver one-off management, administrative, or reporting tasks in this situation? Yes. But, the team already understands that it does not want to depend on the Azure portal for these one-off actions. Hence, both Azure PowerShell and Azure CLI are great options. We will hone in on which tool the team should apply in a moment.

Second, does Tailwind Traders need a repeatable and reliable means of deploying its entire infrastructure in this situation? No, not in this situation. Hence, Azure Resource Manager templates are not the correct choice.

When the Tailwind Traders team is doing scripting, does it come from a Windows administration or Linux administration background? This team has Windows administration experience. It would probably be most convenient to use Azure PowerShell because this tool permits it to utilize the syntax it is most comfortable with to perform one-off administration tasks.

Azure PowerShell is the most suitable choice for this situation.

Use the Azure CLI for One-Off Administrative Tasks

As we saw in the previous section, Tailwind Traders uses technologists with many diverse skills. The DevOps team is mainly concerned with keeping external systems, such as the company's e-commerce site, up and running. This team has Linux administration experience. It often needs to complete administrative tasks associated with the health of the cloud environment. The team soon understood

that managing Azure from the portal takes too much time and is not repeatable. Which tool should it apply for one-off tasks?

Which service should you choose?

Implement the decision criteria you studied earlier to find the correct option.

Because this scenario is almost identical to the one in the previous unit, you can jump over the first two criteria. In other words, you can instantly drop Azure Resource Manager templates and the Azure portal as possible choices for this situation. So, let's go to the third decision criterion.

The team's history should determine the best option in this situation. Because this team has a Linux administration background, it would probably be most suitable to use the Azure CLI. The Azure CLI permits the team to utilize the Bash shell and its syntax to execute one-off administration tasks.

The Azure CLI is the most suitable choice for this situation.

Use the Azure Mobile App to Manage Azure on the Go

Tailwind Traders encounters surges in e-commerce traffic that match national holidays and weekends. In the company's first few years, managers of critical systems had to assemble at the office of the director of cloud operations during these crucial times. But, now that Tailwind Traders has successfully operationalized the most important systems, the director desires to relax this condition and enable employees to spend these dates with their families. Is there a product that can assist in supporting this scenario?

Which service should you choose?

Let's go through our decision criteria again.

First, does Tailwind Traders require to perform one-off management, administrative, and reporting actions? Yes. The real question is, how? A phone or tablet answer could support key employees in keeping an eye on the health of the cloud environment when they are not in the office. The Azure mobile app is probably a great compromise because it allows employees to be absent from work and deliver essential, one-off management and administrative tasks.

We can skip the rest of the decision criteria in this unusual situation. The Azure mobile app is the best choice.

Use ARM Templates to Deploy an Entire Cloud Infrastructure

Tailwind Traders aspires to operationalize their cloud deployments. The company requires a repeatable, safe way to scale its operations during top sales times. Because you will be picking a process for scaling your production environment, you want to guarantee that your chosen service:

- It is effective and can create many resources in parallel
- Creates all dependencies in the correct order
- It can be utilized without worrying that it crashed in the middle of provisioning the necessary infrastructure

Which service should you choose?

Let's go through the decision criteria one more time.

First, does Tailwind Traders need to perform one-off management, administrative, or reporting actions in this scenario? We are not looking to help with one-time or one-off management or administration tasks this time. We are aiming for a technology to automate the deployment of complete infrastructure, as required.

Second, does Tailwind Traders need a repeatable and reliable way to deploy its entire infrastructure? Yes, this is precisely what the company requires. Our decision criteria can guide us to adopt Azure Resource Manager templates.

You could apply Azure PowerShell or the Azure CLI, but these scripting technologies have notable limitations when deploying infrastructure. ARM templates can aid in overcoming these limitations.

The third decision criterion is writing a script by utilizing imperative code. However, when you utilize ARM templates, you determine your infrastructure declaratively using JSON code. Sometimes, you still might require imperative code for configuration or clean-up tasks. In these situations, you can trigger the execution of scripts by utilizing either Azure PowerShell or the Azure CLI to execute these tasks.

In this situation, ARM templates are the right choice.

Lab 7-02: Azure AI Service

Service Introduction

Azure AI services encompass a suite of artificial intelligence tools and capabilities offered by Microsoft Azure, enabling developers to integrate advanced AI functionalities into their applications with ease. These services cover a wide range of AI capabilities, including machine learning, natural language processing, computer vision, and speech recognition. Azure AI services, such as Azure Machine Learning, Azure Cognitive Services, and Azure Bot Services, provide pre-built models, APIs, and development frameworks that facilitate the creation of intelligent applications. Developers can leverage these services to build sophisticated features like image recognition, language understanding, and conversational interfaces, ultimately enhancing the overall user experience and functionality of their applications. Azure AI services empower organizations to harness the power of artificial intelligence without the need for extensive expertise, accelerating the adoption of AI-driven solutions across various industries.

Problem

A company wants to improve its office attendance and surveillance system by enabling face recognition service. How can this be done?

Solution

The company can use the Azure Artificial Intelligence (AI) service for Face Recognition. This service will analyze the picture of a person by facial expression, hair, age, and accessories, then declare the result based on the information collected.

Step-by-Step Guide
1. Open **Microsoft AI**.

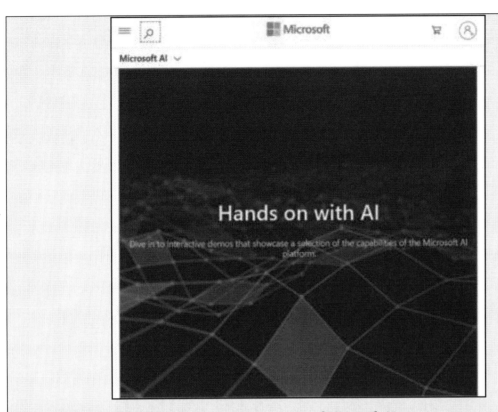

2. Go to the Face and Emotion Recognition service of Microsoft AI.
3. Click on the **Try it out** button.

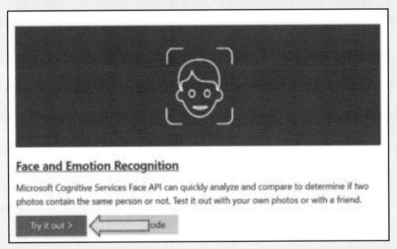

4. The face and Emotion Recognition service page will open and display as shown below.
5. Click on **Add Photo** in both PHOTO 1 and PHOTO 2.

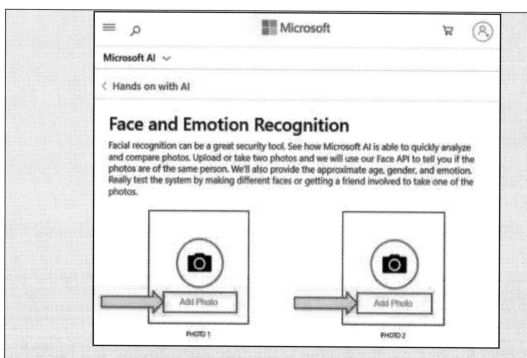

6. On PHOTO 1, upload the picture of the company's employee from the company's library.
7. On PHOTO 2, upload the picture of an unknown person.
8. The face recognition service will scan the photos and declare the result, as shown below.

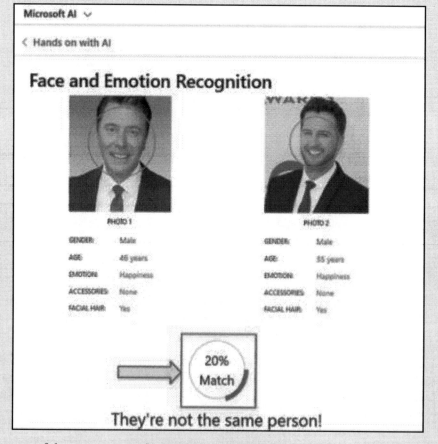

9. Take pictures of the same person for PHOTO 1 and PHOTO 2.

10. The result will show a 100% match, which means both persons are the same.

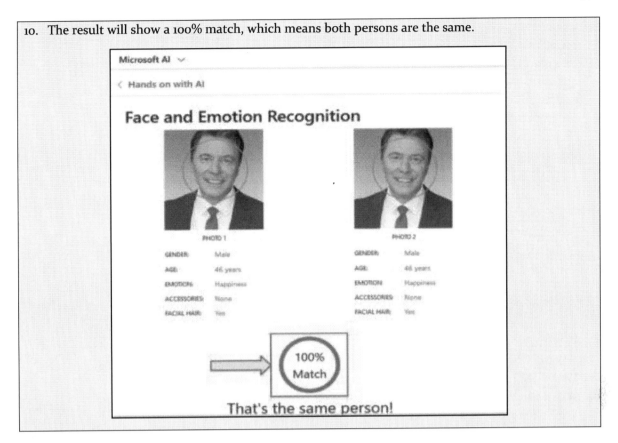

Mind Map

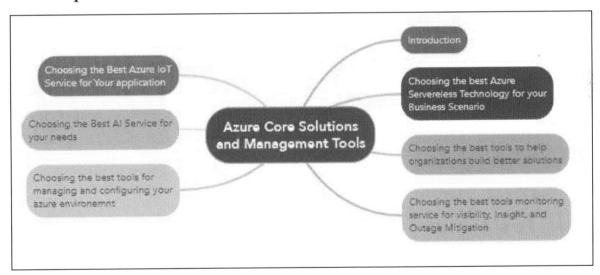

Figure 7-06: Mind Map

Practice Questions

1.	What is the purpose of "models" in Machine Learning and Artificial Intelligence?
A.	To define what you want your Machine Learning implementation to learn

B. To define the framework for integrating other Azure services with your particular Machine Learning instance

C. To define the version of your Machine Learning application

D. To define the size and capacity of the Machine Learning service

2. What are some of the likely outcomes of using Big Data analytics? (Choose 3)
A. Cost reduction on data storage
B. Cheaper and more accessible cloud computing products
C. Products created better aligned with customer needs
D. Better decision-making from immediate analysis
E. A decoupling of business decisions from the development of new products
F. More secure access to company infrastructure

3. When would you use Azure Logic Apps to solve a problem?
A. When a function is not able to solve a problem as a single task
B. When you have to send emails as part of your workflow while processing data from multiple data sources
C. When you have to integrate different systems inside and outside of Azure
D. When you have to use more than one Azure subscription
E. When there are too many integration points to handle with Azure Functions

4. What is the best definition of Azure DevOps?
A. It is a specific section of the Azure Portal where you can manage operational parts of your infrastructure
B. It is a way to write better code and find bugs faster
C. It is a platform to manage Azure resources meant for development, such as App Services, Azure Functions, and Visual Studio Online
D. Azure DevOps is a suite of 5 different tools to create more robust software, faster

5. Which of the following are tools in Azure DevOps? (Choose 3)
A. Azure Automation
B. Azure Artifacts
C. Azure Deployment
D. Azure Operations
E. Azure Pipelines
F. Azure Boards

6. Which are Internet of Things services on Azure? (Choose 2)
A. IoT Services
B. IoT Management Studio
C. IoT Central
D. IoT App Services

E. IoT Hub
F. IoT Virtual Box

7. What is the purpose of "Knowledge Mining" in Machine Learning and Artificial Intelligence?
A. To define what you want your Machine Learning implementation to learn
B. To define the framework for integrating other Azure services with your particular Machine Learning instance
C. To define the version of your Machine Learning application
D. To find existing insights in your data-the size and capacity of the Machine Learning service

8. What are some of the likely outcomes of using HDInsight? (Choose 2)
A. Cheaper and more accessible cloud computing products
B. Allows storing massive amounts of data easily, efficiently and cost-effectively
C. A wide range of scenarios such as Extracting, Transforming, and Loading (ETL), data warehousing, Machine Learning, and IoT can be enabled
D. A decoupling of business decisions from the development of new products

9. Which Azure service is based on Events?
A. HDInsight
B. Databricks
C. Logic Apps
D. Event Grid

10. Which of the following two services is likely similar to each other? (Choose 2)
A. HDInsight
B. Databricks
C. Logic Apps
D. Azure Functions

11. What are the three main features of Cognitive service? (Choose 3)
A. Vision
B. Emotion
C. Decisions
D. Speech

12. What is the best definition of Azure Machine Learning Studio?
A. A specific section of the Azure Portal where you can manage operational parts of your infrastructure
B. A way to write better code and find bugs faster
C. It provides a centralized location for data scientists and developers to work with all the artifacts for developing, training, and deploying machine learning models
D. Azure Machine Learning Studio is a suite of 5 different tools to create more robust software, faster

13. What are the three main services of Machine Learning? (Choose 3)
A. End-to-End Service
B. Tooling
C. Automation
D. Orchestration

14. What are the benefits of a Serverless Model?
A. Dynamic Scalability
B. End-to-End Delivery
C. Faster Time to Market
D. More efficient use of resources

15. What is the purpose of Azure DevTest Labs?
A. To offer developers the tools to support teams in preparing projects, working on application creation, and designing and deploying software
B. To create labs that consist of pre-configured bases or templates for Azure Resource Manager
C. To provide customizable team dashboards with configurable widgets to share information, progress, and trends
D. To test the latest versions of your software

16. Which Azure service provides serverless workflow orchestration to let you integrate apps, data, systems, and services across enterprises or organizations?
A. Logic Apps
B. Functions
C. Apps Grid
D. Bot Service

17. You must use Azure Big Data solutions to query and transform data to extract insights. What is the most appropriate solution for this?
A. Azure SQL Database
B. Data Lake Analytics
C. Cosmos DB
D. Blob Storage

18. In which situation should you use an Azure Function app?
A. When you want to execute a visual studio graphical workflow that provisions an order when the order is received
B. When you want to execute Javascript code that sends a maintenance email every Sunday evening
C. When you want to execute a batch file that removes records from an Azure SQL Database on Demand
D. When you want to use Functions to write code without having to worry about deploying that code or creating VMs to run your code

19. Which Azure analytics service is based on Apache Spark?
A. HDInsight
B. Data Lake
C. Databricks
D. Event Grid

20. What are the outcomes of using Big Data for business value?
A. Better service
B. Better products
C. More profits
D. All of the above

21. Which services are used to manage the computing workload on edge devices?
A. IoT Hub
B. IoT Central
C. Azure Sphere
D. IoT Edge

22. Which of the following components is located on the edge device?
A. IoT Edge module
B. IoT Edge runtime
C. IoT Edge cloud interface
D. None of the above

23. Which of the following online simulators is used to connect IoT devices to the IoT Hub?

A. ExpressRoute

B. FPGA

C. GreenCloud
D. Raspberry Pi

24. Which of the following IoT services provides bi-direction communication?
A. IoT Hub
B. IoT Edge
C. IoT Central
D. Azure Sphere

Chapter 08: Security

Introduction

Microsoft is responsible for the security of the cloud. The user, as a cloud administrator, is responsible for the security of the cloud. Azure security is the most important part of Azure. Azure security services protect data, technologies, and infrastructure from working simultaneously. With Microsoft, security can be successfully achieved through the role of Microsoft and a cloud administrator. Microsoft administrator follows the principles of security, compliance, and integrity to protect customers' data and access. The administrator needs to follow the rules and regulations according to the Microsoft trusted cloud to get access to data.

Why Security is Important

Security is a set of policies or rules allowing traffic to be directed to the network correctly. Network security is very important, especially when there is a communication of infrastructure with the internet. Multiple access is possible on the internet at a time, so there is a need to secure the cloud infrastructure with a set of security rules.

For example, multiple subnets are present in VNet, as shown in Figure 8-01. By default, all virtual machines within the subnet communicate with each other. Within the same VNet, some Virtual Machines (VM) store complex and sensitive data. For this, especially security policies are required to protect data within the same network. For security purposes, the VM with sensitive data is separately available in a subnet with no connection with other subnets in VNet.

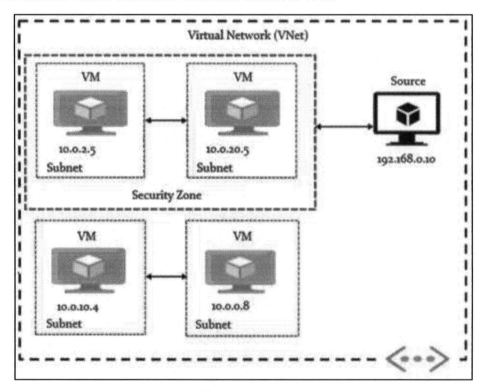

Figure 8-01: VNet with Security feature

This chapter explains the Azure security aspect that makes strong cybersecurity of the cloud.

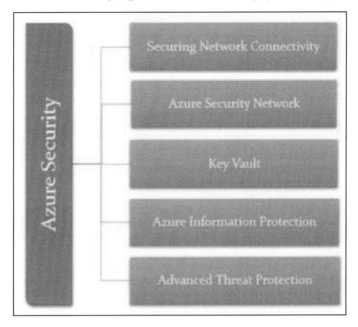

Figure 8-02: Azure Security Services

Azure security services include:

- **Securing Network Connectivity:** Azure built-in resources and services can efficiently secure network connectivity. Azure users can secure the entire network or small parts of the network depending on their cloud architecture need
- **Microsoft Defender for Cloud:** Microsoft Defender for Cloud helps and guides an Azure user to make a secure Azure platform for the utilization of optimum services
- **Azure Key Vault:** Azure Key Vault is an amazing way to hide and save key passwords and uses key hardware for the provision of security when needed
- **Azure Information Protection:** Azure Information Protection (AIP) protects e-mail, complex information, and sensitive data
- **Advanced Threat Protection (ATP):** Advanced Threat Protection (ATP) identifies special users and device activity. It enables the protection of sensitive data and applications against hacking approaches. It also provides a way of single-console management for protection

Zero Trust Model

A security concept known as "Zero Trust" guards resources by preparing for the worst-case situation. Zero Trust checks each request as though it came from an uncontrolled network at first, assuming there has been a breach.

Organizations now require a new security paradigm that adapts to the complexity of the contemporary environment, embraces the mobile workforce, and safeguards people, devices, apps, and data no matter where they are.

Microsoft strongly advises the Zero Trust security architecture, which is founded on the following tenets, to address this new computing world:

Verify explicitly - Authenticate and authorize consistently depending on all accessible data points.

Use least privilege access - Use Just-In-Time and Just-Enough-Access (JIT/JEA), risk-based adaptive rules, and data protection to restrict user access.

Assume breaches - Consider a breach; reduce blast radius and segment access. Make sure the encryption is end-to-end. Use analytics to get visibility, support threat identification, and strengthen defenses.

Adjusting to Zero Trust

Corporate networks have typically been regulated, safeguarded, and seen as secure. The network was restricted to managed computers, VPN access was strictly monitored, and personal devices were regularly barred or restricted.

In the Zero Trust model, the situation is reversed. It demands that everyone authenticate rather than presuming that a device is secure just because it is connected to the corporate network. Then, rather than granting access based on location, it does so after authentication.

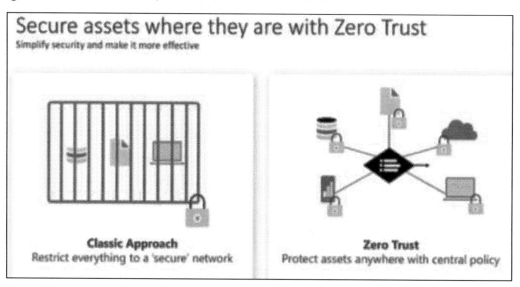

Figure 8-03: Concept of Zero Trust

Defense in Depth

Having just a solitary security measure for cloud infrastructure is never enough. Defense in depth is always required. Let's start with a scenario—a castle with a king, for example. The king is the prize the attackers want and must be defended at all costs. There is often a moat around the castle. It has bare walls with no doors. There are guards at the top. They might have hot oil. There is an inner wall. The throne room is fortified, and so on. There are many layers of defense for the king. This situation portrays defense in depth.

Let us move to the cloud with on-premises infrastructure. This is where you are in charge of all your physical hardware, buildings, staff, and computing capabilities. Like the castle, it needs to protect your on-premises assets and has several layers of defense. You will have swipe cards to get into the building, security guards, restricted access to servers, usernames, passwords, firewalls, and so on. Most of the defense of your assets is up to you because you own the infrastructure.

Some key points of Defense in Depth:

- Strategy to slow the advance of an attack to get unauthorized access to information
- Layered approach: Each layer provides protection, so if one layer is breached, a subsequent prevents further exposure
- Applied by Microsoft, both in physical data centers and across Azure services

There are seven general layers of security in cloud computing, and that goes for Azure:

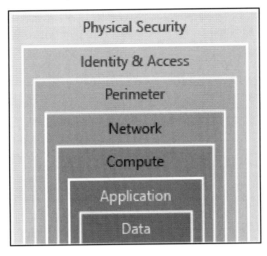

Figure 8-04: Defense in Depth

Physical

This is the actual data center or the first step of defense. It is used for building security & controlling access to computing hardware. Only authorized personnel have access.

Identity and Access

It relates to the Microsoft Entra ID that controls all access to Azure and the identity of all users, applications, and connections.

- Control access to infrastructure and change control
- Access granted is only for what is needed
- Use single sign-on and multi-factor authentication
- Audit events and changes

Perimeter

It protects against Distributed Denial-of-Service (DDoS) attacks, volumetric attacks, protocol attacks, etc.

- Use DDoS protection to filter large-scale attacks before they can cause a denial of service for end-users
- Use perimeter firewalls to identify and alert on malicious attacks against your network

Network

It filters traffic to and from Azure using virtual networks and applying security standards.

- Limit communication between resources
- Deny by default. It only allows what is required
- Restrict inbound internet access and limit outbound, where appropriate
- Implement secure connectivity to on-premises networks

Compute

The compute component protects against intruders entering your virtual machines or databases.

- Secure access to virtual machines
- Implement endpoint protection and keep systems patched and current
- Malware, unpatched systems, and improperly secured systems open your environment to attacks

Application

It is the gateways and firewalls that provide security to your Azure applications.

- Ensure applications are secure and free of vulnerabilities
- Store sensitive application secrets in a secure storage medium
- Make security a design requirement for all application development
- Integrate security into the application development life cycle

Data

The data on Azure is encrypted and protected against anyone unauthorized reading or making sense of it.

- In almost all cases, attackers are after data
- Data can be in the database, stored on disk inside VMs, on a SaaS application such as Office 365, or in cloud storage
- Those storing and controlling access to data ensure that it is properly secured
- Often regulatory requirements dictate controls & processes
- To ensure confidentiality, integrity, and availability

So, Defense-in-Depth on Azure is how Microsoft provides multiple layers of security for your cloud infrastructure.

Securing Network Connectivity

The networks on Azure give access to everything to the user. All the resources and services of Microsoft Azure are connected to a network to provide communication between users, processes, and other services. To run these services of azure, smooth network behavior is required that efficiently provides all the network services within Azure. To achieve optimum network performance, secure network connectivity is very important. Figure 8-05 shows ways to ensure secure network connectivity.

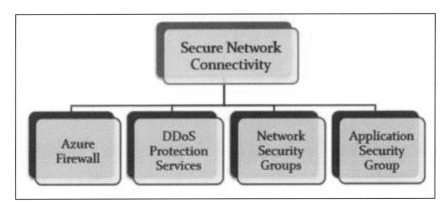

Figure 8-05: Ways of Secure Network Connectivity

Azure Firewall

A firewall is a network security device that analyses incoming and outgoing network traffic and determines whether specific traffic should be allowed or blocked based on a set of security rules. Firewall rules that specify IP address ranges can be created. Clients can only access the destination server with IP addresses in specified ranges. Specific network protocol and port information can also be included in firewall rules.

Azure Firewall is a managed, cloud-based network security service that aids in the protection of Azure virtual network resources. A virtual network functions similarly to a traditional network in your data center. It is a key component of your private network, allowing virtual machines and other computational resources to securely connect to each other, the internet, and on-premises networks.

- **Rules:** Azure firewall must have a certain set of rules that permits to allow and not allow the traffic according to the connected devices and services attached to the network.
- **Variation:** The firewall may have certain hardware and software according to the size of the network.
- **Compulsory Bit:** A firewall is considered a compulsory network section to ensure network security.

Figure 8-06 shows the network performance employing network security with the help of the Azure firewall.

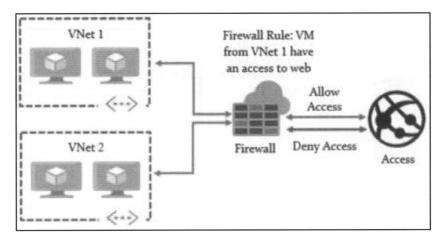

Figure 8-06: Network Configuration with Azure Firewall

What can you configure with Azure Firewall?

You can configure Azure Firewall to:

- Fully Qualified Domain Names (FQDNs) that can be accessed from a subnet are defined by application rules
- Source address, protocol, destination port, and destination address are all defined by network rules
- Inbound requests are translated using Network Address Translation (NAT) rules that define destination IP addresses and ports

Distributed Denial-of-Service Attacks (DDoS)

History: In 2012, six banks in the USA were targeted with a series of Distributed Denial-of-Service attacks. The banks were located in small town and nearby areas. The attack was created from many hackers' servers, each creating a 60 Gb traffic load per second. In 2014, the security provider and content delivery network "Cloud Flare" was targeted with DDoS attacks. The attack was created with a 400 Gb traffic load per second. In 2018, a famous development platform "GitHub" was targeted by a DDoS attack with 1.35 Tb of traffic load per second. All these DDoS made the companies suffer from a massive disaster. Companies lost business and users' trust due to this attack. In addition, companies also need to invest billions of dollars in remaking the networks.

Figure 8-07: Companies Affected by DDoS Attack

DDoS Scenario

Distributed Denial-of-Service is the most common attack on services attached to the internet. Let's suppose a website runs on a server, as shown in Figure 8-08. This server can serve a limited number of user requests. The number of users in the given network is 50,000, and the webservers, at most, have 5000 requests every second. When the entire users send the request simultaneously, the webserver would not be able to serve the demands of the user request. In the end, the web server suddenly stops working due to many user requests. This is because of the Denial-of-Service (DoS) attack. If the web server received the same number of requests from many different sources and computers, then web servers would suddenly stop working due to the multiple simultaneous requests. This attack on the service is called a Distributed Denial-of-Service attack.

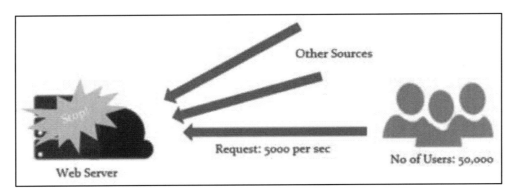

Figure 8-08: DDoS Attack

DDoS Protection Service

- **Target a Website:** Many servers target the same website or computer to stop it from working. For example, GitHub was a target with 127 Mb requests every second.
- **Azure Protection Service:** Microsoft Azure has a protection service against DDoS attacks. Depending on the application's user needs, this service has a different protection level. Azure protection service detects DDoS attacks and works against them.
- **No Halt:** Azure Protection service would not interrupt the routine process of other services on the website due to Azure's global presents.

EXAM TIP: Azure Firewall controls the inflow and outflow of traffic to the network based on a set of rules.

A DDoS attack is an attack of a huge amount of traffic from many different sources to a single website and server. Azure protection service protects from this type of attack globally with no downtime.

Network Security Groups

The security group provides a secure management environment for the network. A Network Security Group (NSG) is required to configure a virtual network where different virtual machines within the subnet connect.

- **Resource Firewall:** NSG has a private resource firewall that allows the connection of VNet, subnet, or another network interface with VM
- **Rules:** NSG has a set of security rules that enable some special VMs to allow or not allow the inbound and outbound traffic load from other resources

Figure 8-09 illustrates the concept of the Network Security Group in the network. There is a virtual machine present in the network. The network can be behind the Azure firewall to protect everything (i.e., complex information, sensitive data, resources, or devices) on the network. The virtual machine has its NSG that specifies the machine's rules and regulations.

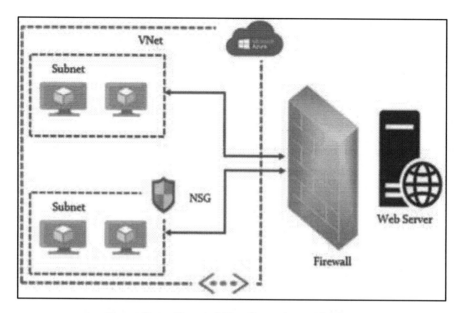

Figure 8-09: Network Configuration with NSG

Application Security Group

NSG protects the traffic flow from and to the specific virtual machine or subnet in the network. Application Security Group (ASG) protects the application running on that particular VM or subnet in the network. ASG provides application security, and NSG provides the security of traffic flow.

- **Shielding Application Infrastructure**: ASG is responsible for providing security to the application (website or Azure resources) running on a particular VM in the network.
- **Natural Integration:** With ASG, network performance is optimized with multiple levels of security rules for application and traffic flow. VMs from a different subnet is combined into NSG based on the application running on those VMs.

Figure 8-10 shows a network configuration with both NSG and ASG.

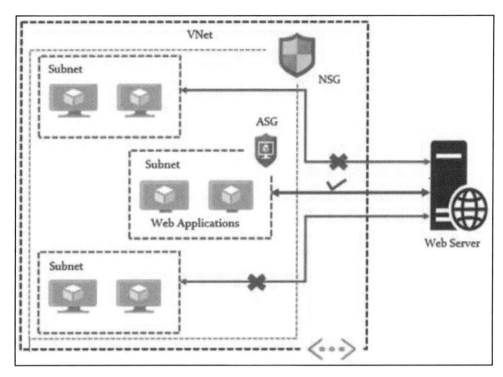

Figure 8-10: Network with ASG and NSG

> **EXAM TIP:** Network Security Group (NSG) is required in the configuration of a virtual network (VNet) where different Virtual Machines (VM) within the subnet are connecting with each other. NSG uses Access Control List (ACL) rules to allow or deny network traffic access to the subnet or VM.
>
> Application Security Group (ASG) protects the application running on that particular VM or subnet in the network.

Microsoft Defender for Cloud

Defender for Cloud is a threat and security posture monitoring tool. It keeps an eye on your on-premises, cloud, hybrid, and multi-cloud environments and sends alerts and advice to help you improve your security posture.

The tools you need to harden your resources, monitor your security posture, defend against cyberattacks, and simplify security management are all included in Defender for Cloud. Defender for Cloud's native integration with Azure makes deployment simple.

Microsoft Defender for Cloud portal contains a summarized view of policy, compliance and subscription coverage, networking, and Resource integrity hygiene, as shown in Figure 8-11.

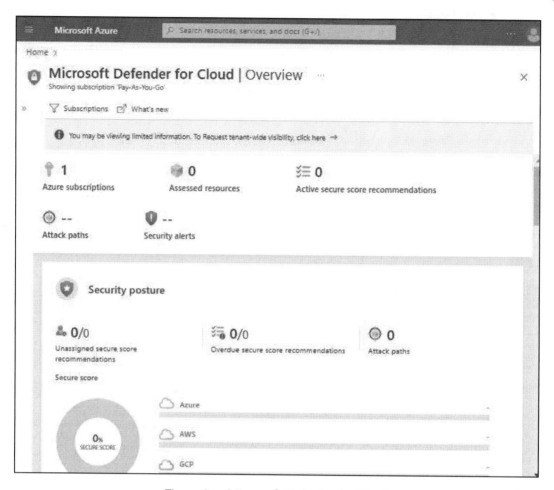

Figure 8-11: Microsoft Defender for Cloud

Protection wherever you deploy

Defender for Cloud is an Azure-native service; thus, it can monitor and secure numerous Azure services without any deployment. However, monitoring Azure services might not provide a clear picture of your security position if you operate in another cloud environment or have an on-premises data center.

Defender for Cloud can automatically deploy a Log Analytics agent to gather security information. The deployment process is handled directly for Azure machines. Microsoft Defender plans are extended to non-Azure computers with the aid of Azure Arc for hybrid and multi-cloud scenarios. Without the use of any agents, Cloud Security Posture Management (CSPM) functions are extended to multi-cloud machines.

Azure Native Protection

You can identify threats with Defender for Cloud across:

- **Azure PaaS services** - Spot attacks aimed at data services, including Azure App Service, Azure SQL, and Azure Storage Account. Additionally, you may utilize Microsoft Defender for Cloud Apps' native integration to detect anomalies on your Azure activity logs (formerly known as Microsoft Cloud App Security)

- **Azure data services** - You can automatically categorize your data in Azure SQL with the aid of Defender for Cloud's Azure data services. Additionally, you can obtain analyses of potential vulnerabilities in the Azure SQL and Storage services and suggestions for mitigating them
- **Networks** - Your exposure to brute force attacks can be reduced using Defender for Cloud. You may secure your network by limiting access to virtual machine ports and preventing unauthorized access by employing just-in-time VM access. Secure access policies can be established on specific ports, for only approved users, permitted source IP address ranges or IP addresses, and for a predetermined period.

Defend your hybrid resources

To safeguard your non-Azure servers in addition to your Azure environment, you can add Defender for Cloud capabilities to your hybrid cloud setup. You will get tailored threat intelligence and prioritized warnings based on your particular surroundings to help you concentrate on what matters the most.

Deploy Azure Arc and turn on the increased security capabilities of Defender for Cloud to extend protection to on-premises machines.

Defend running resources on other clouds

The defender can also protect resources in other clouds (such as AWS and GCP).

For example, if you have linked an Azure subscription to an Amazon Web Services (AWS) account, you can activate any of the following safeguards:

- Your AWS resources can use the CSPM functionalities of Defender for Cloud. This agentless approach evaluates your AWS resources in accordance with security guidelines specific to AWS and factors the results into the secure score. Additionally, the resources will be evaluated for conformity with AWS-specific internal requirements (AWS CIS, AWS PCI DSS, and AWS Foundational Security Best Practices). The asset inventory page in Defender for Cloud is a multi-cloud capability that enables you to manage both your Azure and AWS resources
- Microsoft Defender protects your Amazon EKS Linux clusters for Kubernetes' powerful protection and threat detection for containers
- Due to Microsoft Defender for servers, your Windows and Linux EC2 instances are protected by threat detection and cutting-edge defenses

Access, Secure, and Defend

As you manage the security of your resources and workloads in the cloud and on-premises, Defender for Cloud satisfies three essential needs:

- **Continuous access** - Understand your security stance. Determine and monitor vulnerabilities
- **Secure** - Using Azure Security Benchmark, make resources and services more secure.
- **Defend**- Spot threats to resources, workloads, and services and take appropriate action.

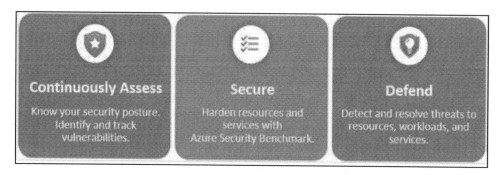

Figure 8-12: Essential needs of Cloud Defender

Continuously Access

You may continually evaluate your environment with the aid of Defender for Cloud. For your virtual machines, container registries, and SQL servers, Defender for Cloud offers vulnerability assessment options.

Microsoft Defender for Endpoint is automatically and natively integrated with Microsoft Defender for Servers. If this integration is turned on, you will have access to Microsoft threat and vulnerability management's vulnerability discoveries.

Due to these assessment tools, you will have consistent, thorough vulnerability scans that include your infrastructure, data, and computation. You may analyze the scan results from inside Defender for Cloud and take action.

Secure

Security in the cloud is a fundamental requirement that must be properly implemented, from authentication techniques to access control to the idea of Zero Trust. You must make sure your workloads are secure if you want to be secure in the cloud. You must have security policies in place that are specific to your environment and circumstances if you want to protect your workload. You receive the entire breadth and flexibility of a top-notch policy solution since Defender for Cloud policies are built on top of Azure Policy controls. You can configure Defender for Cloud to apply your policies to management groups, all subscribers, or even the entire tenant.

The flexibility to develop and extend as needed, adding additional services and resources as required, is one advantage of switching to the cloud. Defender for Cloud continuously scans your workloads for the deployment of additional resources. Defender for Cloud determines whether newly acquired resources are set up in accordance with security best practices. If not, they are identified, and you receive a prioritized list of fixes that need to be made. You can lessen the attack surface on all of your resources by following recommendations.

The Azure Security Benchmark enables and supports the list of suggestions. This benchmark for Azure, created by Microsoft, offers the best recommendations for security and compliance practices based on widely used compliance frameworks.

Defender for Cloud gives you this ability, allowing you to apply secure configuration standards across your resources and set security policies.

Defender for Cloud organizes the recommendations into security controls and assigns a secure score value to each control to make it easier for you to understand how essential each piece of advice is to your overall security posture. The controls provide a working list of things to consider to improve your security

score and overall security posture. In contrast, the secure score provides you with a quick indicator of the state of your security posture.

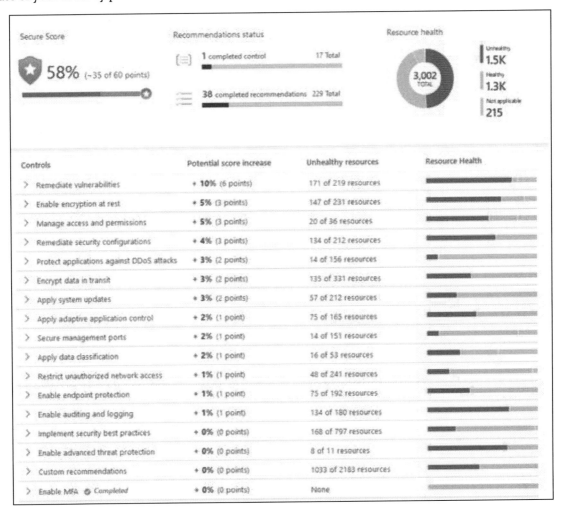

Figure 8-13: Microsoft Defender for Cloud

Defend

The first two areas concern examining, keeping an eye on, and caring for your surroundings. Defender for Cloud offers security alerts and cutting-edge threat protection capabilities that assist you in defending your environment.

Security Alert

Defender for Cloud creates a security alert if it finds a threat in any component of your environment. Security warnings can be:

- Give specifics about the impacted resources
- Suggest corrective measures
- Provide a choice to launch a logic app in some circumstance

You can export an alert whether it was produced by Defender for Cloud or received by Defender for Cloud from a combined security solution. Fusion kill-chain analysis, a Defender for Cloud's threat protection feature, automatically correlates alerts in your environment based on cyber kill-chain analysis to better

understand an attack campaign's full history, where it began, and what kind of impact it had on your resources.

> EXAM TIP: Microsoft Defender for Cloud is a portal within the Azure portal that monitors the resource security hygiene for Azure VMs resources. It contains a security alert timeline that defines the policy for efficient protection response in case of any incident.

Advanced Threat Protection

For many of your deployed resources, including virtual machines, SQL databases, containers, web apps, and your network, Defender for Cloud offers cutting-edge threat protection features. One form of protection is just-in-time access security for your VMs' management ports. Another is adaptive application controls, which let you make lists of which applications are allowed and not allowed to operate on your machines.

Sections in Microsoft Defender for Cloud

Each section in the Microsoft Defender for Cloud portal shows the performance behavior of security features in graphical representation.

- **Policy, Compliance, and Subscription Coverage:** Policy, compliance, and Subscription coverage are monitored by Azure; there is a secure score that represents the implementation of the Azure resource as secure as possible

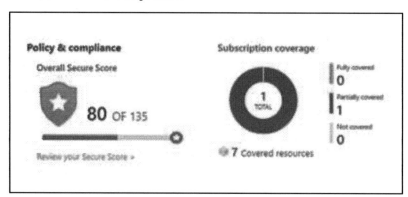

Figure 8-14(a) – Species of Microsoft Defender for Cloud

- **Integrate with Other Cloud Providers:** With this, you can get security information from multiple cloud providers like AWS and GCP directly into Microsoft Defender for Cloud
- **Alerts for resources security:** If any VM is not updated, the defender for cloud quickly updates the VM, stores encrypted data with an IP address, and traffic loads for processing

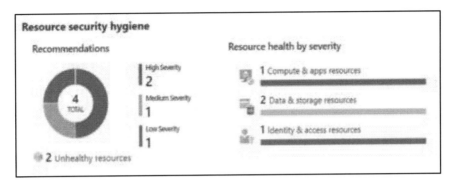

Figure 8-14(b) – Species of Microsoft Defender for Cloud

- **Networking:** The configuration of secure resources in the network within Azure is successfully represented in the networking block of the Microsoft Defender for Cloud.

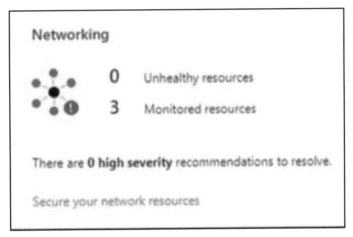

Figure 8-14(c) – Species of Microsoft Defender for Cloud

How to use Microsoft Defender for Cloud?

Azure users must follow this three-step process to take advantage of Microsoft Defender for Cloud infrastructure security.

- **Define Policies:** The user needs to define the security policies Azure can use to monitor cloud infrastructure. Security policies are a set of rules (such as Access Control List) that Azure can use to evaluate the valid configuration of service
- **Resource Protection:** Users need to protect resources, and Microsoft Defender for Cloud can help the user to protect the resources against a threat
- **Response:** In case of any security incident, the defender for the cloud can raise the alerts. Users can investigate the traffic load within Azure implementation after the security alert

Azure Key Vault

Most cloud users need multiple ID numbers and passwords per their usage. However, there rises the problem of how many people will remember multiple passwords and secrets for different users. It isn't easy to memorize the entire list of passwords. One option is that users may share their passwords with

different people on who they rely. As the number of secrets increases, this approach fails to protect the user's key from hackers.

Microsoft gives you a service known as Azure Key Vault to hide the key password and other information. It is the best option for key storage. With Azure Key Vault, you can share your secrets with others without revealing the actual secrets. Azure Key Vault is present in the storage account of the VM. Storage accounts store keys in disk-encrypted form. Azure Key Vault allows user to store their key passwords in an encrypted form so that no one else can view them. This key protection is defined by some rules and followed by the access policy criteria. On the application level, the app developer needs such protection based on their information that no one can expose.

Figure 8-15 shows the application of the Azure Key Vault. There is a database in a network. The data in the network is successfully used for internal services such as applications. A user wants to share access to the network with other trusted outsiders. However, outsiders need an ID and password to access the application. One way to do this is to place a password in Azure Key Vault that efficiently allows an outsider to access individual applications easily. The application identifies itself using the Azure Key Vault to grant access to the database. In this way, the password is never sent to others.

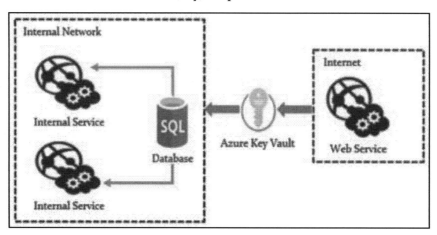

Figure 8-15: Azure Key Vault

Features of Key Vault

Azure Key Vault has some key features.

- **Secure Hardware:** Azure Key Vault has hardware and software protection. Azure Key Vault uses Hardware Security Module (HSM) to store a password and a secret so that no one can see it
- **Application Isolation:** Using Azure Key Vault, applications cannot pass on secrets. Access to the application can be removed easily without having to change the password
- **Global Scaling:** Azure Key Vault can be scaled globally as other managed Azure services resulting in high cryptographic performance

EXAM TIP: Azure Key Vault is a secure way to share secrets and passwords to applications and other resources outside the organization using a defined access policy. It can be scaled globally; not even Microsoft can reveal the secret.

Azure Information Protection

When you store your data on the company's server, how can you know who can access that data? Azure Information Protection provides a way of protecting the sharing of resources. Azure Information Protection enables sharing of files, documents, and sensitive information inside and outside Azure while maintaining full control over that data. Microsoft 365 takes full advantage of the Azure Information Protection service. It makes many new enhancements with AIP, such as support PDF document protection, outlook relicensing, and message protection for the shared mailbox.

With Azure Information Protection, the data can be secured in the following ways:

- **Data Configuration:** An organization can establish data and protection parameters according to AIP services for security purposes
- **Classification of Data**: Organizations can make data secure data by classifying it according to sensitivity and priority. This can be done automatically by Azure Information Protection services or manually by users themselves
- **Track Activities:** With AIP, an organization has full control over data activities. If some irregular activities occur, an organization may cancel access to that data
- **Share Data with Others:** An organization has full control over data sharing. In addition, the organization can manage and carefully supervise those who can edit, view, print, and forward it
- **Integration:** Controlling, protecting, and classifying are integrated with applications like Microsoft Office and other applications that give the security of data and documents within a click

The security of a document can be guaranteed by using Azure Information Protection services. An application of Azure Information Protection is discussed in the scenario, as shown in Figure 8-16. There are two users, User 1 and User 2. User 1 wants to send an email with a sensitive document attachment to User 2 within Azure. User 1 uses a secure label defined in Azure to tag the document and create a link to information protection; then, the email will be securely received by User 2. The document will be opened if User 2 is a valid user.

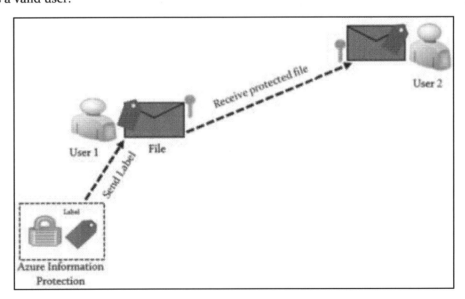

Figure 8-16: Azure Information Protection

Advanced Threat Protection

Advanced Threat Protection (ATP) is the advanced and secure option for providing the security of the links compared to the standard one. It gives an extra layer of security and management of the users to make a more secure and protected system.

Are Users Unreliable?

The need for Advanced Threat Protection is due to the users, whether they are customers or employees. If users have access to the organization's server, file, or document, they might be weak to attackers or hackers. For example, an organization has continuously received threats from the user side, as shown in Figure 8-17. The Business Corporation has sensitive data that makes the attacker target that corporation. One way to get sensitive data is through users. Users are often the weakest link within the organization, and attackers usually take this as their target point. Attackers continuously pin one specific user to give them access to a corporation and ultimately hack the sensitive data.

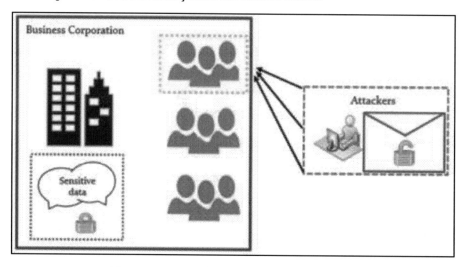

Figure 8-17: Attacker's Target in the Network

Features of Advanced Threat Protection

Azure Advanced Threat Protection has many features that provide the safety of links and analyze security threats.

- **Monitor Users:** Azure ATP helps to monitor users in an on-premises environment and their behavior. Azure ATP analyzes user's activity and information across the network, including permission and membership across each user
- **Supervised User's Behavior:** Azure ATP continuously focuses on users' activities. If there occurs any irregular activity, ATP will be logged as a doubtful activity
- **Propose Changes:** ATP also offers some suggestions regarding security policy to provide the best security practices. Profiling and analyzing users will help to reduce the risk against threats on-premises and in the cloud. ATP will make changes based on the required security policy

Cyber-Attack Kill-Chain

The cyber-attack kill chain is a phrase that defines how the attack is prepared and executed. This deployed model, called Cyber-Attack Kill-Chain, allows detecting and reacting upon the attack. The model reveals seven stages according to which reaction and cyber-attack detection are available.

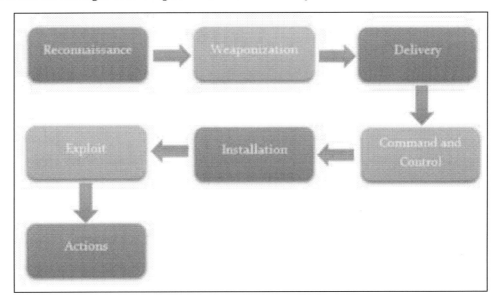

Figure 8-18: Cyber-Attach Kill-Chain

Azure Advanced Threat Protection is responsible for monitoring any aspect of the cyber-attack Kill-Chain. Here, we will discuss the Cyber Attack kill chain as per Azure.

- **Reconnaissance:** If the user is performing a survey, it means searching the device's IP address and finding the other's information to check out the system. ATP will raise the alert to protect the system from any inappropriate incident.
- **Brute Force:** Identifying attempts to compromise users' credentials using brute force that tries various combinations of user names and passwords
- **Increasing Privileges:** Any attempt to gain access to a user with access to more resources and areas within the network

EXAM TIP: Azure Information Protection (AIP) enables the secure sharing of files, documents, and sensitive data inside and outside an organization using protection labels and tags. Azure users can control who can edit, view, and print the information.

Azure Advanced Threat Protection (ATP) provides advanced-level security to prevent the network from threats. It monitors user behavior, creates a baseline, and immediately reports in case of any anomalies.

Azure Sentinel

Sentinel is a security information and event management tool, often just called S-I-E-M or SIEM. This is a commonly used tool for any cloud infrastructure. Azure Sentinel involves five working steps as described below:

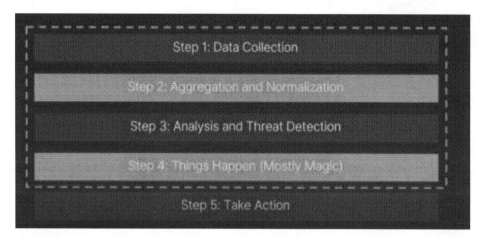

Figure 8-19: Steps in Azure Sentinel

The initial step is to collect data from various sources, such as your network controllers, virtual machines, DNS traffic managers, and much more. The data is aggregated and normalized.

EXAM TIP: Azure Sentinel has suggested queries; you can find samples or build your own. Another option is Azure Notebook, which is more interactive and has the potential to use your data science analysis.

Sentinel is a Security Information and Event Management (SIEM) tool.

This only means that it is sorted and made a bit more usable. The important data is analyzed, and any threats are detected. Sentinel will do 90% of the heavy lifting before you even start investigating a potential security alert. One feature that sets Sentinel apart from other SIEMs is behavioral analytics. Using artificial intelligence, Sentinel will learn about patterns and behaviors to identify if something is out of the ordinary. With AWS integration, you can get all the data from your AWS services fed directly into Sentinel for analysis and threat detection with limitless speed and scale.

Sentinel will take advantage of the huge resources on Azure to be even faster and scale to match your needs. Sentinel has a free Netflix subscription for all plans, and it could use it to protect its infrastructure. Of course, a million features in Sentinel make sense to the security professionals who use it. Sentinel also protects your cloud functionality.

EXAM TIP: Azure Sentinel collects security events and data and keeps them for 31 days by default using connections from multiple vendors or operating systems. This is extendable up to 730 days.

Azure Dedicated Host

Virtual machines in Azure run on Microsoft-managed shared hardware. Your VM workloads are segregated from other Azure users' workloads, despite the shared hardware.

Some businesses must adhere to regulatory requirements that state they must be the sole customer using the real computer that hosts their virtual machines. Azure Dedicated Host provides dedicated physical servers for Windows and Linux Azure VMs.

Azure Dedicated Hosts is a full physical server you get full control over. You provision it just like a VM in Azure, but there are some significant differences and benefits.

- The hardware isolation is at the physical layer, so no one else can sneak onto your server
- No other VMs will be placed on the hardware unless they are the ones you choose and you create
- Control over the maintenance schedule. You will have some choice when sensitive workloads are updated, which can reduce the impact on your service a lot

There are lots of advantages of cloud computing benefits, like:

- Availability Zones
- Fault Isolation
- High Availability
- Scale Sets

You can use Windows, Linux, or SQL Server as your VM image. Save some coins by using existing software licenses that you might have, for example, Windows Server or SQL Server. A Dedicated Host is a good alternative for the hardware-conscious cloud user, but it can also get expensive. Use it wisely.

Combine Azure Services to Create a Complete Network Security Solution

Secure the Perimeter Layer

The perimeter layer is responsible for defending your company's resources against network-based threats. It is critical to recognize these attacks, notify the proper security teams, and eliminate their impact to keep your network secure. To do so, follow these steps:

- Filter large-scale attacks with Azure DDoS Protection before they may cause a denial-of-service for consumers
- With Azure Firewall, you can use perimeter firewalls to detect and notify of dangerous threats on your network

Secure the Network Layer

At this layer, the goal is to limit network connectivity across all your resources to only what is necessary. Limit communication to only what is required by segmenting your resources and using network-level rules.

You can limit the possibility of lateral migration across your network by blocking connectivity. Create rules that define allowed incoming and outbound communication at this tier using network security groups. Here are some best practices to follow:

- By segmenting your network and implementing access rules, you can limit communication between resources
- By default, deny
- Limit inbound internet access and outgoing internet access as needed
- Implement a secure network to an on-premises network

Combine Services

You may mix Azure networking and security services to manage your network security and give more layered protection. You can integrate services in two ways:

Network Security Groups and Azure Firewall

The Azure Firewall adds to the capabilities of network security groups. They give superior defense-in-depth network security when used together.

Network security groups enable distributed network-layer traffic filtering to limit traffic to resources within virtual networks in each subscription.

Azure Firewall is a centralized network firewall that is fully stateful. It protects networks and applications at the network and application levels across many subscriptions and virtual networks.

Azure Application Gateway Web Application Firewall and Azure Firewall

Web application firewall (WAF) is an Azure Application Gateway feature that provides centralized, inbound security against common exploits and vulnerabilities for your web applications.

Azure Firewall offers the following features:

- Non-HTTP/S protocols are protected from inbound traffic (for example, RDP, SSH, and FTP)
- All ports and protocols are protected at the network level for outbound traffic
- Outbound HTTP/S protection at the application level

Lab 8-01: Azure Key Vault

Service Introduction

Azure Key Vault is a secure and centralized cloud service provided by Microsoft Azure for managing and safeguarding cryptographic keys, secrets, and certificates used by cloud applications and services. It acts as a key management solution that helps organizations protect sensitive information, such as API keys, connection strings, and encryption keys, by storing them in a highly secure and compliant manner. Azure Key Vault provides features like access policies, access logging, and hardware security modules (HSMs) to ensure robust security and compliance with regulatory requirements. Developers can seamlessly integrate Azure Key Vault into their applications, and it plays a crucial role in enhancing overall security posture by allowing for the separation of application secrets from the application code, enabling secure and dynamic management of cryptographic keys and other sensitive information.

Problem

An organization must share a secret with a third party for business enhancement. How can the organization build an access policy for others to share its secret without revealing the encryption and security rules, ensuring secure internet traffic?

Solution

Azure Key Vault is a useful tool for managing and sharing secrets. First, Azure Key Vault is created, then a secret is built in the given Key Vault that can be accessible to others. In the given situation, the organization can allow others to access the secret without revealing the secret by using Azure Key Vault.

1. Log in to the Microsoft Azure portal, go to the search bar, and type **"Key Vaults"** in the given space.

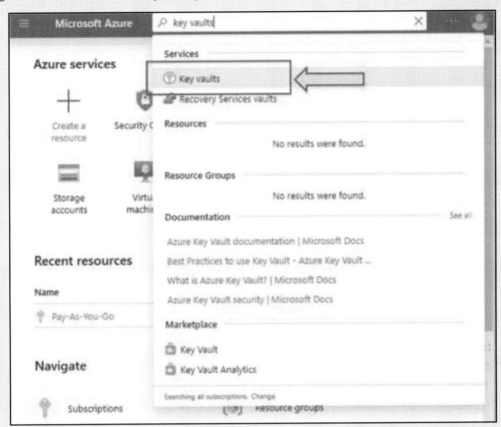

2. The **"Key Vaults"** tab will appear. Click on **"+ Add"** to create a Key Vault.

3. Click on **"Create new"** to enter the Resource group.

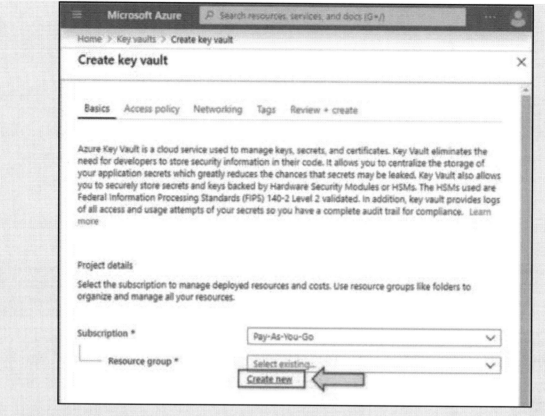

4. Write the name of the Resource group as "**keyvaultrg.**"
5. Then click on "**OK.**"

6. Write "**Key Vault name*,**" "**Region*,**" and "**Pricing tier***" in the "**Instance details.**"
7. Now, click on "**Next: Access policy >.**"

8. The access policy tab will appear. Now, click on "**Review + create.**"

9. Once the validation is passed, click on **"Create."**

10. **"IPSKeyvault1"** has been created.
11. Click on **"Go to resource."**

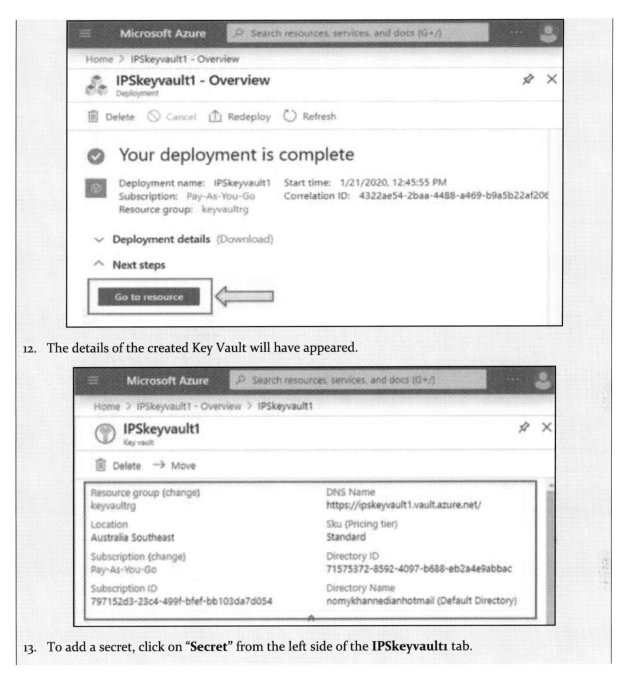

12. The details of the created Key Vault will have appeared.

13. To add a secret, click on "**Secret**" from the left side of the **IPSkeyvault1** tab.

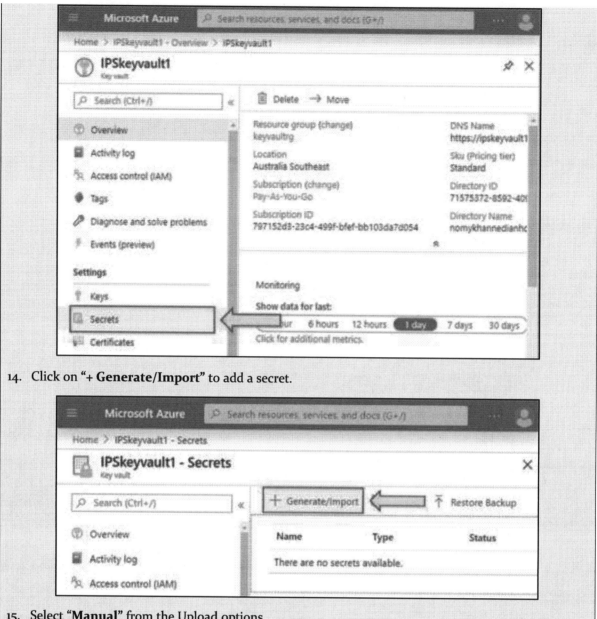

14. Click on "**+ Generate/Import**" to add a secret.

15. Select "**Manual**" from the Upload options.
16. Write "**Name***" and "**Value***" of the secret.
17. Click on "**Create.**"

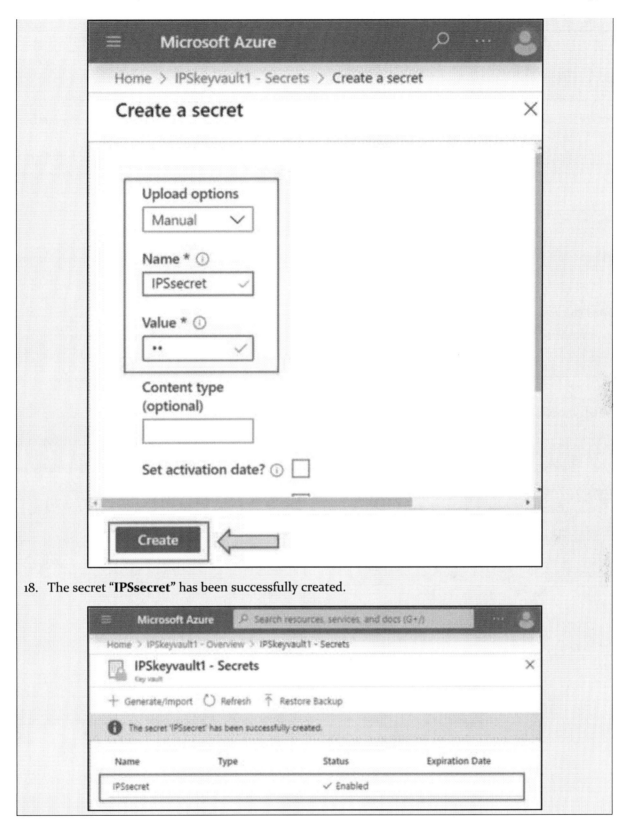

18. The secret **"IPSsecret"** has been successfully created.

Lab 8-02: Network Access to VM using NSG

Service Introduction

Network Security Groups (NSGs) in Microsoft Azure play a pivotal role in controlling network access to virtual machines (VMs). NSGs act as virtual firewalls, allowing or denying inbound and outbound traffic to VMs based on defined rules. By associating NSGs with VMs, administrators can regulate access by specifying allowed protocols, source IP addresses, and destination ports. This fine-grained control enhances security by restricting unnecessary traffic and mitigating potential vulnerabilities. Whether applied at the subnet or individual VM level, NSGs provide a crucial layer of network defense, helping organizations maintain a secure and compliant network environment within the Azure cloud infrastructure. Through thoughtful configuration of NSG rules, administrators can enforce network access policies tailored to their specific security requirements, ensuring a robust defense against unauthorized access to virtual machines.

Problem

A company has recently shifted all its on-prem resources to the Azure cloud and now wants to explore the services offered by Azure. The security and management team is currently assigned to create a secure way to access the web server through a virtual machine. How can they do that?

Solution

By using the Network Security Group feature of Azure, the organization can easily make secure network access to Azure virtual machines.

1. Log in to the **Microsoft Azure** portal.

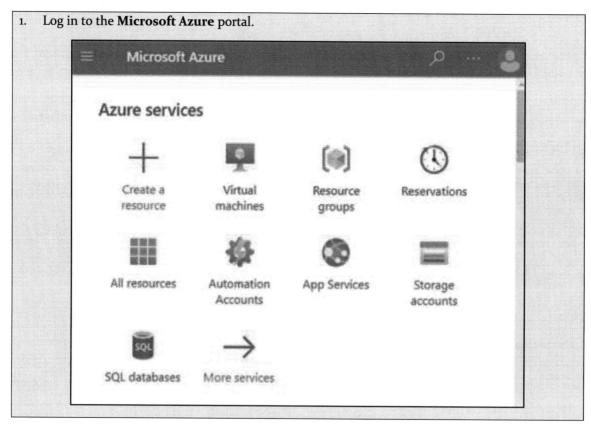

2. Go to the options present at the top of the portal page.
3. Click on **Azure Cloud Shell**.

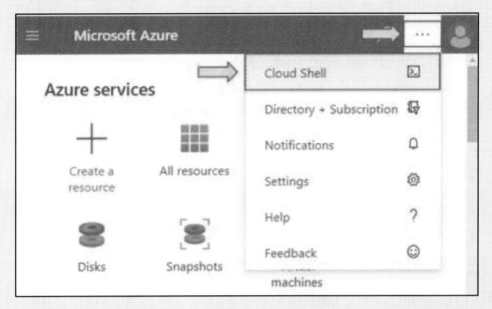

4. Click on **"Create storage."**

Note: Azure Cloud Shell requires an Azure files share to persist files. This will create a new storage account with some monthly costs.

5. The Azure Cloud Shell session will be connected in a moment.

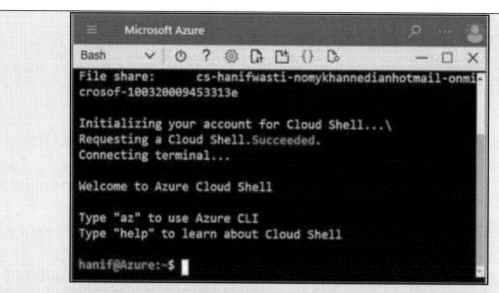

6. Run "**az**" to connect to the Azure CLI session.

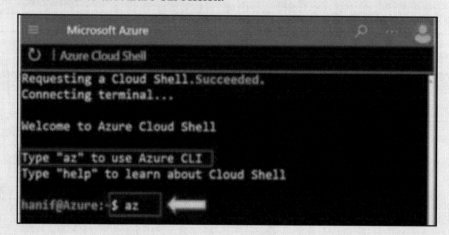

Note: Azure CLI enables you to set the default values. Azure CLI allows you to create and place your desired virtual machine in several default locations and regions.

7. The Azure CLI session will be connected in a moment.
8. After that, run the following set of commands to create a virtual machine.

az vm create \

  --resource-group learn-3894d88b-13a0-4bf7-ad8b-13861b5a2e4f \

  --name ipsvm01 \

  --image UbuntuLTS \

  --admin-username azureuser \

  --generate-ssh-keys

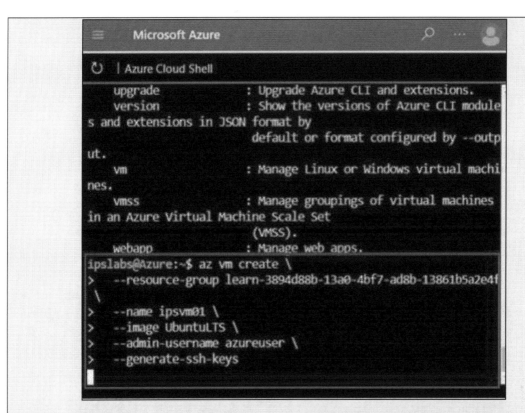

9. The command will take some time to deploy the VM and display the following updates:

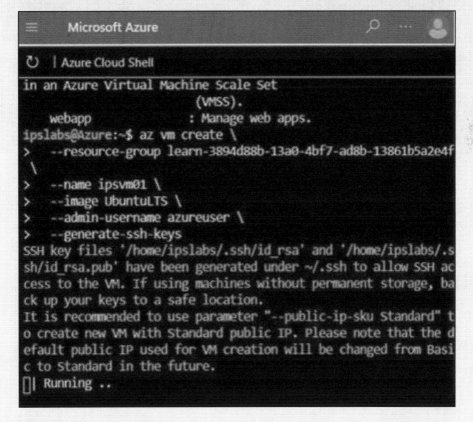

10. After the deployment, the following output will appear, showing all the configuration details.

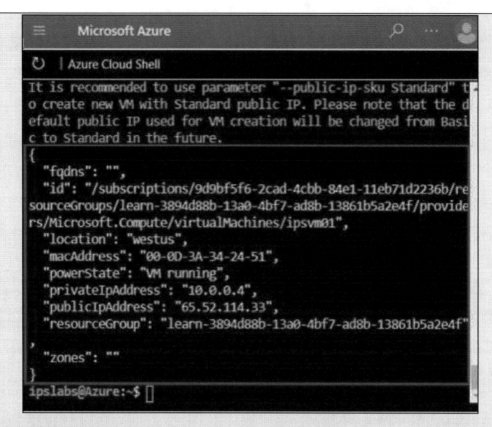

Note: You can verify the deployment of the VM from Azure Portal.

11. After deployment, run the following command to configure the Nginx on the recently deployed virtual machine.

az vm extension set \

  --resource-group learn-3894d88b-13a0-4bf7-ad8b-13861b5a2e4f \

  --vm-name ipsvm01 \

  --name customScript \

  --publisher Microsoft.Azure.Extensions \

  --version 2.1 \

  --settings   '{"fileUris":["https://raw.githubusercontent.com/MicrosoftDocs/mslearn-welcome-to-azure/master/configure-nginx.sh"]}' \

  --protected-settings '{"commandToExecute": "./configure-nginx.sh"}'

```
"privateIpAddress": "10.0.0.4",
"publicIpAddress": "65.52.114.33",
"resourceGroup": "learn-3894d88b-13a0-4bf7-ad8b-13861b5a2e4f"
,
"zones": ""
}
ipslabs@Azure:~$ az vm extension set \
    --resource-group learn-3894d88b-13a0-4bf7-ad8b-13861b5a2e4f
\
    --vm-name ipsvm01 \
    --name customScript \
    --publisher Microsoft.Azure.Extensions \
    --version 2.1 \
    --settings '{"fileUris":["https://raw.githubusercontent.com
/MicrosoftDocs/mslearn-welcome-to-azure/master/configure-nginx.
sh"]}' \
    --protected-settings '{"commandToExecute": "./configure-ngi
nx.sh"}'
```

12. The following output will appear.

```
    --protected-settings '{"commandToExecute": "./configure-ngi
nx.sh"}'
{
  "autoUpgradeMinorVersion": true,
  "enableAutomaticUpgrade": null,
  "forceUpdateTag": null,
  "id": "/subscriptions/9d9bf5f6-2cad-4cbb-84e1-11eb71d2236b/re
sourceGroups/learn-3894d88b-13a0-4bf7-ad8b-13861b5a2e4f/provide
rs/Microsoft.Compute/virtualMachines/ipsvm01/extensions/customS
cript",
  "instanceView": null,
  "location": "westus",
  "name": "customScript",
  "protectedSettings": null,
  "provisioningState": "Succeeded",
  "publisher": "Microsoft.Azure.Extensions",
  "resourceGroup": "learn-3894d88b-13a0-4bf7-ad8b-13861b5a2e4f"
,
  "settings": {
```

13. To see the list of Azure VM IP addresses, run the following command:

IPADDRESS="$(az vm list-ip-addresses \

--resource-group learn-3894d88b-13a0-4bf7-ad8b-13861b5a2e4f \

--name ipsvm01 \

--query "[].virtualMachine.network.publicIpAddresses[*].ipAddress" \

--output tsv)"

```
≡        Microsoft Azure                    🔍   ...   👤

 ↻  | Azure Cloud Shell

ipslabs@Azure:~$ IPADDRESS="$(az vm list-ip-addresses \
>     --resource-group learn-3894d88b-13a0-4bf7-ad8b-13861b5a2e4f
 \
>     --name ipsvm01 \
>     --query "[].virtualMachine.network.publicIpAddresses[*].ipA
ddress" \
>     --output tsv)"
ipslabs@Azure:~$
```

Note: The above set of commands will store the IP address of the virtual machine in the bash variable.

14. After that, run the following command to download the homepage of the webserver.

curl --connect-timeout 5 http://$IPADDRESS

```
≡        Microsoft Azure                    🔍   ...   👤

 ↻  | Azure Cloud Shell

ipslabs@Azure:~$ IPADDRESS="$(az vm list-ip-addresses \
>     --resource-group learn-3894d88b-13a0-4bf7-ad8b-13861b5a2e4f
 \
>     --name ipsvm01 \
>     --query "[].virtualMachine.network.publicIpAddresses[*].ipA
ddress" \
>     --output tsv)"
ipslabs@Azure:~$ curl --connect-timeout 5 http://$IPADDRESS
curl: (28) Connection timed out after 5000 milliseconds
ipslabs@Azure:~$
```

15. Run the following command to get the VM IP address.

echo $IPADDRESS

16. Copy this IP address and open it in a new browser.

17. You will find that access is currently blocked to access this VM.

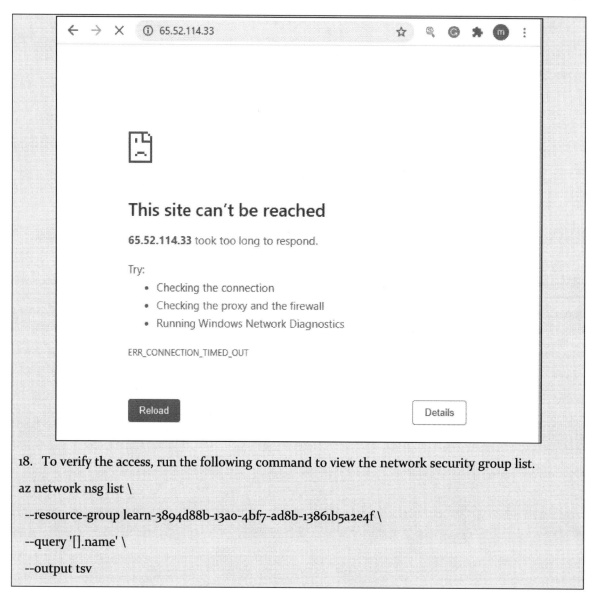

18. To verify the access, run the following command to view the network security group list.

az network nsg list \

  --resource-group learn-3894d88b-13a0-4bf7-ad8b-13861b5a2e4f \

  --query '[].name' \

  --output tsv

```
≡      Microsoft Azure                        ⌕  ···  👤

↻  |  Azure Cloud Shell

ipslabs@Azure:~$ curl --connect-timeout 5 http://$IPADDR
curl: (28) Connection timed out after 5000 milliseconds
ipslabs@Azure:~$ echo $IPADDRESS
65.52.114.33
ipslabs@Azure:~$ az network nsg list \
>     --resource-group learn-3894d88b-13a0-4bf7-ad8b-13861
b5a2e4f \
>     --query '[].name' \
>     --output tsv
```

19. You will get the NSG name in the output.

```
≡      Microsoft Azure                        ⌕  ···  👤

↻  |  Azure Cloud Shell

ipslabs@Azure:~$ az network nsg list \
>     --resource-group learn-3894d88b-13a0-4bf7-ad8b-13861
b5a2e4f \
>     --query '[].name' \
>     --output tsv
ipsvm01NSG
ipslabs@Azure:~$ []
```

20. After that, run the set of commands and see the output.

az network nsg rule list \

  --resource-group learn-3894d88b-13a0-4bf7-ad8b-13861b5a2e4f \

  --nsg-name ipsvm01NSG

```
≡    Microsoft Azure                              ⌕   ...    👤

 ↻   |  Azure Cloud Shell

ipslabs@Azure:~$ az network nsg rule list \
>    --resource-group learn-3894d88b-13a0-4bf7-ad8b-13861b5
a2e4f \
>    --nsg-name ipsvm01NSG
[
  {
      "access": "Allow",
      "description": null,
      "destinationAddressPrefix": "*",
      "destinationAddressPrefixes": [],
      "destinationApplicationSecurityGroups": null,
      "destinationPortRange": "22",
      "destinationPortRanges": [],
      "direction": "Inbound",
      "etag": "W/\"22f2ec3a-d374-4317-bf89-61e2df141617\"",
      "id": "/subscriptions/9d9bf5f6-2cad-4cbb-84e1-11eb71d2
236b/resourceGroups/learn-3894d88b-13a0-4bf7-ad8b-13861b5a
2e4f/providers/Microsoft.Network/networkSecurityGroups/ips
```

22. Run the following set of commands to view the NSG rule list.

az network nsg rule list \

  --resource-group learn-3894d88b-13a0-4bf7-ad8b-13861b5a2e4f \

  --nsg-name ipsvm01NSG \

  --query '[].{Name:name, Priority:priority, Port:destinationPortRange, Access:access}' \

  --output table

```
     "sourceApplicationSecurityGroups": null,
     "sourcePortRange": "*",
     "sourcePortRanges": [],
     "type": "Microsoft.Network/networkSecurityGroups/secur
  ityRules"
    }
  ]
ipslabs@Azure:~$ az network nsg rule list \
>    --resource-group learn-3894d88b-13a0-4bf7-ad8b-13861b5
a2e4f \
>    --nsg-name ipsvm01NSG \
>    --query '[].{Name:name, Priority:priority, Port:destin
ationPortRange, Access:access}' \
>    --output table
Name              Priority    Port    Access
----------------  ----------  ------  --------
default-allow-ssh  1000         22     Allow
ipslabs@Azure:~$
```

25. To create an NSG rule, run the following set of commands:

az network nsg rule create \

  --resource-group learn-3894d88b-13a0-4bf7-ad8b-13861b5a2e4f \

  --nsg-name ipsvm01NSG \

  --name allow-http \

  --protocol tcp \

  --priority 100 \

  --destination-port-ranges 80 \

  --access Allow

```
a2e4f \
>    --nsg-name ipsvm01NSG \
>    --query '[].{Name:name, Priority:priority, Port:destin
ationPortRange, Access:access}' \
>    --output table
Name                    Priority      Port     Access
-------------------     ----------    ------   ---------
default-allow-ssh  1000              22        Allow
ipslabs@Azure:~$ az network nsg rule create \
>    --resource-group learn-3894d88b-13a0-4bf7-ad8b-13861b5
a2e4f \
>    --nsg-name ipsvm01NSG \
>    --name allow-http \
>    --protocol tcp \
>    --priority 100 \
>    --destination-port-ranges 80 \
>    --access Allow
\ Running ..
```

26. The following output will appear.

```
{
  "access": "Allow",
  "description": null,
  "destinationAddressPrefix": "*",
  "destinationAddressPrefixes": [],
  "destinationApplicationSecurityGroups": null,
  "destinationPortRange": "80",
  "destinationPortRanges": [],
  "direction": "Inbound",
  "etag": "W/\"2bb96f9a-cbd8-4acc-bcbf-cbe62ef70b2a\"",
  "id": "/subscriptions/9d9bf5f6-2cad-4cbb-84e1-11eb71d223
6b/resourceGroups/learn-3894d88b-13a0-4bf7-ad8b-13861b5a2e
4f/providers/Microsoft.Network/networkSecurityGroups/ipsvm
01NSG/securityRules/allow-http",
  "name": "allow-http",
  "priority": 100,
  "protocol": "Tcp",
  "provisioningState": "Succeeded",
```

27. Now, run the following commands to check the NSG rule list.

az network nsg rule list \

  --resource-group learn-3894d88b-13a0-4bf7-ad8b-13861b5a2e4f \

  --nsg-name ipsvm01NSG \

  --query '[].{Name:name, Priority:priority, Port:destinationPortRange, Access:access}' \

  --output table

28. You will see the new NSG rule in the list.

```
"sourceApplicationSecurityGroups": null,
"sourcePortRange": "*",
"sourcePortRanges": [],
"type": "Microsoft.Network/networkSecurityGroups/securit
yRules"
}
ipslabs@Azure:~$ az network nsg rule list \
>     --resource-group learn-3894d88b-13a0-4bf7-ad8b-13861b5
a2e4f \
>     --nsg-name ipsvm01NSG \
>     --query '[].{Name:name, Priority:priority, Port:destin
ationPortRange, Access:access}' \
>     --output table
Name                Priority    Port      Access
------------------  ----------  --------  --------
default-allow-ssh   1000        22        Allow
allow-http          100         80        Allow
ipslabs@Azure:~$
```

28. Now, run the following command to access the webserver again.

curl --connect-timeout 5 http://$IPADDRESS

```
ipslabs@Azure:~$ curl --connect-timeout 5 http://$IPADDRES
S
<html><body><h2>Welcome to Azure! My name is ipsvm01.</h2>
</body></html>
ipslabs@Azure:~$
```

29. Verify the above output by navigating to the same VM IP address.

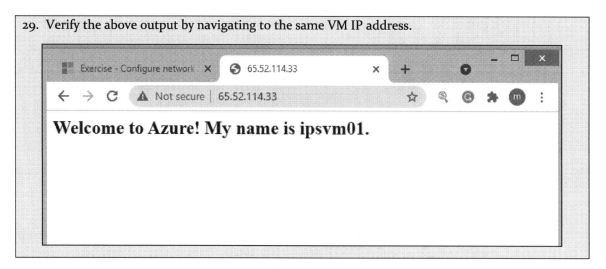

Mind Map

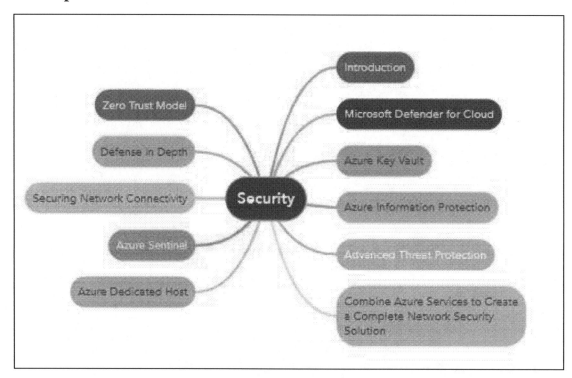

Figure 8-20: Mind Map

Practice Questions

1. What is the most crucial part of Microsoft Azure in the configuration of a network?
A. Security
B. Networking
C. Authentication and Authorization
D. Computation

2. How many ways of securing network connectivity can be possible in Microsoft Azure?
A. Only One
B. Four
C. One Hundred
D. Infinite

3. What is the purpose of the Azure Firewall?
A. Protects sensitive information
B. Helps monitor user's behavior in on-premises and cloud environment
C. Provide a set of rules that ensure the security of network resources.
D. All of the above

4. Which Azure service may use secure hardware to protect the password and secret?
A. Azure Information Protection
B. Network Security Group
C. Advanced Threat Protection
D. Azure Key Vault

5. There is a web server that receives a consecutive number of requests from different sources at the same time; these continuous requests make the server stop working abruptly. This type of attack is called _____.
A. Cross-site Scripting (XSS) Attack
B. Password Attack
C. Distributed Denial-of-Service (DDoS) Attack
D. Malware Attack

6. How is the Network Security Group different from the Application Security Group?
A. NSG defines traffic policies, whereas ASG defines network security based on application policies.
B. NSG is responsible for tracking the attacks, whereas ASG configures attacks.
C. ASG is limited to two VMs, whereas NSG has unlimited resources
D. None of the above

7. Which services use the Access Control List (ACL) to allow or deny network traffic access to the subnet or VM?
A. Azure Key Vault
B. Azure Firewall
C. Network Security Group
D. Azure Information Protection

8. Which of the following is responsible for protecting a subnet or VM?

A. Azure Privacy Services
B. Secure Network Connections
C. Azure Key Vault
D. Microsoft Entra ID

9. What is the function of the Azure Key Vault?
A. Provides secure access to secrets
B. Ensures the network connectivity
C. Allows sharing of user's credential
D. Prevents the use of resources

10. Which services help share files and sensitive information inside and outside Azure?
A. Advanced Threat Protection
B. Azure Key Vault
C. Application Security Group
D. Azure Information Protection

11. Which Azure service can monitor the user's behavior?
A. Azure Firewall
B. Microsoft Defender for Cloud
C. Advanced Threat Protection
D. Azure Networking Services

12. Which Azure service can you use to share the secret with the third party without revealing the actual secret?
A. Azure DNS
B. Azure Key Vault
C. Azure Monitor
D. Azure ATP

13. Which of the following service has its portal within the Azure portal?
A. Microsoft Defender for Cloud
B. Azure Key Vaults
C. Microsoft Entra ID
D. Azure SQL

14. In 2018, a popular developer platform "GitHub" was targeted by a DDoS attack with _____.
A. 60 Gb traffic per second
B. 400 Gb traffic per second
C. 1.23 Gb traffic per second
D. 1.35 Tb traffic per second

15. Which Azure service acts as a resource firewall?
A. Azure Monitor
B. Azure DNS
C. Network Security Group
D. Content Delivery Network

16. Which Azure service configures network security as a network extension of an application structure?
A. Network Security Group
B. Application Security Group
C. Azure Firewall
D. Advanced Threat Protection

17. Which of the following service gives the single unified view of security in hybrid cloud architecture?
A. Microsoft Entra ID
B. Storage Account
C. Microsoft Defender for Cloud
D. SQL Database

18. When data is stored in company servers and resources, customers and employees can get it and share it inside and outside the company. Which service can you use to provide the protected sharing of data?
A. Azure Information Protection
B. Advanced Threat Protection
C. Azure App Services
D. None of the above

19. Why does Azure ATP need a security alert timeline?
A. To protect resources from threats
B. To enable attackers to get access to resources through users
C. To monitor the protection of sensitive data
D. All of the above

20. Which of the following allows us to limit the access of Key Vault to the users?
A. Networking Policy
B. Access Policy
C. Tags
D. All of the above

21. Which of the following allows us to encrypt and protect data against anyone unauthorized reading it or making sense of it?

A. Physical
B. Application
C. Network
D. None of the above

22. Which of the following is a key element in Defense-in-Depth?
A. Strategy to slow the advance of an attack to get unauthorized access to information
B. Each layer provides protection, so if one layer is breached, a subsequent prevents further exposure
C. Both A and B
D. None of them

23. Which of the following is a famous DDoS attack against the developer on which website where attackers sent 127 million requests per second?
A. website GitHub in 2018
B. website GitHub in 2020
C. website Amazon in 2018
D. website Amazon in 2020

24. Which of the following service is the protection against DDoS attacks, volumetric attacks, and protocol attacks?
A. Physical
B. Identity and Access
C. Perimeter
D. Network

25. Which services filter traffic to and from Azure using virtual networks while applying security standards?
A. Physical
B. Identity and Access
C. Perimeter
D. Network

Chapter 09: Privacy, Compliance, and Trust

Introduction

Every company needs the privacy of its data. They want to trust that their data is stored quickly and privacy is looked after. In Azure, you have a service that performs your company's privacy, trust, and compliance. Azure Monitor has various tools to detect, diagnose, visualize, and analyze the response and integrate the data from Azure services' logs and metrics. This chapter will discuss Governance in Azure, its context, why it needs to be done with perfection, and which tools Azure provides you for governance.

As we all know, downtime is a serious problem globally. With Azure Service Health, you can ensure the maximum uptime of your business. In this chapter, we will discuss the compliance and privacy of your applications. Microsoft has its Trust Center in Azure, which they want you to read to get more trust.

Build a Cloud Governance Strategy on Azure

Azure Resource Manager enables us to organize and monitor all the resources after deployment. Azure Resource Manager (ARM) template is used to specify the deployment parameters, list of variables, list of resources, and output. It also provides the file named JSON for the faster deployment of resources.

Governance

We all know that most companies use the Azure platform for its agility to make it easier for the developers to create, manage, update and delete the resources as per requirement. However, sometimes unwanted access to the resource may cause unintended cost consequences. To overcome this, Azure provides a resource access governance solution, which manages, monitors, and audits resource usage to meet goals and requirements.

Consider you have developers and a system administrator who both have their thoughts on upgrading the resource at its best. This may cause a mess, and there are a lot of resources that may be wrongly created. Therefore, by using Governance, you can overcome this, as it has a set of rules, policies, and roles that define acceptable use of Azure resources. To implement good governance, Azure provides you with multiple tools.

 EXAM TIP: Governance keeps you compliant and out of trouble.

Concept of Resource Groups

Azure Resource Manager has several features that you can use to organize the resources, enforce standards, and protect your critical Azure resources from accidental deletion. Resource groups are the containers for the resource deployed on Azure. By placing similar usage, type, or location resources in the same resource groups, you can provide some order and organization to your Azure resources. Tags allow you to improve the organization of your resources even further. You can use tags to associate the custom details with a resource or resource group, such as the cost center and billing department. Resource groups and tags are great for helping in organizing the existing resource and resource group.

Azure policies ensure that new resources use the same tags as existing resources, keeping things organized. To protect the resources after their deployment, the Role-Based Access Control (RBAC) policy provides fine-grained access management for your Azure resources, allowing you to grant users the specific rights they need to perform their jobs. IT personnel can easily manage settings, developers can have read-only access, and the administrator can have complete control simultaneously. You can even prevent resources from being deleted accidentally by enabling resource locks. You can block the ability to delete a resource or prevent changes by marking it as read-only. Azure Resource Manager provides the tools you need to organize and secure your resources.

Resource Groups

The resource group is like a bucket that holds all the components you want to manage together from initiation to retirement. For example, it is much easier to delete a resource group and all the objects that contain it than to delete the VM. Then, the disk storage counts the virtual network and all the objects individually.

Logical Grouping

The main purpose of the resource group is to group resources and perform bulk action upon that group. Different resource groups may be present to perform some specific task. Each resource group is isolated logically from another resource group. There is complete security available for each of the resources present inside the resource group.

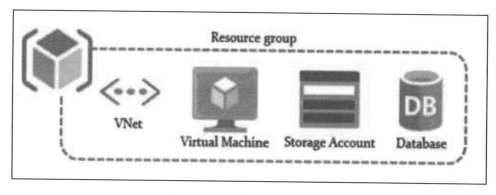

Figure 9-01: Resource Group

Life Cycle

The resource group contains several users with the same region and other specifications. When you have completed an experiment, you can easily delete all the resources by removing the resource group that contains those resources. It saves time and manual processing.

Authorization

Resource groups also enable the security policies when applying a Role-Based Access Control policy into that resource group. You can easily restrict unauthorized users from accessing the resource group with RBAC access.

Use resource groups for Organization

Following are some guidelines that help to create a resource group when working with the organization.

Compatible Naming Convention

For your organization, you can easily start by creating multiple resource groups. Each resource group contains several specific resources to perform a certain task.

Organizing Principles

For example, your solution will consist of several virtual networks, virtual machines, and databases. To simplify the implementation, you can create three resource groups. One is responsible for holding the VMs only, the other holds VNets, and the third holds the database with some unique resource group name, as shown in Figure 9-02.

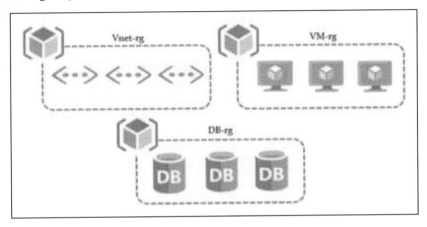

Figure 9-02: Segregated Resource Groups

You could also organize the resources into resource groups so that if you have three tasks to implement, each requires one VM, one VNet, and one Database. Therefore, to simplify this type of implementation, you can organize the resources in the resource group.

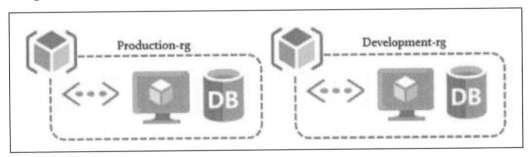

Figure 9-03: Organize Resources in the Resource Group

In addition, if your solution requires the same resources on the input and output side, you could organize these resources into the following resource groups.

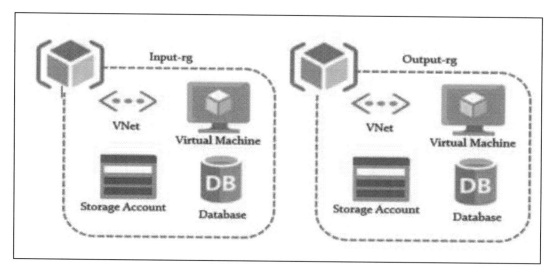

Figure 9-04: Input/Output Resource Group

Some factors are very important to consider when organizing the resource group resources.

Organizing for Authorization

To make the resource as secure as possible, you could organize the resources and use the RBAC policy that allows only authorized users to access this resource group.

Organizing for Lifecycle

You can organize the resources into a resources group that provides you easy working environment with the resource groups. Once you are done with the implementation and have built a solution successfully, you will be required to delete the resources; otherwise, they will be charged to your account according to the Pay-As-You-Go model. You can easily remove resources from the resource groups by just eliminating the resource group. This will immediately remove all the resources present inside the resource group at once and minimize the manual process as well.

Organizing for Billing

Suppose you organized your resources in the resource group to correspond to a single task. So, with this approach, you can easily understand and estimate the billing report produced due to those resources.

Tagging

As discussed earlier, we can organize several resources into the resource group. But what happens if your resources in the resource group are responsible for performing several tasks? Tags are important in distinguishing the same resource according to the task.

What are Tags?

Tagging in Azure is a label with key-value pairs that can be assigned to the resources so that resources can be easily identified. Key indicates the name ad value contains some specified number.

Using multiple virtual machines, you can easily identify VM types using tags.

A single resource can have a maximum of 50 tags. The length of the tag name is limited to 512 characters. You can use 512 characters in length for the name. This allows all types of resources to be present in the

resource group. However, storage resources have a name limit of 128 characters. A value length of 256 characters is allowed. The tag features cannot be applied to all types of resources except the classic ones.

You can create tags for the resources by using Azure Portal, Azure CLI, Azure PowerShell, ARM templates, and SDKs like REST API. For example, if you are using Azure CLI, you can easily add the tag to a virtual network resource by executing the following commands.

```
az resource tag --tags Department=Finance \

    --resource-group msftlearn-core-infrastructure-rg \

    --name msftlearn-vnet1 \

    --resource-type "Microsoft.Network/virtualNetworks"
```

EXAM TIP: Azure Policy automatically adds a resource tag to the resources that you created for your Azure solution. The tags are added according to the policy rules that you define.

Apply Tags to Resources

To apply resource tags to the resources, follow the given steps.

1. Go to the home portal page of Azure.
2. Navigate to your created resource group.
3. Inside the resource group, you will see the list of resources that this resource group holds.
4. To simplify the responsibilities of these resources, you can apply tags.
5. Select any resource from the list and go to the top to give options.
6. Click on "Assign tags."
7. The tag tab will appear, requiring you to give the key-value pair for that resource.
8. Give this resource's unique name and value and click on "Save."
9. After that, go back to the resource. You will see the same resource with the tag.

Edit Tags

To edit the tag, follow the given steps.

1. Go to the portal menu.
2. Click on "Resource groups."
3. The list of several created resource groups will appear.
4. Click on the resource group in which your tagged resource is present.
5. Open the resource in which you apply the tag.
6. Click on the "Edit tags."
7. Edit tags dialog box will appear. You can easily change the name and value and click "Save."

To see the resources of the same tags in the Azure portal, follow the given steps.

1. Go to the portal home page, and click "All resources."
2. The "All resources" page will appear, containing multiple resources.
3. Select "Add filter" present at the top of the page.
4. In the "Tags," select "your assigned key and value," You will immediately see the resources having that assigned tag.

Use Tags for Organization

Similarly, suppose you are working for an organization with several resources, and some resources have multiple responsibilities. In that case, you can simplify the work by assigning the tags with names and values. For example, if one storage account holds data in blob form and the other holds data in queue form, you can assign the tag to distinguish the performance of the storage account.

Azure Role-Based Access Control

To understand Role-Based Access Control, it is necessary to understand the role.

Usually, when using Microsoft Azure to build any solution, you must use certain Azure resources. For example, you have multiple resources like disk, virtual machine, SQL databases, and web applications. For all of these services, you can perform certain actions like creating a disk, updating it, attaching it to a virtual machine, starting and stopping the virtual machine, scaling up the SQL database, or deploying a web app. All these things that can be done with the Azure resources are called actions. Actions define what can be done with a certain type of service. Potentially, you could assign specific actions to users and applications to allow them to manage Azure resources. However, this process becomes very time-consuming as the number of resources increases.

In Azure, creating a bundle of actions to combine the actions like updating the disk, starting or stopping the VM, attaching the disk, and creating a role with a name like VM operator is easier. In the same way, you can create as many roles as you want for your organization. You can fine-grain permissions for your applications and users by using roles. Azure has several built-in roles allowing you to manage access to your resources.

RBAC

Role-Based Access Control (RBAC) can easily secure your Azure resources. A virtual machine, websites, network, storage, and all the critical resources for any organization using a cloud. When it comes to protecting these types of resources, security is paramount. These certain resources and assets need to be locked down and secure. However, it is also very important to grant employees and partners the access they need to perform their duties. Role-Based Access Control is used to grant access from one resource to another. RBAC is the security system that controls and manages who can access the resource.

RBAC role is used to grant access to Azure resources. Figure 9-05 illustrates how classic subscription administrator, RBAC, and Azure AD administrator roles are related. In the figure, a subscription role has an Azure AD tenant with users or a group of users. An Azure AD tenant has access to the root management group that allows users or groups of users to access certain resources present within the resource group.

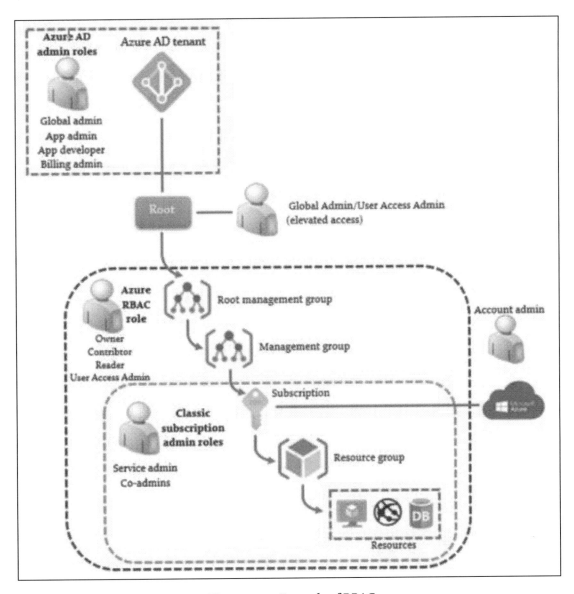

Figure 9-05: Example of RBAC

What can we do with RBAC?

The Role-Based Access Control policy provides fine-grained access management for your Azure resources, allowing you to grant users the specific rights they need to perform their duties.

In addition, using RBAC, you can:

- Allow a single user to manage and control the virtual machine in the given subscription and other users to manage the virtual network
- The database administrator group is responsible for managing the SQL databases in the subscription
- A single user can manage and control all the resources in the resource group, such as VM, VNet, storage account, etc.
- Allow an application to access all the available resources present in the resource group

How does RBAC work?

The way you control access to resources is to create a role assignment. You can enforce the permissions by creating a role assignment. There are three elements required to create a role assignment.

- Security Principal
- Role Definition
- Scope

Security Principal

The security principle is for users, groups, or applications you want to grant access to. This element is not just for people; one application can be a principal with access to another resource. The visualization of the security principle is shown in Figure 9-06.

Figure 9-06: Security Principal

Role Definition

What the service principal can do is specify with role definition. Role definition is a collection of permission or actions. It is also referred to as a role. It lists the permissions you can perform, such as read, write, and delete. Azure has multiple roles you can use, such as an owner or virtual machine contributor. An example of the role definition is shown in Figure 9-07.

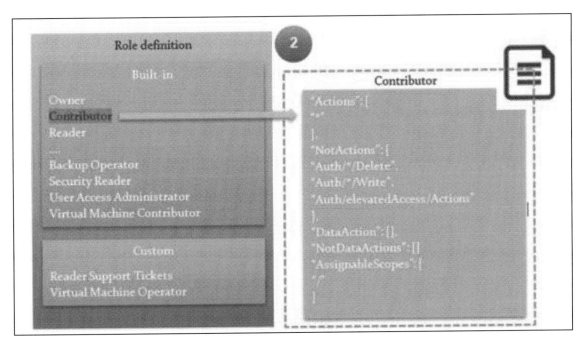

Figure 9-07: Role Definition

There are several built-in roles defined in the role definition. The four most common built-in roles are:

- **Owner** – It has full access to all Azure resources, including reading and writing the resources or deleting access to others
- **Contributor** – This role can create and manage all the Azure resources. However, this role is unable to delete access to others
- **Reader** – The role can only view the existing Azure resource. It is not able to delegate the resource or have access to others
- **User Access Administrator** – This role allows you to control and manage the user access to Azure resources

> **EXAM TIP:** If the common built-in role does not match your requirements, you can create a "custom role."

Scope

After defining the service principal and role definition, you must be given access. This is called scope. In Azure, you can specify a scope at multiple levels, such as a management group, subscription, resource group, or individual resources, and sub-levels inherit those permissions. The parent-child structure given by scope is shown in Figure 9-08.

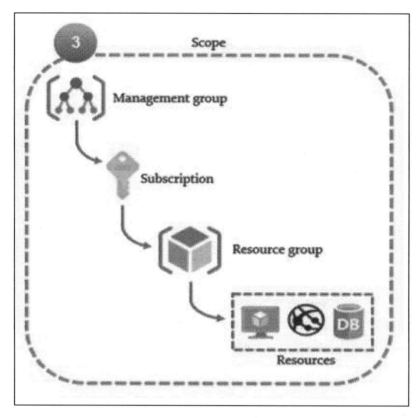

Figure 9-08: Scope

Role Assignment

When you are done with the service principal (who has access), role definition (what can access), and scope (where they can access), you combine these three elements to grant access with a role assignment. You can easily create a role assignment using the Azure portal, Azure CLI, Azure PowerShell, or other methods.

The role assignment method combines a role to a security principal at some particular scope to grant access. Figure 9-09 defines the role assignment by combining the security principal, role definition, and scope defined earlier.

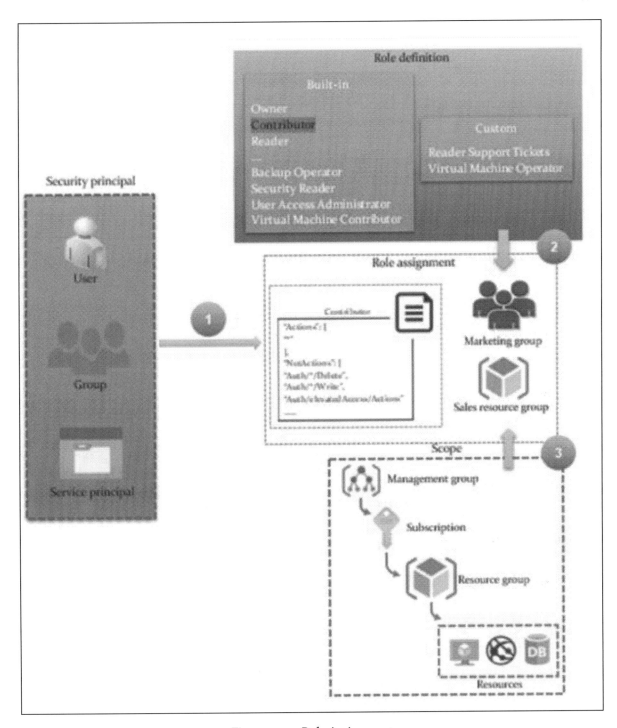

Figure 9-09: Role Assignment

> 💡 **EXAM TIP:** You grant access to a resource by creating a role assignment, then revoke the granted access by removing the same role assignment.

RBAC Uses Allow Model

Role-Based Access Control uses an allow model to define access. You can easily read, write, and delete the resources when assigned to a role. Thus, if one role assignment allows you to read resources, another

allows you to write in the same resource group. You will both be permitted to read and write in the resource group.

Role-Based Access Control has several permissions. One of which is "NotActions." With "NotActions" permission, you can easily create a set of several allowed permission to a specific bunch of users or groups of users. This type of access is granted by defining a role, the powerful permission. You can easily create this role assignment by removing the "NotActions" operations from the "Actions" operation.

For example, usually "Contributor" role has both "NotActions" and "Actions" permissions. When you open the list of permissions in the Azure portal, you will see wildcard "(*)" in the "Actions" operation, indicating that the assigned users or group can perform all types of operations. To make effective permission, you must move the following permissions.

- Delete and create roles and role assignments
- Create, update and delete blueprint artifacts
- Grants the User Access Administrator at the AD tenant scope

RBAC in Azure Portal

The Azure portal allows you to manage identity and access by creating the role assignment. The steps to use Role-Based Access Control (RBAC) using the Azure portal are as follows:

1. Log in to the Azure portal with your credentials.
2. Create a resource group by filling in all the required details.
3. After the deployment of the resource group, open the overview page.
4. Go to the left side given menu, and click on the "Access control (IAM)" option.
5. Initially, no access will be assigned to any resource. Open the "Role assignments" tab.
6. You will see the following list, which categorizes the role assignment concerning Contributor, Owner, and User Access Administrator.

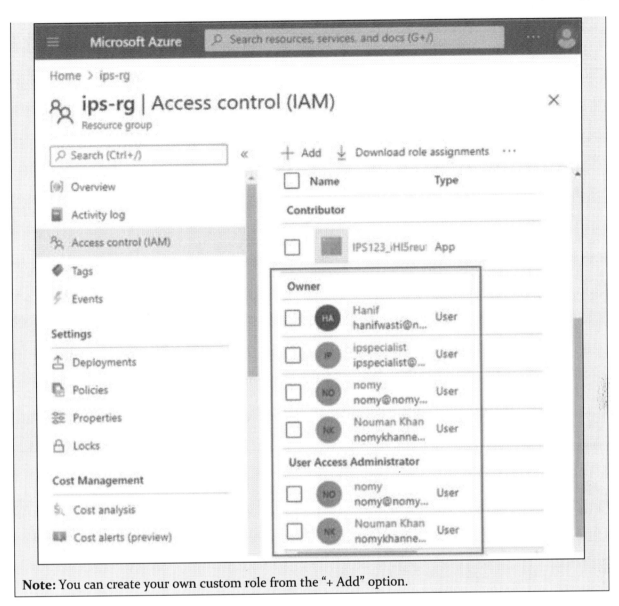

Note: You can create your own custom role from the "+ Add" option.

Secure Azure Resources with RBAC

Introduction

Protecting Azure resources, such as virtual networks, websites, virtual machines, storage, etc., is very difficult for any company or organization, especially when using the cloud. Companies and organizations use Azure-based resources and services to build their solutions. In addition, they want to secure and protect their resource from accidental issues such as data loss, hacking, etc. Companies also want to grant resource access to their employees so they can easily perform their duties.

Role-Based Access Control is used to manage and secure the Azure resource, grant these resources access to multiple employees and allow them to access resources in a certain location. RBAC is the authorization system that provides security and protection to your Azure resource. It also grants access to the employees and managers who has access to these resources and where they can access them (location).

Role-Based Access Control

To understand Role-Based Access Control, it is necessary to understand the role.

Usually, when using Microsoft Azure to build any solution, you must use certain Azure resources. For example, you have multiple resources like disk, virtual machine, SQL databases, and web applications. For all of these services, you can perform certain actions like creating a disk, updating it, attaching it to a virtual machine, starting and stopping the virtual machine, scale-up the SQL database, or deploying a web app. All these things that can be done with the Azure resources are called actions. Actions define what can be done with a certain type of service. Potentially, you could assign specific actions to users and applications to allow them to manage Azure resources. However, this process becomes very time-consuming as the number of resources increases.

In Azure, creating a bundle of actions to combine the actions like updating the disk, starting or stopping the VM, attaching the disk, and creating a role with a name like VM operator is easier. In the same way, you can create as many roles as you want for your organization. You can fine-grain permissions for your applications and users by using roles. Azure has several built-in roles allowing you to manage your access to your resource.

Azure Subscription

When working with RBAC, Microsoft Entra ID (former name Azure AD) is also used for identity and access management. When you start working work Azure, it is mandatory to use an Azure subscription. Azure subscription is linked with a single Microsoft Entra ID. Users, groups, and applications in that particular directory can manage and control the Azure resources in the Azure subscription. Each Azure subscription uses a single Microsoft Entra ID for sign-on (SSO) and access management. You can increase your on-premises AD directory to the cloud by using the Azure feature called Azure AD Connect. This feature allows us to manage and monitor Azure subscriptions with the existing work identities.

Note: When you disable the on-premises AD account, you will lose access to the Azure subscription connected with Microsoft Entra ID.

Microsoft Entra ID (Azure AD) and Role-Based Access Control (RBAC) work together because Azure AD is the centralized service for identity and access management, and that access management for Azure resources is done with the RBAC feature.

EXAM TIP: Microsoft Entra ID services are available for everything present on Azure. It is the first service given when a user creates an account in Azure.

Secure Resources with RBAC

As discussed earlier, Azure policy restricts resource access and allows resource access to only specified users. To control resource security, Role-Based Access Control can be used.

In Microsoft Azure, a role is a list of actions you can or cannot do. Your role definition could allow you to create and manage a virtual machine. However, it prevents you from deleting them. The following are the most common and known back roles:

- **Owner** – Provides full access to resources in Azure, and you can delegate access to other users
- **Contributor** – It is like an owner role; it provides full access to resources in Azure. However, you cannot delegate control. The reader can only view the resources

- **User Access Administrator** – It is granted permission to manage access to Azure resources

In addition, by using RBAC, you can:

- Allow a single user to manage and control the virtual machine in the given subscription and other users to manage the virtual network
- The database administrator group is responsible for managing the SQL databases in the subscription
- A single user can manage and control all the resources in the resource group, such as VM, VNet, Storage account, etc.
- Allow an application to access all the available resources present in the resource group

View Access Permission

To view the access permission, go to your resource group's "Access control (IAM)" option.

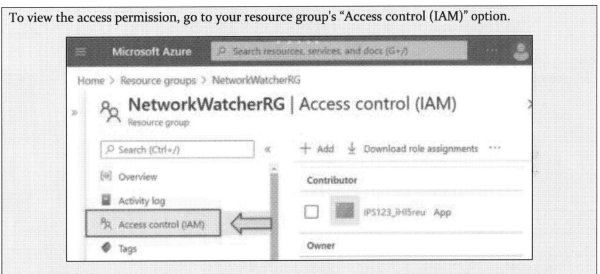

In this panel, you can see who can access an area and their assigned role. You can add and remove the role access as well.

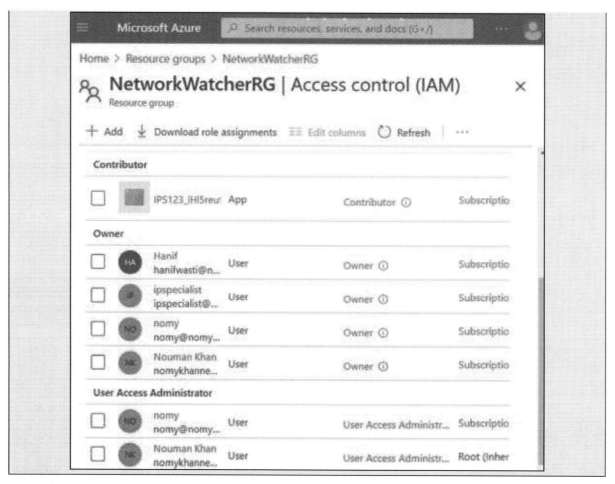

Define Access using RBAC

Role-Based Access Control uses an allow model to define access. You can easily read, write, and delete the resources when assigned to a role. Thus, if one role assignment allows you to read resources, another allows you to write in the same resource group. You will both be permitted to read and write in the resource group.

Best Practices for RBAC

The following are some best practices for RBAC.

- Separate responsibilities within your squad and allow only the amount of access to users that they require to perform their duties
- It is not good to restrict the users from using any resource in the subscription. Instead, you should assign a single role to the user so that they can access it at a particular scope
- Plan your access control strategy in such a way that grants users the least privileged access that they require to perform their jobs
- Use of resource locks. It restricts the users from deleting and modifying any resource

Azure Policy

Azure Policy is used to create policies in Azure. With Azure Policy, you can manage and assign policies to the resources with multiple rules so that specific resources are compliant with your business standard

and SLAs. You can use Azure Policy to make sure that the use of resources does not become a mess. Azure Policy is a default allow and explicit deny system.

If you have a group of resources with the policies for each resource, then Azure Policy is a service that ensures that these resources are compliant with the policies. Azure enforces that.

 EXAM TIP: Azure Policy ensures compliance with policies applied to the resources.

A policy is a set of rules to ensure compliant resources.

Use Policies to Enforce Standards

When you have built multiple resources in the resource group and assigned tags to some resources, you can easily simplify the working responsibilities of these resources. But what if you implement the new resource in the same resource group, and how do you ensure that the new resource will follow the same tagging and grouping rule? With Azure policy, you can easily design certain rules that apply to your Azure environment.

Azure Policy

When an Azure Policy is assigned to a particular resource group. The resources in the resource group would remain to exist as it is. Azure Policy is responsible for highlighting the issues of some particular service using a definition that affects the resource present Resource Groups.

Normally, you can use Azure policies to enforce things like creating a policy or rule that allows access to only a specific resource or resource group. You can also create a policy that assigns tags to resources belonging to some specific region. In this chapter section, you will learn how to create an Azure policy and use it to enforce standards.

Create a Policy

There are three steps involved in the creation of the Azure policy. These are:

1. Create a Policy Definition
2. Create a Policy Assignment
3. Test out a Policy

Create a Policy Definition

The first step in creating policy is to create a policy definition. The following steps could be used to create a policy definition.

1. Go to **Azure** Portal, and click on **"Policy"** from the resources available.

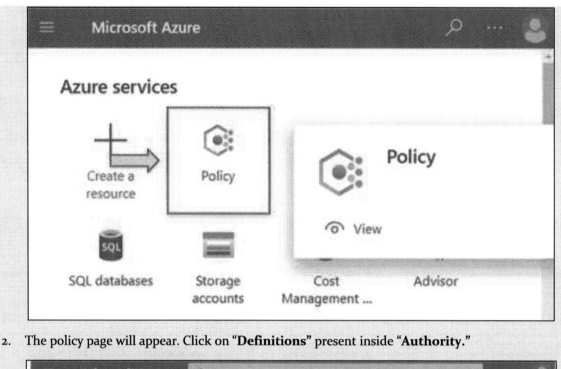

2. The policy page will appear. Click on **"Definitions"** present inside **"Authority."**

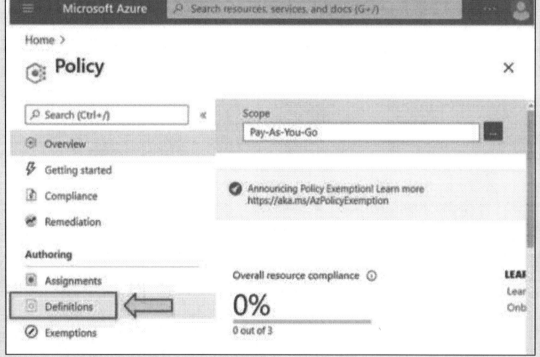

3. To create a custom policy, click on "+ **Policy definition**" present at the top given options.

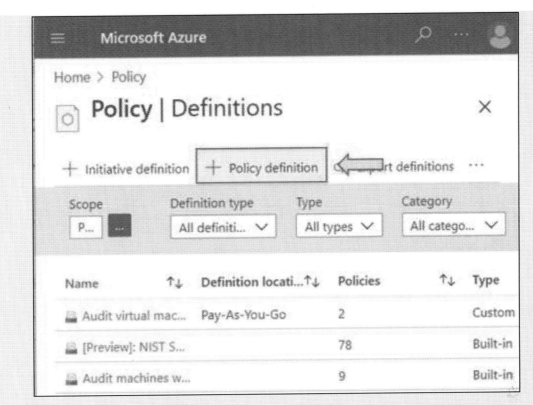

4. On the **"Policy definition"** page, select the definition location (subscription) by clicking on the right-corner option.

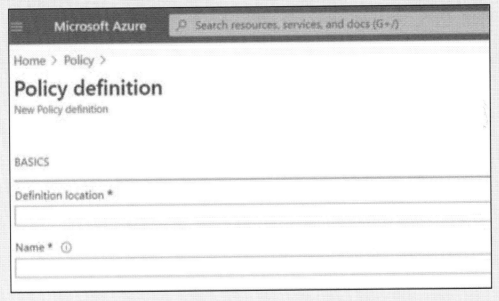

5. Select your subscription and click on **"Select."**

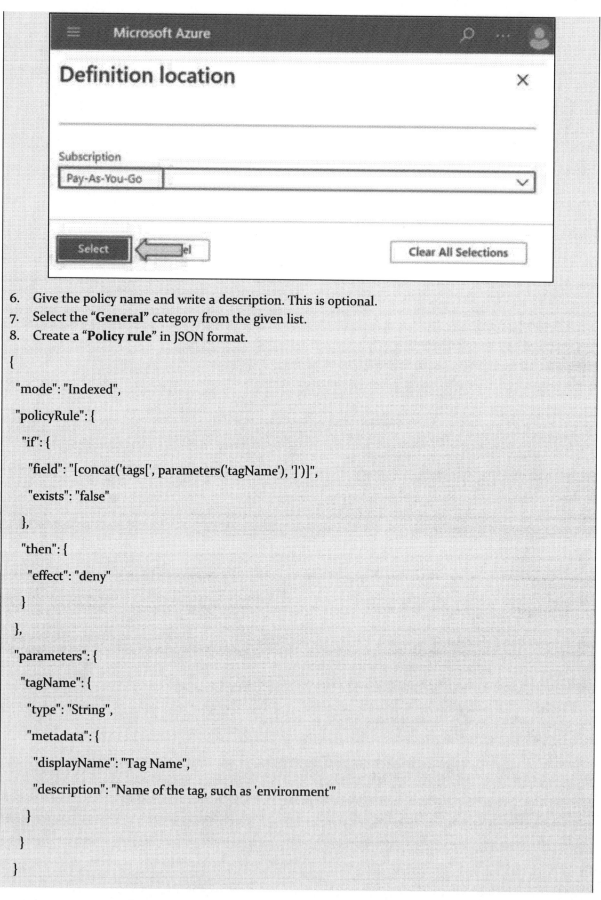

6. Give the policy name and write a description. This is optional.
7. Select the "**General**" category from the given list.
8. Create a "**Policy rule**" in JSON format.

```json
{
  "mode": "Indexed",
  "policyRule": {
    "if": {
      "field": "[concat('tags[', parameters('tagName'), ']')]",
      "exists": "false"
    },
    "then": {
      "effect": "deny"
    }
  },
  "parameters": {
    "tagName": {
      "type": "String",
      "metadata": {
        "displayName": "Tag Name",
        "description": "Name of the tag, such as 'environment'"
      }
    }
  }
}
```

}

9. Click on **"Save."**

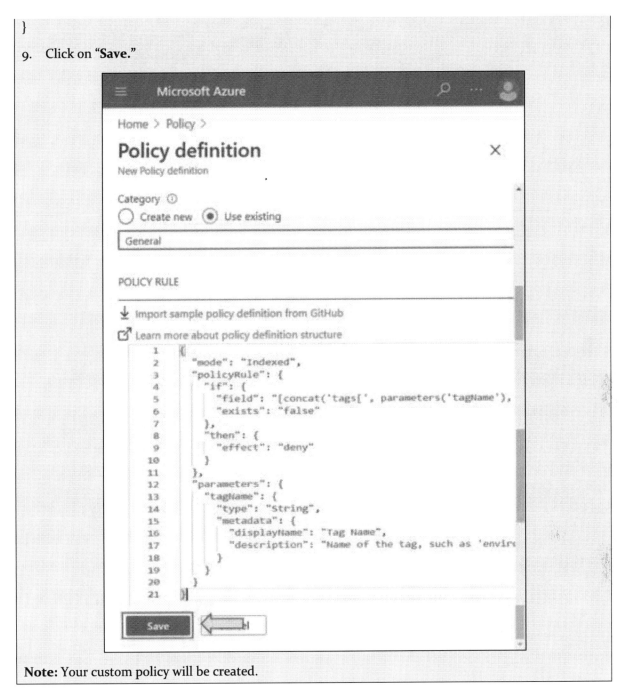

Note: Your custom policy will be created.

Create a Policy Assignment

After creating a policy definition, the next step is to create a policy assignment. For policy assignments, follow the given steps.

1. Go to **Azure** Portal, and click on **"Policy"** from the resources available.

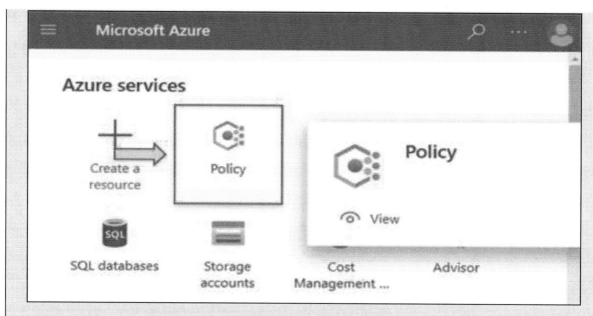

2. The policy page will appear. Click on **"Assignments"** present inside **"Authority."**

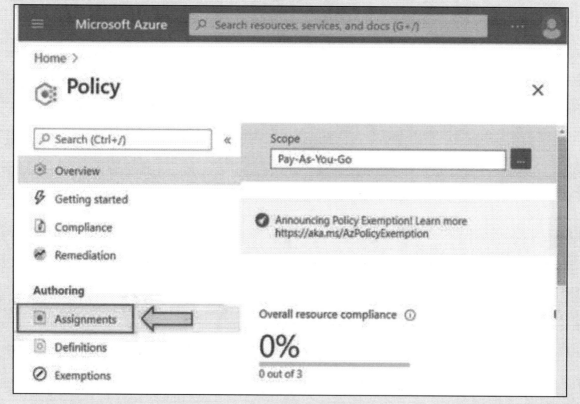

3. In the **"Assign Policy"** pane, you will assign the policy to your resource group. Click on **"Assign Policy"** present at the top given options.

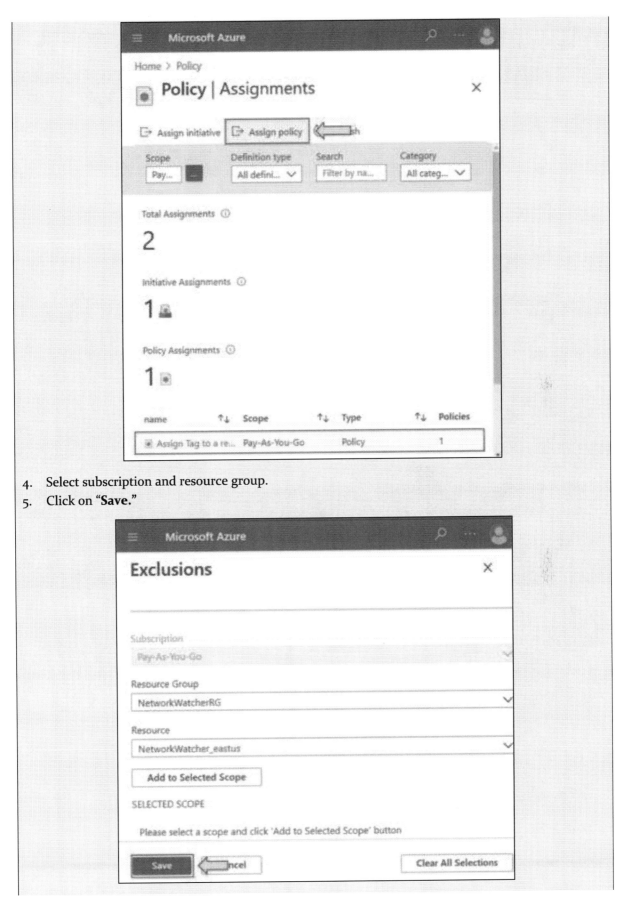

4. Select subscription and resource group.
5. Click on "**Save.**"

6. Select the "Custom" type from the list for the policy type.
7. Select **"Enforce tag a resource"** and click on **"Select."**

8. Now, verify the **"Basic"** details.
9. Click on **"Next."**

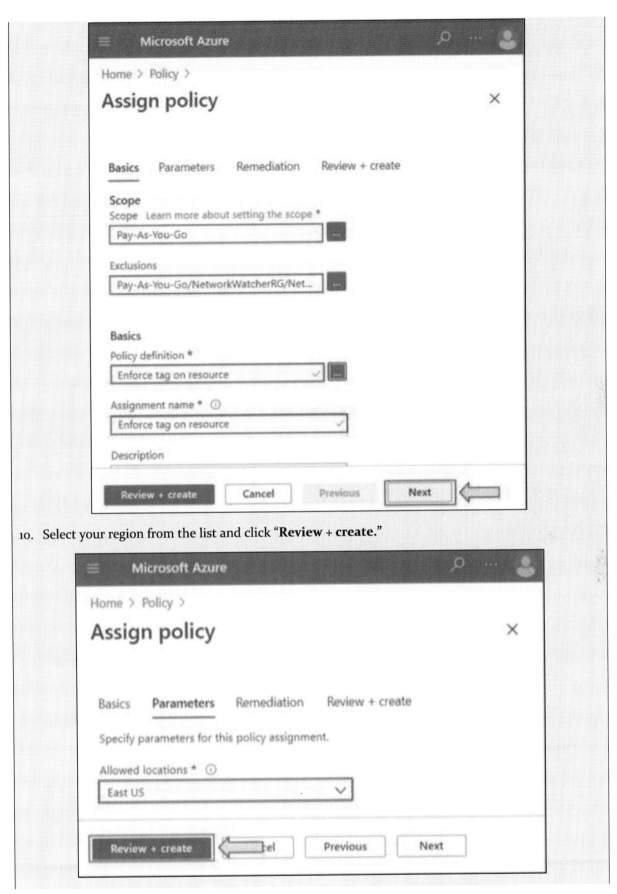

10. Select your region from the list and click "**Review + create.**"

11. When the validation is passed, click on **"Create."**

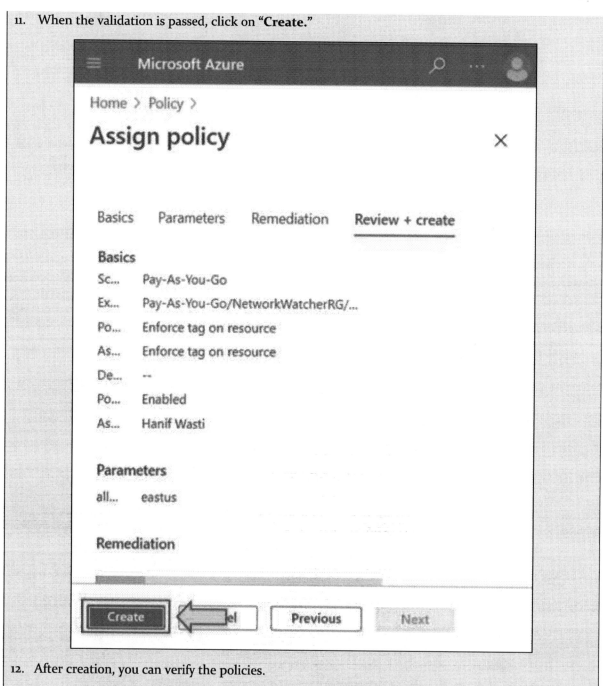

12. After creation, you can verify the policies.

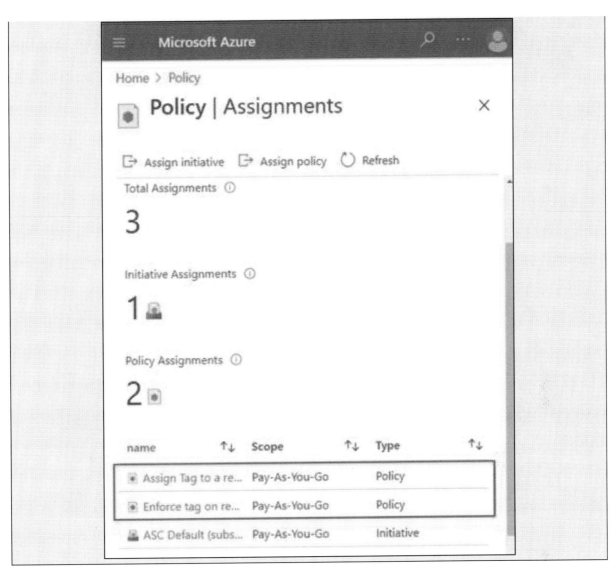

Test out a Policy

After assigning the policy, you can test this policy by creating any resource in your assigned resource group.

1. Go to **Azure** Portal and click on **"Create a resource."**

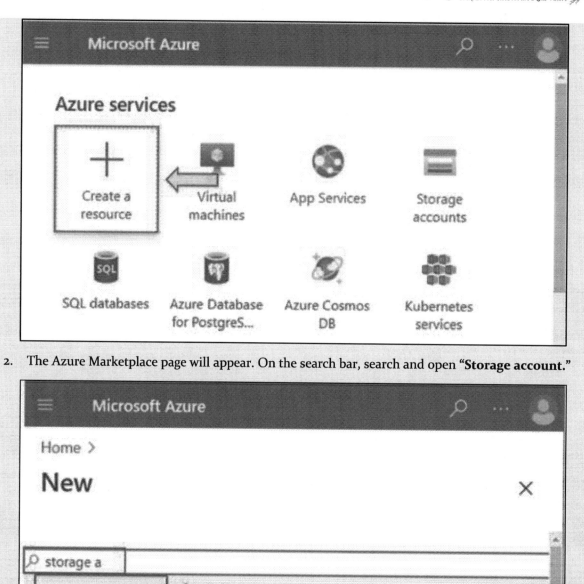

2. The Azure Marketplace page will appear. On the search bar, search and open **"Storage account."**

3. Click on **"Create."**

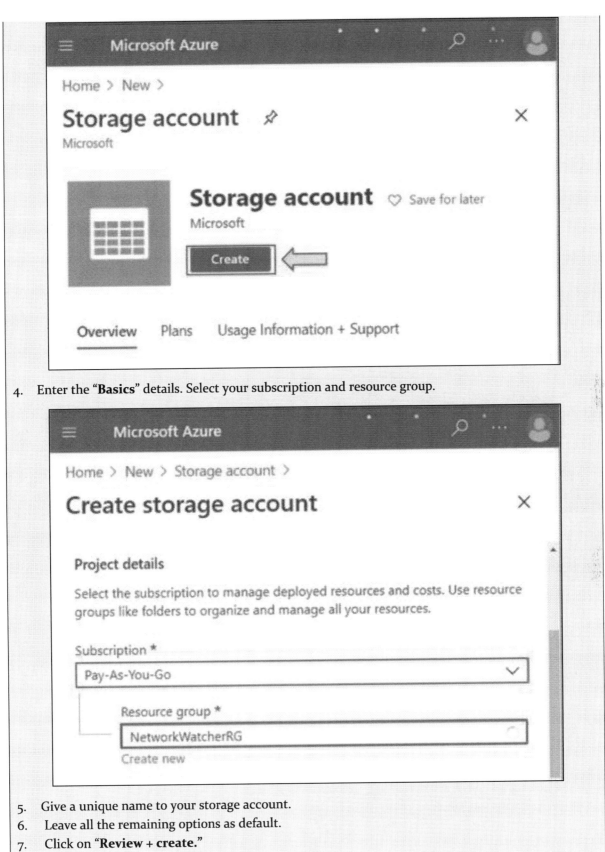

4. Enter the **"Basics"** details. Select your subscription and resource group.

5. Give a unique name to your storage account.
6. Leave all the remaining options as default.
7. Click on **"Review + create."**

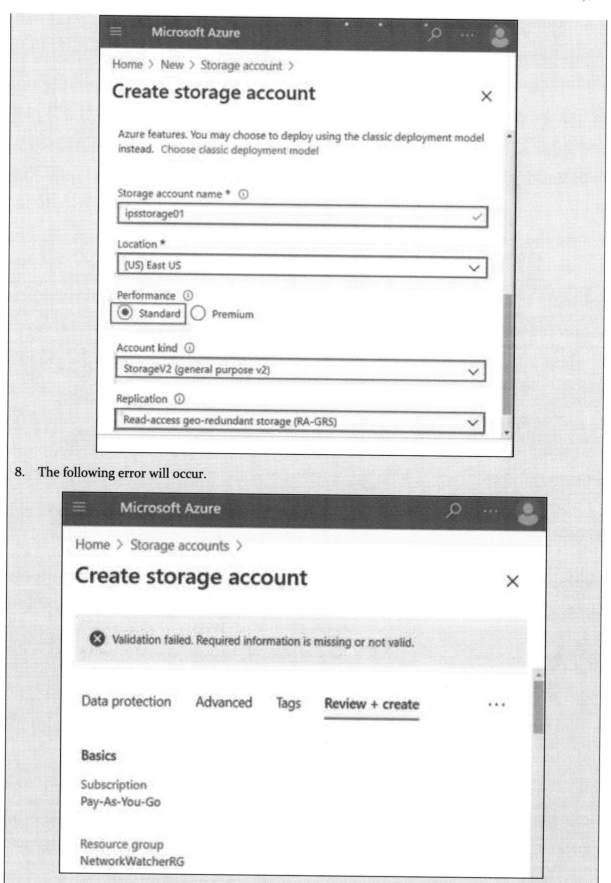

8. The following error will occur.

Note: This happened due to the assigned policy.

9. Go back to the **"Tags"** pane from the top.
10. Enter the key-value pair of your own choice.
11. Click on **"Review + create."**

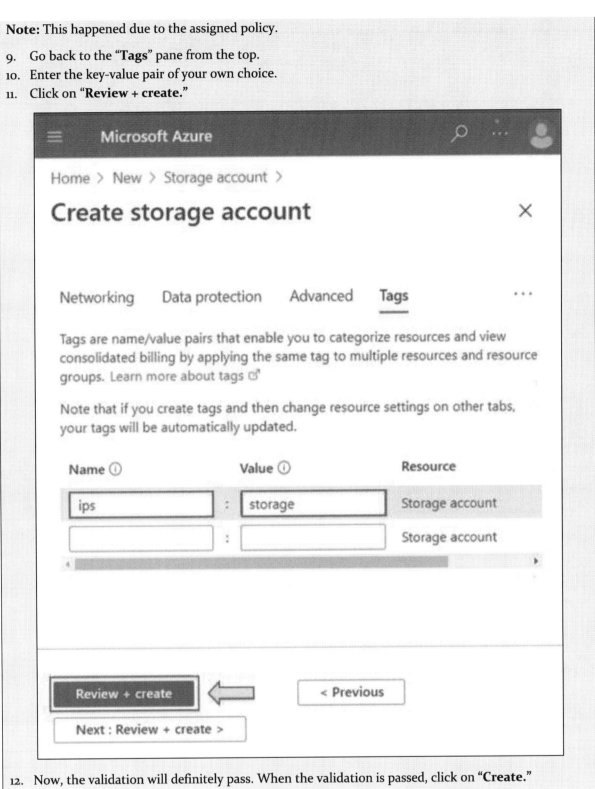

12. Now, the validation will definitely pass. When the validation is passed, click on **"Create."**

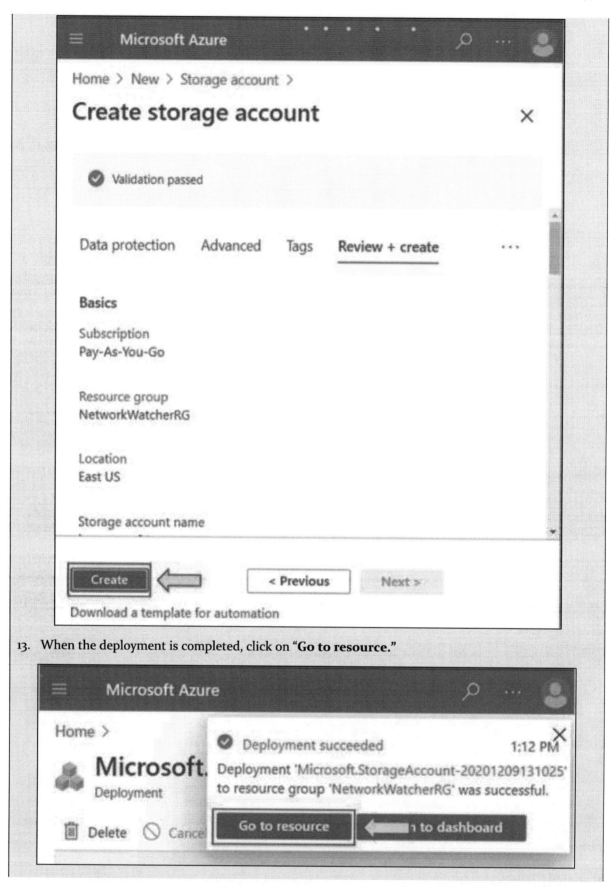

13. When the deployment is completed, click on "**Go to resource.**"

14. You can verify the configuration details from the overview page of the storage account.

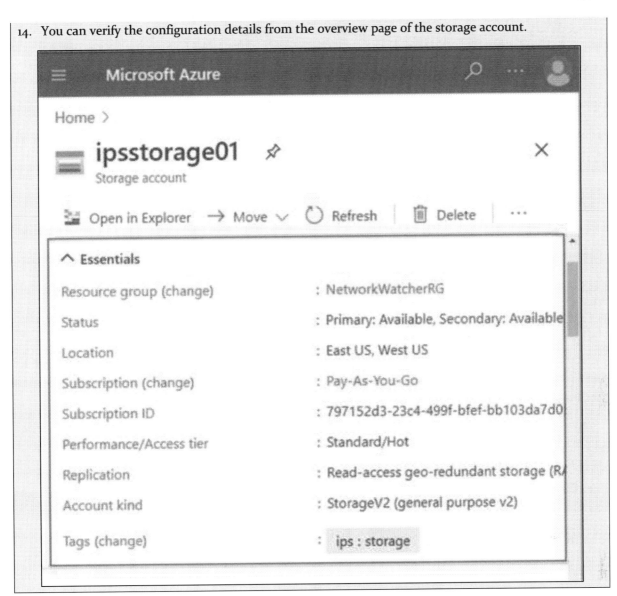

The main purpose of Azure policy is to restrict access from an unauthorized source. Organizations normally use this type of policy to secure their resources, and these types of policies are designed with legal and regulatory restrictions. These assigned policies control resources. For example, you can assign an Azure policy that says that your organization can create only Linux-based VMs. If anyone from your organization tries to create a Windows-based VM or another type of VM, this policy will not allow them to create such virtual machines.

Azure Policy Initiatives

An Azure Policy initiative serves as a mechanism for organizing the related policies, allowing for the collective management of compliance goals. It consolidates various policy definitions to streamline the assessment of compliance status for broader objectives. As an illustration, consider the "Enable Monitoring in Microsoft Defender for Cloud" initiative within Azure Policy. This initiative is designed to oversee the monitoring of all available security recommendations across diverse Azure resource types in the Microsoft Defender for Cloud. Within this overarching initiative, specific policy definitions are encapsulated, such as monitoring unencrypted SQL Databases, ensuring compliance with OS

vulnerability baselines, and verifying the presence of an endpoint protection agent on servers. Each of these policy definitions contributes to the comprehensive goal of enhancing monitoring capabilities within Microsoft Defender for Cloud.

Azure Blueprint

It is a template for creating Azure resources. Everything you need to deploy in the standard cloud environment of Azure is defined in the blueprint. Consider an example of creating a new Azure environment and meeting specific governance rules and regulations. Now, doing this manually can be quite difficult. Azure Blueprints enables cloud architects and central information technology groups to define a repeatable set of Azure resources that implements and adheres to an organization's standards, patterns, and requirements. Some common scenarios have built-in samples, like situations with specific governance, regulations, and guidelines.

 EXAM TIP: To create a standard Azure Environment, Azure Blueprint is used.

Cloud Adoption Framework for Azure

The Azure Cloud Adoption Framework provides a tried-and-true direction for your cloud adoption journey. The Cloud Adoption Framework assists you in developing and implementing the business and technological strategies required for cloud success.

A good cloud environment must support organization strategy, be easy to manage, and comply with government or industry regulations. Setting up your cloud environment requires a lot of decisions, each of which can have a significant impact on your outcome.

The Cloud Adoption Framework for Azure guides you toward cloud adoption in five key stages and offers a collection of documentation, implementation guidance, best practices, and tools for each.

- Define your approach.
- Make a strategy.
- Prepare your company.
- Adopt cloud computing.
- Administrate and control your cloud infrastructures.

Azure Advisor for Security Assistance

Azure Advisor is a separate portal within Azure that has Security Assistance as part of the Microsoft Defender for Cloud. We have already discussed the Microsoft Defender for Cloud in Chapter 8.

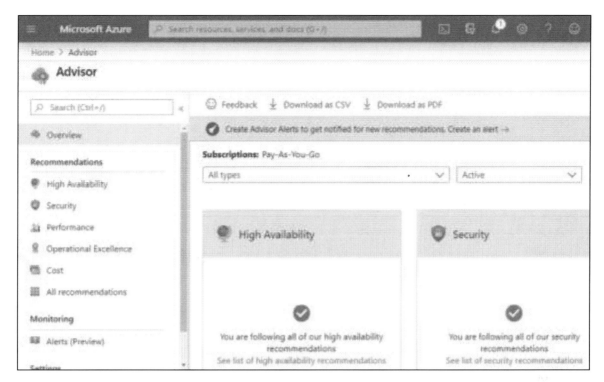

Figure 9-10: Azure Advisor

Use Locks to Protect Resources

Locking the Azure resources is the ultimate way of protecting the resource. It prevents you from deleting and changing any resource mistakenly.

Resource Locks

In Azure, resource locks are the settings that can be applied to restrict the user from unneeded modification and deletion. These locks have two types of modes. One is to delete, and the other is read-only. With delete lock, you will be allowed to make all the changes in that resource except to delete it. You can also view the resource without changing, modifying, or deleting it with read-only access. Resource locks can be applied to subscriptions, resource groups, or any resource present in the resource group.

Note: The "Read-only" lock can create some unpredicted outcomes due to the additional actions required for a read operation.

When the resource lock is applied to any particular resource, you first remove the lock from that resource to perform any operation. Resource locks prevent your resource from accidental actions and protect you from doing something you may not have intended to do. This type of lock is applied regardless of RBAC permissions.

Purpose of Azure Resource Locks

Resources cannot be mistakenly altered or destroyed with a resource lock.

Even with Azure RBAC restrictions in place, there is still a possibility that someone with the necessary degree of access might destroy crucial cloud resources. Resource locks stop resources from being modified or removed depending on the type of lock. Resource locks may be used to restrict access to specific resources, entire resource groups, or even an entire subscription. Since resource locks are inheritable, if you apply one to a resource group, it automatically applies to all of the resources in that group as well.

Types of Resource Locks

There are two different kinds of resource locks: one restricts users from removing resources, and the other from modifying or deleting resources.

Delete - Delete implies that a resource is no longer available for reading or editing by authorized users.

ReadOnly - A resource that is marked as readonly can only be updated or deleted by authorized users. Applying this lock is equivalent to limiting all authorized users to the Reader role's permissions.

Manage resource locks

Resource locks can be effectively managed through various methods, including the Azure portal, PowerShell, the Azure CLI, or an Azure Resource Manager template. To access, add, or remove locks in the Azure portal, navigate to the Settings section within the Settings pane of any specific resource. This provides a user-friendly interface for efficiently handling resource locks based on your requirements.

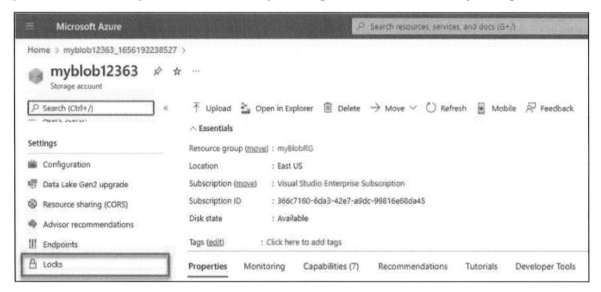

Figure 9-11: Manage resource locks.

Delete or change a locked resource

Managing locked resources involves a two-step process to enable modifications despite the presence of locks. Although locks are valuable in preventing inadvertent changes, users can navigate this restriction by first removing the existing lock on the resource. This initial step is essential for any subsequent actions, regardless of the user's RBAC (Role-Based Access Control) permissions. Even users with the owner role for the resource must initiate the removal of the lock before executing any activities previously restricted. Once the lock is successfully removed, users can proceed to apply the desired changes to the resource, ensuring that they possess the necessary permissions to perform the intended actions and adhere to

RBAC policies throughout the process. This structured approach ensures a systematic and secure method for users to manage and modify locked resources.

Use Resource Locks in Practices

The use of resource locks is a way of protection from accidents. To delete any resource, you have first to move the lock. This feature is usually used to protect some special resources of Azure that could have a large impact if they are accidentally deleted or modified. Examples of such resources are the ExpressRoute circuit, domain controller, virtual network, databases, etc.

Use Locks to Protect Resources

Locking the Azure resources is the ultimate way of protecting the resource. It prevents you from deleting and changing any resource mistakenly.

Resource Locks

In Azure, resource locks are the setting that can be applied to restrict the user from unneeded modification and deletion. These locks have two types of modes. One is to delete, and the other is read-only. With delete lock, you will be allowed to make all the changes in that resource except to delete it. You can view the resource without changing, modifying, or deleting it with read-only access. Resource locks can be applied to subscriptions, resource groups, or any resource present in the resource group.

> **Note:** The "Read-only" lock can create some unpredicted outcomes due to the additional actions required for a read operation.

When the resource lock is applied to any particular resource, you first remove the lock from that resource to perform any operation. Resource locks prevent your resource from accidental actions and protect you from doing something you may not have intended to do. This type of lock is applied regardless of RBAC permissions.

How to create a resource lock?

Follow the given steps to create a resource lock in the resource group.

1. Go to the portal page of Azure. Navigate to the resource group.
2. On the resource group pane, note the available resources.
3. From the left side given menu, click on "Locks" present inside the "Settings" option.
4. Click on "+Add" to create a lock.
5. Write the "Lock name" and "Lock type."
6. Click on "OK."

7. Select any resource present in that resource group and delete it. You will see the following error message.

Note: To remove any resource from the locked resource group, you should first delete that lock and then delete the resource.

Use Resource Locks in Practices

The use of resource locks is a way of protection from accidents. To delete any resource, you have first to move the lock. This feature is usually used to protect some special resources of Azure that could have a

large impact if they are accidentally deleted or modified. Examples of such resources are the ExpressRoute circuit, domain controller, virtual network, databases, etc.

Lab 9-01: Azure Resource Locks

Service Introduction

Acme Software, a rapidly growing software development company, embraced the cloud for its infrastructure. However, their agile development process resulted in concerns about accidental deletions or modifications of critical resources, potentially causing outages and data loss. They needed a way to prevent human error while still enabling agile development.

Problem

The fast-paced environment led to accidental resource deletions or modifications by developers, causing service disruptions and costly downtime. Lack of control over resource configuration raised compliance concerns and made it difficult to enforce internal security policies consistently.

Solution

Acme Software's success story showcases the power of Azure Resource Lock for cloud-based companies prioritizing both agility and security. By introducing preventive measures, granular control, and seamless integration, Acme achieved peace of mind knowing its infrastructure was protected from accidental disruptions while still empowering its developers to innovate.

1. Log in to the **Azure Portal** using your credentials.

Azure RBAC Role Assignment

2. From the portal home page, search and open **Resource groups.**

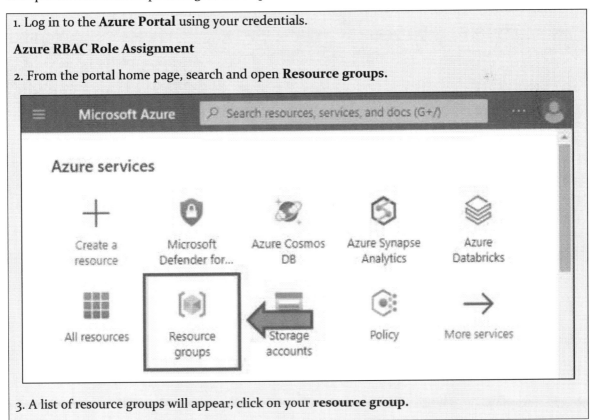

3. A list of resource groups will appear; click on your **resource group.**

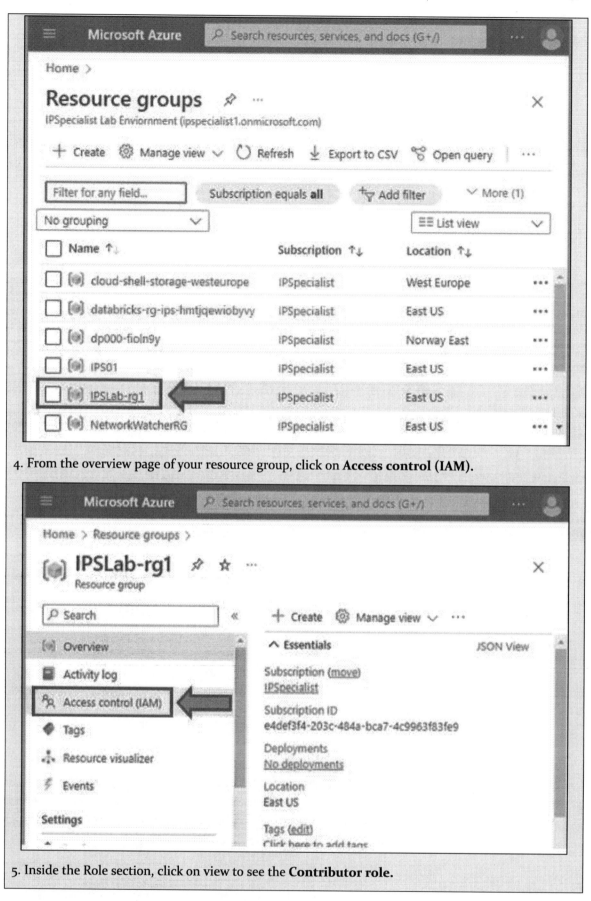

4. From the overview page of your resource group, click on **Access control (IAM)**.

5. Inside the Role section, click on view to see the **Contributor role.**

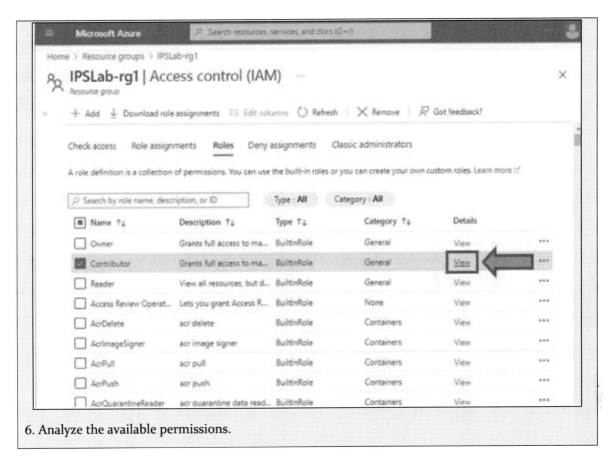

6. Analyze the available permissions.

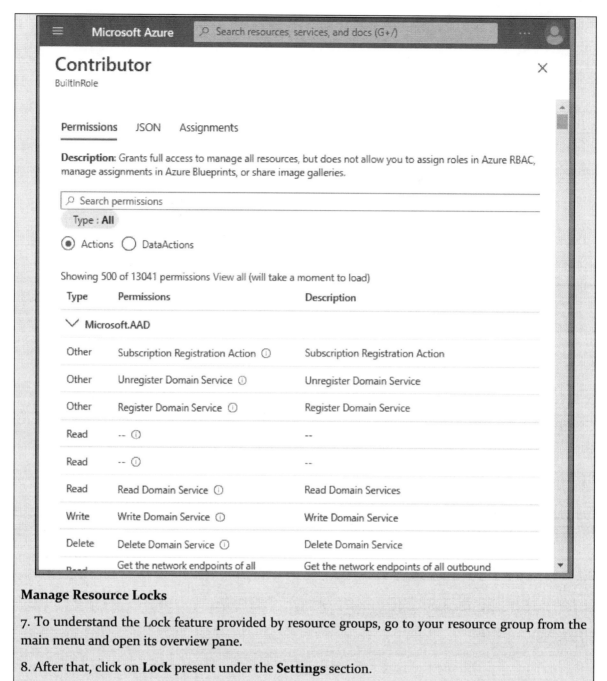

Manage Resource Locks

7. To understand the Lock feature provided by resource groups, go to your resource group from the main menu and open its overview pane.

8. After that, click on **Lock** present under the **Settings** section.

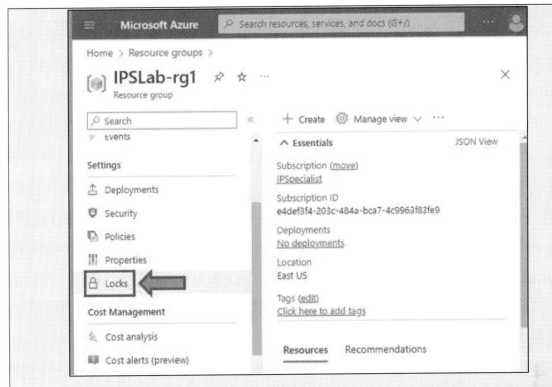

9. Specify the lock name, and to prevent the deletion of your resource group, you should set **Delete** lock. Click on **OK**.

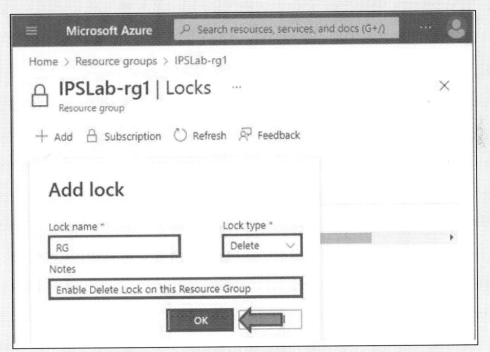

Note: You need to specify the notes to enable it.

10. You will see that the lock has been successfully created.

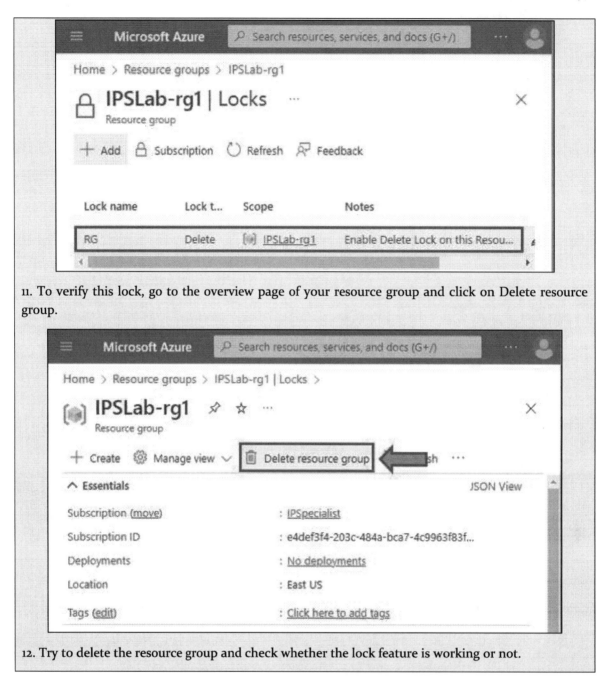

11. To verify this lock, go to the overview page of your resource group and click on Delete resource group.

12. Try to delete the resource group and check whether the lock feature is working or not.

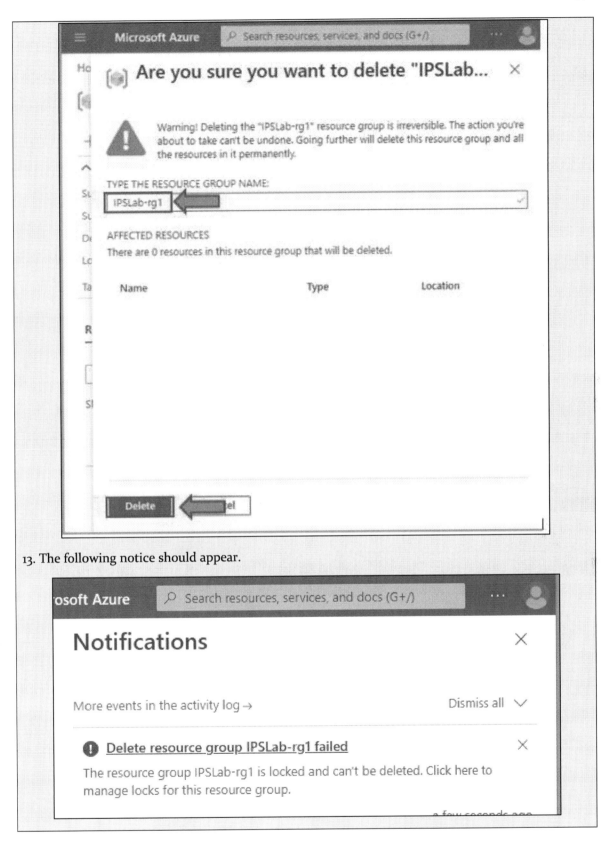

13. The following notice should appear.

Subscription Governance Strategy

You identify a cloud organization structure that suits your company's needs at the start of any cloud governance project. Typically, this phase entails building a cloud center of excellence team (also called a cloud enablement team or a cloud custodian team). This group can establish governance policies for the entire organization from a centralized place.

The subscription level is frequently where teams begin their Azure governance plan. When it comes to creating and managing subscriptions, there are three primary factors to consider:

- Billing
- Access Control
- Subscription Restrictions

Billing

Per subscription, you can only create one billing report. Organizing subscriptions by department or project is one option if you have many departments and need to "chargeback" cloud charges.

Resource tags can also be beneficial. Consider your internal billing requirements when determining how many subscriptions you need and what to call them.

Access Control

A subscription is an Azure resource deployment boundary. Every Microsoft Entra ID tenant is linked to a subscription. Using Azure role-based access control, managers can set granular access through defined roles for each tenant.

Subscription Limit

Subscriptions have some resource constraints as well. For example, the maximum number of network Azure ExpressRoute circuits per subscription is 10. Those constraints should be taken into account throughout the design phase. If you need to go above those limits, you may need to purchase additional subscriptions. There is no way to extend a hard limit maximum once you have reached it.

Subscription management can also be done with the use of management groups. Access, policies, and compliance are all managed by a management group across several Azure subscriptions.

Azure Monitor

Azure Monitor maximizes flexibility and application efficiency by offering a comprehensive solution to capture, monitor, and use the cloud and on-site telemetry. To improve your Azure experience, Azure Monitor uses telemetry data. It helps you understand how your applications operate and detect problems and the resources they depend on proactively.

We know that managing cloud services means lots of resources and a lot of individual processes. And on top of that, you need to monitor the system's health to check whether things are running smoothly or not. In a scenario where one of the services is not performing well or fails, then identifying it becomes the aim of the Azure Monitor.

Telemetry is the collection of measurements of other data at remote or inaccessible points and their automatic transmission to receive equipment for monitoring. It is the information about how services or devices are performing. This information is then passed to the central server to perform the analysis.

The data collected in Azure are of two types: logs and metrics. Metrics are numerical values, while logs are different kinds of data, like events or traces.

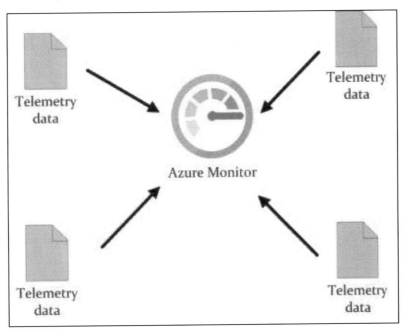

Figure 9-12: Pushing Telemetry Data to Azure Monitor

In Azure, all the telemetry data goes into Azure Monitor. Consider an example in which multiple VMs are running; Azure Monitor verifies that they are running smoothly. If anyone VM is not performing, you need to know which one, and for that, you need telemetry data about the machine. This telemetry data constantly feeds into the Azure Monitor. Through Azure Monitor, you can analyze all of your data in one place. It is a fully managed centralized service. You can also use interactive query language to query the telemetry data. To detect problems faster, you can use Machine Learning with your resources.

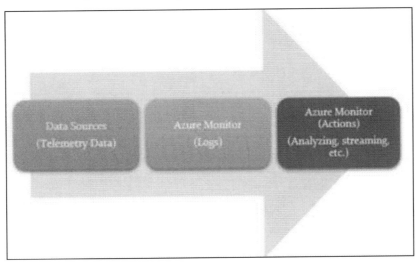

Figure 9-13: Working process of Azure Monitor

Outcomes

The outcome of using Azure Monitor:

- Maximize Performance
- Maximize Availability
- Identify Issue

Azure Service Health

Whenever there is a plan of maintenance or service incident, you get notified about it with the use of Azure Service Health. The Azure platform needs to be updated and maintained like any infrastructure by mitigating the risk and taking necessary steps to protect your infrastructure and applications. Downtime is one of the enemies of your application or service. To help with this, there is a Service Health Dashboard in Azure.

With Azure Service Health, you get notified about the planned or unplanned maintenance of the platform. It has the following features:

- **Dashboard** – There is a personalized dashboard to highlight the service issues that affect your resources
- **Custom Alerts** – There are custom alerts to notify about any outages. These are simple to set up and customize
- **Real-time Tracking** - In case any issue occurs, it finds the root cause of the issue in real-time, and after resolving the issue, it downloads the official report
- **Free Service** – It is a free service

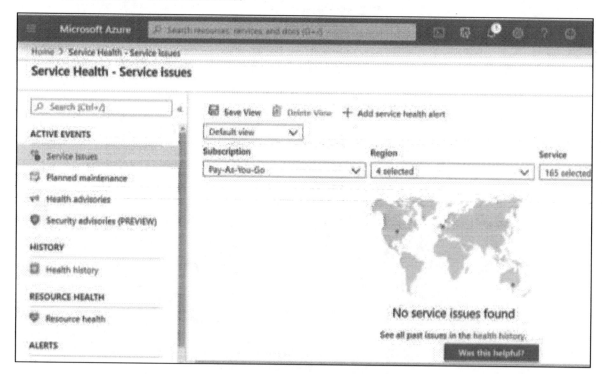

Figure 9-14: Service Health Dashboard

Demo 9-01: Azure Monitor

1. Login to Azure Portal and go to **"Monitor."**

2. Here is an overview of the monitor.

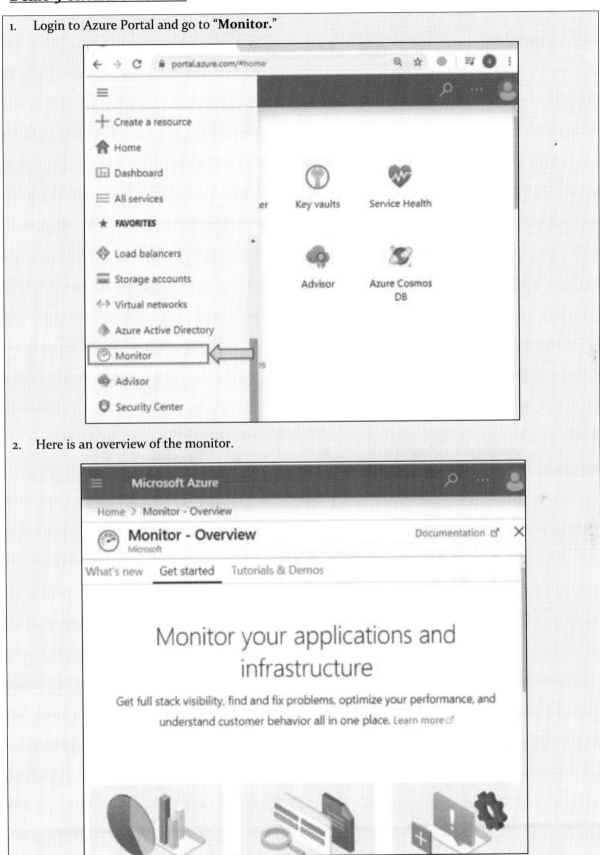

3. Now, go to **"Service Health"** from the left side of the window.

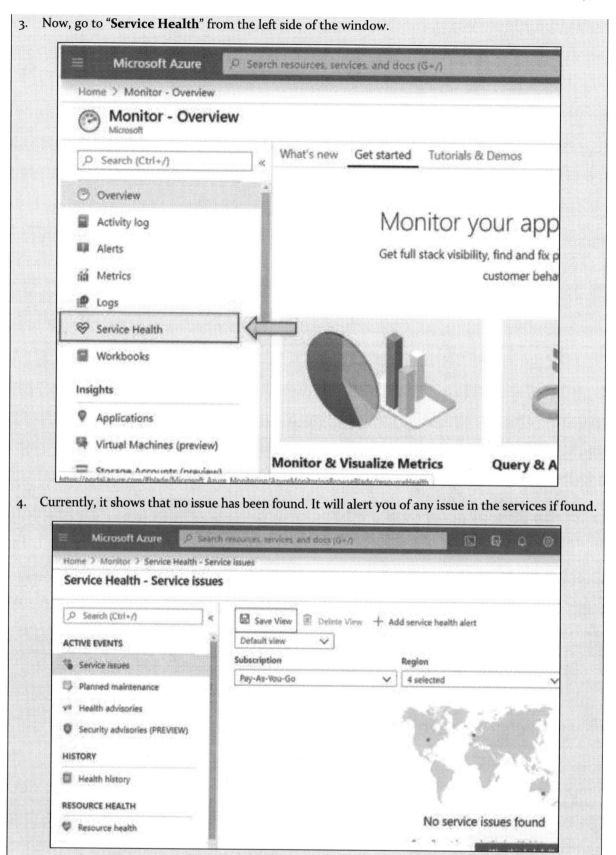

4. Currently, it shows that no issue has been found. It will alert you of any issue in the services if found.

5. If you click "Planned maintenance," it will show any upcoming or scheduled planned maintenance events.

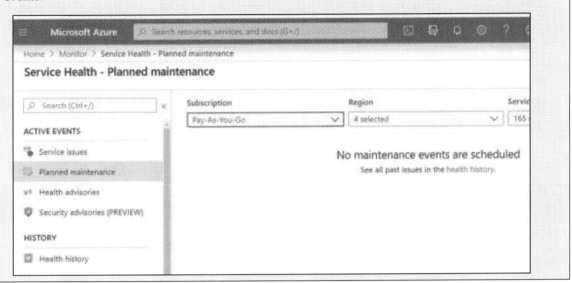

Compliance

The general principle that cloud services deliver must adhere to the requirements faced by cloud customers is strongly compliant. This is a very important issue with new cloud computing services, and many IT professionals are thoroughly looking at it. If any company in the EU does not take compliance seriously, it must pay a massive fine. For example, suppose any company is dealing with paying customers and does not comply with privacy and regulations about personal data. In that case, the company could be fined 4% of the annual global turnover. Below are some different standards and regulations cloud customers need to comply with.

EXAM TIP: Compliance is not negotiable.

Industry Compliance

This refers to the legislation and rules the industry generally has to comply with. The most common three legislations and rules are:

- **General Data Protection Regulation (GDPR)** - Its main objective is to protect individuals and the processing of their data. With this, you get personal data back to an individual rather than a company that owns it. Protecting consumers' data forces companies to implement a lot of tools.

EXAM TIP: GDPR compliance is needed to interact with EU-based customers.

- **ISO Standards** - ISO is the International Standardization Organization, and they have a huge number of compliance categories. Generally, it is compliant with quality and customer satisfaction, which is ISO 9001:2008
- **NIST** – NIST is the National Institute of Standards and Technology and focuses purely on the technology industry. NIST guidelines are designed so that compliance with NIST also means

compliance with multiple Federal US regulations. CyberSecurity Framework is one of the most famous frameworks there is

> EXAM TIP: GDPR, NIST, and ISO are the regulations and standards that ensure your application legislation.

Azure Compliance Manager

For Compliance, Azure provides you the Azure Compliance Manager because the company knows about compliance and as it knows about your resources, so it can easily combine the tools and give you a recommendation as per that. There are many benefits of using Compliance Manager in Azure, some of which are:

- It gives you a recommendation on ensuring compliance with GDPR, NIST, ISO, or others
- It assigns tasks to your team and tracks the progress of the task; each member is responsible for a certain compliance area
- With that, you have a compliance score to chase perfect compliance
- It gives you secure storage for uploading the compliance documents to prove compliance
- It gives you a report on compliance with data so that you can give that report to your managers and auditors

Azure Government Cloud

To know what compliance is, who makes guidelines, bodies, and framework, and how Azure manages it all, you have two regions and offerings that are unique when there is compliance.

First is Azure Government Cloud; if you are a US government body or are contracted for one, you can access Azure resources in Azure Government Cloud regions. They are separate dedicated data centers. With these dedicated data centers, you get guaranteed that only US federal, state, and local governments have access to this dedicated instance with operations controlled by Screened US citizens.

It ensures compliance with required US government agencies and level 5 Department of Defense approval. With this, you can get all the benefits of Azure, like HA, scalability, and managed resources.

> EXAM TIP: Azure Government Cloud provides dedicated data centers purely for US government bodies.

China Region

It is the second specific region when it comes to compliance. As a country, China has very specific and strict requirements when there are data, internet, or online entities, so when you need to provide cloud services here, you have to use the China region in Azure. This means that Azure has physically separated data centers in China without any connection to the other regions of Azure. All data is stored in China at all times. For example, if China is included in the region for DynamoDB, it will not work globally. Within that, you are completely compliant with all Chinese regulations. All of these physically separated locations are managed by Chinese companies.

> EXAM TIP: The Azure China region fully complies with Chinese regulations, data centers, and data.

Azure China 21Vianet

21Vianet operates Azure China 21Vianet. It is a geographically segregated instance of cloud services in China. Shanghai Blue Cloud Technology Co., Ltd. ("21Vianet"), a wholly-owned subsidiary of Beijing 21Vianet Broadband Data Center Co., Ltd., operates and transacts Azure China 21Vianet independently.

According to the China Telecommunication Regulation, cloud service providers, infrastructure (IaaS), and platform (PaaS) providers must have value-added telecom permits. These permits are only available to locally registered businesses with less than 50% foreign participation. To comply with this regulation, 21Vianet operates the Azure service in China based on Microsoft-licensed technologies.

Azure products and services available in China

The Azure services have similar service standards and are built on the same Azure, Office 365, and Power BI technologies that make up the Microsoft global cloud service. Where applicable, customers and 21Vianet execute Azure agreements and contracts in China.

The fundamental elements of IaaS, PaaS, and software as a service are all present in Azure (SaaS). Network, storage, data management, identity management, and numerous other services are among these elements.

The majority of the capabilities offered by worldwide Azure, including geosynchronous data replication and autoscaling, are supported by Azure China 21Vianet. Even if you already use global Azure services, you may need to rehost or modify any or all of your apps or services to run in China.

Privacy

Privacy is an extension of compliance. In Azure, privacy is the core power of the platform, so there is no single service or place for it. Microsoft also has its privacy statement, which you can see from the following link:

https://privacy.microsoft.com/en-gb/privacystatement.

Instead of building privacy control, including tools and services.

- **Azure Information Protection** - It is used for classifying, labeling, and helping protect data based on its sensitivity
- **Azure Policy** – As discussed earlier, it is used to define and enforce the rules to ensure regulations and privacy
- **Guides** - When dealing with GDPR privacy requests from European user data, Guides are used on Azure to comply
- Use Compliance Manager to follow the privacy guidelines

Trust

In Azure, there are two services in terms of Trust. One is Trust Center, and the other is Service Trust Portal. Trust Center is a shortcut to knowing all the things that Microsoft does to ensure you do not lose trust in Azure and other services. With this, you have a link to learn about security, privacy, GDPR, the location of your data, compliance, and more. This link lets you know more about security implementations, privacy implementations, etc.

Service Trust Portal is a location to review all the independent reports about Azure. It is a portal of proof that they comply with many millions of different standards and certifications. It is crucial to know that Azure complies with the various quality and security standards more than any other cloud provider. In short, we can say that it is a one-stop-shop for security, regulatory and compliance, and privacy information related to Azure Cloud.

Service Trust Portal

A site that gives access to numerous tools, content, and other resources about Microsoft's security, privacy, and compliance standards is called the Microsoft Service Trust Portal.

The Service Trust Portal provides information on the policies and procedures that Microsoft has put in place to safeguard our cloud services and the customer data they contain. You must sign in as an authenticated user with your Microsoft cloud services account in order to access some of the resources on the Service Trust Portal (Microsoft Entra ID organisation account). For compliance materials, you must read and agree to the Microsoft non-disclosure agreement.

How to Access?

To explore Service Trust Portal, you can visit the given URL:

https://servicetrust.microsoft.com/

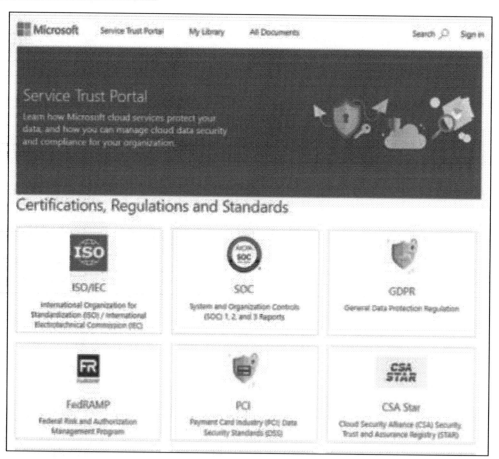

Figure 9-15: Service Trust Portal

The main menu provides access to the Service Trust Portal's content and functionality. On the primary menu, there are the following categories:

- The Service Trust Portal offers a quick access option to take users back to the homepage.
- You can save (or pin) documents to your My Library page to easily access them later. Additionally, you can set up notifications for when your My Library's documents are updated.
- On the service trust portal, All Documents serves as a central hub for all documents. You can pin documents to have them appear in your My Library from the All Documents page.

Mind Map

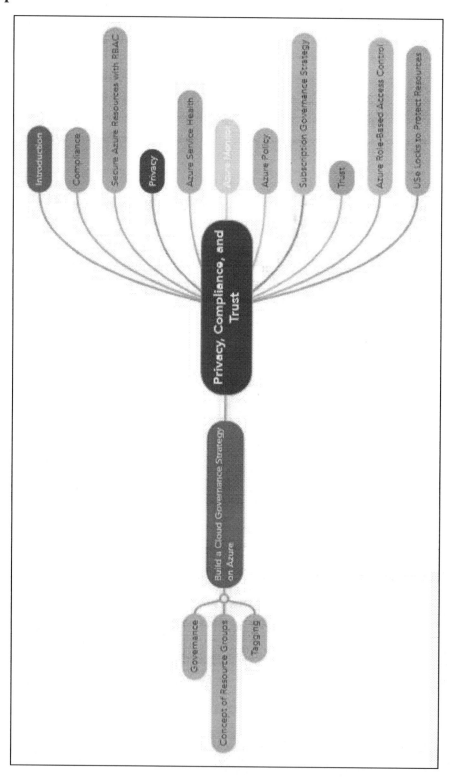

Figure 9-16: Mind Map

Practice Questions

1. Which two customers can develop a cloud solution using Azure Government?
A. A European government entity
B. A Canadian government contractor
C. A European government contractor
D. A United States government entity

2. From the following options, which one provides organizations the ability to manage compliance of Azure resources across multiple subscriptions?
A. Azure App Service Plans
B. Azure Policy
C. Azure Resource Group
D. Management Group

3. If you want to restrict access to Azure resources per the company's policy so that only the admin can create a resource in the region where their office is located, then which Azure resource will you use to define this policy?
A. A Reservation
B. A Management Group
C. An Azure Policy
D. Read-only lock

4. For migrating the services from on-premises to Azure cloud, you need to identify the compliance of Azure with your organization's regional requirements. From the following, which one is helpful?
A. Azure Trust Center
B. Azure Portal
C. Azure Marketplace
D. None of the above

5. For what region is DRP compliance needed?
A. US Region
B. EU Region
C. Asia Region
D. All of the above

6. Which is used to track an incident in real-time and get its report?
A. Azure Network Watcher
B. Azure Policy
C. Azure Service Health
D. Azure Blueprint

7. RBAC has a feature to define which action can be performed by which user on specific resources. True or false?
A. True
B. False

8. In Azure Monitor, which services can feed data?
A. On-Premises
B. Azure Services
C. Both On-Premises and Azure Services
D. Only Premium Services

9. In Azure, what types of locks can you apply? (Choose 2)
A. Closed
B. Read-only
C. Update
D. Create only
E. Delete

10. To trust the Azure Portal more, you can view the Service Trust Portal and Azure Privacy Portal in Azure. True or false?
A. True
B. False

11. In the China region, all Azure Services are globally located. True or false?
A. True
B. False

12. In RBAC, how many elements are present?
A. 2
B. 3
C. 4
D. 5

13. To create a standard Azure Environment, you can take help from _____.
A. Azure Advisor
B. Azure Policy
C. Trust Center
D. Azure Blueprint

14. For compliance in Azure, which service can be used?

A.   Azure Trust Center
B.   Azure Privacy Portal
C.   Azure Compliance Manager
D.   Azure Monitor

15.   To classify, label, and help protect data based on its sensitivity, which Azure Service can you use?
A.   Key Vault
B.   Defender for Cloud
C.   Azure Dedicated HSM
D.   Azure Information Protection

16. To define a subscription strategy, there are _____ primary factors to consider.

A. Two

B. Three

C. Four

D. Five

17. How many key stages are used in Cloud Adoption Framework for Azure?

A. Four

B. Three

C. Five

D. None of the above

18.   Which of the following is China's geographically segregated cloud service instance?

A. Huawei Cloud

B. Baidu Cloud

C. Tencent Cloud

D. Azure China

Chapter 10: Pricing

Introduction

For migration to the cloud, we have discussed many topics, but we did not examine the primary concern, which is pricing. It is one of the most important parts of any cloud computing service.

Pricing does not only mean understanding the price of Azure services. Organizations often want to know about the cost of computing services before applications are deployed to the cloud. After the application is deployed, they want to reduce costs as much as possible and have insights into Azure's resource costs.

For managing costs in Azure, you need to be familiar with some areas of pricing, i.e., Subscriptions, Cost Management, Pricing Factors, and Best Practices.

Azure Pricing Structure

Azure pricing structure depends upon the following criteria:

- Pay for the resources you access
- Pay for the number of hours you use
- Pay depending upon the size of the resource
- Service payment is tiered
- Pricing as per the location of service

Subscriptions

The pricing structure of Microsoft Azure works on a subscription price that is tied to what you are using within the Azure infrastructure. All resources in Azure reside within the subscription; you cannot access any resources until you are subscribed.

Once you sign up for Azure, you immediately get an Azure subscription, and all the services you create are created within that subscription. Additional subscriptions are useful in cases where you want to have some logical groupings for Azure resources or if you want to be able to report on resources used by specific groups of people.

Like any other Azure resource, you can manage your subscription in the Azure portal. You can monitor and manage costs, give access to it through RBAC to other users, add locks to it, and do so much more.

Subscription in Azure can be defined as:

Multiple Subscriptions: Any Azure account can have multiple subscriptions. It is very useful for organizing who pays for what.

Billing Admin: One or more users can be a 'billing admin,' which manages anything and everything that has to do with billing and invoicing on Azure. It ensures invoice separation of responsibility.

Billing Cycle: A billing cycle on Azure is either 30 or 60 days.

> **EXAM TIP:** Each subscription is associated with a unique identifier called a subscription ID. To help you identify it, you may assign your subscription a descriptive name, but Azure will always use

the ID to identify your subscription. If you inquire about your Azure account with Microsoft, you will often be asked for your subscription ID too.

Offer Types

At any given time, Azure has a lot of active offer types. You can get the offer depending on your subscription type. You can get many more offers with popular subscription types, such as pay-as-you-go and enterprise-level agreements. You can check the offer types when you are signing up for Azure.

Figure 10-01: Azure Offer Types

Management Groups

Management Groups is a very useful feature on Azure regarding subscriptions. Management groups may indicate the following:

Group Subscriptions: You can group your subscriptions to allow taking actions in bulk across subscriptions. This is very useful in organizations that deal with many subscriptions.

Organize: You can simultaneously manage access, policies, and compliance in multiple subscriptions.

Billing Logic: You maintain the billing associated with the right budgets. You have the Nest management groups to indicate the hierarchy, which means each management group has a single parent group but many child groups and their relationship.

Azure Cost Management

Azure Cost Management is a handy tool in Azure that allows the study of your costs on a granular level. Cost management allows you to create a budget for your Azure expenses, set up notifications so that you will know if you are hitting a budgeted limit, and evaluate your costs in detail.

Azure Cost Management is accessible from the Azure portal. You can get a detailed view of the current and future projected costs of all the resources within your area of accountability. Azure Cost Management is free of cost and included with all Azure subscriptions.

You can download reports on spending and get recommendations on how to save on costs and analyze them. You can optimize your resources to save money and monitor the charges of other cloud service providers, such as Amazon Web Services.

To start with Cost Management, open the Azure portal, search for Cost Management, and click on Cost Management + Billing.

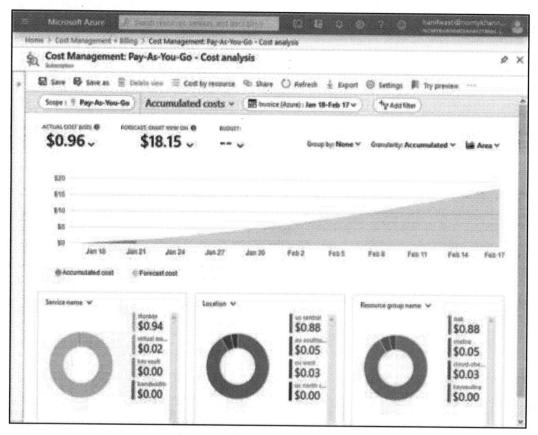

Figure 10-02: Azure Cost Management

Cost alerts in the Cost Management service provide a consolidated view of three types of alerts: Budget alerts, Credit alerts, and Department spending quota alerts.

Budget Alerts

These alerts notify users when spending, based on usage or cost, reaches or exceeds the predefined amount in the budget conditions. Budgets can be created through the Azure portal or Azure Consumption API, supporting both cost-based and usage-based budgets. When triggered, budget alerts are automatically generated, become visible in the Azure portal, and sent via email to the specified recipients.

Credit Alerts

Credit alerts are relevant for organizations with Enterprise Agreements (EAs). These alerts notify users when Azure credit monetary commitments are consumed, automatically triggered at 90% and 100% of the Azure credit balance. Credit alerts are reflected in the cost alerts section of the portal and sent via email to account owners.

Department Spending Quota Alerts

These alerts notify users when department spending reaches a fixed threshold of the quota. Spending quotas are configured in the EA portal, and alerts are generated when thresholds, such as 50% or 75% of the quota, are met. Department spending quota alerts trigger email notifications to department owners and appear in the cost alerts section.

Budgets

Budgets allow users to set spending limits for Azure based on various criteria, such as subscription, resource group, or service type. Configuring a budget also involves setting a budget alert. When the budget reaches the defined alert level, it triggers a budget alert displayed in the cost alerts area. Additionally, if configured, budget alerts send email notifications indicating that the budget alert threshold has been reached. Advanced budget use involves triggering automation for resource management based on budget conditions.

We know that when resources and services are running, cost management can be quite an expensive task. To manage all of these costs, you have cost management. When you use resources or services in Azure, you need to buy them, as, without them, you cannot access them. You need a service that automates cost management because tracking costs is difficult. When you start thinking about moving to the cloud, you will probably want to decide the cost of the resource. Once you have started deploying and using Azure services, managing costs to remain within your budget becomes important. Azure has tools to help you schedule and manage your Azure costs. The management of cost in Azure can be done in many different ways; some of these are given below:

Azure Free Account

If you have never had a free Azure trial and have never been a paying Azure user, then you are eligible for a free Azure account. A free account gives you cost-free access to the most popular Azure services for 12 months, and many other Azure services offer free usage even after the 12 months have passed. You also get a $200 credit, which you can use for 30 days of Azure services after you sign up for a free account.

Free accounts provide a range of benefits, such as 750 hours of computing on virtual machines, 5 GB of storage, 250 GB of SQL database, 5 GB storage on Cosmos DB, and a bundle of Artificial Intelligence services, all for 12 months.

Microsoft places a $200 free-account spending limit. If you reach the spending limit, you can upgrade your subscription to a Pay-As-You-Go subscription, with which you can create additional resources.

At the end of the 30 days, any resources that are not free are automatically deleted. So if you want to continue using your resources, you must upgrade your Azure subscription before the 30 days expire.

> **EXAM TIP:** The $200 credit cannot be used to pay for Azure Marketplace offerings. Many Azure Marketplace offerings, however, provide their free trials.
>
> You can have only one free account per Microsoft Account.

Pricing Factors

In cloud computing, pricing is very tricky to predict and calculate. An Azure account has a lot of resources, such as networks, connections, virtual machines, firewalls, storage accounts, functions, etc.

When you plan your Azure deployments, you should consider the factors that can influence your costs. The primary factors influencing costs are the size, the type of resource, the Azure regions you are using, and the bandwidth.

Resource Size

The pricing depends upon the size of the resource. A more powerful virtual machine will cost more than the less powerful one.

Resource Type

Resource type is also an important factor in pricing. This also makes sense as there is a very big difference in the number of hardware resources needed to run a virtual machine compared to a machine learning service or big data analytics. There is also a big difference in the complexity of maintaining and running various Azure services.

Location

Azure has a global network of data centers from the US to Australia and from Norway to South Africa; they are all treated equally with slightly different pricing. Exchange rates, labor costs, etc., influence the prices.

Bandwidth

Bandwidth refers to data moving in and out of Azure data centers and between Azure data centers. The bandwidth your services are using incurs a cost . as well.

Zones & Bandwidth

To make things clear, Azure has designed three billing zones; each has many Azure regions. Any data transfer between the regions in the same billing zone is free; this process is called Ingress. Any data transfer between two billing zones is charged; this process is called Egress.

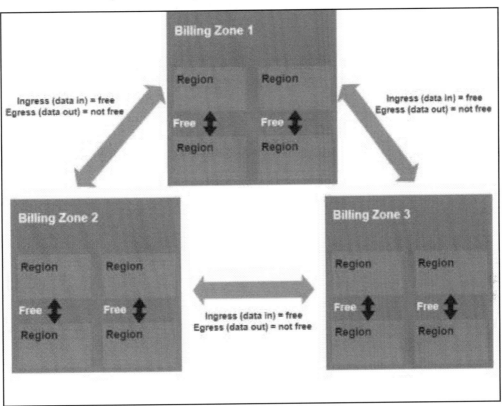

Figure 10-03: Data Transfer in Billing Zones

> EXAM TIP: Each Azure service has a pricing page that outlines the estimated pricing for that resource based on typical usage.

Pricing Calculator

The Azure pricing calculator helps you estimate costs depending on the products you plan to use, where those products will be deployed, and so on. You can access the pricing calculator by going to https://azure.microsoft.com/en-us/pricing/calculator.

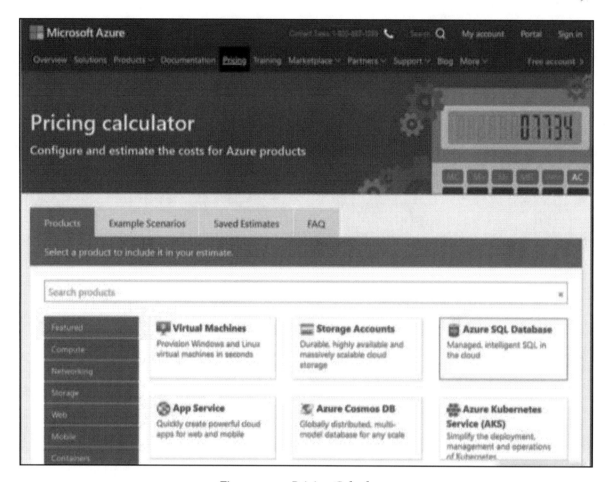

Figure 10-04: Pricing Calculator

Steps for Using Pricing Calculator

1. The first step in calculating your Azure expense estimate is to select which products you wish to use. Some of the more popular Azure products are shown by default, and by clicking on their title, you can select any of those products.

2. Then, scroll down to customize each service's specifics after selecting the products you want to use. These specifics vary according to how Microsoft pays for the product.

3. Clicking "Pricing Details" will open the product pricing page in a new tab.

4. You can also click on "Product Details" or "Documentation" to read more about the service to help you make better decisions about the options you select.

5. Once you have configured the product according to your needs, you can click the "Clone" button to add another product instance to your estimate.

6. To check your estimate of prices, scroll down to the bottom of the page.

7. You can pick a support plan to add to your estimate.

8. You can click "Export" to save your estimate as an Excel file, then select "Save" to save your estimate in the price calculator to make changes later or select "Share" to build a sharable link to your estimate so that others can view it too.

Total Cost of Ownership (TCO) Calculator

The pricing calculator helps estimate your expenses for new applications in Azure, but if you have on-premises applications that you want to migrate to Azure and want an estimate of how much you can save, the TCO calculator is a better choice. You can access the TCO calculator by browsing to:

https://azure.microsoft.com/en-us/pricing/tco/calculator.

Information about your on-premises servers, databases, storage, and network usage should be included when using the TCO calculator. Figure 10-05 configures an on-premises server for a Web App.

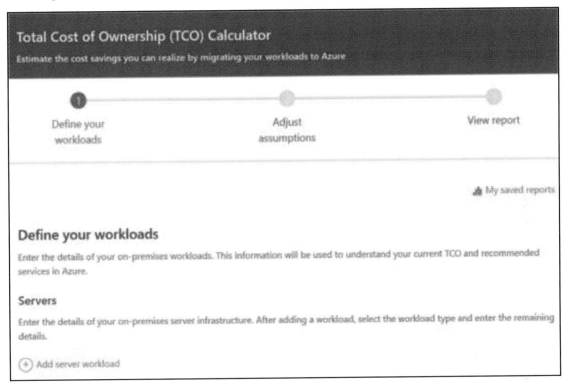

Figure 10-05: TCO Calculator

Your TCO report shows you how much you can save by moving your app to Azure over the next five years, as shown in Figure 10-06.

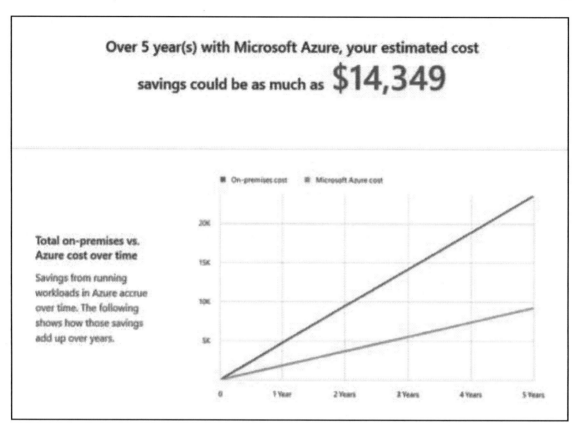

Figure 10-06: TCO Report

A TCO report includes detailed charts of expenses. You will also find a breakdown of on-premises and Azure costs at the bottom of the report so that you can easily determine where you will be saving money.

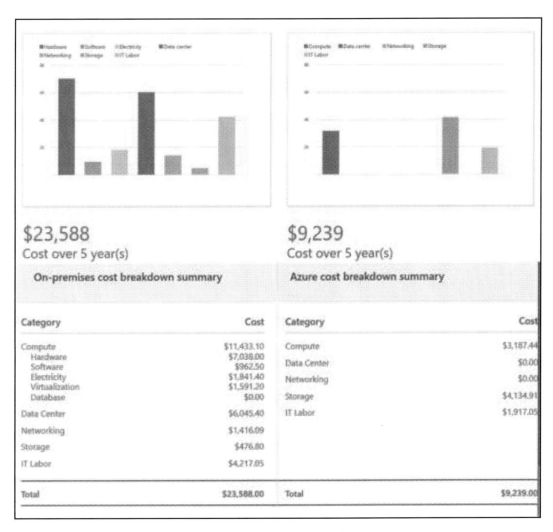

Figure 10-07: TCO Report Chart

Lab 10-01: Estimate and Compare Workload Costs by using the Pricing Calculator

Service Introduction

Ecomify, a fast-growing e-commerce platform, experienced significant traffic surges during peak season, leading to performance bottlenecks and concerns about escalating cloud costs. They lacked transparency in their Azure spending and struggled to compare cost-effectiveness across different configurations for their e-commerce platform.

Problem

Ecomify's pay-as-you-go model meant fluctuating cloud bills, making it difficult to budget and optimize spending. They lacked insight into resource utilization and cost drivers. Ecomify needed a solution to handle peak traffic without incurring excessive costs, but scaling resources without understanding potential expenses was risky.

Solution

Ecomify's success story demonstrates the transformative power of Azure Pricing Calculator and TCO for cloud-based businesses seeking to optimize costs and achieve financial clarity. By leveraging these tools, Ecomify achieved cost transparency, improved decision-making, and gained confidence in its cloud scalability, letting it focus on its core business and growth.

This lab demonstrates how to estimate the Total Cost of Ownership with the Azure TCO calculator.

1. Navigate to the web browser and go to the Total Cost of Ownership website.

https://azure.microsoft.com/en-us/pricing/tco/calculator/

2. The default page of the TCO calculator will appear.
3. Click on "**Start assessment.**"

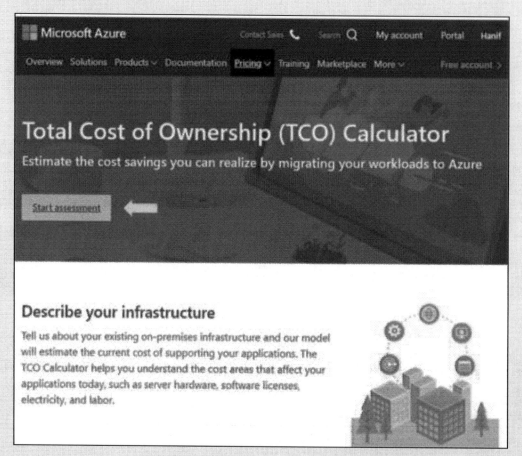

4. There are three steps to estimate cost savings. To estimate any cost, you must first define the workload weightage.

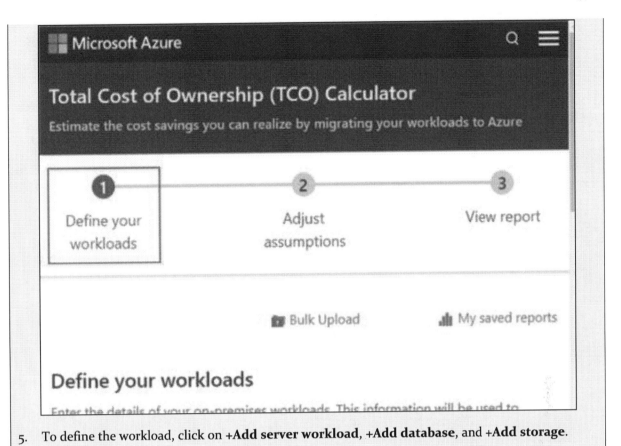

5. To define the workload, click on **+Add server workload**, **+Add database**, and **+Add storage**.

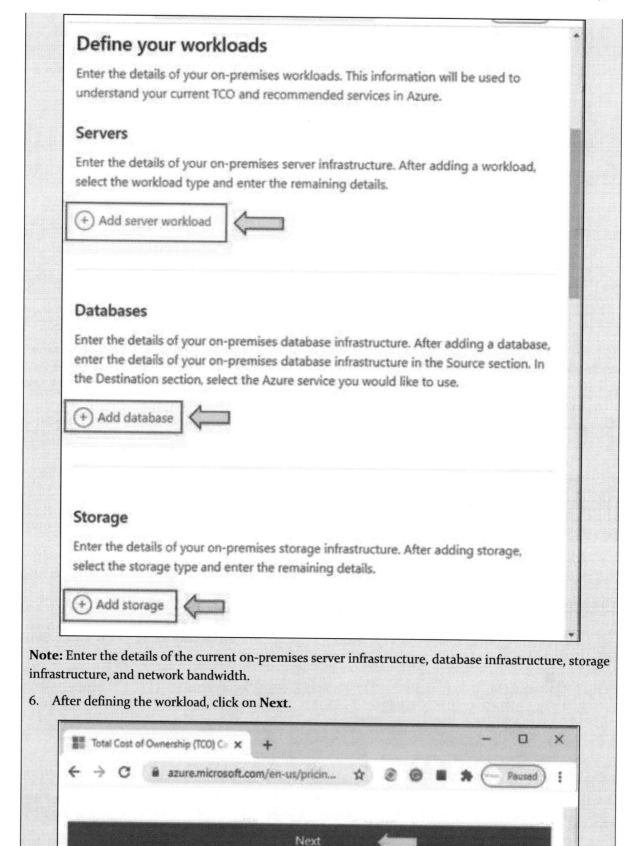

Note: Enter the details of the current on-premises server infrastructure, database infrastructure, storage infrastructure, and network bandwidth.

6. After defining the workload, click on **Next**.

7. After defining the workload, the next step is **"Adjust assumptions."**
8. Select the currency of your choice.

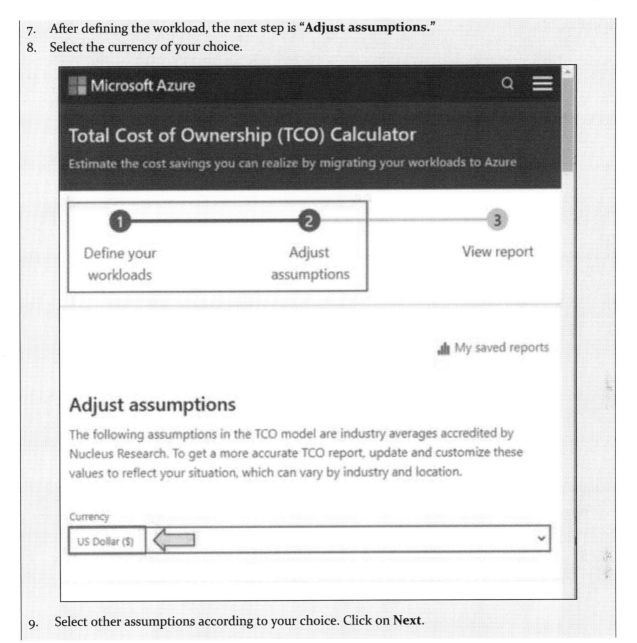

9. Select other assumptions according to your choice. Click on **Next**.

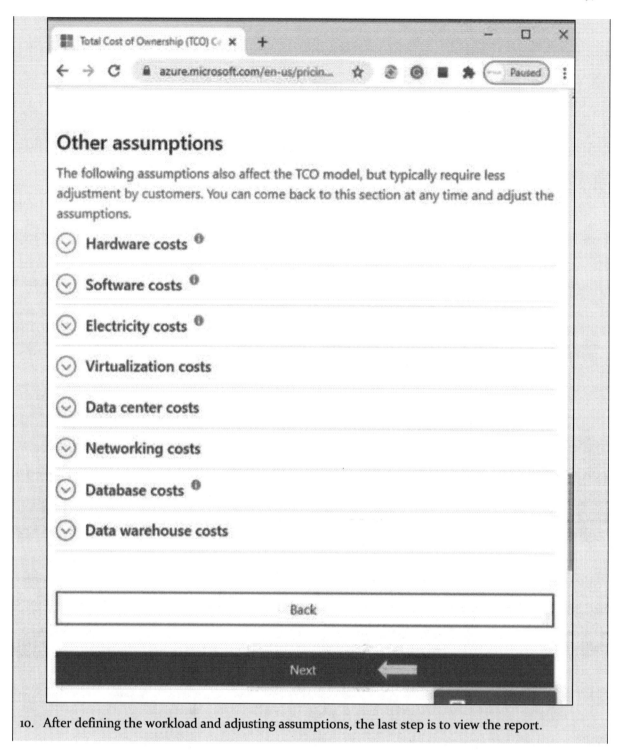

10. After defining the workload and adjusting assumptions, the last step is to view the report.

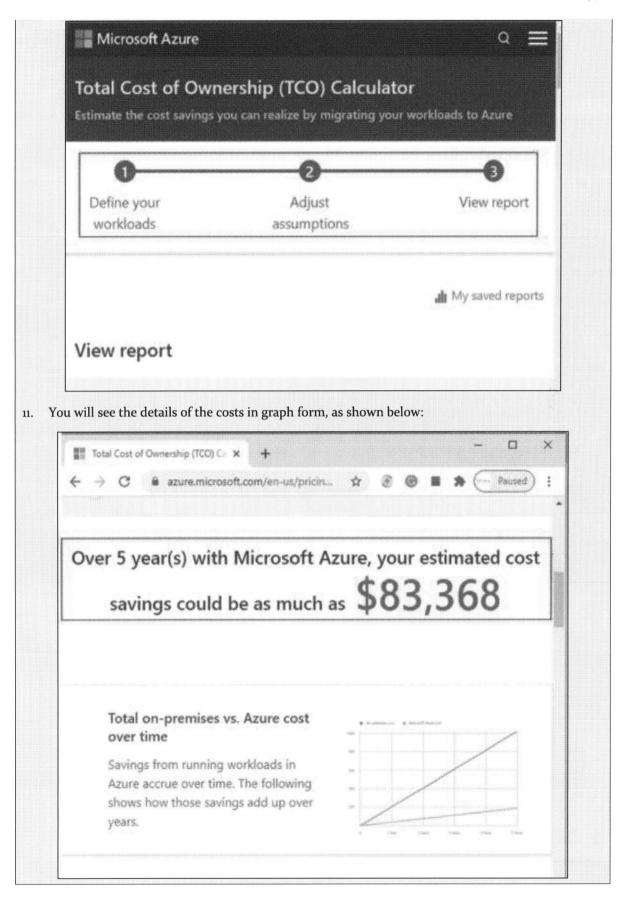

11. You will see the details of the costs in graph form, as shown below:

Best Practices for Minimizing Azure Costs

Cost management is an operational challenge and should be an ongoing practice that begins before spending money on cloud services. To implement cost control effectively and reduce costs, you need to:

- Be equipped with the right tools for performance
- Be responsible for costs
- Take appropriate action to reduce expenses

Spending Limits

Azure spending limits are the recommended means to manage your Azure subscription's total spending and do not spend over the credit amount when your usage leads to charges that exhaust your spending limit; the services you deployed will be disabled for the rest of that billing period.

Default Limit: Some Azure accounts with monthly credits will have default spending limits. This could be 0$ for a free account and 150$ for a Microsoft subscription account. When the credits are used, the limit kicks in.

No Increase: When the credits are gone, either remove the spending limit entirely or leave it in effect.

No Spending Limit: Pay-as-you-go subscription has no spending limit functionality.

> **EXAM TIP:** An important part of cutting off Azure costs is to ensure that all the cloud services are fully utilized. Since most cloud use is based on resource consumption, not using parts of a network reflects unnecessary expenses. Proper planning can help avoid unused resources in the cloud.

Quotas

A quota is a limit on certain properties of an Azure service. For example, a maximum of 100 namespaces per subscription is allowed for Event Hub. The quotas are necessary to ensure Azure can maintain its high service level. If you need to increase the quota for a particular service, you can ask Microsoft to increase them.

Tags

Tags are non-functional labels attached to resources or resource groups to manage the cost of resources. You can attach as many to each resource as you want. Tags provide an excellent way of attributing costs. The tags can be used as a filter, and when you analyze data to evaluate costs, you can use them to be grouped. They are non-functional attributes.

Some common best practices for using tags are:

Identify Roles: Protect sensitive data by defining which roles can access a resource.

Related Resources: To make bulk processing and updating easier, define which resources are related.

Filter: Filter resources per project, customer, or for reporting purposes.

Unambiguous: Create a list of tags that includes: a description, tag name, and potential values.

💡 **EXAM TIP:** Pay-as-you-go is a very common pricing model in which you pay only for what you use per month. It is one of the most expensive models for Azure usage.

Reserved Instances

With Reserved Instance, you can prepay for the virtual machine or SQL Database computing capacity for one or three years. Pre-paid allows you to get a discount on the resources you are using. You cannot reserve all the services. It will dramatically reduce the cost of computing up to 72 percent on pay-as-you-go pricing with an upfront commitment of one year or three years. Reservations offering a billing discount do not affect your instance's runtime status.

Azure Advisor

Azure Advisor is a tool that detects low-usage virtual machines from a CPU or network cost standpoint. You can shut down or resize the system to continue running the machines based on estimated costs. The advisor also makes recommendations for purchases in reserved instances. The recommendations are based on your virtual machine used for the last 30 days. With the help of this recommendation, you can reduce your expenditure when you act upon them.

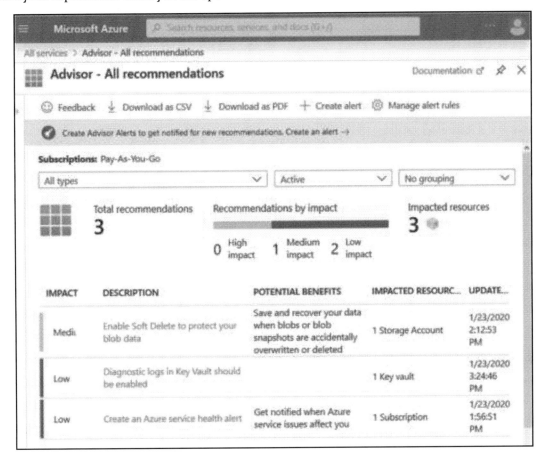

Figure 10-08: Azure Advisor

Lab 10-02: Using the Pricing Calculator

Service Introduction

The Azure Pricing Calculator is a valuable tool for organizations and individuals looking to estimate and understand the costs associated with deploying resources and services in the Microsoft Azure cloud. Accessible through the Azure portal, the calculator allows users to select and configure various Azure services, regions, and deployment options to generate accurate cost projections. Users can input details such as the number of virtual machines, storage capacity, and network resources to tailor the estimate to their specific requirements. Additionally, the Azure Pricing Calculator provides visibility into potential cost savings through reserved instances or specific pricing tiers. This tool empowers users to make informed decisions about resource provisioning and optimize their Azure spending based on their unique needs and budget constraints, contributing to a cost-effective and efficient cloud deployment strategy.

Problem

An organization is planning to upgrade its infrastructure with Azure services but wants to know the estimated cost for requesting the Virtual Machine and Azure Function service.

Solution

Microsoft Azure provides a free pricing calculator to estimate the cost of any services. You select the service and add the features you want to find the estimated result of the cost that you can download in the form of an Excel Sheet, which can be useful for decision-making.

1. Open a browser and go to the Azure pricing calculator using the given URL.

   https://azure.microsoft.com/en-au/pricing/calculator/

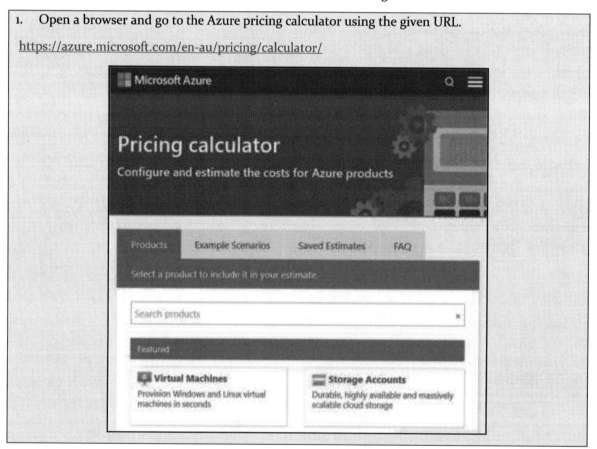

2. Click on the **"Virtual Machines."**

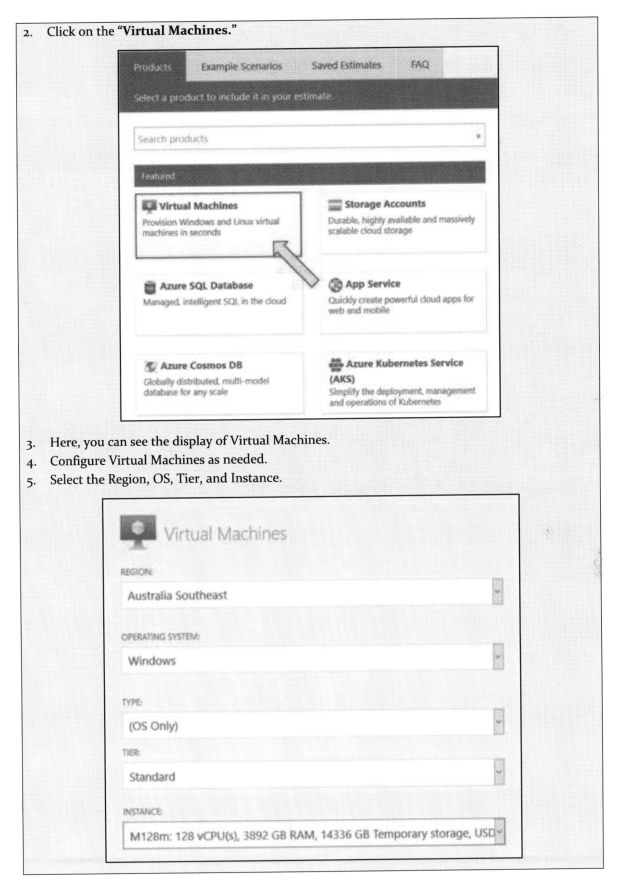

3. Here, you can see the display of Virtual Machines.
4. Configure Virtual Machines as needed.
5. Select the Region, OS, Tier, and Instance.

6. On the billing options, select the number of Virtual Machines and the number of hours for utilizing this VM.

7. You can see the estimated cost of 1 VM with 1 hour of utilization.

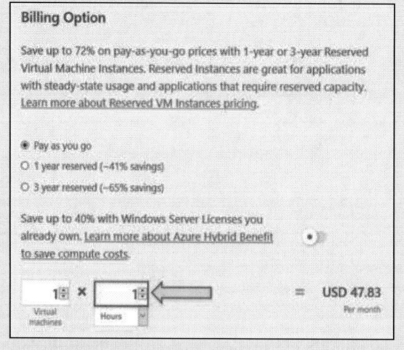

8. Now, click on **"Azure Functions"** to add functions.

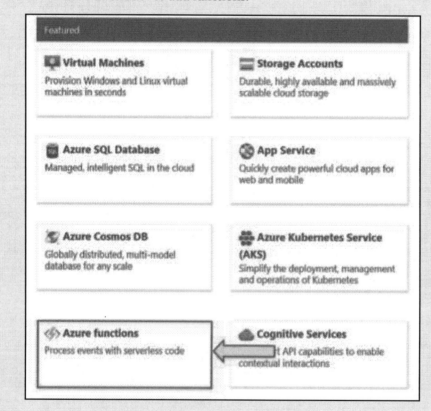

9. Configure Azure functions by selecting regions, memory size, execution time, and number of executions.
10. You can see the estimated cost for 4 million requests in 100 seconds, as shown below.

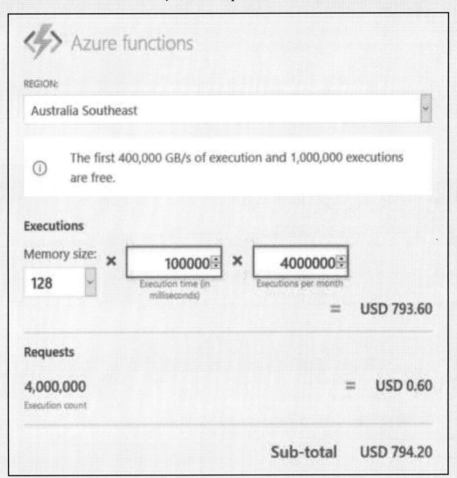

11. Select the support level that charges 100 USD.
12. See the total estimated cost of all the added services.
13. Save and export the result.

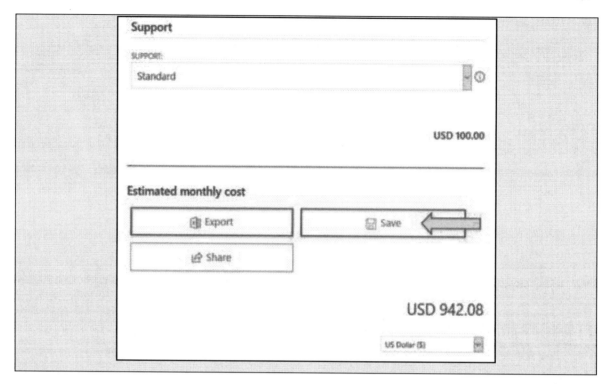

Mind Map

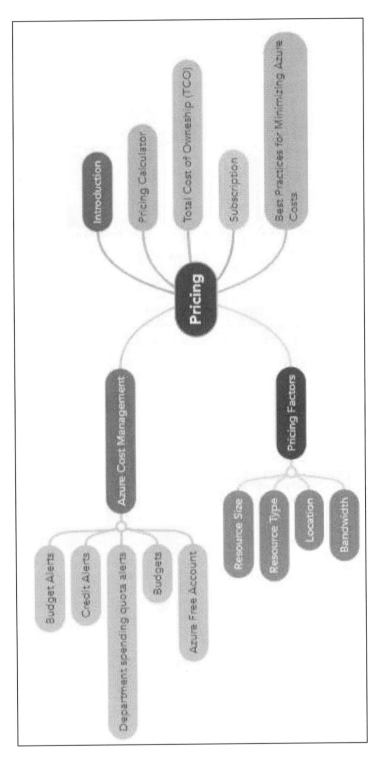

Figure 10-09: Mind Map

Practice Questions

1. A billing cycle on Azure is _____.
   A. Bi-monthly
   B. Yearly
   C. Monthly
   D. Hourly

2. Which of the following terms is not indicated by the Management Group?
   A. Group Subscriptions
   B. Organize
   C. Billing Admin
   D. Billing Logic

3. A free account gives you free access to the most popular Azure services for _____.
   A. 30 days
   B. 60 days
   C. 6 months
   D. 12 months

4. Which of the following allows you to create a budget for your Azure expenses, set up configurable notifications, so you will know if you are hitting a budgeted limit, and evaluate your costs?
   A. Management Groups
   B. Cost Management
   C. Pricing Calculator
   D. TCO Calculator

5. Which of the following can you download reports on spending and get recommendations on how to save on costs and analyze them?
   A. Cost Management
   B. Management Groups
   C. Pricing Calculator
   D. TCO Calculator

6. Which of the following is the least influencing factor of pricing?
   A. Resources Size
   B. Resources Type
   C. Bandwidth
   D. Location

7. Any data transfer between the regions in the same billing zone is free; this process is called Egress. True or false?

A. True
B. False

8. Any data transfer between two billing zones is charged; this process is called Egress. True or false?
A. True
B. False

9. From the following, which one will help you estimate costs depending on the products you plan to use and also get to know where those products will be deployed?
A. Cost Management
B. Azure Advisor
C. Pricing Calculator
D. TCO Calculator

10. You have on-premises applications that you want to migrate to Azure. What would be the best choice if you want to estimate how much you can save in Azure?
A. Cost Management
B. Azure Advisor
C. Pricing Calculator
D. TCO Calculator

11. TCO report shows the estimated result of how much money you can save by moving your app to Azure over the next _____.
A. 3 years
B. 4 years
C. 5 years
D. 1 year

12. Select the three primary groups that must be coordinated within the company to ensure you handle the costs effectively.
A. Finance
B. Managers
C. App teams
D. Billing Admin

13. Which cost analyzing tool can monitor the charges of other cloud service providers such as Amazon Web Services?
A. Cost Management
B. Azure Advisor
C. Pricing Calculator
D. TCO Calculator

14. What are the best practices to implement cost control effectively and reduce costs?
A. Be equipped with the right tools for performance

B. Be responsible for costs

C. Take appropriate action to reduce expenses

D. Resize your resources

15. Which tool can make recommendations for purchases in reserved instances?
A. Azure Reservations
B. Azure Advisor
C. Pricing Calculator
D. TCO Calculator

16. How are Azure subscriptions related to pricing?
A. If you lock subscriptions in for 1 or 3 years, the services within it go down in price
B. The more subscriptions you have, the cheaper each service will get
C. The billing of each service in your account is within a single subscription
D. The price of a subscription depends on the location of your company or personal address

17. To manage expenses on Azure, what is a recommended best practice?
A. Monitor frequently used services and keep track of any excess usage using the Azure Spending Manager
B. Use Azure Alerts to get notified when spending exceeds the subscription limits
C. Use the subscription credit limits, which are built into all Azure subscriptions
D. Use Azure spending limits on resources and services

18. Which Azure calculator would you use to determine monthly costs for Azure services?
A. Azure Service Calculator
B. Azure Portal Service Estimation
C. Total Cost of Ownership Calculator
D. Azure Pricing Calculator

19. From the following, which features are in Azure Cost Management? (Choose 2)
A. Recommendations to move services between Azure regions to save on cost
B. Visualize future costs for your Azure account
C. Visualize current costs for your Azure account
D. Automatic shutdown of services that have not been used for a set time

20. Which factors influence the cost of using products and services on Azure? (Choose 3)
A. The location of the service or resource
B. Resource usage. The more you use it, the cheaper it gets
C. The age of the resource
D. Resource size
E. How much bandwidth will you use

Chapter 11: Managing and Deploying Azure Resources

Introduction

This chapter focuses on the Azure core architectural components, including Resource Groups, Resource Manager Template, Geography, and Azure App Service. The ARM template is a JavaScript Object Notation (JSON) file, a deployment code that defines the resources deployed in the resource group.

Hopefully, by the end of this chapter, you will understand the core components and their purposes while learning how to manage and use Azure Resource Manager (ARM) templates and the importance of managing and deploying Azure resource options.

Azure Resource Groups

Azure Resource Groups contain a different number of Azure resources. Azure Resource Groups help to monitor, manage, and provide access control of resources. With the resource group all resources within the resources group can span different Azure regions.

Azure Resource Group provides a managed group of Azure resources like Virtual Machines, SQL Databases, storage accounts, etc. Resource groups allow one to add and remove resources and apply role-based access information easily. Within a resource group, the same type of resources is created depending upon the company's requirements. There is no extra charge required for the creation of resource groups.

Azure Resource Manager

Azure Resource Manager enables us to organize and monitor all the resources after deployment. The ARM template is used to specify the deployment parameters, list of variables, list of resources, and output. It also provides the file named JSON for the faster deployment of resources.

Purpose of ARM Templates

It is an underlying service or interfaces where the Azure resource deployment and management occur. It provides a management layer, which lets you create, upgrade, and uninstall your Azure subscription tools with a single action Azure resource group and does not allow you to consider all the related resources as a single item. You can use management features such as access control, locks, or tags to ensure your resources are protected and organized after deployment. The main purpose of ARM templates includes:

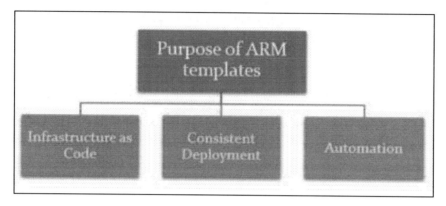

Figure 11-01: Purpose of ARM

Infrastructure as Code

When you are using the ARM templates, the main goal is referred to as "Infrastructure as Code." You can use ARM templates to declare a certain infrastructure of a solution. It is a text-based (declarative JSON) representation of Azure resources and configuration used to create a solution. We use ARM templates by defining the JSON script because it provides many benefits.

Consistent Deployment

With ARM templates, we can achieve consistent deployments. It makes the repeatable deployment of infrastructure with clearly defined input and output.

For example, ARM gives you a common language to deploy any resource. You do not need to be careful about the tools or SDKs for deploying, as ARM deploys the necessary resources to build your solution.

Automation

With ARM templates, you can automate the deployments. ARM templates provide automation and orchestration deployments through scripts and Azure services.

For example, when managing an Azure subscription, you have certain projects, and each project needs common resources like a virtual network, virtual machine, and storage accounts. In this case, if you have been regularly deploying this infrastructure, you have to spend some time on the deployment of these resources regularly as well. To avoid this, you can deploy these common resources with ARM templates and automate the deployment of that infrastructure using Azure Automation, PowerShell, CLI, etc.

> EXAM TIP: The ARM template is a JSON file in which you define each Resource Manager resource that needs to be deployed. You can define this template with a single action in the Resource Manager.

Benefits of Azure Resource Manager

Azure Resource Manager allows you to:

- Use declarative templates rather than scripts to manage your infrastructure. What you wish to deploy to Azure is specified in a Resource Manager template, which is a JSON file
- Instead of managing each resource separately, deploy, manage, and monitor them all as a single unit for your solution

- Re-deploy your solution as needed during the development life cycle, and be sure that your resources are set up consistently.
- Establish the connections between the resources so that they can be distributed in the proper sequence.
- Due to RBAC's inherent integration with the management platform, all services should be subject to access control.
- To order the resources in your subscription logically, apply tags to each resource.
- Viewing pricing for a collection of resources with the same tag will help you understand how your company bills.

Bicep: A Declarative Language for Azure Resource Deployment

Bicep is a language designed for deploying Azure resources, utilizing a declarative syntax that simplifies the provisioning of infrastructure. In essence, a Bicep file serves as the blueprint defining the desired infrastructure and configuration. The Azure Resource Manager (ARM) then deploys the specified environment based on this Bicep file. While akin to ARM templates, typically written in JSON, Bicep files adopt a more streamlined and concise style.

Here are some key benefits of using Bicep:

1. Support for All Resource Types and API Versions:

Bicep offers immediate support for both preview and General Availability (GA) versions of Azure services. As new resource types and API versions are introduced by resource providers, Bicep allows users to seamlessly incorporate them into their files without waiting for tool updates.

2. Simple Syntax:

Compared to equivalent JSON templates, Bicep files boast a more concise and readable syntax. Bicep requires no prior knowledge of programming languages, making it accessible to a broader audience. Its declarative nature precisely specifies the desired resources and their properties for deployment.

3. Repeatable Results:

Bicep files are designed to provide consistent results throughout the development lifecycle. They are idempotent, meaning the same file can be deployed multiple times, yielding identical resource types in the same state. This ensures confidence in the reproducibility of the infrastructure.

4. Orchestration:

Bicep leverages Azure Resource Manager to orchestrate the deployment of interdependent resources. Users are relieved from the complexities of ordering operations as the Resource Manager ensures resources are created in the correct order. Additionally, deployments are optimized through parallel execution, enhancing overall efficiency.

5. Modularity:

Bicep supports modularization, allowing users to break down their code into manageable parts known as modules. These modules deploy sets of related resources, promoting code reuse and simplifying development efforts. Integrating a module into a Bicep file becomes a straightforward way to deploy specific resources when needed.

> **EXAM TIP**: The ARM template is a JSON file in which you define each Resource Manager resource that needs to be deployed. You can define this template with a single action in the Resource Manager.

Structure of ARM Templates

Resource as Code

With the ARM template, we can deploy any resource in terms of code.

For example, when you want to create a virtual machine, the first thing that needs to be considered is to create a virtual machine to define the resource group. The resource group will hold this VM. The ARM template will define what will exist in terms of Azure resources and configuration within a resource group, where you will define the resource (virtual machine). After that, you define some important properties of a virtual machine, like name, location, and size in terms of code. You will have to define operating system images like Linux, data disk, and a network interface for functionality. The pictorial representation of this example is shown in Figure 11-02.

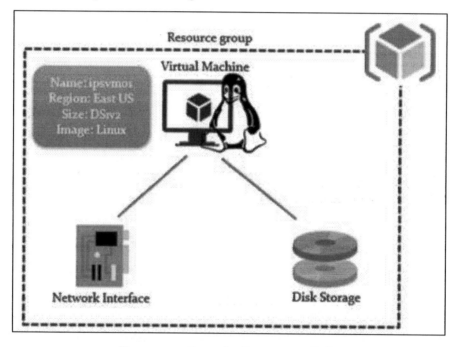

Figure 11-02: Example: Resource as Code

The creation of the resource (VM) can be obtained by using the code shown below.

Resource: "Virtual Machine" {

Virtual Machine Properties: {

Name: "vm1"

Location: "US East"

Size: "DS1 V2"

Storage: {

> OSImage: "Linux"
>
> DataDisk: "DataDisk1"}
>
> Network: {
>
> NIC: "NIC1"}   }   }

Template Format

Everything is defined in a specified format when we use an ARM template.

```
{
"$schema": https://schema.management......,

"contentVersion": "1.0.0.0",

"parameters": {.......},

"variables": {.....},

"resources": [......],

"outputs": {......},

"functions": [......],

}
```

Azure Resource Manager Template is a simple template that contains: $schema, contentVersion, parameters, variables, functions, resources, and outputs.

$schema

It is an important and necessary element that needs to define the location of the JSON schema file. It describes the language of the template.

contentVersion

It describes the details and format of the template. Microsoft uses it to define the template structure.

Parameters

Parameters define the custom value taken as input when the template runs for resource deployment. There is a limit of 256 parameters in a template. Examples of parameters are VM name, location, size, etc.

Variables

It is where you define the specific values that can be used in the entire template, largely to help simplify the template's usability and readability. For example, you can use multiple virtual machines in the same virtual network; instead of going into each virtual machine and configuring the details, you can use variables. You can set the VM name as a variable used throughout the template. When you need to change the name, you change the variable.

Resources

The resources section in the ARM template is necessary to define the resource that you need to deploy through the ARM template. The resources can be deployed by following Microsoft's definition of each of

these resources. This is because a range of different properties is needed during the configuration of resources—for example, a VM or VNet.

Outputs

The output allows you to return values from the ARM template deployment. For example, let's consider you are deploying five virtual machines. When you create your ARM template, you do not know what public and private IP addresses are. If you are automating the deployment of the ARM template, you can set the output section that returns only the IP addresses.

> **Note:** You must define the output name and type for outputs. In value, you define where you got the value, which is evaluated and returned to output.

Functions

You can define complex expressions through functions that do not need to be used repeatedly in the template. You can create your user-defined functions, different from the standard (built-in) template function. A user-defined function is usually used repeatedly throughout the ARM template.

> **EXAM TIP:** With functions and variables, you can maintain your template easily.

Example – VM Resource

The ARM template in terms of Visual Studio code is shown in Figure 11-03 (a) and (b). This code specifically defines the "resources" section of the virtual machine.

```
"resources": [
  {
    "type": "Microsoft.Storage/storageAccounts",
    "apiVersion": "2019-06-01",
    "name": "[variables('storageAccountName')]",
    "location": "[parameters('location')]",
    "sku": {
      "name": "Standard_LRS"
    },
    "kind": "Storage",
    "properties": {}
  },
  {
    "type": "Microsoft.Network/publicIPAddresses",
    "apiVersion": "2020-06-01",
    "name": "[parameters('publicIPName')]",
    "location": "[parameters('location')]",
    "sku": {
      "name": "[parameters('publicIpSku')]"
    },
    "properties": {
      "publicIPAllocationMethod": "[parameters('publicIPAllocationMethod')]",
      "dnsSettings": {
        "domainNameLabel": "[parameters('dnsLabelPrefix')]"
      }
    }
  },
  {
    "type": "Microsoft.Network/networkSecurityGroups",
    "apiVersion": "2020-06-01",
    "name": "[variables('networkSecurityGroupName')]",
    "location": "[parameters('location')]",
    "properties": {
      "securityRules": [
```

Figure 11-03 (a): ARM Template

```
    },
    "storageProfile": {
      "imageReference": {
        "publisher": "MicrosoftWindowsServer",
        "offer": "WindowsServer",
        "sku": "[parameters('OSVersion')]",
        "version": "latest"
      },
      "osDisk": {
        "createOption": "FromImage",
        "managedDisk": {
          "storageAccountType": "StandardSSD_LRS"
        }
      },
      "dataDisks": [
        {
          "diskSizeGB": 1023,
          "lun": 0,
          "createOption": "Empty"
        }
      ]
    },
    "networkProfile": {
      "networkInterfaces": [
        {
          "id": "[resourceId('Microsoft.Network/networkInterfaces', variables('n
        }
      ]
    },
    "diagnosticsProfile": {
      "bootDiagnostics": {
        "enabled": true,
        "storageUri": "[reference(resourceId('Microsoft.Storage/storageAccounts'
```

Figure 11-03 (b): ARM Template

There are different key components present inside the resource section. The description of each key component is explained in table 11-01.

Field	Description
Type	The type of resource being created: a virtual machine
Name	The name to be assigned to the resource: uses a parameter
dependsOn	Resources this VM depends on a Network Interface Card (NIC)

Properties	Properties of the resource: Virtual machine properties
> osProfile	Important OS properties, like admin username and password
> hardwareProfile	Property: The hardware characteristics of the VM
> storageProfile	Property: The storage properties, including OS disk, etc.
> networkProfile	Property: The connected Network Interface Card

Table 11-01: Key Components in Resource Section

In this template, you can see different parameters like resource type, location, size, etc. You can use automation scripting tools like the Azure CLI, Azure PowerShell, or even the Azure REST APIs with your favorite programming language to deploy resources from templates. You can also use Visual Studio, Visual Studio Code, and Azure portal to deploy your templates.

In the above example, the resource section specifies the version of the definition of the resource from Microsoft. You must define the resource name in terms of a variable. After that, define the resource group location. Figure 11-04 defines the general definition of the resource section.

```
},
"resources": [
    {
        "type": "Microsoft.Storage/storageAccounts",
        "apiVersion": "2019-06-01",
        "name": "[variables('storageAccountName')]",
        "location": "[parameters('location')]",
        "sku": {
            "name": "Standard_LRS"
        },
        "kind": "Storage",
        "properties": {}
    },
```

Figure 11-04: General Resource Section

Properties

This section resides in the resources. It holds osProfile, hardwareProfile, storageProfile, and networkProfile.

osProfile – It defines the computer name, username, and type of authentication used.

storageProfile – It defines the type of image used for the VM. This section also contains some terms to define the marketplace image that will be used to build the operating system for the virtual machine.

The publisher can be a Linux operating system or Microsoft Windows Server.

Offer is the actual type of image—for example, Ubuntu, Windows, etc.

SKU defines the version of the operation system.

The version shows the current version of an image. Usually, "latest" is used.

osDisk – The code shows only an operating system attached to the virtual machine. There is no data disk associated with the virtual machine.

```
"storageProfile": {
  "imageReference": {
    "publisher": "MicrosoftWindowsServer",
    "offer": "WindowsServer",
    "sku": "[parameters('OSVersion')]",
    "version": "latest"
  },
  "osDisk": {
    "createOption": "FromImage",
    "managedDisk": {
      "storageAccountType": "StandardSSD_LRS"
    }
  },
```

Figure 11-05: storageProfile Section

networkProfile – Once we depend on the resource, we need the pre-built network interface card.

At last, the resource section includes the Azure Monitor to monitor the virtual machine. Azure Monitor stores the diagnostic information in the storage account.

```
"networkProfile": {
  "networkInterfaces": [
    {
      "id": "[resourceId('Microsoft.Network/networkInterfaces', variables('ni
    }
  ]
},
"diagnosticsProfile": {
  "bootDiagnostics": {
    "enabled": true,
    "storageUri": "[reference(resourceId('Microsoft.Storage/storageAccounts',
```

Figure 11-06: networkProfile Section

EXAM TIP: Use https://azure.microsoft.com/en-us/resources/templates/ to explore other Azure templates and understand how to deploy resources using ARM templates.

Working with ARM Templates

After understanding the ARM template's concept and what is inside it, in this section, we will learn how to retrieve ARM templates, export the ARM template, and deploy resources using Cloud Shell.

When using the ARM template, you should perform the following deployments:

Deploy to a Resource Group

ARM templates are commonly used to represent the resources within a single resource group. The deployment defines what the resources are and what configurations within the resource group are.

If you have multiple resource groups, you can also deploy them using an ARM template. However, the deployment of multiple resource groups has become advanced and complex. For such cases, you can use linked ARM templates.

Deployment Modes

If you have already used the ARM templates and you want to deploy the resource in the resource group, the condition is that you have to deploy multiple resources within the same resource. To do so, there are two different ways available.

- **Complete Mode** – The ARM template will delete all the resources that do not exist in the template or are no longer in use
- **Incremental Mode** – This deployment will not delete anything. It will only update the properties of the resources in the resource group. This is a default mode

Deployment Tools

When working with Azure Resource Manager (ARM) template, several options are available. You can use Azure Portal, Visual Studio Code, Azure PowerShell, Azure CLI, etc. You can get advanced integration with tools like Visual Studio Code, CI/CD, and Azure pipelines.

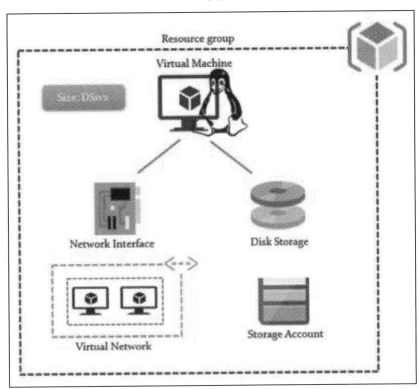

Figure 11-07: Working with ARM Template

Deploy a Resource with Azure CLI

There are two options available to deploy a resource by using Azure CLI.

Standalone Template

You can deploy any resource by using a single standalone ARM template. With this option, the ARM template contains all the information required to deploy resources within a single file. This is the common way to deploy any resource with the ARM template.

```
# Standalone deployment
az deployment group create \
        --name "deployvm" \
        --resource-group "ips-rg" \
        --template-file "ips.json"
```

Template with Parameters File

The second option is to deploy a resource with a parameters file. The parameters file can be used to provide some flexibility toward consistent deployment. This template has a separate command argument used to specify the parameters file.

```
# With parameter file
az deployment group create \
        --name "deployvm" \
        --resource-group "ips-rg" \
        --template-file "ips.json" \
        --parameters "@devparams.json"
```

Both templates can be used with Azure CLI. For example, when you want to build a solution, you can build a template that defines a range of resources used to build a solution. You might set a range of properties within the ARM template as parameters. If you want to build high-performance resources, use an ARM template to deploy the solution both in production and development. Then, you can use the ARM template to build a high-performance resource for production and development using the above CLI commands.

Benefits of Azure Resource Manager

Azure Resource Manager allows you to:

- Use declarative templates rather than scripts to manage your infrastructure. What you wish to deploy to Azure is specified in a Resource Manager template, which is a JSON file
- Instead of managing each resource separately, deploy, manage, and monitor them all as a single unit for your solution
- Re-deploy your solution as needed during the development life cycle, and be sure that your resources are set up consistently

- Establish the connections between the resources so that they can be distributed in the proper sequence
- Due to RBAC's inherent integration with the management platform, all services should be subject to access control
- To order the resources in your subscription logically, apply tags to each resource
- Viewing pricing for a collection of resources with the same tag will help you understand how your company bills

Lab 11-01: Working with ARM Templates

Service Introduction

PayFast, a rising FinTech startup offering secure online payments, needed to quickly deploy and manage its cloud infrastructure but faced complexity and manual work with traditional configuration methods. They required a solution to automate deployments, enforce consistency, and enable self-service provisioning for developers.

Problem

PayFast relied on manually configuring resources through the Azure portal, a slow and error-prone process hindering DevOps agility and developer productivity. Manual deployments led to inconsistencies in resource setup, creating environment drift and making infrastructure troubleshooting challenging.

Solution

PayFast's success story showcases the power of ARM templates for companies seeking to boost DevOps agility, improve developer productivity, and ensure consistency in their Azure cloud infrastructure. By utilizing the power of automation and code-driven infrastructure, PayFast achieved faster deployments, streamlined operations, and empowered their developers to innovate at a rapid pace.

Task 1: Working with ARM Template

1. Log in to the **Microsoft Azure** portal and go to the portal menu.

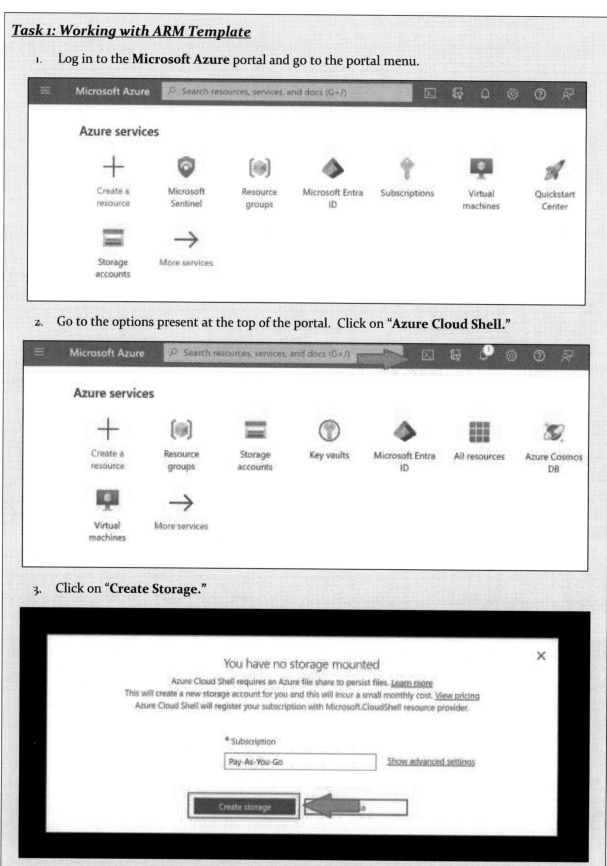

2. Go to the options present at the top of the portal. Click on **"Azure Cloud Shell."**

3. Click on **"Create Storage."**

4. The Cloud Shell session will start in a moment.
5. Type "**ls**" to see the list of available items.

```
faizan [ ~ ]$ ls
clouddrive  ips.json
faizan [ ~ ]$ █
```

6. You will see the .json file in the drive with the name "**ips.**"

```
faizan [ ~ ]$ ls
clouddrive  ips.json
faizan [ ~ ]$ █
```

7. To see the code, open the code editor by typing "ips.json."

```
faizan [ ~ ]$ ls
clouddrive  ips.json
faizan [ ~ ]$ code ips.json
faizan [ ~ ]$ □
```

8. You will see the available code in the ips.json file.

```
Microsoft Azure

Bash          ⏻ ? ⚙ ...

ips.json

1  {
2      "$schema": "https://schema.management.azure.com/schemas/2
3      "contentVersion": "1.0.0.0",
4      "parameters": {
5          "storageAccountType": {
6              "type": "string",
7              "defaultValue": "Standard_LRS",
8              "allowedValues": [ "Standard_LRS", "Standard_GRS"
9
10         }
11     },
12     "variables": {
13         "storageAccountName": "ipsstorage01"
14     },
15     "resources": [
16         {
17             "type": "Microsoft.Storage/storageAccounts",
18             "name": "[variables('storageAccountName')]",
19             "apiVersion": "2018-02-01",
```

```
≡   Microsoft Azure                                    ⌕  ...  👤

Bash      ∨  |  ⏻  ?  ⚙  ⯮  ⯐  {}  ⯑              —  ☐  ✕

                              ips.json                           ...
 18            name . [variables( storageAccountName )] ,
 19            "apiVersion": "2018-02-01",
 20            "location": "[resourceGroup().location]",
 21            "sku": {
 22                "name": "[parameters('storageAccountType')]"
 23            },
 24            "kind": "Storage",
 25            "properties": {
 26            }
 27        }
 28    ],
 29    "outputs": {
 30        "storageAccountName": {
 31            "type": "string",
 32            "value": "[variables('storageAccountName')]"
 33        }
 34    }
 35 }
```

9. Press "**CTRL+Q**" to close the code editor.
10. Type the following command in the Cloud Shell session to create a resource group.

```
faizan [ ~ ]$ az group create --name Myips --location eastus
{
  "id": "/subscriptions/797152d3-23c4-499f-bfef-bb103da7d054/resourceGroups/Myips",
  "location": "eastus",
  "managedBy": null,
  "name": "Myips",
  "properties": {
    "provisioningState": "Succeeded"
  },
  "tags": null,
  "type": "Microsoft.Resources/resourceGroups"
}
faizan [ ~ ]$ ▮
```

11. You will see output in JSON format.

```
faizan [ ~ ]$ az group create --name Myips --location eastus
{
  "id": "/subscriptions/797152d3-23c4-499f-bfef-bb103da7d054/resourceGroups/Myips",
  "location": "eastus",
  "managedBy": null,
  "name": "Myips",
  "properties": {
    "provisioningState": "Succeeded"
  },
  "tags": null,
  "type": "Microsoft.Resources/resourceGroups"
}
faizan [ ~ ]$ █
```

12. After the resource group, we will deploy the resource in that resource group according to the **"ips.json"** code.

13. To do that, run the following sets of commands:

```
Bash                                                                              — □ ×
faizan [ ~ ]$ az deployment group create --name ipsdeploy --resource-group Myips --template-file ips.json
{
  "id": "/subscriptions/797152d3-23c4-499f-bfef-bb103da7d054/resourceGroups/Myips/providers/Microsoft.Resources/deploy
ments/ipsdeploy",
  "location": null,
  "name": "ipsdeploy",
  "properties": {
    "correlationId": "56782e86-bc76-4efc-b1a2-22c89dbfa2b5",
    "debugSetting": null,
    "dependencies": [],
    "duration": "PT1.09462895",
    "error": null,
    "mode": "Incremental",
    "onErrorDeployment": null,
    "outputResources": [],
    "outputs": null,
    "parameters": {},
    "parametersLink": null,
    "providers": [],
```

14. This command will take some time to complete the execution.

15. After the execution process, the following output will appear.

```
Bash                                                                              — □ ×
faizan [ ~ ]$ az deployment group create --name ipsdeploy --resource-group Myips --template-file ips.json
{
  "id": "/subscriptions/797152d3-23c4-499f-bfef-bb103da7d054/resourceGroups/Myips/providers/Microsoft.Resources/deploy
ments/ipsdeploy",
  "location": null,
  "name": "ipsdeploy",
  "properties": {
    "correlationId": "56782e86-bc76-4efc-b1a2-22c89dbfa2b5",
    "debugSetting": null,
    "dependencies": [],
    "duration": "PT1.09462895",
    "error": null,
    "mode": "Incremental",
    "onErrorDeployment": null,
    "outputResources": [],
    "outputs": null,
    "parameters": {},
    "parametersLink": null,
    "providers": [],
```

16. Go to the Azure Portal page, and open **"Resource groups."** Click on the resource group that was just created from the CLI session.

Home > Resource groups >

[●] **Myips**
Resource group

+ Create ⚙ Manage view ∨ 🗑 Delete resource group ↻ Refresh ↓ Export to CSV ⟨⟩ Open query | 🏷 Assign tags

∨ **Essentials**

Resources Recommendations

Filter for any field... | Type equals **all** ✕ | Location equals **all** ✕ | ⁺ᵧ Add filter

Showing 0 to 0 of 0 records. ☐ Show hidden types ①   No grouping ∨

Name ↑ Type ↑↓ Location ↑↓

17. Go to the options present at the left corner of the page. Click on **"Deployments"** present inside **"Settings."**

Home > Resource groups > Myips

⬆ **Myips | Deployments** ☆ ⋯
Resource group

🔍 Search « ↻ Refresh ⊘ Cancel Redeploy 🗑 Delete ↓ View template

Settings Filter by deployment name or resources in the deployment...

⬆ Deployments ⬅ ☐ **Deployment name** **Status** **Last modified**
🛡 Security ☐ ipsdeploy ✅ Succeeded 1/30/2024, 9:09:16 PM
⚙ Deployment stacks
📄 Policies
☰ Properties
🔒 Locks

18. Click on the deployment. From the left corner option, click on **"Template."**

Home > Resource groups > Myips | Deployments > ipsdeploy

ipsdeploy | Template ⋯ ✕
Deployment

🔍 Search « ↓ Download 📚 Add to library ⬆ Deploy

⬇ Overview ① Automate deploying resources with Azure Resource Manager templates in a single, coordinated operation. Define resources and configurable input parameters and deploy with script or code. Learn more about template deployment.
🔲 Inputs
☰ Outputs
📄 Template ⬅ **Template** Parameters Scripts

⚙ Parameters (0) 1 {
📄 Variables (0) 2   "$schema": "http://schema.management.azure.com/schemas/2015-01-01/
🔲 Resources (0)   deploymentTemplate.json",
  3   "contentVersion": "1.0.0.0",
  4   "parameters": {},
  5   "resources": []
  6 }

19. You will see that you can get access to the ARM template that was deployed using CLI.

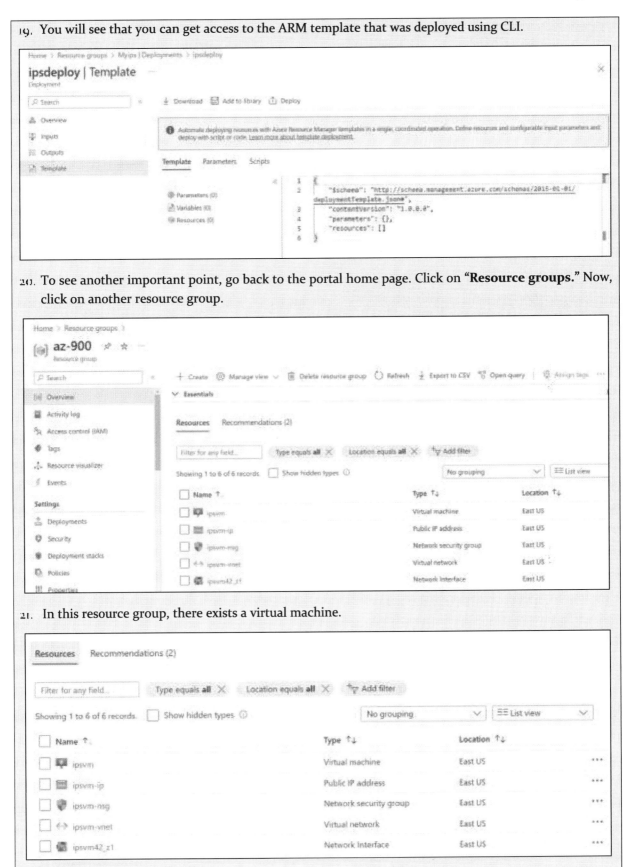

20. To see another important point, go back to the portal home page. Click on **"Resource groups."** Now, click on another resource group.

21. In this resource group, there exists a virtual machine.

22. From the left corner option, click on "**Deployments**" present inside "**Settings.**"

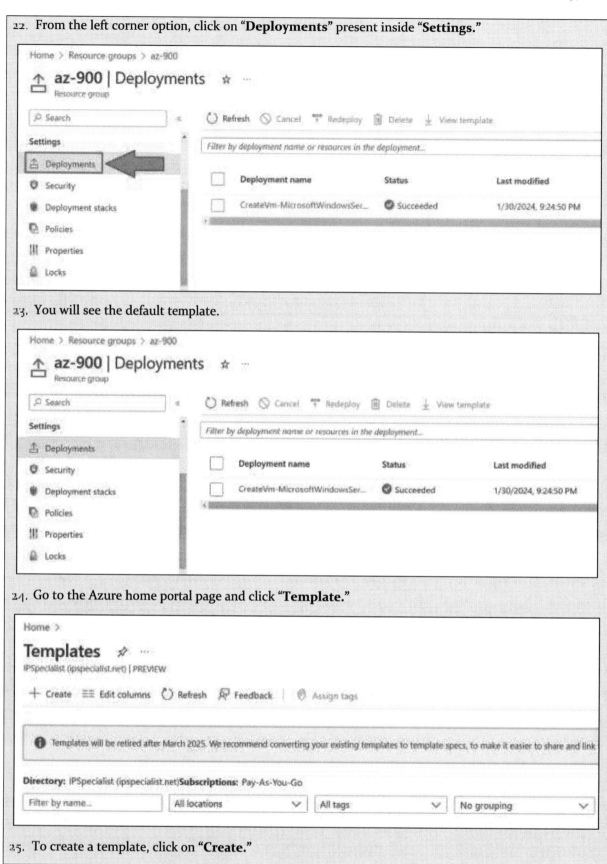

23. You will see the default template.

24. Go to the Azure home portal page and click "**Template.**"

25. To create a template, click on "**Create.**"

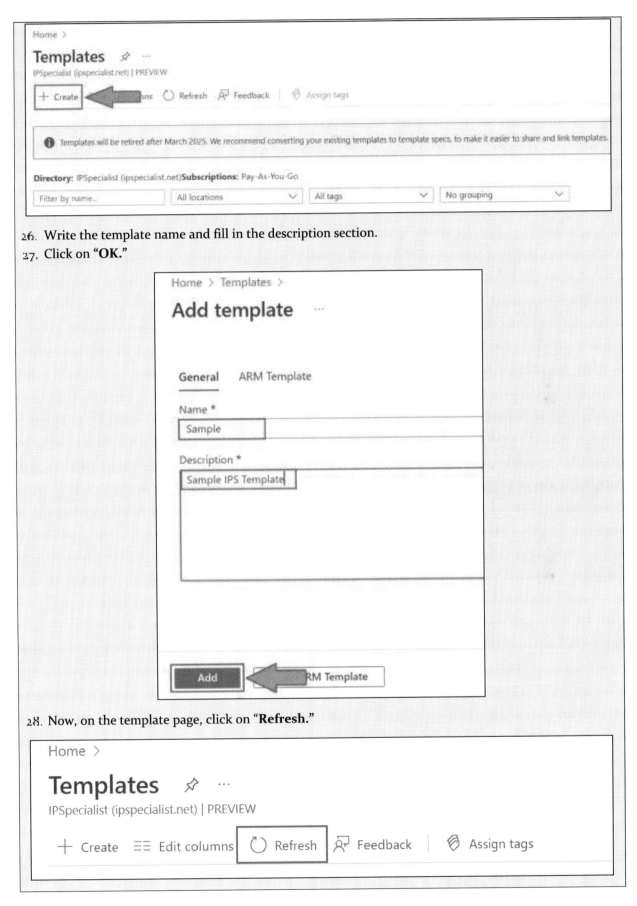

26. Write the template name and fill in the description section.
27. Click on **"OK."**

28. Now, on the template page, click on **"Refresh."**

29. You will see that your created template has appeared. Click on it. You will see the **"Publisher"** and **"Modified"** fields.

30. With the template option, you can easily deploy a template. When you click **"deploy,"** you will see the **"Custom deployment,"** which will allow editing the template and parameters.

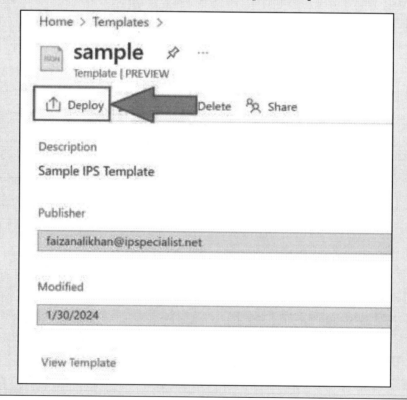

Azure Arc

The management of hybrid and multi-cloud settings can become very challenging. Various tools are available to provision, configure, and monitor Azure resources. What about cloud resources in a multi-cloud configuration or on-premises resources in a hybrid configuration?

Arc enables you to expand Azure compliance and monitoring to your hybrid and multi-cloud settings using Azure Resource Manager (ARM). Azure Arc simplifies governance and management by providing a unified multi-cloud and on-premises management platform.

Azure Arc offers a centralized, integrated method to:

- By projecting your current non-Azure resources into ARM, you can manage your complete environment as one unit
- Manage databases, Kubernetes clusters, and multi-cloud and hybrid virtual machines as though they were running on Azure
- Use familiar Azure services and management tools no matter where they are located.
- As you implement DevOps techniques to accommodate new cloud and native patterns in your environment, keep employing traditional ITOps
- Create custom locations as an abstraction layer on top of Kubernetes clusters and cluster extensions that Azure Arc supports

<u>What can Azure Arc do Outside of Azure?</u>

You can currently manage the following resource types located outside of Azure using Azure Arc:
- Servers
- Kubernetes Clusters
- Azure Data Services
- SQL Server
- Virtual Machines (Preview)

> **EXAM TIP**: Azure Arc is a Microsoft service that extends Azure's management and services to any infrastructure, allowing organizations to manage resources, deploy applications, and apply Azure services across on-premises, multi-cloud, and edge environments. Azure Arc provides a centralized management platform, enabling consistent and unified operations for diverse resources, regardless of their location. This service is designed to enhance flexibility and control by bringing Azure's capabilities to the customer's own data center or other cloud providers.

Azure App Service

In Microsoft Azure, Azure App Services are usually used to provide the hosting environment for web applications. Azure App Service manages various instances to handle the traffic, and the load balancer spreads the incoming traffic request to all the available VM instances of the web application.

In Azure, the App Service plan defines the features and resources available to the instances. This service can configure the virtual machine's computing resources, including CPU, memory, storage, custom

domain, scalability, traffic manager, and more. It also describes the operating system (Windows or Linux) and the availability of the service in terms of backup.

Additionally, the Azure App Service plan defines:

- Region
- Number of VM Instances
- Size of the Instance
- Pricing Tier

Lab 11-02: Create a Website Hosted in Azure

Service Introduction

Creating a website hosted in Azure is a straightforward process that leverages Azure App Service, a fully managed platform allowing developers to build, deploy, and scale web applications seamlessly. To initiate the process, users can utilize the Azure portal to create an App Service plan and a corresponding web app. Developers can then deploy their website code, whether it is developed in .NET, Java, Node.js, Python, or other supported languages, using various deployment options like Git, Azure DevOps, or Visual Studio integration. Azure provides features such as automatic scaling, continuous deployment, and integration with Azure DevOps, streamlining the development workflow. Moreover, custom domains and SSL certificates can be easily configured through Azure App Service, ensuring a secure and personalized web presence. With built-in monitoring, logging, and integration with Azure services, hosting a website in Azure offers a robust and scalable solution for delivering web content to users worldwide.

Problem

An organization has shifted its resources from on-premises to the cloud. The developer wants to create a new website for the organization using the Azure service. How could this be possible?

Solution

Using Azure App Service, the developer can host the website by following the given steps.

1. Log in to the **Microsoft Azure** portal and go to the portal menu.
2. Before creating a website, we will first create a resource group in which the website will reside. Therefore, click on "**Resource groups**" from the portal home page.

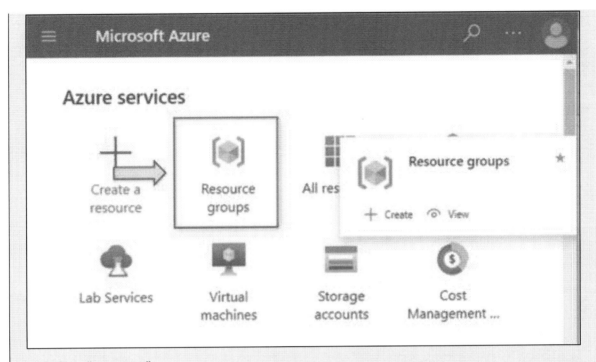

3. Click on "**+ Create.**"

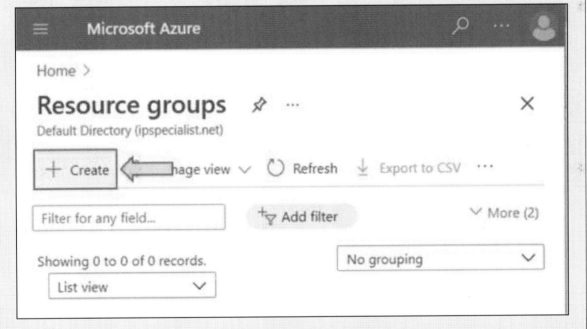

4. Enter the configuration for the resource group. Inside the "**Project details,**" select your subscription.
5. Write the unique name for the resource group.
6. Inside the "**Resource details,**" select your nearest location from the list.
7. Click on "**Review + create.**"

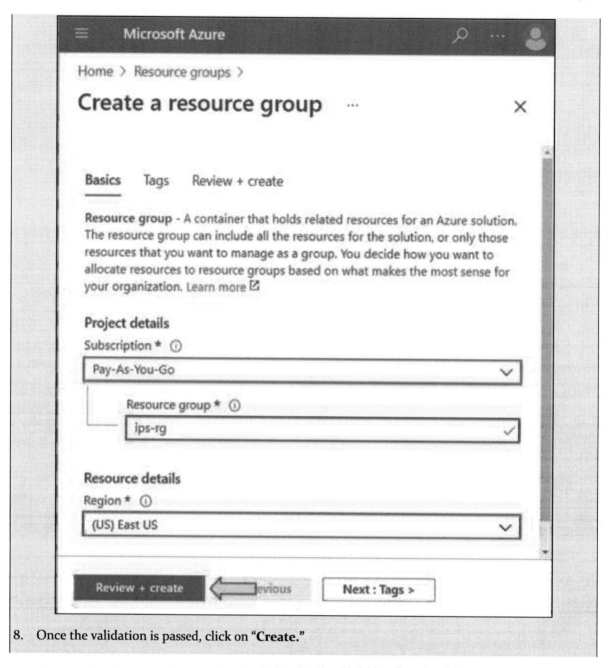

8. Once the validation is passed, click on **"Create."**

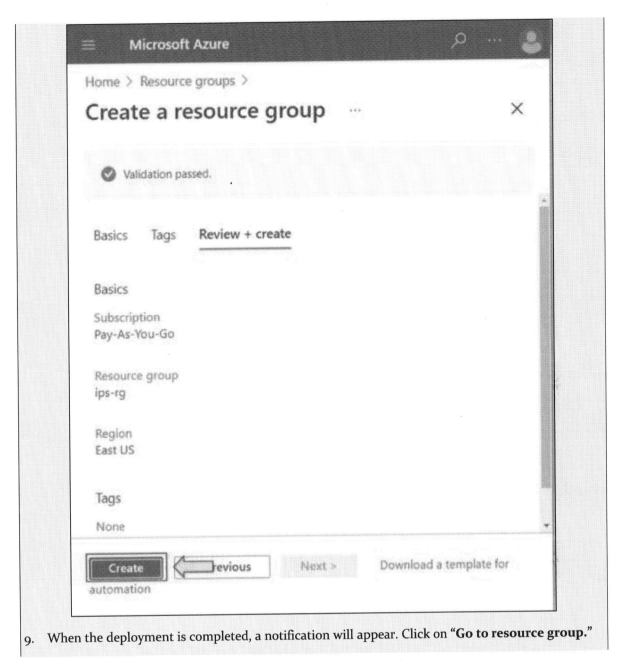

9. When the deployment is completed, a notification will appear. Click on **"Go to resource group."**

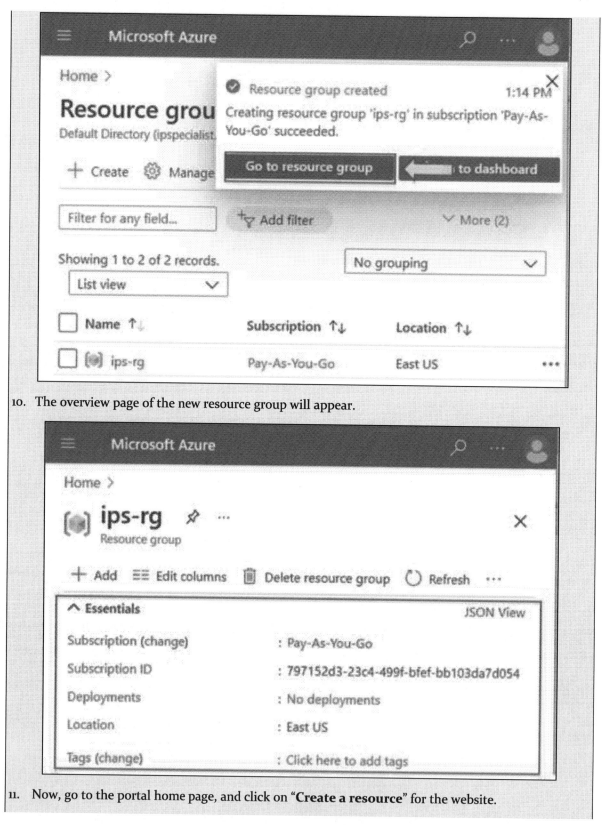

10. The overview page of the new resource group will appear.

11. Now, go to the portal home page, and click on **"Create a resource"** for the website.

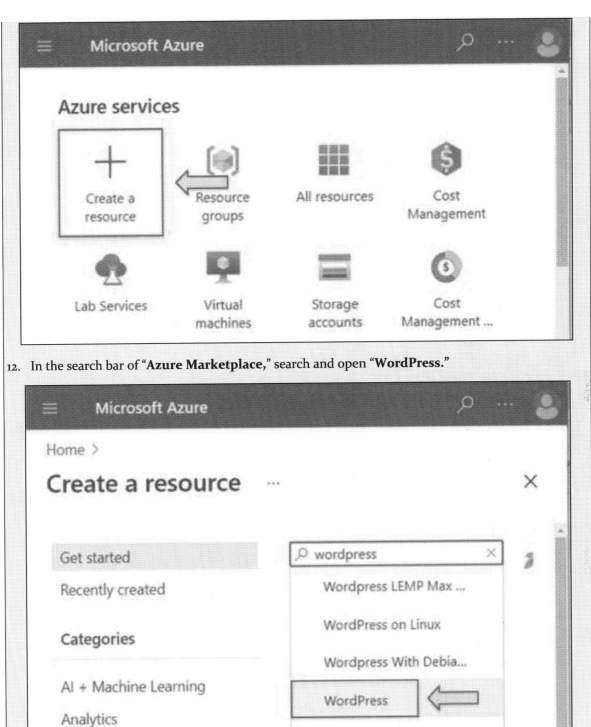

12. In the search bar of "**Azure Marketplace,**" search and open "**WordPress.**"

13. Click on "**Create.**"

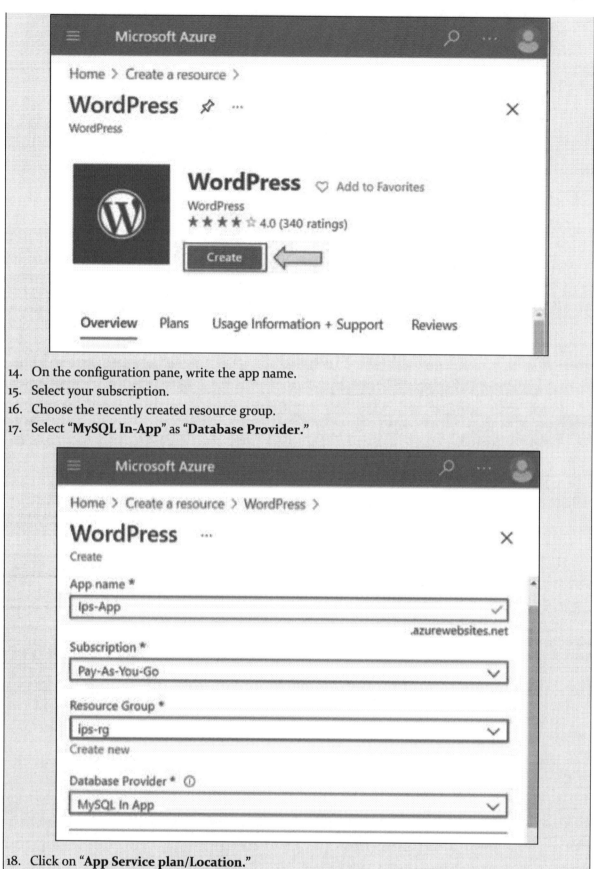

14. On the configuration pane, write the app name.
15. Select your subscription.
16. Choose the recently created resource group.
17. Select "**MySQL In-App**" as "**Database Provider.**"

18. Click on "**App Service plan/Location.**"

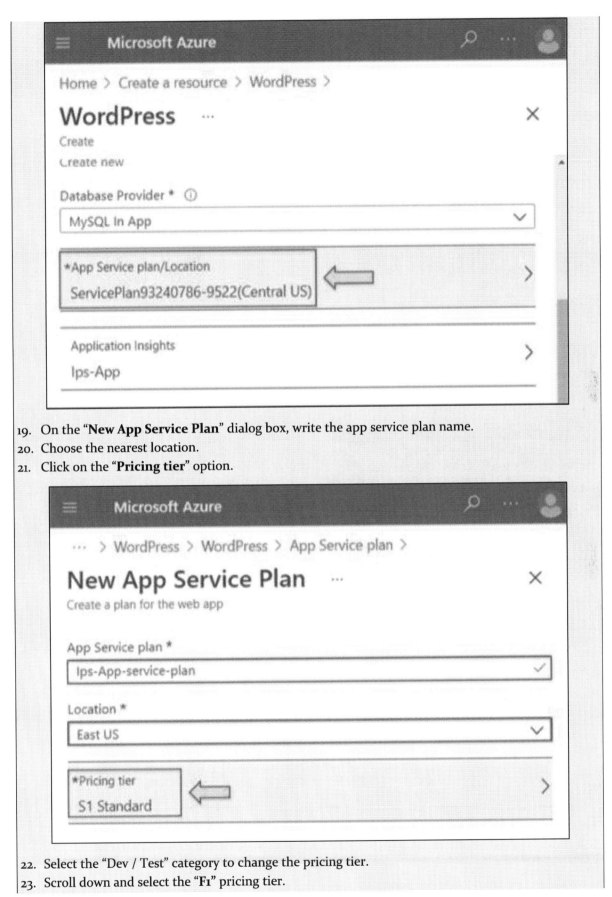

19. On the "**New App Service Plan**" dialog box, write the app service plan name.
20. Choose the nearest location.
21. Click on the "**Pricing tier**" option.

22. Select the "Dev / Test" category to change the pricing tier.
23. Scroll down and select the "**F1**" pricing tier.

24. Click on **"Apply."**

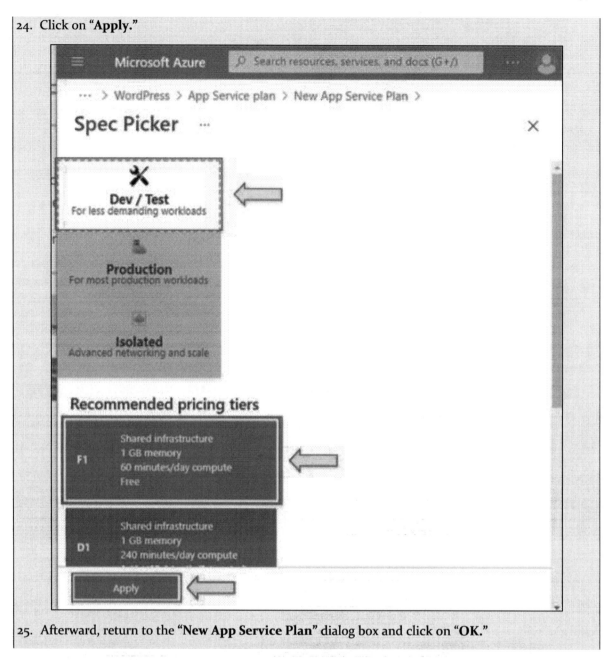

25. Afterward, return to the **"New App Service Plan"** dialog box and click on **"OK."**

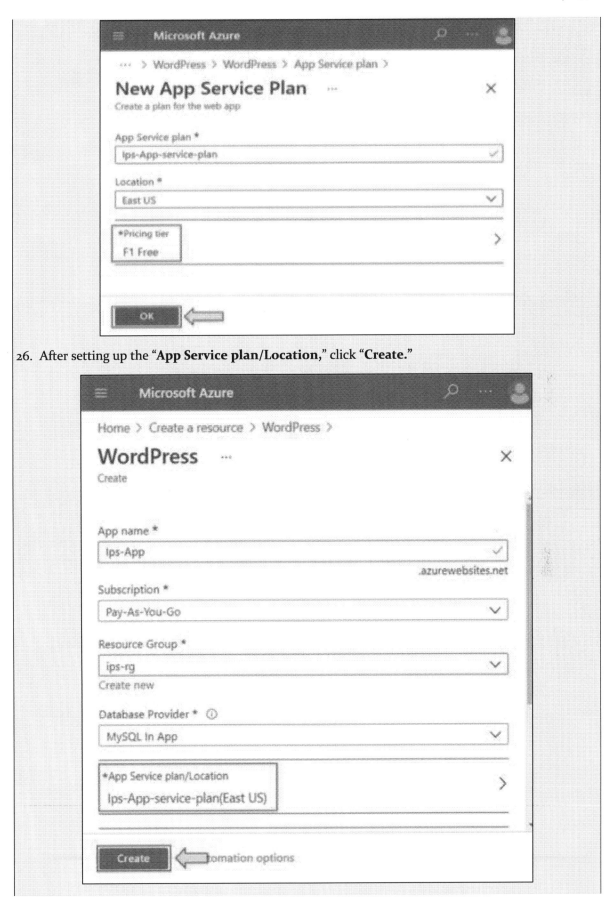

26. After setting up the "**App Service plan/Location,**" click "**Create.**"

27. A notification will appear as soon as the deployment is successful. Click on **"Go to resource."**

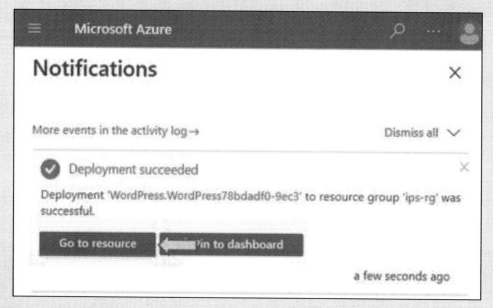

28. The overview page of the website will appear, containing all the configuration details.
29. Navigate to the given **"URL."**

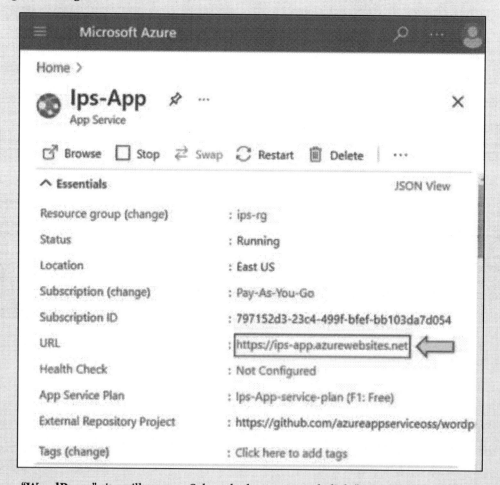

30. A new **"WordPress"** site will appear. Select the language and click **"Continue"** to add the content.

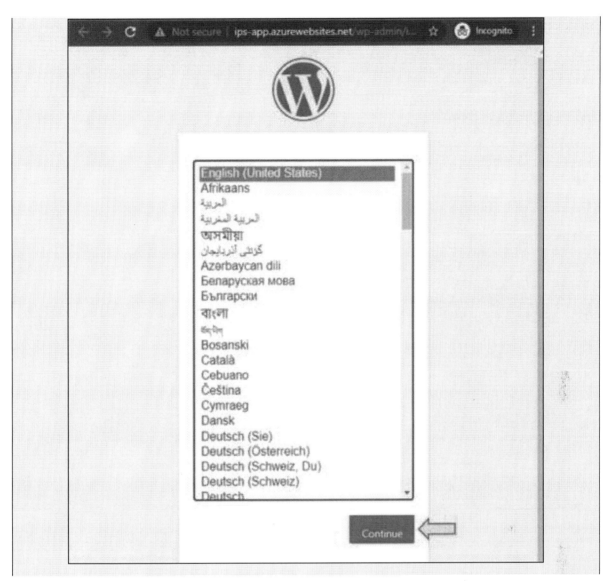

Mind Map

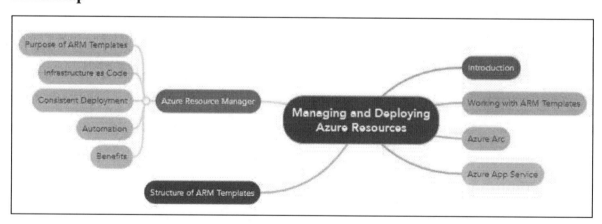

Figure 11-08: Mind Map

Practice Questions

1. Which provides the management layer to create the resources?

A. Azure Hybrid Benefits
B. ARM
C. RBAC
D. Tags

2. Which of the following is used for the ARM template?

A. JSON
B. YAML
C. XML
D. None of the above

3. Which of the following features helps to get the orchestration deployment?
A. Infrastructure as Code
B. Consistent deployment
C. Automation
D. None of the above

4. Which attribute defines the fixed value that can be used in the entire template?

A. Variables
B. Parameters
C. Functions
D. $schema

5. With Custom Script Extension, adding a resource in a template is easy, but it is not a good idea to continuously add and delete a resource. True or false?

A. True
B. False

6. Which of the following best defines the Azure App Service?

A. Function as a Service (FaaS)
B. Infrastructure as a Service (IaaS)
C. Software as a Service (SaaS)
D. Platform as a Service (PaaS)

7. Which App Service plan tiers can manually scale up to 3 dedicated instances?

A. Basic Tier

B. Premium Tier

C. Isolated Tier
D. Standard Tier

8. How many elements are present in the ARM template?
A. Four
B. Eight
C. Six
D. Two

9. How many options are there to deploy resources using Azure CLI?
A. Only One
B. Zero
C. Three
D. Two

10. Which of the following Azure service is used to host web applications?
A. Azure Monitor
B. Azure App Service
C. Azure Virtual Network
D. Azure AI Services

11. Which of the following helps to deploy the solution with readymade tools?
A. Azure Marketplace
B. Azure App Service
C. Azure Monitor
D. Azure Resource Manager

12. Which of the following provides the protected area for deployment solutions?
A. Availability Sets
B. Azure Marketplace
C. Availability Zones
D. None of the above

Chapter 12: Support

Introduction

Support plays an important role in the cloud environment. As we have learned, at least some portion of infrastructure management moves to the cloud provider when we move to the cloud. When something goes wrong, you must get the help you need to keep your applications available. It is also important to understand what level of support is being provided for specific services, in particular services that may be in previewing and not published officially. We also know that some changes have always been performed to upgrade features or new products for which you need an extensive support infrastructure for Azure and its users.

In this chapter, we will look at all the aspects related to Azure. We will cover various support plans you can purchase and benefit from, tickets to generate a query, available support channels, knowledge center, Service Level Agreements, and the release cycle for Azure services.

Plans

Microsoft offers numerous support plans for Azure customers to find the right level of support for your organization. There are five different support plans available in Azure; Basic, Developer, Standard, Professional Direct, and Premier. Choosing the right plan balances how much access you require for resources and how much you are willing to spend.

 EXAM TIP: The higher the support plans, the higher the amount you need to pay.

The things which are included in all support plans are:

- *24/7 Access:* Around-the-clock access to billing and subscription support as Microsoft wants to make sure you can pay them
- *Online Self-Help:* Includes Azure documentation and white papers that guide you through complex issues or scenarios
- *Forums:* Supports forums that offer a great way to ask questions to other Azure users about what they use and how they use it
- *Azure Advisor:* Best practice recommendations for multiple Azure services from Azure Advisor
- *Service Health:* Access to the service health status of current issues and future planned maintenance on the Azure platform

These are included in all the support plans free of charge, and coincidentally, all of these are a part of the (free) Basic Support Plan.

Plan Inclusions- Paid Plans

The following table shows the features of various Azure paid plans.

	Developer	Standard	Professional Direct	Premier
Price	$	$$	$$$	$$$$
Technical Support	Access to support engineers via email only during business hours	Access to support engineers 24x7 via email or phone	Access to support engineers 24x7 via email or phone	Access to support engineers 24x7 via email or phone
Support Cases	Unlimited	Unlimited	Unlimited	Unlimited
Azure Configuration	Guidance Troubleshooting	Guidance Troubleshooting	Guidance Troubleshooting	Guidance Troubleshooting
Response Time	Sev. C: < 8 hours	Sev. C: < 8 hours Sev. B: < 4 hours Sev. A: < 1 hour	Sev. C: < 4 hours Sev. B: < 2 hours Sev. A: < 1 hour	Sev. C: < 4 hours Sev. B: < 2 hours Sev. A: < 1 hour <15 minutes (with Azure Rapid Response or Azure Event Management)
Architecture Support	General Guidance	General Guidance	Architecture Guidance	Customer Specific
Operations Support			Onboarding Reviews	Tech Reviews Reporting Tech Account Manager
Training			Webinars	On-demand

Table 12-01: Azure Paid Plans

Apart from the premier, all these support services can be used by signing up online. Your support service will start immediately.

Tickets

Azure enables you to create and manage support requests, also known as support tickets. A ticket is usually a number that uniquely identifies your inquiry. All communication and details of your support request are recorded with a ticket number attached to them. So, a ticket is a single reference to the whole support request.

Submitting a Ticket

There are a few steps to submitting a ticket.

1. You submit a ticket through the Azure portal after logging in.

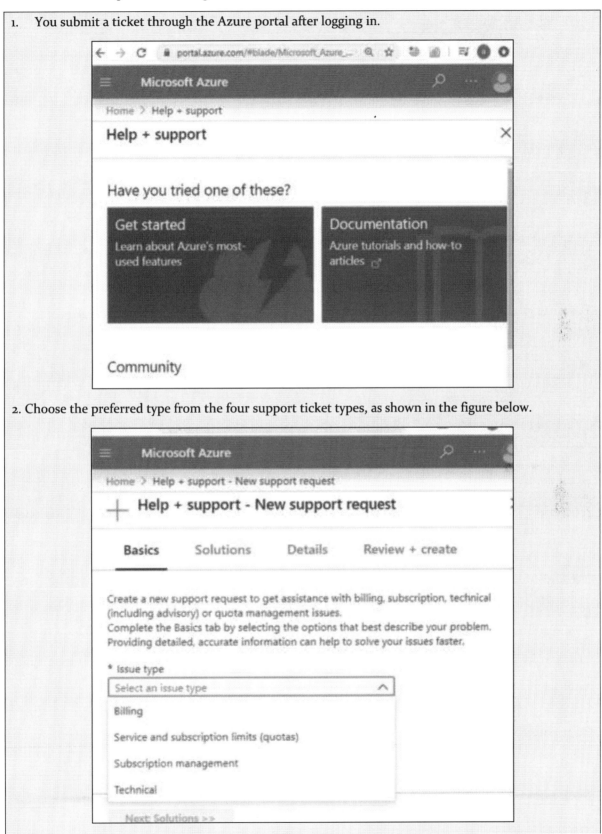

2. Choose the preferred type from the four support ticket types, as shown in the figure below.

3. Fill in the details regarding the issue you create a ticket for.

Microsoft Azure   Search resources, services, and docs (G+/)

Home > Help + support - New support request

Help + support - New support request

Basics   Solutions   Details   Review + create

Create a new support request to get assistance with billing, subscription, technical (including advisory) or quota management issues.
Complete the Basics tab by selecting the options that best describe your problem. Providing detailed, accurate information can help to solve your issues faster.

* Issue type

| Billing   ⌄ |

* Subscription

| Pay-As-You-Go (797152d3-23c4-499f-bfef-bb103da...   ⌄ |

Can't find your subscription? Show more ⓘ

* Summary

| In a few words, describe your issue |

* Problem type

Let's begin by understanding more about your issue

4. Microsoft's support agent will attend to your request within a specific time and according to your support plan.

EXAM TIP: Azure's basic support plan allows creating a ticket for billing and subscription only, nothing technical.

Channels

Azure supports various channels that are free to everyone, through which you get more help from Azure. The support channels are:

1. **Azure Documentation:** Azure documentation is a collection of thousands of articles on Azure products and services. The Azure product managers write them, and technical experts and the community contributes. These are constantly updated and provide in-depth knowledge of products and services.

2. **Forums:** Forums attract everyone, from beginners to experts. On forums, people ask questions, some give answers, and some search for past knowledge.
   https://azure.microsoft.com/en-au/support/community/
3. **Social Media:** Social media is an effective way to get direct support from Azure and the team behind every service. You can ask questions by searching for experts on various social media platforms.

Knowledge Center

The knowledge center is the place of common Azure knowledge. In the knowledge center, you can find basic questions common for all those new to Azure; these are called Common questions. Azure knowledge center aims to answer those common questions.

In the knowledge center, you are provided with the following guidelines:

1. **No New Question:** You cannot add a new question or add to an existing one.
2. **Search:** Search the knowledge center by category, product, and free text. Azure knowledge centers also give links to Azure documentation and more.
3. **Complements to Other Channels:** You cannot find all the answers in the knowledge center, so you can also use the other support channels.
   https://azure.microsoft.com/en-au/resources/knowledge-center/

Service Level Agreement

When using Azure Services, you need some form of guarantee that the service will be running stably. Service Level Agreement (SLA) helps ensure that the services you are subscribed to are available to you as mentioned in the agreement. It describes Microsoft's commitment to uptime and connectivity.

It is like a contract between the service provider and the client. It is an agreement on certain service levels, like how long the service will be available in case of unavailability. If your service does not go up for the given time defined in the agreement, then you will be compensated by claiming it from Microsoft.

Properties

Some properties of SLAs are:

1. **Confidence:** SLAs give confidence to customers by ensuring the uptime and reliability of services.
2. **Contract:** SLAs ensure a contract between Microsoft and customers that states a commitment to uptime and connectivity.
3. **Multiple SLAs:** There are a lot of SLAs in Azure, generally one for each product. It automatically comes when you subscribe to the service.
4. **Complex:** Some SLAs are very complex as they have various levels depending on the number and variety of services, which region you use, and much more.
5. **Mandatory:** SLAs are given by Microsoft; various service levels apply if you have an Azure account. No SLAs are associated with free products and services.

Service Life Cycle

Every product and service in Azure has its lifecycle, known as Service Lifecycle. Azure is an always-changing environment, and new services are always being introduced. Existing services also evolve and introduce new features. It is important to understand the service lifecycle in Azure, how you can keep up with changes, and how a service's lifecycle might impact your support and your SLA.

Gathering Customers Data

When Microsoft develops the services for the Azure platform, it is necessary to ask questions to customers regarding the new features before adding them. This act can save large investments if the services fail.

Stages

There are two main stages in Service Life Cycle:

1) **Preview:** Most Azure products will go through the preview phase before becoming fully available on the Azure platform. It is categorized into two forms: private preview and public preview.
   a) *Private Preview:* It ensures that *specific* Azure customers have an Azure feature for assessment. This is typically by invite only and issued directly by the product team responsible for the feature or service.
   b) *Public Preview:* This ensures that all Azure customers have an Azure feature for evaluation.
2) **General Availability:** All the services are generally available to all the customers as normal service. These services have an SLA, support team, and all other support that the services need. Azure technologies, which are reviewed and tested successfully, will typically be made available to customers as part of the generally available Azure-based product. Before going fully global, generally, services are rolled out in a few regions.
   https://azure.microsoft.com/en-au/updates/

Demo 12-01: Using Preview Services

1. Go to the following preview portal link: https://preview.portal.azure.com/#home. Here, you will see a preview option on top of the portal. It differs from the Azure portal as it contains all the services and products in the preview state.

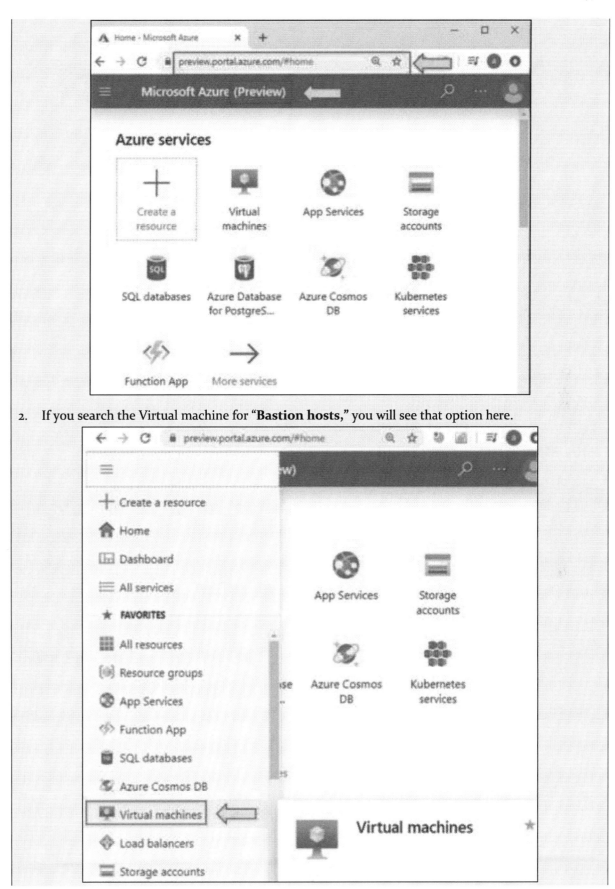

2. If you search the Virtual machine for "**Bastion hosts,**" you will see that option here.

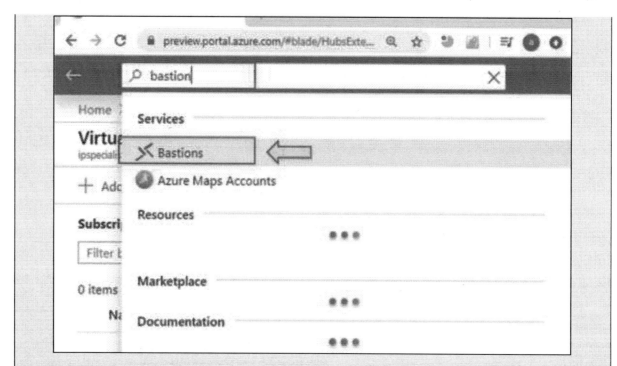

Note: Go into that service and create it if you want. From this preview portal, you can view all the currently unavailable products on the Azure portal.

Mind Map

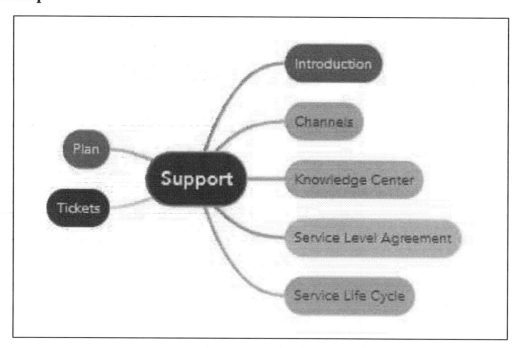

Figure 12-01: Mind Map

Practice Questions

1. From the following options, which are the valid support channels in Azure?
A. Azure Call Support
B. Phone a Friend
C. Azure Documentation
D. Social Media

2. How will you submit a ticket in Azure?
A. Through the Azure Support Portal, which comes with any paid support plan
B. Through the Azure Portal
C. Using the email address support@azure.com
D. Use the phone number for your region and support level

3. What is the response time for Severity B on the Professional Direct Support Plan?
A. 1 hour
B. 3 hour
C. 2 hour
D. 5 hour

4. What is the response time of Severity C cases in the Standard Support Plan?
A. 8 hour
B. 3 hour
C. 2 hour
D. 5 hour

5. How many support plans are available in Azure?
A. 2
B. 3
C. 4
D. 5

6. From the following support plans, which one is free of cost and available with a free account?
A. Standard
B. Basic
C. Developer
D. Premier

7. What questions and answers can the Azure Knowledge Center give you?
A. Architectural diagrams
B. A selection of the Azure documentation and articles found on TechNet
C. Common questions asked when first starting to use Azure

D. Over 100,000 user-submitted questions and answers

8. In Azure Knowledge Center, users can also submit new questions. True or false?
A. True
B. False

9. How do you sign up for a service-level agreement with Azure?
A. Call the regional support number as provided in the Azure Portal to discuss the desired level of the agreement
B. In the Azure Portal, go to the service in question and click on the "Service Level Agreement" section
C. Fill out the form on the Microsoft Azure main support page
D. Service level agreements are included with every Azure service automatically

10. In a private preview, the services will be available for evaluation by all customers. True or false?
A. True
B. False

11. There are no SLAs with the free products. True or false?
A. True
B. False

12. What is an SLA?
A. A contract between the user and Azure
B. A contract between the user and free services
C. A contract between the user and preview services
D. None of the above

13. From the following support plans, which support gives < 15 minutes response time for critical business impact cases?
A. Standard
B. Basic
C. Developer
D. Premier

14. Which support plan has only technical support via email?
A. Standard
B. Professional Direct
C. Developer
D. Premier

15. Which support channel is a collection of thousands of articles on Azure products and services?
A. Azure Documentation
B. Azure Call Support
C. Phone a Friend
D. Social Medi

Answers

Chapter 01: Introduction to Azure

1. Answer: B

Explanation: Consumption-based pricing is based on the usage of resources and is not time-based. It is not limited to free accounts, and the services are not necessarily consumed all the time.

2. Answer: C

Explanation: IaaS is the backbone of cloud computing; in some way, all Azure services depend on IaaS. IaaS Azure services must never be purchased in advance but may be used as required.

3. Answer: A

Explanation: It collects data from various sources and visualizes it from on-premises and the cloud.

4. Answer: C

Explanation: Instead of providing and managing services, Cloud Agility lets them concentrate on other issues such as security, monitoring, and analysis.

5. Answer: A

Explanation: In Azure, this is called Scalability, which means adding or removing resources easily and quickly as per demand. It is important in such situations where you do not know the amount of the needed resources.

6. Answer: D

Explanation: This way, you get high availability for your servers by replacing the failed server instantly with the new one. HA depends on the number of VM you set up to cover in case one goes down.

7. Answer: C

Explanation: Capital Expenditure (CapEx) is the expenditure to maintain or acquire fixed assets by spending money. This includes land, equipment, etc.

Operational Expenditure (OpEx) is the cost of a product or a system that is running on a day-to-day basis, like electricity, printer papers, etc.

8. Answer: A

Explanation: Availability Zones are locations within an Azure region that are physically separate. It comprises one or more independently operating power and network data centers.

9. Answer: B

Explanation: Each region has a minimum of three zones.

10. Answer: C

Explanation: Regions are geographical areas where Azure is present to deploy the Azure resources. It is a set of data centers with a latency-defined perimeter connected via a dedicated regional low-latency network.

11. Answer: D

Explanation: PaaS is designed to facilitate the fast development of web or mobile apps for developers without the need to take concern over the setting or maintaining the underlying server, storage, network, and database infrastructure needed for development.

12. Answer: B

Explanation: VMs are Linux and Windows VM on-demand with your desired configuration hosted in Azure. It is an IaaS resource.

13. Answer: B

Explanation: Resource Manager Template is a JavaScript Object Notation (JSON) file that defines the resources deployed in the resource group. It also defines the dependencies between the deployed resources. With this template, resources can be deployed in a consistent and repeatable way.

14. Answer: B

Explanation: In Azure Storage, you can build a storage account for up to 500 TB of cloud data because it has a limit of 500TB per storage account.

15. Answer: D

Explanation: It is a cloud-based identity and access management service in Azure. It is one of the core services of Azure. This cloud-based IAM service allows users to sign in and access internal or external resources.

16. Answer: C

Explanation: In CLI, command changes rarely, so you can automate the commands for future purposes.

17. **Answer: A**

Explanation: An interactive browser, accessible shell for managing Azure resources, Azure Cloud Shell, is accessible by a browser. The shell experience is the best option, whether you work with Bash or PowerShell, as it offers flexibility.

18. **Answer: B**

Explanation: The limitation of a free Azure Account is that you get free services for 12 months, with credit expiring after 30 days.

19. **Answer: D**

Explanation: Most Azure features for PowerShell are made up of cmdlets. This simplifies the interaction with Azure resources to be consistent and efficient. It is a small, lightweight group of commands to perform actions.

20. **Answer: B**

Explanation: You can use the Azure portal with any form of subscription to access all generally available Azure products and services.

21. **Answer: D**

Explanation: Azure Resource Manager gives you the tools to organize and secure your resources. It is a fundamental service used to install and manage Azure resources. It has a management layer that enables you to create, upgrade, and delete Azure subscription tools. After deployment, you use management tools like access control, locks, and tags to keep your resources safe and organized.

22. **Answer: C**

Explanation: You can get authenticated and authorized access to Azure services with an Azure subscription. It also enables you to allocate resources. An Azure subscription is a logical unit of Azure services linked to an Azure account, which is a Microsoft Entra ID (Azure AD) or a directory that Azure AD trusts identity in.

23. **Answer: D**

Explanation: There are two subscription boundaries.

Billing boundary - How an Azure account is billed for utilizing Azure is determined by this subscription type. For different types of billing requirements, you can create several subscriptions. To

help you organize and manage your costs, Azure creates distinct billing reports and invoices for each subscription.

Access Control Boundary - Azure's access-management policies are applied at the subscription level, and you can build several subscriptions to suit different corporate structures. Within a company, you could have several departments to which you apply different Azure subscription policies. This payment approach enables you to manage and control access to users' resources through subscriptions.

24. **Answer: A**

Explanation: If your company has a lot of subscriptions, you will need a way to keep track of access, regulations, and compliance for all of them. Over and above subscriptions, Azure management groups provide a level of scope. Subscriptions are organized into containers called management groups, and the management groups are subject to your governance rules. All subscribers within a management group automatically inherit the management group's conditions.

Chapter 02: Compute

1. **Answer: C**

Explanation: Virtual machines are an IaaS offering where you can manage the entire machine.

2. **Answer: B and C**

Explanation: Azure charges for Virtual Machines hourly and the resources you used. You also pay more per hour if you use more CPUs and RAMs on your VMs.

3. **Answer: D**

Explanation: Azure Container Instances is the simplest and fastest way to run an Azure container without managing any virtual machines and following a higher-level service.

4. **Answer: C**

Explanation: Concerning Azure, compute is a term that covers many services in Azure, enabling computation in the cloud.

5. **Answer: A**

Explanation: Azure App Service is a fully managed Platform as a Service (PaaS), meaning servers, networks, storage, and other fundamental infrastructures are all managed and controlled by Azure.

6. **Answer: D**

Explanation: Scale sets support up to 1,000 VM instances. If your custom VM images are created and uploaded, the limit is 600 VM instances.

7. Answer: A

Explanation: API is an Application Programming Interface that hosts your data backend services and does not have a graphical user interface, i.e., no user interface, no front end.

8. Answer: C

Explanation: Containers are the preferred way for cloud applications to be packaged, deployed, and managed.

9. Answer: B

Explanation: Kubernetes is an open-source container orchestration system for automating application deployment, management, and scaling.

10. Answer: A, C, and D

Explanation: Azure Kubernetes Service cluster architecture is based on Node, Node pools, Node selector, and Pods.

11. Answer: A

Explanation: Azure Functions is a serverless computing service that is hosted on the public cloud of Microsoft Azure.

12. Answer: C

Explanation:

Easy to create and manage multiple VMs

- Maintaining a consistent configuration across your environment is important when multiple VMs are operating your application. The VM size, disk configuration, and device configurations should be the same across all VMs for the reliable performance of your application
- All VM instances are created from the same base OS image and configuration in the scale set. This approach allows you to easily control hundreds of VMs without additional network management or configuration tasks
- Scale sets allow the Azure load balancer for basic layer-4 traffic distribution and Azure Application Gateway for further advanced layer-7 traffic distribution and SSL termination.

13. Answer: C

Explanation: Azure Functions is a great solution for data processing, systems integration, internet-of-things (IoT) work, and simple APIs and microservices development.

14. Answer: C

Explanation: Concerning Azure, compute is a term that covers any services enabling computation in the cloud.

15. Answer: B

Explanation: Function Service belongs to the Serverless cloud service model.

16. Answer: C

Explanation: Azure virtual machine scale sets allow you to create and manage a pool of identical load-balanced VMs. The number of VM instances will automatically increase or decrease in response to a demand or a given schedule. Scale sets make your applications highly accessible and allow you to manage, configure, and upgrade many VMs centrally.

17. Answer: C

Explanation: Azure Functions is an easy way to run small pieces of code or "functions" in the cloud. A user can create and upload code serverless and then define the triggers or events to execute the code. Triggers may come from various sources, including another user's application or cloud services, such as databases, events, and hubs for notification.

18. Answer: B

Explanation: Azure App Service is a fully managed Platform as a Service (PaaS). This means servers, networks, storage, and other fundamental infrastructures are all managed and controlled by Azure; you have to focus on business values and logic.

19. Answer: A, D, and E

Explanation: Azure provides three types of app services. Web Apps, Web Apps for Containers, and API Apps cover a specific use case. App Services can all run on Linux, but it is not a particular type of service. Event Grid is a separate service on Azure.

20. Answer: C

Explanation: Each virtual machine has hardware, including CPUs, memory, hard drives, network interfaces, and other devices. The virtual hardware is then mapped to the actual hardware on the physical computer, which saves costs by reducing the need for physical hardware systems and related maintenance costs, and the power and cooling demand.

21. **Answer: A**

Explanation: Azure Virtual Desktop is a cloud-based desktop and application virtualization service. It allows your users to access a cloud-hosted version of Windows from anywhere. Windows, Mac, iOS, Android, and Linux are all supported by Azure Virtual Desktop. It is compatible with apps that let you access distant desktops and apps. Most recent browsers can also be used to access Azure Virtual Desktop-hosted experiences.

22. **Answer: D**

Explanation: Remote Desktop Protocol is the graphical terminal or terminal server used to connect to another computer through a network connection. It listens for TCP on port 3389. RDP allows the client to protect the server from the software interface connection. It can run an application mode that loads the shortcut from the user's desktop and appears as if it is the standard application.

23. **Answer: B**

Explanation: An RDP file is a text file consisting of name/value pairs that define the RDP clients' connection to the remote computer using RDP.

Chapter 03: Networking

1. **Answer: A**

Explanation: Azure networking provides the connectivity between Azure resources and the on-premises network.

2. **Answer: C**
Explanation: Azure load balancer and application gateway can distribute the traffic load among the service.

3. **Answer: A**

Explanation: CDN with Dynamic Site Acceleration (DSA) provides the web application update features to the customers. The user can route the dynamic request through CDN without a cache.

4. **Answer: D**

Explanation: Azure CDN places the data replicas at the data center closest to the user side. The data center present closest to the users is called the edge node, which contains a cache of files that provides the edge of the internet to users.

5. **Answer: A**

Explanation: VPN gateway provides secure connectivity between Azure and on-premises networks. A VPN gateway comprises a VNet gateway and a virtual private network.

6. Answer: A

Explanation: It is considered the most advanced load balancer that enables the balancing of web traffic to manage web applications using an HTTP request. Because of its services, the gateway is called the layer 7 load balancer within Microsoft Azure.

7. Answer: B

Explanation: CDN can provide information like images, dynamic changes of video, or website content that is regularly changing. Users can experience good performance and access the resources more quickly.

8. Answer: C

Explanation: VPN gateway is useful for establishing a private connection between Azure resources and an on-premises environment, office, the cloud, or other premises within the cloud in order to establish a secure private connection.

9. Answer: A

Explanation: The main purpose of creating a subnet is to make multiple networks within the same VNet. With multiple subnets, two or more VMs are developed within the subnet. Such a subnet is called a gateway subnet, and a virtual network gateway is used to connect these gateway subnets.

10. Answer: C

Explanation: Azure load balancer provides the load-balancing feature to the connected virtual machines within Microsoft Azure. It manages the network traffic load and enables all VMs to process.

11. Answer: D

Explanation: Azure portal is the console of Microsoft Azure, providing numerous features, services, and a way to create networks with multiple Azure resources and services. It gives GUI representation for the customer to use Azure services. It provides constant availability for using these services.

12. Answer: A

Explanation: Cloud networking enables cloud computing to develop a network with low latency, better security, and optimized performance.

13. Answer: B

Explanation: There are 3 possible connections for connecting the hybrid networks. These are:

- Site-to-Site Connection
- Point-to-Site Connection
- Multi-Site Connection

14. Answer: D

Explanation: A company's data is distributed in Azure and on-premises infrastructure to make it a hybrid solution. A specific VNet gateway called a VPN gateway is used to connect the two. VPN gateway is responsible for creating encrypted communication within the hybrid cloud architecture.

15. Answer: A

Explanation: A simple VNet must consist of a virtual machine (one or more than one), an internet resource, and an on-premises network. VNet can provide secure connections using gateways.

16. Answer: A

Explanation: Content Delivery Network (CDN) provides networking services, which can lead to network failure. CDN proves reliable to its end users, but when it stops working due to technical issues, it cannot get any information from the server side.

17. Answer: C

Explanation: Azure load balancer delivers high availability and network performance to online applications. It distributes the traffic load to the virtual machine present in the network.

18. Answer: B

Explanation: The attributes of VNet, while being created in the Azure portal, define a way to improve network performance and provide scalable service from the designed network. These attributes include address space, public IP address, location, and subnet.

19. Answer: B

Explanation: Using the Azure portal, a VNet should first be created; once the VNet has been deployed, the next step is to add some resources from the resource group to the VNet present in the Azure portal. The resources can be added as long as there is space available in the address space, and each resource should have a unique IP address.

20. Answer: C

Explanation: The load balancer belongs to layer 4. It has multiple virtual IP addresses to route TCP/UDP traffic. It is also responsible for connecting the virtual network and on-premises. The application gateway

is an advanced load balancer that provides gateway services to the application layer. It is responsible for routing traffic to specific applications like web apps. Application gateway secures application services using firewalls.

21. **Answer: B**

Explanation: VPN gateway provides secure connectivity between the Azure and on-premises network. A VPN gateway is made up of a VNet gateway and a virtual private network.

22. **Answer: C**

Explanation: ExpressRoute is one of the Azure services capable of providing a private and secure connection between Azure and on-premises networks that provide a more secure and reliable connection. This route comprises a circuit and provides two types of connectivity: primary and secondary.

23. **Answer: A**

Explanation: Site-to-Site VPN or S2S provides a way to connect your on-premises network to the Azure virtual network. This type of connection requires a VPN device on-premises with an externally facing IP address. A secure connection called a tunnel enables multiple encrypted connections for security purposes.

24. **Answer: C**

Explanation: There are three ExpressRoute connectivity models:

- Any-to-any (IPVPN) networks
- Virtual cross-connection through an Ethernet Exchange
- Point-to-point Ethernet Connection

25. **Answer: D**

Explanation: Azure ExpressRoute provides global connectivity to all regions with high availability, better security, and reliability.

Chapter 04: Storage

1. **Answer: D**

Explanation: Disk storage is a complete virtual hard drive to be accessed. The disk storage is created when you create a virtual machine.

2. **Answer: C**

Explanation: In file types and sizes, Azure blob containers are the most flexible. Any file sizing up to 2GB can be stored in an Azure blob container.

3. Answer: B

Explanation: Drive mapping is how operating systems like Microsoft Windows link a local drive to another device (such as a File Server) via a network using a shared storage area. So, the shared storage solution is File storage.

4. Answer: B

Explanation: Archive storage is the cheapest form of blob storage to store data, which is rarely used, like device backups.

5. Answer: B

Explanation: When creating a Storage Account, the name must be between 3 to 24 characters in length and may only contain numbers and lowercase letters.

6. Answer: A

Explanation: Every storage account on Azure must have a unique name, which is used by giving it a web address to identify it on the Internet. Access management of storage accounts is done via Microsoft Entra ID.

7. Answer: C

Explanation: You can use the file storage as an extension to your on-premises file system so that it never runs out of space and prioritizes which data you keep on-site.

8. Answer: B and D

Explanation: Azure offers four types of managed disk storage: Standard HDD, Standard SSD, Premium SSD, and Ultra Disk.

9. Answer: B

Explanation: All storage accounts are encrypted for data at rest using SSE (Storage Service Encryption).

10. Answer: D

Explanation: Append blobs are used for log data and can be up to 195GB. It is usually used for optimizing the append operation.

11. Answer: B

Explanation: **The hot tier** is for frequently accessed data and is the most optimized. Access costs are lower (read-write), but storage costs are the highest.

12. Answer: C

Explanation: Premium SSD is super-fast and high-performance storage for critical workloads. It is recommended for database installation, in particular with low latency.

13. Answer: C

Explanation: Data on your Azure Storage Account are durable, highly accessible, safe, and scalable. The unique namespace means that every storage data has its webpage with its unique name. It is written in the format: "https://<Storage-Account-Name>.<Storage-type>.core.windows.net.

14. Answer: A

Explanation: A Storage Account is like an access point for Azure Storage. All your Azure Storage Data Objects, like blobs, files, queues, tables, and disks, are on an Azure storage account. So first, you need to create a storage account and then use any storage option.

15. Answer: D

Explanation: Block blobs store text and binary data up to 4.7 TB. It is made up of blocks of data that can be managed individually. In one block blob, you can have 50,000 blocks.

Chapter 05: Databases

1. Answer: B

Explanation: Cosmos DB is a NoSQL, globally distributed DB.

2. Answer: B

Explanation: Latency is the time taken by the data to travel. The higher the latency, the longer it takes for data to reach the user.

3. Answer: A

Explanation: With Cosmos DB, latency is limited to single-digit milliseconds (0-9) anywhere in the world.

4. Answer: D

Explanation: With Azure SQL, you can easily migrate your on-premises SQL database to Azure SQL and get all its benefits; this is done without any code change and with a frictionless process.

5. Answer: C

Explanation: With Azure SQL, you can store 100TB of data within a minute.

6. Answer: A

Explanation: With Azure SQL, you can also take advantage of integrated Machine learning tools. Database optimization and performance improvement suggestions are given depending on the usage pattern. With ML, you get notified about any degradation or anything bad happening in your database.

7. Answer: D

Explanation: Azure Server for MySQL was designed to provide high availability with 99.99% SLA and does not require additional setup, replica features, or costs to guarantee that your apps run as required.

8. Answer: C

Explanation: Azure Database for MySQL is the database built-in by the community, while Azure SQL is Microsoft's product. MySQL is an open-source project where anyone can contribute to the community.

9. Answer: C

Explanation: Azure Database for MySQL is PaaS, which Microsoft manages.

10. Answer: B

Explanation: PostgreSQL is the default database for macOS.

11. Answer: D

Explanation: A database can sort and index the data and retrieve them. Databases are cheaper, safer, and have more efficient space than other data storage options.

12. Answer: A

Explanation: Cosmos DB has a globally distributed database and includes an extremely low latency, several collaborative software, and unlimited scaling to meet demand. Cosmos DB is not meant for cheap storage or data backup.

13. Answer: C

Explanation: Database Migration Service on Azure has a range of destinations to which the data can be migrated. These include Azure SQL, Azure SQL Server, and Cosmos DB. Big data tools like Azure Data Lake or HDInsight are not currently supported.

14. **Answer: A**

Explanation: It is deployed as a single server and as a Citus cluster. The Hyperscale (Citus) choice scale queries horizontally through multiple sharding tools and offers more scaled and productive applications.

15. **Answer: C**

Explanation: For geometric data (GIS), the government mostly uses Postgres. PostGIS is the GIS extension that gives hundreds of functions to process geometric data in multiple formats.

16. **Answer: C**

Explanation: When you are required to store large volumes of data not frequently used, search for a data warehouse or data lake. Transactional applications such as SQL, PostgreSQL, and CosmosDB are useful for frequently accessed data.

17. **Answer: A**

Explanation: Azure Synapse is a data warehouse that blends data, big data analytics, and data integration into a unified service that provides end-to-end analytics at a cloud scale. It stores big data of size petabytes and runs queries on relational and non-relational data.

Chapter 06: Authentication and Authorization

1. **Answer: A**

Explanation: The identity services of Microsoft Azure are responsible for providing the platform to the users and ensuring the validity of users for the application through the process of authentication, authorization, and access management tools.

2. **Answer: B**

Explanation: Authentication is a way to verify the customer's or user's identity. Once authenticated, the user can access files, databases, emails, etc. This is called authorization.

3. **Answer: D**

Explanation: Identity service is responsible for access management, ensuring the restriction of access to service towards other or unauthorized users. It provides confidentiality, integrity, and availability.

4. Answer: C

Explanation: Authentication is the user's identification through a user ID and password. Other verification approaches are also used to authenticate Azure users.

5. Answer: B

Explanation: Identity service is the management tool that secures the user's identity by first authenticating it. After authentication, authorization will give access rights to Azure users.

6. Answer: A

Explanation: Multi-Factor Authentication provides the most advanced security and protection features to Azure users. MFA has the most efficient throughput protection using multiple authentication processes. MFA uses the principle of "something you know (user ID and password), something you have (app on mobile to receive the confirmation code), and something you are (biometric)".

7. Answer: C

Explanation: Authorization is a part of identity management that provides access rights to Azure users after the authentication process.

8. Answer: A

Explanation: Tenant is the first AAD instance after creating an Azure account. One user belongs to a single tenant only.

9. Answer: C

Explanation: Microsoft Active Directory (AD) only provides directory services for physical access. It is most commonly used in on-premises networks like offices, educational institutes, etc.

10. Answer: D

Explanation: Hybrid cloud architecture is a requirement for many organizations. Microsoft Entra ID (AAD) can help users manage resources and services on both on-premises and Azure clouds.

11. Answer: B

Explanation: Multi-Factor Authentication (MFA) performs user authentication in multiple steps. The first step is to verify the user with a user ID and password. The second step is to send a code to the user's phone for further verification. The third step is biometric verification. This step is optional.

12. Answer: C

Explanation: Authorization is a granular part of identity service that provides the rights to authenticated users to access particular data.

13. **Answer: A**

Explanation: Microsoft Entra ID and Active Directory (AD) are directory services. Directory services are databases that store information distributed across different locations. AAD is the main tool to manage services on Azure. At the same time, AD is the management tool for the on-premises network.

14. **Answer: A**

Explanation: Azure subscription is very important for both the end-user and Microsoft. An Azure subscription allows the user to use Azure resources for cloud computing.

15. **Answer: D**

Explanation: Multi-Factor Authentication combines multiple authentication processes to provide an advanced level of a secure environment for accessing the data. Sometimes, biometrics is the only authentication way to provide security.

16. **Answer: B**

Explanation: Access management provides user access to IT resources. Access management only allows a correct user (i.e., authorized user) to access the system applications for security.

17. **Answer: C**

Explanation: Microsoft Entra ID is the first service when a user creates an Azure account. Without AAD, Azure users can use Azure resources and services.

18. **Answer: B**

Explanation: Microsoft Entra ID is a very important tool in the Azure portal because it is also responsible for handling users' information and assigning access to other resources such as Cosmos DB, Virtual Machine, etc.

19. **Answer: A**

Explanation: Active Directory is designed to access on-premises network resources and users. AD does not support the management of web-based services.

20. **Answer: C**

Explanation: Tenant is the first directory service when a new user creates an account in Azure. A user belongs to a single tenant, and tenants may have multiple users. Sometimes, the user can be a guest of other tenants.

Chapter 07: Azure Core Solutions and Management Tools

1. Answer: A

Explanation: A model is a set of rules for how to use the data provided. The model finds patterns based on the rules.

2. Answer: A, C, and D

Explanation: Azure Data Lake Analytics is an on-demand job analytics service that simplifies big data. Instead of hardware tuning, deploying, and configuring, you write queries to transform the data and extract valuable insights. The analytics service can promptly handle jobs of any size by changing the dial to how much power you need. You pay for your job only when it works, making it cost-effective.

3. Answer: C

Explanation: Logic Apps simplifies how you design and build flexible applications for application integration, data integration, system integration, Enterprise Application Integration (EAI), and Business-to-Business (B2B) communication, whether in the cloud, at the premises, or both.

4. Answer: D

Explanation: Azure DevOps offers developer tools to support teams in preparing projects, working on application creation, and designing and deploying software. Developers can use Azure DevOps Services or on-premises with Azure DevOps Server to operate in the cloud. Azure DevOps provides integrated features that can be accessed via your web browser or client IDE.

5. Answer: B, E, and F

Explanation: There are currently 5 services in Azure DevOps:

Azure Boards- Provides a suite of Agile tools to help plan and monitor code bugs and issues using Kanban and Scrum processes.

Azure Pipelines- provides services to develop and release continuous integration and distribution of your apps.

Azure Repos- Provides the source control of your code to Git repositories or Team Foundation Version Control (TFVC).

Azure Test Plans- Provides various software testing tools, including manual/exploratory testing and continuous testing.

Azure Artifacts: Allows teams to share public and private Maven, Npm, and NuGet packages and incorporate package sharing into your CI/CD pipelines.

6. **Answer: C and E**

Explanation: There are many Azure services for the Internet of Things. Two of them are IoT Hub and IoT Central. The others listed are not valid Azure services.

7. **Answer: D**

Explanation: Use Azure Search to find existing insights in your data. File relationships, geography connections, and much more.

8. **Answer: B and C**

Explanation: Azure HDInsight allows storing massive amounts of data easily, efficiently, and cost-effectively. The most popular open-source frameworks, such as Hadoop, Spark, Hive, LLAP, Kafka, Storm, R, and more, are available. A wide range of scenarios such as Extracting, Transforming, and Loading (ETL), data warehousing, machine learning, and IoT can be enabled with these frameworks.

9. **Answer: D**

Explanation: Azure Event Grid lets you easily build applications with event-based architectures.

10. **Answer: C and D**

Explanation: Logic Apps are similar to Function Apps because a trigger kicks them off, but what happens after that is completely different. Unlike Function Apps, to create some efficient workflows with Logic Apps, you do not have to write code.

11. **Answer: A, C, and D**

Explanation: Cognitive services bring AI within every developer's reach — without requiring expertise in machine learning. All it takes is an API call to embed the feature to see, hear, speak, search, understand, and accelerate decision-making in your apps.

12. **Answer: C**

Explanation: The Azure Machine Learning Studio is the top-level tool for the machine learning service. It provides a centralized location for data scientists and developers to work with all the artifacts for developing, training, and deploying machine learning models.

13. **Answer: C**

Explanation: Machine Learning Services are:

End-to-End Service: The service to use AI and machine learning almost anywhere on Azure.

Tooling: The Machine Learning service is a collection of tools to help you build AI applications.

Automation: Azure automatically recognizes trends in your applications and creates models for you.

14. **Answer: A, C, and D**

Explanation: The benefits of the Serverless Model are:

- **No Infrastructure Management:** Use fully managed infrastructure. Developers can avoid administrative tasks and concentrate on the core business logic. You simply deploy the code with a serverless platform, and it runs with great availability.
- **Dynamic Scalability:** The infrastructure can automatically scale up and down within seconds to match any workload requirements for serverless computing.
- **Faster Time to Market:** Serverless applications reduce the dependencies of operations on each development cycle, increasing the agility of development teams to produce more features in less time.
- **More Efficient Use of Resources:** Shifting to serverless technology allows companies to reduce TCO and resource reallocation to speed up the pace of innovation.

15. **Answer: B and D**

Explanation: DevTest Labs creates labs that consist of pre-configured based or templates for Azure Resource Manager. These have all the tools and applications you can use to create environments. You can create environments in a couple of minutes instead of taking hours or days.

By using DevTest Labs, you can test the latest versions of your software when performing the following tasks:

- Using interchangeable templates and artifacts to provision Windows and Linux environments quickly
- Easily integrating the DevTest Labs delivery system for the provision of on-demand environments
- Scaling up the load testing by providing multiple testing agents and building pre-provisioned training and demo environments

16. **Answer: A**

Explanation: Azure Logic Apps is a cloud service that helps you plan, automate, and orchestrate business processes, activities, and workflows when businesses or organizations need to integrate apps, data, and services.

17. **Answer: B**

Explanation: Azure Data Lake Analytics is an on-demand job analytics service that simplifies big data. Instead of hardware tuning, deploying, and configuring, you write queries to transform the data and extract valuable insights.

18. **Answer: D**

Explanation: Azure Functions is the compute component of serverless services offered by Azure. This means you can use Functions to write code without worrying about deploying that code or creating VMs to run your code.

19. **Answer: C**

Explanation: Azure Databricks is an analytics platform based on Apache Spark, enhanced for the Microsoft Azure cloud services platform.

20. **Answer: D**

Explanation: Businesses use the big data accumulated in their systems to improve operations, provide better customer service, create customized marketing campaigns based on specific customer preferences, and, ultimately, increase profitability.

21. **Answer: D**

Explanation: Azure IoT Edge is the cloud-based computing service used to manage and ensure the smooth running of workflow on the edge device. It enables moving cloud analytics and custom business logic to IoT devices. The device can easily process logic directly without pushing data to the cloud.

22. **Answer: B**

Explanation: The IoT Edge runtime enables custom logic and cloud logic on the IoT Edge device. It is located on the edge device. The runtime is responsible for receiving the program code at the edge and communicating the devices with Azure IoT Hub. It executes management and communication operations. It also ensures the state of IoT Edge modules and continuously reports the module's health to the cloud.

23. **Answer: D**

Explanation: Microsoft has launched a Raspberry Pi Azure IoT online simulator to connect the devices to the Azure IoT Hub. It consists of three different sections.

- **Assembly area:** It defines the visualization of circuit simulation
- **Coding area:** It gives the brief code in Java
- **Integrated Console Window:** It displays the output in response to the given code

24. **Answer: A**

Explanation: Azure IoT Hub allows for bi-directional communication between the cloud and IoT devices and allows developers to take advantage of this information to provide insights monitoring and develop custom solutions for their IoT platform.

Chapter 08: Security

1. Answer: A

Explanation: In the configuration of networks, network security is a very important part that protects access to files, directories, and information in a computer network against hacking and unauthorized changes in the network.

2. Answer: B

Explanation: There are four possible ways defined to make secure network connections. The Azure firewall defines a set of rules for the protection of resources. Distributed Denial-of-Service (DDoS) protection services prevent the system from receiving excessive requests. Network Security Group (NSG) makes the security of network resources, and Application Security Group (ASG) is used to provide application-level security.

3. Answer: C

Explanation: Azure firewall is a layer 7 protocol introduced by Microsoft. It defines a set of rules for the incoming and outgoing traffic in the network to ensure the security of resources in the network.

4. Answer: D

Explanation: To hide the key password, secrets, and other information from third-party Azure Key Vault is the best option for key storage. It allows sharing a secret with others without revealing the actual credentials for security reasons. Azure Key Vault has hardware and software protection. Azure Key Vault uses a Hardware Security Module (HSM) to store passwords and secrets that no one can view.

5. Answer: C

Explanation: When the web server receives the same number of requests from many different sources and computers at once, the webserver suddenly stop working due to the multiple simultaneous requests. This attack on the service is called a Distributed Denial-of-Service (DDoS) attack.

6. Answer: A

Explanation: Network Security Group (NSG) is required in the configuration of a Virtual Network (VNet) where different Virtual Machines (VM) within the subnet are connecting with each other. A Network Security Group can secure the traffic load across the network, whereas an Application Security Group (ASG) protects the application running on that particular VM or subnet in the network.

7. Answer: C

Explanation: Network Security Group (NSG) is required in the configuration of a Virtual Network (VNet) where different Virtual Machines (VM) within the subnet are connecting with each other. NSG uses Access Control List (ACL) rules to allow or deny network traffic access to the subnet or VM.

8. Answer: B

Explanation: To provide secure and protected communication between the resources, services, and processes, a secure network connection should be required to configure a network.

9. **Answer: A**
Explanation: Azure Key Vault is a useful service that hides other parties' actual passwords and keys. It secures the network by defining the access policy that allows secure access to secrets and passwords.

10. **Answer: D**
Explanation: Azure Information Protection provides a way of protecting the sharing of resources. Azure Information Protection (AIP) enables sharing of files, documents, and sensitive information more securely outside the organization.

11. **Answer: C**
Explanation: Advanced Threat Protection (ATP) is an advanced and secure option for providing the security of the links compared to the standard one. It gives an extra layer of security and management of the users to make a more secure and protected system.

12. **Answer: B**
Explanation: Azure Key Vault stores secrets and passwords. It allows sharing of passwords and secrets with others in a hidden form so that nobody can view the actual secret.

13. **Answer: A**
Explanation: Microsoft Defender for Cloud is itself a portal that monitors the various security features of Azure. Security features include policy, compliance, networking, subscription coverage, and resource security hygiene. Defender for Cloud enables threat alerts as well.

14. **Answer: D**
Explanation: A DDoS attack is an excessive number of requests from different sources, resulting in server or website failure. GitHub experienced the recent record-break DDoS attack with 1.35 TB traffic per second.

15. **Answer: C**
Explanation: Network Security Group (NSG) acts as a resource firewall to prevent network resources from unwanted traffic loads. It defines rules called the Access Control List (ACL) to make network resources as secure as possible.

16. **Answer: B**
Explanation: Application Security Group (ASG) protects applications currently running on a particular VM or subnet.

17. **Answer: C**
Explanation: Microsoft Defender for Cloud provides an overview of security features in Azure. It also provides its advantage towards a hybrid cloud infrastructure where data is present on both on-premises and cloud.

18. **Answer: A**

Explanation: Azure Information Protection (AIP) protects the sharing of email, file, or sensitive data inside and outside an organization. It uses a label for sensitive information that protects it from threats and other activities throughout the process.

19. **Answer: A**

Explanation: Azure Advanced Threat Protection service has a security alert timeline that contains a timeframe for the activities in the network. It also highlights and detects the issues in the network.

20. **Answer: B**

Explanation: Azure Key Vault the limited access to secrets and passwords. It defines an access policy to ensure who can access the secret.

21. **Answer: C**

Explanation: The data on Azure is encrypted and protected against anyone unauthorized reading or making sense of it. In almost all cases, attackers are after data.

22. **Answer: A and B**

Explanation: A strategy to slow the advance of an attack to get unauthorized access to information and a layered approach that each layer provides protection. So if one layer is breached, a subsequent prevents further exposure.

23. **Answer: A**

Explanation: A famous DDoS attack was, as it is against the developer website GitHub in 2018, where attackers sent 127 million requests per second, which is huge. To protect against DDoS, Azure has the DDoS Protection service.

24. **Answer: C**

Explanation: Perimeter is the protection against DDoS attacks, volumetric attacks, protocol attacks, and so on. It uses DDoS protection to filter large-scale attacks before they can cause a denial-of-service for end-users.

25. **Answer: D**

Explanation: Network is the traffic filter to and from Azure using virtual networks and applying security "standards. Limit" communication between resources.

Chapter 09: Privacy, Compliance, and Trust

1. **Answer: D**

Explanation: First is Azure Government Cloud; if you are a US government body or are contracted for one, you can access Azure resources in Azure Government Cloud regions. It is a physically separated instance of Azure, dedicated to U.S. government workloads only.

2. Answer: B

Explanation: Azure Policy is used to create policies in Azure. With Azure policy, you can manage and assign policies to the resources with multiple rules so that specific resources are compliant with your business standards and SLAs.

3. Answer: C

Explanation: With the use of Azure Policy, you can define the company policy so it will enforce the resource to comply with this policy.

4. Answer: A

Explanation: Trust Center is a shortcut to knowing all the things that Microsoft does to ensure you do not lose trust in Azure and other services. With this, you have a link to learn about security, privacy, GDPR, the location of your data, compliance, and more.

5. Answer: B

Explanation: Any company that wishes to interact with users located in the European Union must adhere to the many GDPR rules around privacy.

6. Answer: C

Explanation: Azure Service Health informs you of incidents and planned maintenance related to Azure Service. This information can be used to take adequate measures to limit downtime. Azure Service Health cannot receive data from any of your applications or third-party services. It is Azure only.

7. Answer: A

Explanation: With RBAC, you can outline fine-grained access management to the resources. You can define specific user access to an individual resource, for example, what they can do with that specific resource and in which specific area of resource they have access.

8. Answer: C

Explanation: Azure Monitor can accept data from almost any application to monitor their activities and health. You have a single dashboard for all the current measurements, or you can use the collaborative query language to dive into the archived data.

9. Answer: B and E

Explanation: Locks are of two types: delete or read-only. You cannot delete the resource in the delete lock type, while in the read-only lock type, you cannot change the resource.

10. Answer: B

Explanation: The Trust Center can be used to find evidence of all the various compliance specifications Azure complies with. You can read audit reports on any part of Microsoft products, like Azure, through the Service Trust Portal.

11. Answer: B

Explanation: Azure has physically separated data centers located in China without any connection to the other regions of Azure. All data is stored in China at all times according to Chinese regulations.

12. Answer: B

Explanation: In RBAC, there are three main elements: Security Principal, Scope, and Role Definition.

13. Answer: D

Explanation: Azure Blueprint is a template for creating Azure resources. Everything you need to deploy in the standard cloud environment of Azure is mentioned in the blueprint.

14. Answer: C

Explanation: Azure, for Compliance, provides you the Azure Compliance Manager because Azure knows about compliance and as it knows about your resources, so it can easily combine the tools and give you a recommendation as per that.

15. Answer: D

Explanation: Azure Information Protection is used for classifying, labeling, and helping protect data based on its sensitivity.

16. Answer: B

Explanation: The subscription level is frequently where teams begin their Azure governance plan. When it comes to creating and managing subscriptions, there are three primary factors to consider:

- Billing
- Access control
- Subscription restrictions.

17. **Answer: C**

Explanation: The Cloud Adoption Framework for Azure guides you toward cloud adoption in five key stages and offers a collection of documentation, implementation guidance, best practices, and tools for each.

- Define your approach.
- Make a strategy.
- Prepare your company.
- Adopt cloud computing.
- Administrate and control your cloud infrastructures.

18. **Answer: D**

Explanation: 21Vianet operates Azure China 21Vianet. It is a geographically segregated instance of cloud services in China. Shanghai Blue Cloud Technology Co., Ltd. ("21Vianet"), a wholly-owned subsidiary of Beijing 21Vianet Broadband Data Center Co., Ltd., operates and transacts Azure China 21Vianet independently.

Chapter 10: Pricing

1. **Answer: C**

Explanation: A billing cycle on Azure is either 30 or 60 days.

2. **Answer: C**

Explanation: Management groups may indicate the following:

- **Group Subscriptions:** You can group your subscriptions to allow taking actions in bulk across subscriptions. This is very useful in organizations that deal with many subscriptions.
- **Organize:** You can manage policies and compliance in multiple subscriptions simultaneously.
- **Billing Logic:** You can maintain the billing associated with the right budgets. You have the Nest management groups to indicate the hierarchy and their relationship.

3. **Answer: D**

Explanation: A free account gives you access to the most popular Azure services for 12 months.

4. **Answer: B**

Explanation: Cost management allows you to create a budget for your Azure expenses, set up configurable notifications so you will know if you are hitting a budgeted limit, and evaluate your costs in detail.

5. **Answer: A**

Explanation: With Azure Cost Management, you can download reports on spending, get recommendations on saving on costs, and analyze them.

6. Answer: C

Explanation: The bandwidth slightly influences the pricing factor; the bandwidth your services use incurs a cost.

7. Answer: B

Explanation: Any data transfer between regions in the same billing zone is free; this process is called Ingress.

8. Answer: A

Explanation: Any data transfer between two different billing zones is charged. This process is called Egress.

9.   Answer: C

Explanation: The Azure price calculator will help you estimate costs depending on the products you plan to use, where those products will be deployed, and so on.

10.   Answer: D

Explanation: The TCO calculator is the best choice when you have applications on site that you want to migrate to Azure, and you want an estimate of how much you can save in Azure.

11.   Answer: C

Explanation: TCO report shows you how much you can save by moving your app to Azure over the next 5 years.

12.   Answer: A, B, and C

Explanation: Three primary groups listed below need to be coordinated within the company to ensure you handle the costs effectively.

- **Finance:** Person responsible for authorizing budget requests across the enterprise based on projections of cloud spending. They pay the corresponding bill and assign the costs to different teams to drive accountability.
- **Managers:** Business decision-makers in an organization need to understand cloud spending to find the best outcomes for spending.

- **App Teams:** Engineers manage cloud infrastructure daily and create applications that meet the needs of the enterprise. These teams need flexibility in their defined budgets to deliver the most value.

13. Answer: A

Explanation: By Azure Cost Management, you can optimize your resources to save money and monitor the charges of other cloud service providers, such as Amazon Web Services.

14. Answer: A, B, and C

Explanation: To implement cost control effectively and reduce costs, you need to:

- Be equipped with the right tools for performance
- Be responsible for costs
- Take appropriate action to reduce expenses

15. Answer: B

Explanation: The advisor makes recommendations for purchases in reserved instances. The recommendations are based on your virtual machine used for the last 30 days. The recommendations can help you reduce your expenditure when you act upon them.

16. Answer: C

Explanation: The pricing structure of Microsoft Azure works on a subscription price that is tied to what you are using within the Azure infrastructure. All resources in Azure require a subscription; you cannot access any resources until you subscribe.

17. Answer: D

Explanation: Azure spending limits are the recommended means to manage your Azure subscription's total spending. When your usage leads to charges that exhaust your spending limit, the services you deployed will be disabled for the rest of that billing period, and manual monitoring of the spending of Azure services is ineffective.

18. Answer: D

Explanation: The Azure price calculator will help you estimate costs depending on the products you plan to use and where those products will be deployed.

19. Answer: B and C

Explanation: Azure Cost Management is accessible from the Azure portal. You can get a detailed view of the current and future projected costs of all the resources within your area of accountability. Azure Cost Management is free of cost and includes all Azure subscriptions.

20. Answer: A, D, and E

Explanation: The primary factors influencing costs are;

- **Resource Size** - Different sizes of resources will have different pricing. A more powerful virtual machine will cost more than the less powerful one.
- **Resource Type** - The choice of resource type greatly influences price. This also makes sense as there is a very big difference in the number of hardware resources needed to run a virtual machine compared to a machine learning service or big data analytics. There is also a big difference in the complexity of maintaining and running various Azure services.
- **Location** - Azure has a global network of data centers from the US to Australia and from Norway to South Africa; they are all treated equally with slightly different pricing. Exchange rates, labor costs, etc., influence the price.
- **Bandwidth** - The bandwidth your services are using incurs a cost as well.

Chapter 11: Managing and Deploying Azure Resources

1. Answer: B

Explanation: It is an underlying service where the Azure resource deployment and management are done. It provides a management layer that lets you create, upgrade, and uninstall your Azure subscription tools. You use management features such as access control, locks, or tags to ensure that your resources are protected and organized after deployment.

2. Answer: A

Explanation: Resource Manager Template is a JavaScript Object Notation (JSON) file that defines the resources deployed in the resource group. It also defines the dependencies between the deployed resources. With this template, resources can be deployed in a consistent and repeatable way.

3. Answer: C

Explanation: With ARM templates, we can automate the deployments. ARM templates provide automation and orchestration deployments through scripts and Azure services.

4. Answer: A

Explanation: Variables are where you define the specific values that can be used in the entire template. It is unnecessary, but you can use it to reduce the complexity of the template, as it makes your template simpler to maintain.

5. Answer: B

Explanation: "Custom Script Extension," through which you can download and run the script on your VMs, helps configure and download applications, or for other setup or management tasks after deployment. These scripts can either be stored in Git or Azure Storage. These scripts may be executed manually or in an automatic deployment. You can describe a resource that you will need to be added to the template of your Resource Manager. It is the most useful and best technique for continuously adding resources. When you are done with the service principal (who has access), role definition (what can access), and scope (where they can access). You combine these three elements to grant access with a role assignment.

6. Answer: D

Explanation: In Microsoft Azure, Azure App Service is a Platform as a Service (PaaS) used to host your Azure code. Because of the PaaS service, you do not need to maintain the infrastructure like you would if you manage the virtual machine. It enables you to build and host web applications and mobile backends without manually maintaining an operating system or a web server.

7. Answer: A

Explanation The basic tier provides 10 GB storage of disk space and supports an unlimited number of applications with 32 bits and 64 bits. The pricing tier has 3 sizes (B1, B2, and B3) for compute power, memory, and disk storage. It supports manual scaling of up to 3 dedicated instances only. This pricing tier is used for the dev/test application before production. It provides a guaranteed SLA of 99.95%.

8. Answer: C

Explanation: Azure Resource Manager Template is a simple template that contains: $schema, contentVersion, Parameters, variables, functions, resources, and outputs.

9. Answer: D

Explanation: There are two options available.

- **Standalone Template** - You can deploy any resource by using a single standalone ARM template. With this option, the ARM template contains all the information required to deploy resources within a single file.
- **Template with Parameters File** - The parameters file can provide flexibility toward consistent deployment. This template has a separate command argument used to specify the parameters file.
-

10. Answer: B

Explanation: Azure App Service is a powerful tool for hosting web apps, mobile, and APIs. It also offers auto-scaling, high availability, and applications running in Windows and Linux environments. Azure App Service has several designs available for the development of an application.

11. Answer: A

Explanation: Azure Marketplace enables the development of applications by seeking help and using tools available in Azure Marketplace.

12. Answer: C

Explanation: Availability Zones are present within Azure regions. These zones provide highly available protected areas to run applications and data.

Chapter 12: Support

1. Answer: C and D

Explanation: In Azure, the supported channels are used to interact with experts and professionals Azure. These include The Azure documentation, technical forums, and official Azure social media accounts.

2. Answer: B

Explanation: You can go through the "Support" section of the Azure Portal for support tickets. There, you will have a choice of various tickets, and you can choose the kind of support level you want.

3. Answer: C

Explanation: The response time for Severity B cases in the Professional Direct Support plan is <2 hours.

4. Answer: A

Explanation: The response time of the severity C cases in the Standard Support plan is <8 hours and in the Developer support plan.

5. Answer: D

Explanation: There are five different support plans available in Azure: Basic, Developer, Standard, Professional Direct, and Premier.

6. Answer: B

Explanation: A basic support plan is free of cost and given along with the Azure Free account.

7. Answer: C

Explanation:

The knowledge center is the place of common Azure knowledge. In the knowledge center, you can find basic questions common for all those new to Azure; these are called Common questions. Azure knowledge center aims to answer those common questions.

8. Answer: B

Explanation: No New Question: You cannot add a new question or add to an existing one.

9. Answer: D

Explanation: All Azure services are subject to Service Level Agreements. Each SLA includes a subscription and support level.

10. Answer: B

Explanation: Public preview: This ensures that all Azure customers have an Azure feature for evaluation.

11. Answer: A

Explanation: Microsoft gives SLAs; various service levels apply if you have an Azure account. No SLAs are associated with free products and services.

12. Answer: A

Explanation: SLA describes Microsoft's commitment to uptime and connectivity. It is like a contract between the service provider and the client. It is an agreement on certain service levels, like how long the service will be available in case of unavailability.

13. Answer: D

Explanation: For high-severity business impact cases, the response time is <15 minutes (with Azure Rapid Response or Azure Event Management).

14. Answer: C

Explanation: Access to support engineers via email only during business hours is given in the developer support plan.

15. Answer: A

Explanation: Azure documentation collects thousands of articles on Azure products and services. The Azure product manager writes them, and technical experts and the community contribute.

Acronyms

AAD	Azure Active Directory
ACI	Azure Container Instances
ACL	Access Control List
AD	Active Directory
ADC	Application Delivery Controller
AES	Advanced Encryption Standard
AI	Artificial Intelligence
AIP	Azure Information Protection
AKS	Azure Kubernetes Service
API	Application Program Interface
APU	Accelerated Processing Unit
ARM	Azure Resource Manager
ASG	Application Security Group
AWS	Amazon Web Service
AZ	Availability Zone
Azure ATP	Azure Advanced Threat Protection
B2B	Business-to-Business
CapEx	Capital Expenditure
CDN	Content Delivery Network
CLI	Command Line Interface
CPU	Central Processing Unit
DB	Database
DC/OS	Distributed Cloud Operating System
DDoS	Distributed Denial-of-Service
DevOps	Development and Operations
DMS	Database Migration Services
DNS	Domain Name System
DoD	Department of Defense
DoS	Denial-of-Service
DR	Disaster Recovery

DSA	Dynamic Site Acceleration
EAI	Enterprise Application Integration
ELT	Extract, Load, and Transform
ETL	Extract, Transform, and Load
EU	European Union
FaaS	Function as a Service
FIPS	Federal Information Processing Standards
GCP	Google Cloud Platform
GDPR	General Data Protection Regulation
GPU	Graphics Processing Unit
HA	High Availability
HDD	Hard Disk Drive
HDFS	Hadoop Distributed File System
HSM	Hardware Security Model
HTTP	Hypertext Transfer Protocol
HTTPS	Hypertext Transfer Protocol Secure
IaaS	Infrastructure as a Service
IOPS	Input/Output Operations per Second
IoT	Internet-of-Things
IP	Internet Protocol
ISO	International Standardization Organization
IT	Information Technology
JSON	JavaScript Object Notation
KEDA	Kubernetes-based Event Driven Autoscaling
MCU	Micro-Controller Unit
MFA	Multi-Factor Authentication
ML	Machine Learning
MPLS	Multiprotocol Label Switching
NIST	National Institute of Standards and Technology
NSG	Network Security Group
OpEx	Operational Expenditure
OS	Operating System
PaaS	Platform as a Service

PCI	Payment Card Industry
POP	Point of Presence
RBAC	Role-Based Access Control
RCAs	Root Cause Analyses
SaaS	Software as a Service
SDKs	Software Development Kits
SLA	Service Level Agreement
SOC	Standard Occupational Classification
SQL	Structured Query Language
SSD	Solid State Drive
SSE	Storage Service Encryption
SSL	Secure Sockets Layer
SSO	Single Sign-On
TCO	Total Cost of Ownership
TCP	Transmission Control Protocol
TFS	Team Foundation Server
TFVC	Team Foundation Version Control
UIDs	Unique Identifiers
URL	Uniform Resource Locator
US	United State
VM	Virtual Machine
VMs	Virtual Machines
VNet	Virtual Network
VPN	Virtual Private Network

References

https://azure.microsoft.com/en-gb/global-infrastructure/regions/

https://docs.microsoft.com/en-us/learn/paths/azure-fundamentals/

https://searchcloudcomputing.techtarget.com/definition/Windows-Azure

https://searchcloudcomputing.techtarget.com/definition/cloud-computing

https://azure.microsoft.com/en-us/global-infrastructure/locations/

https://docs.microsoft.com/en-us/learn/modules/protect-against-security-threats-azure/6-host-virtual-machines-dedicated-hosts

https://docs.microsoft.com/en-us/azure/cloud-adoption-framework/

http://www.azurespeed.com/Information/AzureRegions

https://docs.microsoft.com/en-us/azure/azure-resource-manager/management/overview

https://docs.microsoft.com/en-us/learn/modules/azure-architecture-fundamentals/resources-resource-manager?ns-enrollment-type=LearningPath&ns-enrollment-id=learn.az-900-describe-cloud-concepts

https://en.wikipedia.org/wiki/Cloud_computing_security

https://www.forcepoint.com/cyber-edu/cloud-security

https://acloud.guru/course/az-900-microsoft-azure-fundamentals/learn/security-/introduction/watch?backUrl=~2Fcourses

https://acloud.guru/course/az-900-microsoft-azure-fundamentals/learn/pricing/introduction/watch

https://learning.oreilly.com/library/view/exam-ref-az-900/9780135732199/ch04.xhtml#ch04

https://daryusman.wordpress.com/2019/01/24/access-public-and-private-preview-features/

https://azure.microsoft.com/en-us/support/legal/preview-supplemental-terms/

https://www.lynda.com/Azure-tutorials/Understand-service-lifecycle-Azure/2815127/2246786-4.html

https://docs.microsoft.com/en-us/learn/paths/az-900-describe-core-azure-services/

https://docs.microsoft.com/en-us/azure/azure-resource-manager/templates/syntax

https://docs.microsoft.com/en-us/azure/azure-resource-manager/templates/template-functions-resource

https://azure.microsoft.com/en-us/services/app-service/

https://cloudacademy.com/blog/understanding-core-azure-architectural-components/

https://searchcloudcomputing.techtarget.com/definition/Microsoft-Azure-Marketplace

https://www.otava.com/reference/how-to-use-azure-resource-groups-a-simple-explanation/

https://docs.microsoft.com/en-us/azure/availability-zones/az-overview

https://azure.microsoft.com/en-us/features/resource-manager/?cdn=disable

https://docs.microsoft.com/en-us/azure/cost-management-billing/costs/cost-mgt-best-practices

https://docs.microsoft.com/en-us/azure/role-based-access-control/overview

https://docs.microsoft.com/en-us/azure/role-based-access-control/overview

https://www.petri.com/getting-started-with-role-based-access-control-in-azure

https://docs.microsoft.com/en-us/azure/governance/policy/overview

https://azure.microsoft.com/en-us/solutions/governance/

https://docs.microsoft.com/en-us/azure/governance/blueprints/overview

https://docs.microsoft.com/en-us/azure/azure-monitor/overview

https://www.techopedia.com/definition/30551/cloud-compliance

https://docs.microsoft.com/en-us/azure/azure-government/

https://docs.microsoft.com/en-us/azure/azure-government/documentation-government-welcome

https://docs.microsoft.com/en-us/azure/china/overview-operations

https://azure.microsoft.com/en-us/overview/trusted-cloud/privacy/

https://servicetrust.microsoft.com/

https://docs.microsoft.com/en-us/microsoft-365/compliance/get-started-with-service-trust-portal

https://digitalguardian.com/blog/what-advanced-threat-protection-atp

https://docs.microsoft.com/en-us/azure/security/fundamentals/network-overview

https://azure.microsoft.com/en-us/services/azure-firewall/

http://techgenix.com/network-security-groups/

https://docs.microsoft.com/en-us/azure/virtual-network/security-overview

https://www.petri.com/understanding-application-security-groups-in-the-azure-portal

https://medium.com/awesome-azure/azure-application-security-group-asg-1e5e2e5321c3

https://azure.microsoft.com/en-us/blog/applicationsecuritygroups/

https://docs.microsoft.com/en-us/azure/security-center/security-center-intro

https://azure.microsoft.com/en-us/services/security-center/

https://azure.microsoft.com/en-us/services/key-vault/

https://www.winwire.com/azure-key-vault/

https://azure.microsoft.com/en-us/services/information-protection/

https://www.microsoft.com/en-us/itshowcase/protecting-files-in-the-cloud-with-azure-information-protection

https://docs.microsoft.com/en-us/azure/information-protection/reports-aip

https://techcommunity.microsoft.com/t5/azure-information-protection/new-enhancements-to-office-365-message-encryption-with-azure/ba-p/1042617

http://download.microsoft.com/download/B/2/7/B2763D5D-E72A-45CA-AA3A-AD13519886B2/Data_in_Motion_Infographic_EN_US.pdf

https://azure.microsoft.com/en-us/features/azure-advanced-threat-protection/

https://docs.microsoft.com/en-us/azure-advanced-threat-protection/what-is-atp

https://docs.microsoft.com/en-us/azure-advanced-threat-protection/working-with-suspicious-activities

https://en.wikipedia.org/wiki/Kill_chain

https://docs.microsoft.com/en-us/azure/azure-resource-manager/management/resource-providers-and-types

https://azure.microsoft.com/en-us/product-categories/compute/

https://docs.microsoft.com/en-us/learn/modules/welcome-to-azure/3-tour-of-azure-services

https://cloud.netapp.com/blog/storage-tiers-in-azure-blob-storage-find-the-best-for-your-data

http://www.differencebetween.net/technology/difference-between-authentication-and-authorization/

https://acloud.guru/course/az-900-microsoft-azure-fundamentals/learn/azure-solutions/

https://searchitoperations.techtarget.com/definition/DevOps

https://whatis.techtarget.com/definition/HDInsight

https://docs.microsoft.com/en-us/azure/lab-services/devtest-lab-overview

https://azure.microsoft.com/en-us/overview/ai-platform/

https://azure.microsoft.com/en-us/services/cognitive-services/

https://docs.microsoft.com/en-us/azure/devops/user-guide/what-is-azure-devops?view=azure-devops

https://docs.microsoft.com/en-us/azure/event-grid/overview

https://docs.microsoft.com/en-us/azure/logic-apps/logic-apps-overview

https://docs.microsoft.com/en-us/azure/azure-databricks/what-is-azure-databricks

https://azure.microsoft.com/en-us/overview/serverless-computing/

https://docs.microsoft.com/en-us/azure/data-lake-analytics/

https://docs.microsoft.com/en-us/learn/modules/ai-machine-learning-fundamentals/?ns-enrollment-type=LearningPath&ns-enrollment-id=learn.az-900-describe-core-solutions-management-tools-azure

https://docs.microsoft.com/en-us/learn/modules/azure-devops-devtest-labs/?ns-enrollment-type=LearningPath&ns-enrollment-id=learn.az-900-describe-core-solutions-management-tools-azure

https://docs.microsoft.com/en-us/learn/modules/monitoring-fundamentals/?ns-enrollment-type=LearningPath&ns-enrollment-id=learn.az-900-describe-core-solutions-management-tools-azure

https://docs.microsoft.com/cn-us/learn/modules/management-fundamentals/?ns-enrollment-type=LearningPath&ns-enrollment-id=learn.az-900-describe-core-solutions-management-tools-azure

https://docs.microsoft.com/en-us/learn/modules/serverless-fundamentals/?ns-enrollment-type=LearningPath&ns-enrollment-id=learn.az-900-describe-core-solutions-management-tools-azure

https://docs.microsoft.com/en-us/learn/modules/iot-fundamentals/?ns-enrollment-type=LearningPath&ns-enrollment-id=learn.az-900-describe-core-solutions-management-tools-azure

https://docs.microsoft.com/en-us/azure/app-service/overview-authentication-authorization

https://www.youtube.com/watch?v=NRRK3DYeqXU

https://www.youtube.com/watch?v=Iop0T4UxFxE

https://www.youtube.com/watch?v=oxmg-6zUVwc

https://www.slideshare.net/IdentityDays/gouvernance-multitenant-didentits-et-ressources-azure-avec-azure-active-directory-par-marius-zaharia

https://en.wikipedia.org/wiki/Active_Directory

https://searchwindowsserver.techtarget.com/definition/Active-Directory

https://docs.microsoft.com/en-us/azure/active-directory/authentication/concept-mfa-howitworks

https://acloud.guru/course/az-900-microsoft-azure-fundamentals/learn/authentication-and-authorization/quiz/watch?backUrl=~2Fcourses

https://docs.microsoft.com/en-us/power-bi/developer/create-an-azure-active-directory-tenant

https://docs.microsoft.com/en-us/azure/cosmos-db/introduction

https://stackify.com/what-is-azure-cosmos-db/

https://azure.microsoft.com/en-us/services/cosmos-db/

https://docs.microsoft.com/en-us/azure/sql-database/sql-database-technical-overview

http://www.davidchappell.com/writing/white_papers/Introducing_the_Windows_Azure_Platform,_v1.4_--Chappell.pdf

https://azure.microsoft.com/en-us/services/sql-database/

https://docs.microsoft.com/en-us/azure/mysql/overview

https://docs.microsoft.com/en-us/azure/postgresql/overview

https://azure.microsoft.com/en-au/resources/videos/azure-database-services-mysql-postgresql-mariadb/

https://azure.microsoft.com/en-us/services/database-migration/

https://docs.microsoft.com/en-us/azure/dms/faq

https://searchcloudcomputing.techtarget.com/definition/Microsoft-Azure-Data-Lake

https://docs.microsoft.com/en-us/azure/databricks/data/data-sources/azure/sql-data-warehouse

https://azure.microsoft.com/en-us/services/synapse-analytics/

https://docs.microsoft.com/en-us/azure/databricks/data/data-sources/azure/sql-data-warehouse

https://docs.microsoft.com/en-us/azure/storage/blobs/storage-blob-storage-tiers?tabs=azure-portal

https://docs.microsoft.com/en-us/azure/storage/blobs/storage-blobs-overview

https://aidanfinn.com/?p=18415

http://techgenix.com/azure-storage-accounts/

https://docs.microsoft.com/en-us/azure/storage/common/storage-account-overview

https://intellipaat.com/blog/tutorial/microsoft-azure-tutorial/azure-storage/#Azure_Disk_Storage

https://www.dremio.com/azure-storage-explained/

https://docs.microsoft.com/en-us/azure/virtual-machines/windows/disks-types#disk-comparison

https://azure.microsoft.com/en-us/services/storage/archive/

https://www.pluralsight.com/paths/managing-microsoft-azure-networking

https://www.microsoftpressstore.com/store/microsoft-azure-essentials-fundamentals-of-azure-9781509302963

https://www.vmware.com/topics/glossary/content/cloud-networking

https://www.youtube.com/watch?v=kgwqrqKrox8

https://www.vmware.com/topics/glossary/content/cloud-networking

https://en.wikipedia.org/wiki/IP_address

https://www.techopedia.com/definition/4763/address-space

https://www.accessagility.com/blog/benefits-of-subnetting

https://www.c-sharpcorner.com/article/azure-virtual-networks/

https://docs.microsoft.com/en-us/azure/load-balancer/load-balancer-overview

https://kemptechnologies.com/glossary/source-ip-hash-load-balancing/

https://docs.microsoft.com/en-us/azure/vpn-gateway/vpn-gateway-about-vpngateways

https://docs.microsoft.com/en-us/azure/vpn-gateway/vpn-gateway-howto-site-to-site-resource-manager-portal

https://docs.microsoft.com/en-us/azure/vpn-gateway/vpn-gateway-vpn-faq

https://mindmajix.com/microsoft-azure-application-gateway

https://acloud.guru/course/az-900-microsoft-azure-fundamentals/learn/networking/a5b8496d-4af7-8ad6-eef8-9eco4f34103c/watch

https://www.f5.com/services/resources/glossary/ssl-offloading

https://docs.microsoft.com/en-us/azure/application-gateway/overview

https://docs.microsoft.com/en-us/azure/dns/dns-overview

https://practical365.com/blog/how-to-use-azure-cdn-content-delivery-network/

https://docs.microsoft.com/en-us/azure/architecture/best-practices/cdn

https://docs.microsoft.com/en-us/azure/cdn/cdn-dynamic-site-acceleration

https://acloud.guru/course/az-900-microsoft-azure-fundamentals/learn/networking/lab-virtual-network-connection/watch?backUrl=%2Fcourses

https://www.youtube.com/watch?v=rOiSRkxtTeU

Appendix C: References

https://azure.microsoft.com/en-us/product-categories/networking/

https://www.dataversity.net/key-cloud-agility/

https://docs.microsoft.com/en-us/azure/storage/common/storage-introduction#types-of-storage-accounts

https://docs.microsoft.com/en-us/cli/azure/get-started-with-azure-cli?view=azure-cli-latest

https://docs.microsoft.com/en-us/cli/azure/install-azure-cli?view=azure-cli-latest

https://docs.microsoft.com/en-us/azure/app-service/

https://docs.microsoft.com/en-us/azure/app-service/overview

http://www.informit.com/articles/article.aspx?p=2423911

https://www.techopedia.com/definition/6580/compute

https://azure.microsoft.com/en-us/overview/what-is-a-virtual-machine/

https://www.techopedia.com/definition/4805/virtual-machine-vm

https://docs.microsoft.com/en-us/azure/aks/intro-kubernetes

https://docs.microsoft.com/en-us/azure/aks/concepts-clusters-workloads#kubernetes-cluster-architecture

https://azure.microsoft.com/en-in/services/kubernetes-service/

https://azure.microsoft.com/en-us/services/container-instances/

https://searchcloudcomputing.techtarget.com/definition/Microsoft-Azure-Functions

https://docs.microsoft.com/en-us/azure/azure-functions/functions-overview

https://docs.microsoft.com/en-us/azure/virtual-machine-scale-sets/overview?toc=%2Fazure%2Fvirtual-machines%2Flinux%2Ftoc.json

About Our Products

Other products from IPSpecialist LTD regarding CSP technology are:

 AWS Certified Cloud Practitioner Study guide

 AWS Certified SysOps Admin - Associate Study guide

 AWS Certified Solution Architect - Associate Study guide

 AWS Certified Developer Associate Study guide

 AWS Certified Advanced Networking – Specialty Study guide

 AWS Certified Security – Specialty Study guide

 AWS Certified Big Data – Specialty Study guide

 Microsoft Certified: Azure Fundamentals

 Microsoft Certified: Azure Administrator

 Microsoft Certified: Azure Solution Architect

 Microsoft Certified: Azure DevOps Engineer

 Microsoft Certified: Azure Developer Associate

 Microsoft Certified: Azure Security Engineer

 Microsoft Certified: Azure Data Fundamentals

 Microsoft Certified: Azure AI Fundamentals

 Microsoft Certified: Azure Data Engineer Associate

 Microsoft Certified: Azure Data Scientist

 Microsoft Certified: Azure Network Engineer

 Oracle Certified: Foundations Associate

 Microsoft Certified: Power Platform Fundamentals

Other Network & Security related products from IPSpecialist LTD are:

- CCNA Routing & Switching Study Guide
- CCNA Security Second Edition Study Guide
- CCNA Service Provider Study Guide
- CCDA Study Guide
- CCDP Study Guide
- CCNP Security SCOR Study Guide
- CCNP Enterprise ENCOR Study Guide
- CCNP Service Provider SPCOR Study Guide
- CCNP Security SVPN Study Guide
- CCNP Enterprise ENARSI Study Guide
- CCNP Service Provider SPRI Study Guide
- CompTIA Network+ Study Guide
- CompTIA Security+ Study Guide
- Ethical Hacking Certification v11 First Edition Study Guide
- Ethical Hacking Certification v12 First Edition Study Guide
- Fortinet FortiGate Administrator
- Palo Alto Certified Network Security Administrator

Made in the USA
Columbia, SC
14 March 2024

33075562R00298